Good Housekeeping
Guide to Fixing Things
Around the House

Good Housekeeping

Guide to Fixing Things

Around the House

by MARCIA D. and ROBERT M. LILES

with Eileen Stukane and the editors of *Good Housekeeping*

Good Housekeeping Books   New York

HOW TO USE THIS BOOK

The lamp won't light? The hot water runs cold? The bookshelves are sagging? You *can* call a repairman, but if—and when—he comes, the cost of his services will be high. With this book, you can do most of the repairs around the house yourself.

For easy reference, the book is divided into two sections. Section I is a concise "dictionary"; it contains entries for hundreds of items from "Acoustical Tile" to "Zipper." Almost everything that could go out of whack around the house is covered here—including things like broken china, stained lampshades, chairs that need recaning, toilets that won't flush, roofs that leak, and lots more. Finding what you need to know is as easy as saying ABC, since all the entries in Section I are in alphabetical order.

Section II defines terms that may be unfamiliar to you, and illustrates the various tools called for in repairs. This section also gives you a rundown on what you should know about nails and other fasteners, electricity and wiring, gluing and clamping, painting, refinishing wood, and other basic repair skills.

To use this book, look up the item you want to repair in Section I. If any of the background information in Section II would be helpful to you in making that repair, you are referred to it right there in the entry—no turning back and forth to an index is necessary. Or you may want to read Section II, in whole or in part, straight through. Of course, there are some repairs that can only be handled by professionals. This book tells you which these are, and where to find the experts.

Acknowledgments. We wish to thank Mr. Gustav A. Berger, Berger Art Conservation, Inc., of New York City, for his kindness in sharing his expertise on artworks and picture frames; the National Paint, Varnish and Lacquer Association; the Window Shade Manufacturers Association; Stanley Tools; Black & Decker Manufacturing Co.; Ridge Tool Co; and the editors of *Popular Mechanics.*

We also want to thank Ms. Sheila Weller for unflagging devotion to typing chores, and Mr. John E. Walsh for his contributions to the form this book finally took.

Drawings by Loring Eutemy

CONTENTS

Section I

Section II

SECTION I

ACOUSTICAL TILE, CEILING | wood, mineral wool, glass fiber; plastic

Discolored or Stained. Clean the tiles—first with a vacuum cleaner, then with a clean, damp cloth you've dipped in soap (or detergent) and water. Dry thoroughly with a towel.

Stubborn Stains. If you've had no luck with soap and water, touch up the discoloration with a thin layer of paint (flat finish, not gloss) mixed to match the clean portion of the tile.

Note: Experts say one coat of paint is your limit on acoustic tile: More layers of paint will clog the "pores" of the tiles—and keep them from soaking up the sound waves every home is heir to.

Some Tiles Loose or Bulging. Dampness on *Surface* of Tile. Obviously, dampness in the room (laundry, bath, or kitchen) is collecting and condensing on your ceiling. Too much of this with certain types of tile is apt to give you serious problems. The most porous variety—made of wood fiber—may sooner or later come unstuck, and may even land on you or yours while you're doing the chores. There are two ways to reduce the moisture in the room, but both of them require the skills of a professional.

1. Install an Exhaust Fan. If you decide on this, send for the electrician. He can advise you on the proper type and do the installation and wiring.

2. Vent the Moisture-Producing Machinery. (Washing machines, for instance, give off steam, which will condense in the room.) Send for the plumber, and he'll pipe the steam through a tube in the wall to the outdoors, where it will do less damage.

And, till the repairman comes, keep the place as dry as possible: Open windows and doors before the atmosphere gets humid. To replace the loose tiles, see below. (If you decide to replace *all* of the tiles, you may want to choose a glass fiber or polystyrene plastic tile. These materials are not as porous as wood or mineral wool fiber—hence they have greater resistance to dampness. Do not replace tile or retile the area until ceiling and walls are dry.)

A Few Tiles Loose or Bulging. Dampness and Stains *Behind* Tile. Most likely you'll spot the condition and the clue to it at the same time. If the

3

tile is loose and the surface *behind* it is stained or moldering, you can bet a leaky roof is responsible.

First step: remove the tile. If the tile was applied with adhesive, cut any portions that are *not* loose free with a sharp knife. If the tile is nailed or stapled to what's behind it, pry up one of the flanged edges with a sturdy knife or screwdriver. Whatever way you do it, do it gently: Be very kind to the plaster on the ceiling. If you *should* damage it, see below, "Plaster Behind Tile Loose."

Next, locate the leak in the roof and stop it. (See ROOF.) Replace the tile only after the roof and ceiling areas are repaired and dry. (To replace tile, see below.)

Plaster Behind Tile Loose, in Need of Patching. (*Note:* This applies to small cracks in the plaster only. If large areas of plaster are loose, you're in for a full ceiling-repair job, and probably now is the time to call the contractor or carpenter.) You find the small cracks in the plaster after you've removed the loose tile. Scrape or sandpaper the surface—to remove the residue of tile adhesive and to prepare the plaster. Then apply the type of patching plaster the repairman calls *spackle*. (Buy it at the paint or hardware store, follow directions on the container.) For details, see below.

Replacing Damaged Tile by Using Tile Adhesive. If your tile was "glued," not nailed, to the ceiling, follow these four steps to replace the tile:

1. Sandpaper. Remove the old tile cement from the area. Be careful not to scrape off too much plaster when you do this. (If you do, apply spackle, let it dry, sand it smooth.)

2. Cut the *flange* off the edges of the tile. (This border is needed only if a tile is to be nailed in place.)

3. Dab the back of the tile with tile adhesive. (See diagram below, left.)

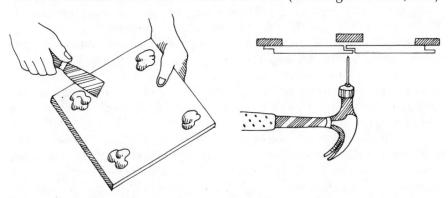

These globs you're dabbing on should be about the size of a normal, healthy grape. Put a dollop of the cement at each (underside) corner, and another in the center of the tile.

4. Press the tile to the ceiling, and be sure to use the same amount of

pressure across the surface of the tile—to squeeze and spread the cement globs evenly across the underside.

Some Tiles Loose. Nails Holding Them Popping Out or Wiggly. If nails hold your tiles in place, and the tiles are loose, it's probably because the nails are not long enough for the job. Usually nails must go through the plaster on the ceiling, then the *lath* (the wood strips behind the plaster), and then, finally, into the *joists* (the wooden inner structure of your house). Take a look at one of the wiggly nails. Is it at least two inches long? If not, see below. *Note:* Some acoustic tiles are nailed to *furring strips* (thin strips of wood attached to the ceiling). If the tiles seem loose, drive 2-inch nails through the overlapping flange of the tile—next to the borders where the two tiles meet (see diagram, opposite right).

Replacing Tile by Nailing It. Trim off the flanges, then nail the tile to the ceiling with 2-inch-long, cement-coated nails. Countersink the nails (see Section II, WORKING WITH NAILS, SCREWS, AND FASTENERS, p. 236). then spackle and paint over the nailheads—to give a professional finish to the job.

Large Area of Tiles Bulging or Loose. This can be a serious (to say nothing of unsightly) hazard. The tiles may all come loose and hit you on the head. Remove the tiles one by one, or call the repairman (a carpenter) and have him do the job. Keep people and pets out of the area until the repair is made. Retile with old or new tiles, after making the checks (above) to find the cause for this condition.

ADHESIVE AND GLUE

See Section II, GLUING AND CLAMPING, p. 248. The GLUE CHART will guide you to the selection of the appropriate glue for the job.

AERATOR

Clogged. If less water than usual comes out of your kitchen faucets, it's possible that the little aerator at the tip of the spout is clogged. This small device looks like a miniature strainer, and it's there to put bubbles in the stream of water from your tap and to lessen the splashing from the spout. In parts of the country where the water is *hard* (that is, contains more calcium salts), the wire basketry-work of the aerator can become filled with deposits of calcium. These will diminish the flow from your tap. To solve the problem, unscrew the aerator and separate the screens and strainers you find inside it. (Make a mental or actual note on how you took these out, because you've got to put them back in proper order.) Clean the parts with a brush, then flush off any residue with a strong jet of water from the tap. Put strainers and screens back into the aerator, and put it back on the spout.

Note: If you can't unscrew the aerator by hand, wrap a cloth around it and use a curve-jawed pipe wrench to loosen it. (See Section II, GLOSSARY OF TOOLS, p. 229.)

AFGHAN AND THROW | crochet

Holes and Tears. The method you use to mend your afghan will depend on your dexterity and on whether the piece is proudly displayed or just intended for plain everyday use. You can:

1. Crochet It. First, find yarn to match the afghan and buy a crochet hook (one smaller than the loops of crochet is preferable to a large hook). Look for the loose ends in the damaged area, tack or pin one of them, temporarily, to keep the afghan from raveling. Knot the other loose end to the new yarn. Then duplicate the stitch of the afghan. When the mend is made, draw the yarn to the back of the afghan, using the crochet hook, and secure it by knotting it to the other end.

2. Darn It. Use matching yarn, if possible. Secure broken and loose ends (tack them down with needle and thread or yarn), then make a neat, woven darn. (See Section II, MENDING BY SEWING, p. 281.)

Worn Spots. Reinforce the underside of the afghan with small running stitches, or, if greater strength is needed, crisscross and weave the stitches, as you do when you make an ordinary darn. (See Section II, as cited above, p. 281.)

Edging Worn. Crochet a picot border all around the afghan. Or, if crocheting is not your thing but sewing is, use contrasting yarn and a large tapestry needle to make a blanket-stitch border. (See Section II, as cited above, p. 280.)

AFGHAN AND THROW | knit

Holes and Tears. There are two ways to mend holes in knits; your choice will depend on your talents, your patience, and whether your afghan or throw was once a thing of beauty, or just a cozy old throw for the attic bed. You can:

1. Knit-Stitch It. This is the way professionals mend knitted pieces, and it's not difficult if the item you're mending has big, loose stitches. If you use matching yarn, your mend will be hard to detect on the right side of the afghan. The knit-stitch method is used mostly for pieces knitted with the stockinette stitch, but if you're handy, you can adapt the technique to the stitch you're mending. (See Section II, MENDING BY SEWING, p. 284.)

2. Darn It. This is the traditional way of mending knitted things, especially socks. Use matching yarn, if possible. The repair will look like

weaving, not knitting, but it will be strong. Catch up loose ends that may keep on raveling. (See Section II, as cited above, p. 281.)

Worn Spots. Reinforce the wrong side of the afghan with tiny running stitches. (See Section II, as cited above, p. 276.) If you prefer a more fastidious technique, reinforce the area on the right side with the duplicate stitch, a variation of the knit-stitch. (See Section II, p. 284.)

Runs and Ravels. You can make these disappear like magic if you use a crochet hook (use one slightly smaller than the loops of the stitches in the afghan). Insert the hook in the loop at the bottom of the run and pull the next horizontal thread through this. Continue on up the "ladder" until you come to the top rung. Tack the last loop in place with needle and thread, on the wrong side of the afghan. (For details, see Section II, MENDING A RUN WITH A CROCHET HOOK, under MENDING BY SEWING, p. 283.)

AFGHAN AND THROW | woven fabrics

Holes and Tears. There are three techniques for mending afghans made of woven fabrics. We recommend the first, *if* your afghan is loosely woven, and if you want to make an invisible mend the way professional re-weavers do.

1. Rewoven Patch. This takes time and it also requires that you have extra material just like that in your afghan. If you do have a square of the fabric (or can take a small piece from a turned-under hem), you're in business! Follow the directions in Section II, MENDING BY SEWING, p. 286.

2. Appliqués. These can be used to mend a hole on finely woven fabric, and if you use contrasting colors and attractive shapes, they'll look like decoration, not mending. You can buy machine-embroidered flowers or other designs and sew these over the damaged area. Or you can make appliqués of your own from brightly colored scraps. Follow directions in Section II, as cited above, p. 286.

3. Darns. These are good for loosely woven fabrics and not as tricky to do as the "Rewoven Patch" (above). For directions, see Section II, as cited above, p. 281.

Edging Worn. There are three ways to cope with this. You can:

1. Bind It. Any binding or ribbon will do, but velvet or satin ribbons are especially attractive fabrics to use to finish the edge. (See Section II, as cited above.)

2. Crochet It. Make a picot border all around the afghan.

3. Blanket-Stitch It. Use contrasting yarn to make this attractive new finish for your afghan. (See Section II, MENDING BY SEWING, p. 280.)

4. Hem It. Just fold the edge under twice, and make a new edging by stitching this with needle and thread. If you machine-sew this hem, be

careful not to let the material bunch up. For hemming, see Section II, as cited above, p. 278.

AIR CONDITIONER | central

CAUTION: *Do not attempt to repair this intricate and expensive piece of equipment. For your own safety, you should call the authorized serviceman or an electrical contractor when your unit fails to operate properly or to operate at all. Always turn off the unit if it produces unusual noises or strange odors. (A motor burnout gives off an acrid odor and means that the motor must be repaired or replaced.)*

There are several important points to check (either *before* you send for help, or while you're waiting for the repairman to come). Some of these are elementary, but others require care and know-how. Check off as many as you really trust yourself to cope with:

1. Has the unit been turned on? Check the *"On-Off"* switch.

2. Is there a power failure in your area? (If there is, your other appliances—including your radio—will not be working.) Check with a neighbor or the utility company to be sure.

3. Have you cleaned the removable filters recently? Clogged filters can hamper the machine's operation. *Disconnect the current to the unit, even if the air conditioner has failed to go on!* If you have disconnected the unit's power supply and the filters are clogged, torn, or not properly inserted, check your owner's manual and follow its directions carefully. (Most units have long-lasting filters that can be vacuumed or washed in soap and water, dried, then reinserted. But each model varies slightly, so your best guide is the set of directions for *your* air-conditioning system.)

4. Have you checked the fuse or circuit breaker for the unit? If not, do so, but first be sure to consult Section II, ELECTRICITY AND WIRING, p. 257.

5. If you've done all of these things, just sit tight, and wait till the repairman comes!

AIR CONDITIONER | room

CAUTION: Play safe with air conditioners by following these rules:

Always turn off the unit if it gives off strange odors. This can be an indication of serious trouble in the motor (a motor burnout gives off an acrid odor, and means that the motor must be repaired or even replaced.)

Always turn unit off if it makes unusual noises during any part of its operation. This is an indication that the fan may be hitting some part of the mechanism, or that something's loose that shouldn't be!

Never open the unit (to examine filters or other parts) unless you have disconnected the cord plug from the electric outlet. You run the risk of getting electric shock if you don't unplug the machine, even after you've turned it off!

Be sure your unit is grounded when it is installed. If it isn't, unplug it and don't operate it until the serviceman comes and does the grounding for you. (For details on this, see Section II, GROUNDING, under ELECTRICITY AND WIRING, p. 269.)

Note: There are few actual repairs you can make on an air conditioner. If you have problems, it's best to call your serviceman or dealer. Experts say, though, that many of the calls air-conditioner repairmen get are from people who've neglected to learn the simple routine for running the machine. Save money by checking out the items below before you call the repairman. Maybe your problem is:

Machine Won't Start. Is the unit plugged in? (Someone may have pulled the plug out when you were not looking.) Switch the button to *off*, plug cord in, and *then* turn the machine to *on*. If the unit still doesn't start, make these checks:

1. Is the plug faulty? Switch the machine to *off*, then remove the plug—carefully—from the outlet (don't yank it out). Examine the cord: Is it damaged? Is the plug cracked or damaged? Are the prongs loose and wiggly? If you spot any of these problems, have the plug and cord repaired by a professional.

2. Has the circuit fuse blown? This fuse is in the main fuse box, probably in the basement of your house, and it should be labeled. (See Section II, p. 257, ELECTRICITY AND WIRING, for details, and pay special attention to the SUPER SAFETY RULES, therein.)

3. Is the plug secure in the outlet? You may find the prongs of the plug need to be spread a little to make the plug fit firmly in the outlet slots. Be sure the unit switch is at *off*, then pull the cord plug out, examine the prongs, and spread them with your fingers *just a little*. Insert the plug again, then turn the machine to *on*.

4. Have you set the dials on the machine properly? Check your owner's manual to be sure.

5. If you've made all these checks and the machine still won't run, call a repairman.

Machine Runs But Doesn't Cool Room. Furniture or draperies may be blocking the flow of cool air. Move them so that they don't. If this is not the cause, check this list:

1. The louvers that direct the air flow may not be in proper position for maximum cooling. Adjust them so that cool air flows to the hot spots in the room. (Because hot air rises, the ceiling is apt to be hotter than the floor. You should send cool currents *up* by moving the louvers.) These

louvers are on the front of your unit, and you can adjust them by hand while the machine is running *or* when it's off.

2. Is the thermostat set properly? Look at the dial. If the day is a scorcher and your thermostat is not at its coldest setting, move the dial to that position, but leave it there! (Do not dial back and forth.)

3. Are doors to other rooms open? Maybe you're asking the machine to cool the whole house and not just the room you bought it for. Give it a chance to work. Shut off other rooms and see if this doesn't solve the cooling problem.

4. Do you have other appliances operating in the room that are adding heat? For instance, are there many lights on? Are you using a washer-dryer? And do you have the oven on, too? If you want to cool the room, save the laundry for later, use just the top of the stove. In other words, alternate the use of your heat-giving appliances in hot weather if you want the best from your air conditioner.

5. Have you checked the filters? If they're clogged with dirt, your machine will not work properly and you'll get less cold air from it. Turn the machine to *off,* unplug the cord from the outlet. Using your owner's manual as a guide, find out where the filters are and remove them. (Usually, they just lift out of the machine by their handles.) Then wash them in sudsy water, rinse and dry, and reinsert them. *Note:* Some units have decorative grilles which can be taken off. Remove the filters behind the grille, and wash, rinse, and dry them. Reinsert, then put the grille back in place. The permanent-type filter should be cleaned about every two weeks, if you use the machine often.

6. Are the filters torn? Are they so badly clogged with dirt that you can't clean them? Buy new filters or have a serviceman install new ones. Don't use the machine until this is done.

7. When you removed the filters, did you notice dirt on the other parts of the works? Dirty filters can spread dirt to the rest of the machine. Be sure the machine is off, then open it, and with the small dusting brush and the radiator tool of your vacuum cleaner, gently siphon off the dirt. Don't hit any of the parts. The machine needs all the kindness and respect it can get!

8. Is the machine icing up? Sometimes frost or ice forms inside the machine, on what are called the cooling coils. This happens when the weather outside is damp or muggy. Switch the machine to *Fan* and let the ice melt off.

The machine will also ice up if the thermostat is set at the coolest position, making the compressor (the cooling part of the machine) run constantly. Turn the thermostat slowly toward the lower numbers on the dial until you hear the compressor click off. Now, leave the dial at this setting until the ice melts. If the machine fails to return to cooling, automatically, after one hour, *turn the thermostat up one number every fifteen minutes, until cooling begins again.* At this setting, the compressor should function properly —alternating between *cool* and *fan* (keeping the machine from icing up).

Note: Do not turn the thermostat back and forth as if you were fiddling with a radio dial. You can blow a fuse by making the compressor go on and off, then on again, in the space of a few minutes.

Machine Labors or Fades. This is caused by a lack of electrical "juice." Your circuits may be overloaded, or it's possible the electric company has cut back on power. Check with your neighbors or the utility company, then call your electrician. You may need to install a special line (additional power) for the machine. Your electrician can advise you on this.

Machine Shimmies and Shakes. Turn the machine off. Unless there's an earthquake going on, your unit needs to be more firmly anchored to the window or wall. Check the installation of the machine from outside the house and from the inside, too. Be sure that supports are secure, that bolts or screws holding the machine in place are tight. Call the man who installed your unit and have him do any work that's needed.

Warm Air Is Seeping into Room. If you feel air coming in from outdoors and you can see daylight between the unit and the wall or window casing, you're not getting the best cooling you could. Turn the machine off. Fill up any cracks between it and the opening it's in with caulking strips. The best caulking for this job is a pliable, puttylike substance that comes in long, coiled strands from the hardware store. Push the caulking, a strand at a time, into the crack, smoothing it out so that it makes a sure seal.

Machine Makes a Loud Clattering Sound. As we've cautioned you (see first paragraph this entry, page 8, *turn the unit off.* Usually this sound means that a fan inside is hitting another part of the machine. This can happen if the unit is not properly set into the window or wall—that is, if it tilts *down* toward the floor, or *up* toward the ceiling. Place a carpenter's level on top of the machine. If the bubble in the little glass window is not centered, your air conditioner needs help. Push wedges of wood (called *shims*) under the conditioner to prop it up and level it. Gently tap these wedges in place (between the bottom of the machine and the windowsill) until the carpenter's level shows that the unit no longer tilts. Depending on the tilt of your air conditioner, shim it from the outside of your house or from indoors. Try the machine after it's level; if it still clatters, turn it off and call the repairman.

Machine Drips Water. This can be caused either by icing (see opposite page) or by a clogged drainage line. If the drainage line is clogged, the drip will appear at the front of the unit. After you've turned the machine off *and* pulled out the electric cord from the wall outlet, remove the grille and try to open the drainage hole at the base of the coils. Use a flexible wire for this, or use your meat baster (the one that looks like a big medicine dropper) to try to force air into the blocked line.

If the drips are on the outdoor side of the machine and they're coming from its base, the unit will have to be leveled (see above, page 11). You can shim it up yourself or get the repairman to do it.

AIR DUCT | heating or air conditioning

Wall or Floor Registers Leading to Ducts Are Dusty. It may surprise you to know that all registers (or grilles) covering your hot or cold air system ducts are removable. Lift them off or remove the screws that hold them in place. Wash them or wipe off both sides with a damp cloth, or clean them with your vacuum cleaner. Anyone who has airborne allergies will thank you if you keep these registers clean. *Note:* It's a good idea to keep pets and children away while you're doing this chore: Small pets can fall into floor ducts and your child may be tempted to throw toys down them.

Ducts Beneath Registers Are Dusty or Dirty. Dust in the air and dirt streaks on your walls may be telling you that you've neglected to clean the ducts *beneath* the registers. Don't wait for these signals—get to work on those ducts! Remove the registers, as above, and with the hose and longest tool attachment to your vacuum, work slowly down the duct. Be careful not to whack or dent the sides of the ducts as you siphon up the dust. This chore should be part of your regular cleaning routine, so that dirt particles are not blown into your rooms when the heating or cooling units are working. Replace the register, and be sure it fits snugly to the top of the duct.

Unpleasant or Oily Odors Coming from Ducts. This should alert you to call your serviceman *immediately.* The trouble can be serious. It may mean that your furnace is acting up or that you have a damaged motor in the cooling system. Turn the unit off. (See also AIR CONDITIONER/CENTRAL, and FURNACE.)

Filters Dusty or Clogged. (See also the above cited items.)

Ducts Damaged. Inspect the duct system—in your basement or crawl space—to be sure it's intact. Broken insulation around the ducts or holes in the surface of the duct will change the temperature in the system and make it work against itself—*and* hike up your fuel or electric bills.

To patch a metal duct, measure the damaged area; from your hardware store, buy enough galvanized iron or aluminum sheeting to cover it, plus an inch to spare all around. Be sure to get the same metal as that used in the duct. Shape the patch to fit the duct. If it's cylindrical, bend it; if rectangular, make a right-angle bend over straight-edged wood (a plank or workbench edge). Spread the underside with metal glue. Use a wire cinch or belt-clamp to hold the patch in place until the glue sets. (See Section II, GLUING AND CLAMPING, p. 248.)

Insulation Covering Ducts Damaged. If you already have insulation but some of it is damaged, remove the metal fasteners that hold the flexible insulation in place. Buy some more pliable insulating material, wrap it around the duct, and fasten the metal bands securely around this new piece of material.

Ducts Need Insulation. If your cooling or heating ducts pass through crawl spaces or parts of the house that don't require cooling or heating (say, the basement), and there's no insulation covering them, chances are that your unit is working overtime when it need not. Buy pliable insulation (you can find a source in the yellow pages of your phone directory). Remember to get the metal fasteners! Wrap the insulation, like a bandage, around the duct. Fasten securely with the metal bands.

ALABASTER OBJECT | bowl, box, statuette

Surface Dull, Stained, or Discolored. See MARBLE.

Broken. See MARBLE.

Parts of Art Objects Broken or Missing. Choice objects and collector's items can be restored by an expert, who uses different techniques, depending on the damage. Mixtures of beeswax and carnauba wax can be molded to replace the missing pieces. The texture, color, and typical translucency of alabaster can be perfectly reproduced by this process. The restorer will also use dowels or sunken rivets if the damage calls for it. Your nearest art museum can recommend a restorer for your treasure.

ALARM CLOCK

See CLOCK.

ALUMINUM AWNING

Metal awnings come with various finishes. Some are unfinished, with a plain metal surface; others have a painted or baked-on enamel surface.

Metal Finish Stained. Get some specially prepared aluminum cleaner from your hardware store, and, using a fine steel-wool pad and the cleaner, scrub the stained area. Rinse with clear water. (You'll probably need a ladder for this chore; if so, consult our LADDER SAFETY RULES in Section II, p. 312.)

Painted Surface Chipped or Damaged. Ask your paint store for the specially prepared paints used for aluminum surfaces. Ordinary oil paints will not cling to aluminum for any length of time, and if you use them you'll just have the job to do again. Follow the directions on the paint can for the number of coats to apply. Prepare the surface by removing any flakes of old paint with steel wool.

Baked-on Enamel Surface Chipped. See above, "Painted Surface Chipped or Damaged."

Awning Shakes or Rattles. If you've had rough weather recently, the screws that fasten your awning may have come loose. Get on a ladder and inspect them, tightening loose screws with a screwdriver. Be sure you follow our "LADDER SAFETY RULES," as cited above, p. 312.

ALUMINUM BEVEL SIDING

See SIDING—LEAKS AROUND TRIM.

ALUMINUM FURNITURE

Surface Pitted. Scrub it with steel-wool pads and detergent or soap, or with a specially prepared aluminum cleaner, which you buy at a hardware store. Wipe the surface dry, and protect it from further pitting by waxing with paste wax or by applying a thin layer of varnish. Use spray-can varnish to get an even, professional-looking finish.

Folding Chairs and Chaise Are Difficult to Open or Close. Use a silicone spray to make the metal joints move more easily. The spray is available at hardware stores.

Plastic Webbing of Seat Is Torn. You can replace this yourself. Look in the yellow pages of your phone directory for dealers in webbing. First, figure out how much material you'll need. Measure the webbing on your chair seat and allow for a few extra feet. Rent or buy a heavy stapler. Use the old seat webbing-weave pattern as your guide, and make a drawing of it. (Or better still, take a picture of it.) Cut off the old webbing, weave the new seat following your drawing or photograph, and staple the loose ends together on the underside of the seat.

ALUMINUM POT AND PAN

Surface Pitted. If you use an electric dishwasher, your pots and pans can be pitted by the dishwasher detergent when some undissolved particles of it are sprinkled on them. The cure for this and other pitting is to rub the surface of the pot with steel wool and a mild detergent or soap. Rinse and dry the pan or pot.

Stains Inside Pan. Fill the pan with water up to (and including) the stained area, and add to this a tablespoon of cream of tartar to a quart of water. Let the solution stand, then wash, rinse, and dry the pan.

Bottom of Pan Is Scorched. Soak the pan for a few hours, then scrub it with steel wool and soap or a soap pad.

Sides or Bottom of Pan Dented. If the dent is on the outside, place the pan, dent-side down, on a wooden workbench or chopping block, and gently hammer the *other* (or convex) side of the dent until it disappears. Your hammerhead should be wrapped in a soft cloth when you do this. If the dent is on the *inside* of the pan, place a wood block against the indentation (the concave side), and hammer gently on the bulging portion. (See diagrams.)

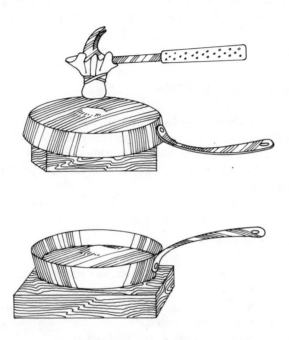

Handle Loose. CAUTION: *There's a safety hazard in using pots and pans that have faulty handles. Hot food may spill on the cook or the server if the handles wobble or come off. Don't use the utensil until the handles are fixed.* Either remove the handle yourself, if it's removable, or take the pan to a local metal shop. You can buy a replacement and attach it with screws yourself, or if need be, the man at the metal shop will rivet the handle on for you.

ALUMINUM SCREEN

Powdering. You may have noticed a fine powder on the window- or door sill beneath your screens. This corrosion will eventually wear away the screening. Brush the screen thoroughly, then vacuum it. Next, to coat the screen, thin a clear varnish with turpentine or other thinner according to directions on the container. (Thinning the varnish is done so that the "pores" in the screen, between the metal strands, will not become clogged and shut out air.) Varnish one side of the screen, then turn it (or go to the other side, if it's propped up), *squeeze out your brush* and run it over the other side. The brush will pick up enough varnish from the first side to cover the wires, but will also be free enough of varnish to leave openings between the wires. Thus, your screen can "breathe." Let dry overnight. Remember, the cleaner your screen before varnishing, the wider the "pores" of the screen after varnishing—*and*, it will look better, too!

ALUMINUM STORM WINDOW

Sticking. Permanently installed storm sash, which have sliding panels of glass and screening, stick when the grooves become corroded—something that happens especially often near the seashore. To unstick, steel-wool the grooves, then clean them and spray with a silicone lubricant bought at the hardware store.

ANDIRON | brass or iron

Brass—Stained By Wood Resins. Rub the stained area with fine steel wool, then polish the andirons with a commercial brass polish.

Iron—Rusted. Steel-wool the area, wipe clean, then paint the portion (or all of the andiron) with a special fire-resistant paint in a flat or glossy finish, depending on your andirons and preference.

Legs Bent, Log Support Sagging. Take the andirons to an ironmonger (look for one in the yellow pages of your phone directory). He will heat and then hammer the legs and support into shape. If you ask him, he'll bolt or weld an extra flange onto the sides of the legs to help them stand up better to hot fires.

Wobbly or Loose. If the ornamental upright front of the andiron is bolted to the log supports, examine the bolt to see if it is loose. Tighten the bolt with a wrench. (See Section II, GLOSSARY OF TOOLS, p. 229.) Be sure that you align the log support correctly with the ornamental front piece.

Finial Loose. Some styles of andirons have decorative finials atop the front of the andiron. If the finial is loose, unscrew it, clean the threads and the screw end, then coat both pieces with plastic steel or other strong metal glue, and replace the pieces. Remember that the thinnest layer of glue makes the strongest bond. (See Section II, GLUING AND CLAMPING, p. 248.)

ANTENNA

INDOOR

Telescoping Poles Bent. Both the single-pole variety and the rabbit-ear antenna are subject to the bends. A bent antenna won't hurt your picture or sound reception, but it's hard (if not impossible) to telescope the poles again when this happens. If you can't straighten the section by hand, place the pole between two blocks of wood, then squeeze them together. Rotate the blocks as you do this, pressing out the kink. Then try sliding the telescoping parts of the antenna up and down. If you still can't move them, you should replace the antenna with a new one, available from a radio/TV shop.

Telescoping Pole Has Come Apart in Middle. First, try reinserting the detached section, then give it a twist or half-turn. If, when you do this, you feel the bottom section grab the next section, you're in business! If the pole still comes apart, coat the smaller (detached) section with glue, insert this in the larger section, and let the glue harden overnight. You won't be able to telescope these two sections anymore, but your antenna will give better reception.

Telescoping Pole Sticks. If you can't slide the sections in and out easily, extend the pole, wipe it clean, and spray the pole with a silicone lubricant, available at a hardware store.

OUTDOOR

Poor Picture or Sound. One of the reasons for this may be that your antenna is not properly aimed at the station that's sending the programs. It takes two to tackle the problem. You can sit and watch the picture on the set while your husband (or a friend who likes high places) goes to the roof. He should move the antenna arms around until you get good reception down below. Tell him he's on target. Then turn off the set and have him tighten the bolts that hold the arms in place and tighten the bands or fasteners that hold the stem of the antenna to the chimney, or side of the house or roof. He'll need a screwdriver and a wrench.

If your antenna is on target for the station but still gives poor reception, the trouble may be in the wiring and connections. Turn off the set, be sure to unplug the cord from the wall outlet, and check the wires at the back of your set that connect with the antenna. Are the wires loose? If they are, wind them around the posts of the small screws on the back of the set, then tighten these screws with a small screwdriver. The wires should be secure now. Also, check the lead-in wire and the connections at the antenna for breaks.

Antenna Badly Damaged. If your antenna has been knocked down by a windstorm and is bent beyond repair, have your television repairman install a new one.

ANT

See Section II, PEST CONTROL, p. 307.

ANTIQUE

See specific items: CHINA, CHAIR, TABLE, etc.

APPLIANCE

See specific items: AIR CONDITIONER/CENTRAL, AIR CONDITIONER/ROOM, etc.

APPLIANCE CORD

See Section II, ELECTRICITY AND WIRING, especially SUPER SAFETY RULES, p. 258, EXTENSION CORDS, p. 269, and GROUNDING, p. 269.

APPLIANCE LIGHT

Note: Appliances usually have special types of light bulbs. You should not assume that you can replace, for instance, the light bulb in your oven or your refrigerator with an ordinary light bulb—even if they look alike.

Won't Work. Some of these special light bulbs are made to withstand extreme heat or extreme cold. Some are decorative; others, like oven lights, are strictly functional. Some have screw-in bases (like the ordinary bulb in a lamp), and others are inserted in the socket by pressing and turning into a slot (there is a slight click when contact is made). Some of these light bulbs are shielded with a protective cover which must be removed before the bulb is taken out. Your best bet is to consult your owner's manual on how to replace the light. If you can't lay your hands on the manual, call your dealer and ask him what to buy, or carefully remove the bulb and take it with you to the hardware store, along with the name and model of your appliance.

AQUARIUM

Broken Sides. Remove the glass fragments and clean the tracks of the frame thoroughly with a scraping tool, screwdriver, knife, or ice pick. Measure the side so that you can have new glass cut for it, and take a piece of the broken glass with you to the glass cutter. He can give you glass of the same thickness as the original. Buy some white roof-caulking compound at the hardware store. Press this compound into the frame-tracks of the tank, then slide the new piece of glass into place. Push it down—gently!—so that the compound oozes from the frame. Now, press the glass outward (from the inside) and smooth the excess compound down into the tracks. Remember, *this tank has to be watertight,* and you are sealing it with the compound. Trim off excess caulking, and let the mend set overnight before you put fish and water back in.

Leaks. First, find that leak! Then take out the fish (give them a temporary home), and bail out the water. If you can't locate the leak, seal *all* of the seams. Scrape the loose compound or cement from the inside seams, then smooth in aquarium sealer (available at stores where aquariums are sold). Follow directions on the label for drying time before you fill the tank.

ARMCHAIR

See CHAIR/SIDE OR ARM CHAIR: WOOD, and CHAIR/UPHOLSTERED.

ARTIFICIAL FLOWER | paper, plastic, silk

Petals or Leaves Torn. You can mend these if you use the proper glue for the material. Consult our GLUE CHART, in Section II, under GLUING AND CLAMPING, p. 248.

ARTWORK

See PAINTING AND DRAWING, and PHOTOGRAPH.

ASBESTOS-CEMENT SHINGLE

See SIDING, and ROOF.

ASHTRAY

Alabaster or Marble—Nicotine Stains and Burns. Make a dab of paste by mixing hydrogen peroxide (available at the drug store) and a pinch of talcum powder. Rub this on the stained area, then add a drop of ammonia and wait a minute or two. Wash off the mixture with clear water, and dry thoroughly. (To polish, see MARBLE.)

Ceramic—Stains and Burns. These will come off easily with water and soap or detergent, if there's a good glaze on the surface. Rinse and dry.

Metal—Stains and Burns. Wash with soap or detergent, then apply metal polish. Rinse and dry.

Broken. Mend by gluing the pieces together. (See CHINAWARE, and Section II, GLUING AND CLAMPING, p. 248.)

Bottom of Ashtray Is Rough—Scratches the Table. Glue a small felt pad to the back of the ashtray. Or use "moleskin" (it usually has an adhesive backing). Stick it to the underside of the ashtray. Or if you have an old cork coaster, you can use this to protect surfaces. Consult the GLUE CHART for the right glue. (See Section II, GLUING AND CLAMPING, p. 248.)

ASPHALT ROOFING

See ROOF.

ASPHALT TILE

See FLOOR TILE.

ATTIC FAN

See FAN/ATTIC.

AWNING

Aluminum. See ALUMINUM AWNING.
Canvas. See CANVAS AWNING.

BABY CARRIAGE | including car beds

Because it carries your baby, it's best to be cautious about repairs on the baby buggy. Don't tinker with the brakes or other mechanical parts if you're not handy. Your friendly bicycle repairer (ours happens to be a woman) or the supplier who sold you the carriage can tackle the job for you.

Carriage dealers and repair-shop people do stress the need for good maintenance. Inspect the carriage and be sure that nuts and bolts are tight. (If not, tighten them with a screwdriver and a wrench. Consult Section II, GLOSSARY OF TOOLS, p. 229 for these.) Test the brake to be sure it holds. If it doesn't, see below. Most important, keep the carriage wheels and axle clean and free from grit, mud, and sand. In other words, wipe or vacuum off the grime when you come home from a muddy buggy trip. Consult your owner's manual, and follow directions about oiling metal parts.

Below are repairs you can do yourself, followed by buggy breakdowns that experts should handle.

Small Rips and Tears in Fabric. You can make most of these inconspicuous by mending with one of the fabric sticky tapes, applied on the wrong side of the hood or carriage compartment. Or you can buy matching fabric or plastic at the fabric shop or department store, cut a neat patch, and glue this to the right side, over the tear, with white glue (polyvinyl resin glue). (For more on gluing, see Section II, GLUING AND CLAMPING, p. 248.)

Wheels Don't Turn Easily. The wheel may be sticking because it's jammed with grit and grime. Wipe it with a clean cloth. If it still doesn't turn easily, take it apart. First, remove the hubcap; this usually snaps off. (Some caps must be loosened by raising the small metal tabs between the spokes of the wheel. Do this with a prying tool like a screwdriver or a dull knife. Be careful not to damage the tabs.) Under the hubcap, you'll find two washers. When you've taken these off, the wheel can be gently worked off the axle. Examine each of these parts for grit, wipe them clean, and if they're made of metal (not plastic, as some are), rub with 3-in-1 oil (available at the hardware store or gas station). *Don't let the parts get slurpy with oil; a drop or two, or just a little dab, will do!* Reassemble the wheel, then test it. If dirt caused the wheel to stick, this cleaning should take care of the problem.

Joints Stiff When You Try to Collapse the Carriage. The carriage that converts into a car-bed has a collapsible frame that can be folded (for storage or for portability when you're traveling). If the joints seem stiff, they need to be oiled. Use 3-in-1 machine oil (it comes in an oilcan with a small nozzle) and be sure you reach the sticking joints. Don't overoil— use one or two drops only!

Brakes Don't Hold. If you have a small pipe, larger than the end of the brake rod, slip this over the end of the rod (for leverage) and bend this part of the rod *slightly,* so that it touches the wheel when the brake is supposed to be "on" or engaged. If the rod won't bend easily or is badly damaged, see below.

Brakes Broken. If you double-check your carriage to find out why the brake doesn't hold, you may discover that the end of the brake rod has been damaged or even sheered off. *Fixing this is a job for an expert.* Most likely the part will have to be rewelded or replaced. Consult your dealer or local repair-shop proprietor.

Fabric Tattered. Many manufacturers nowadays make replaceable fabric fittings for their carriages. You can buy new fittings for most models from your carriage dealer. If the carriage is a hand-me-down and you need to replace the hood or other damaged fabric, look through the yellow pages of your phone directory for an upholsterer who'll make new fittings.

Wheel Off—Damaged. Your supplier or the local bicycle repairer can fix the wheel, or, if it's beyond repair, he or she can order a new wheel from the manufacturer and install it for you.

BAG | fabric or straw

Holes and Tears. Coarse weaves like burlap, or bags made of Mexican sisal or raffia, can be repaired by darning. Arts and crafts stores carry raffia or jute, and shops that sell Mexican imports often have sisal in strands. Use a needle with a large eye (tapestry or upholstery needle) and follow the instructions for an ordinary darn (it's just like the one you'd use for darning socks). (See Section II, MENDING BY SEWING, p. 281.) *Note:* If you can't buy matching mending material, unravel some strands from the seams or hem, and darn with this.

Tightly woven fabrics (canvas, denim, or finely woven cottons and wools) are best mended with patches. Use a scrap of the same material for the patch (try to find this in the seam or hem), and follow the instructions for the ordinary sewed-on patch. (See Section II, as cited above, p. 284.)

If you hate to sew, buy press-on patches at your local fabric store. Follow the manufacturer's directions for applying the patch, and just iron it on over the tear. You can make glued-on patches from any suitable sturdy material. (Sometimes contrasting colors cut in decorative shapes will add style and zing to your beach thing!) Be sure the patch you cut is larger than the damaged area. Trim it neatly, or pink the edges with pinking shears. Spread white glue (polyvinyl resin glue) on the back of the patch and hold it in place for a few minutes until the glue sets.

Handles Coming Off. If the straps or handles are mendable, sew them on. If they have seen better days, replace them. You can:

1. Make new handles with sisal, raffia, or string, just the way you'd do a buttonhole loop. Use a tapestry needle. (See Section II, as cited above, p. 280.)

2. Buy leather or plastic strips and rivets from an arts and crafts supplier, and rivet the strips to the top of the carryall. (This form of riveting is easier than sewing. Follow the directions in Section II, BOLTING AND RIVETING, p. 246.

3. Crochet new handles with a large crochet hook and twine, wool, or string.

Zipper Broken. See ZIPPER.

BAG | handbag or purse

See HANDBAG.

BAG | luggage

See LUGGAGE.

BAG | plastic or leather

Holes and Tears. Patch with matching material and glue. (Consult Section II, GLUING AND CLAMPING, especially GLUE CHART, p. 248, under this heading.)

Handles Coming Off. See BAG/FABRIC OR STRAW and HANDBAG.

BALL, TANK

Replacing tank ball. See TOILET.

BALUSTER

Repairing. See STAIR.

BAMBOO FURNITURE AND ACCESSORIES

Well-cared-for bamboo is as appealing as the tropic lands it comes from. Poorly cared-for bamboo furniture is apt to look disreputable. If you have bamboo pieces, keep this in mind: bamboo gets its light, summery look and pliability from nature. It's an exotic tropical grass or reed, hollow as a pipe, and easily bent to various shapes. Strong as it seems, it is fragile and needs looking after. Don't leave bamboo furniture outdoors all summer long and expect it to perform in November as it did in May.

Bamboo Splitting. Use a contact cement and be sure to follow directions on the container (some contact cements are flammable and some have toxic fumes. *Don't* use any of them in a room with a pilot light, *don't* smoke, and *do* have plenty of windows open). Coat both surfaces to be glued, and let them dry for about half an hour. Now bring them together —accurately, because once they touch you can't pry them apart again! Clamp, lash, or tape the pieces together for a tight bond, and allow this to "cure" for at least a day. (For details on gluing see Section II, GLUING AND CLAMPING, p. 248.)

Small Spots and Stains. Most bamboo pieces are in the *raw* (without any finish) or they've been given a light coat of varnish to protect the surface. With small stains and spots, first try to wash the areas with water and soap or detergent, rubbing them clean with a rag. Be sure to dry. If the spot remains, add an equal amount of vinegar to water. Rub the spot with this, then dry. If the spot is still there, try these remedies:

1. If the stain is *dark,* apply ordinary laundry bleach, full strength, with a rag, to the area. Rinse off and dry, then rinse again with vinegar solution. Rinse with water and dry. Finish the entire piece with a protective coat of furniture wax.

2. If the stain is whitish, use steel wool (ask your hardware dealer for 000-grade) and rub the spot *gently!* Brush off dust, wipe clean, and wax.

3. Cover the spot or stain with an ordinary crayon, matching the color of the undamaged area.

Large Stains and Spots. Unless you are the patient, puttering type, your best bet is to rub the entire surface gently and lightly with 000-grade steel wool and vacuum the dust off carefully. Then take the piece outdoors, prop it up on a stand (over a drop cloth), and spray-paint it with an aerosol paint. Use an enamel paint for style and durability.

If you *are* a putterer, remove the stains and spots with the technique outlined above. If your bamboo piece has had a coat of varnish, you'll have to apply varnish remover, too. Use the water-soluble variety, sold in a spray can. Rinse the remover off with a garden hose (be sure to do this away from the lawn or outdoor plants: The remover may damage them). Next, rub the surface with 000-grade steel wool, vacuum the dust away, and wipe the surface superclean! Save the final steps for clear days with no wind. In a dust-free area, spray on a thin coat of varnish. Again, be guided by the directions on the container: Varnishing is tricky, tacky work. Allow about forty-eight hours for the first coat to dry. You may need a second coat. If so, proceed as above.

BAMBOO-HANDLED UTENSIL

Although bamboo is not strictly a wood (bamboo comes from a giant-size reed or grass and is hollow-stemmed), you should treat it with the same care you give wooden utensils. This means that you should not soak your bamboo-handled steak knives and flatware in the sink. Nor should you wash them in the dishwasher. Instead, wash them quickly in soap and warm water, rinse and dry thoroughly.

Handles Coming Loose. Too much soaking in hot water will do this, and it will spoil the looks of the bamboo, too. Pull the two pieces apart, and clean them carefully. (You may need to dissolve old glue inside the bamboo handle with a cotton swab dipped in vinegar.) Scrape the metal prong so that it's free of glue. To mend, use a superstrong (epoxy) glue. Coat each part lightly, then force them together. Both parts should be under pressure to join tightly and neatly. Press a cork on the tip of the knife blade, then wrap sticky tape from end to end of the implement and let the glue cure for about eight hours. (For details on working with epoxy, see Section II, GLUING AND CLAMPING, p. 248.)

Stains and Spots. (See BAMBOO FURNITURE.) After you've followed the routine described there, finish this way: don't varnish the pieces; just rub on some mineral oil and let this dry for twenty-four hours. Repeat the application as often as possible, until you have a luster that appeals to you.

BARBECUE

Below, we treat simple barbecues that cook with charcoal. For gas or electric broiler-rotisseries, consult ROTISSERIE.

Brick Barbecue—Exterior Bricks Soiled and Stained. Grease and smoke stains won't do any harm to your cookery, but they do detract from the charm of the occasion. First, if you can, vacuum the stained surfaces; if you can't, brush them. Next, with a stiff, clean brush and detergent and water, scrub the stains. Do this carefully, so as not to loosen the mortar (the cement) between the bricks. Allow the surface to dry for about an hour. If the stains remain, buy some trisodium phosphate at your local paint store, mix this with water, and, wearing rubber gloves, scrub the stained bricks *gently!* If you're still not happy with the way the bricks look, buy matching water-base paint and touch up the spots. *Note:* Don't let anyone sell you on the idea of using muriatic acid for this project. You can injure yourself and others with this powerful chemical.

Barbecue Smoky. If wind and weather aren't the causes, maybe your food or your methods are. *Don't* let too much grease accumulate on the sides of the pit or pan, and *do* wait until the coals are gray—not red—on the outside! If your barbecue has a chimney, soot accumulation inside it or a partly closed or defective damper may be the reasons for excessive smoke. To remedy, open the damper or, after the fire is completely dead, examine it for damage. (For more on this, see FIREPLACE.) At this point, too, you can peer down the chimney from above (see CHIMNEY) and then get rid of the encrusted soot. (With an outdoor barbecue, just twirl a bunch of leafy twigs in the chimney, working this up and down like a back scratcher. Cleaning an indoor barbecue chimney requires more preparation. Consult CHIMNEY.)

Small Cracks in Bricks. These are easy to mend, and can be fixed so the mend is almost invisible. (See Section II, BRICK AND MORTAR: CLEANING, REPAIRING, AND REPOINTING, p. 273.)

Mortar Crumbling Between Bricks. Another simple repair. (See Section II, as cited above.)

Line of Bricks and Mortar Cracked—Smoke Leaking Through Cracks. If the barbecue is indoors, put out the fire. Don't use the barbecue until it is repaired: it is a fire hazard. Find a contractor or a good mason to do the job. If the barbecue is outdoors, and if nothing nearby can be ignited by sparks from the cracks, finish your cooking, put out the fire, enjoy your cookout, *then* consult with a mason about repairs.

Grills on All Types of Barbecues—Rusting. If you cook outdoors and don't protect your grill, you may find that it's rusty from dampness or rain. Lift out the grill, scrub it with a steel-wool soap pad, wash it thoroughly in soap and water, dry, then rub it with salad oil and keep it indoors or covered until you barbecue again.

Metal Barbecue (Including Japanese Hibachi)—Rust Marks on the Outside. Rub the rust off with steel wool, then apply stove-black polish. Be sure not to let the polish touch food surfaces. *Note:* If your metal barbecue has a special, baked-on finish (you can tell by the satiny sheen), don't clean it with steel wool. Consult your owner's manual on care and cleaning. Soap and water or detergent should suffice.

Cracks in Metal. If ashes or coals from the barbecue could fall on your wooden deck (or any other ignitable surface), don't use the unit until repairs are made. If the cracks are small, you can tackle these yourself. (See STOVE/WOOD OR COAL BURNING.)

BARBECUE | electric

See ROTISSERIE.

BARBECUE | gas-fuel

See RANGE/GAS.

BAROMETER | aneroid or mercury

If you depend on your barometer to forecast the weather, you'll need an expert's services when the instrument breaks down. (A mercury barometer, by the way, resembles your thermometer, which you probably wouldn't try to fix. The rise and fall of the column of mercury in the barometer tells you whether the oncoming weather will be fair or stormy. The aneroid barometer uses a spring mechanism to record these fluctuations in pressure.)

Not Working. If your barometer is the mercury type, look at the mercury; it may have drained out completely, or it may have separated. Shaking or tapping sometimes can bring separated globs of mercury together, but experts say that this is unlikely. Let them do the work for you. If your barometer is the aneroid type, the spring mechanism may have broken. Most clockmakers can repair either of these breakdowns, but if your local man can't, look in the yellow pages of your phone directory for barometer suppliers and repairers. If you happen to be near a boatyard, take your barometer to the man who fixes marine instruments.

Dial Damaged. A clockmaker can usually fix it.

Case Damaged. If your instrument is an antique, take it to a cabinet-maker or antiques repairer (you can find one through the yellow pages of your phone directory). Metal cases can also be repaired by metalworking specialists. A jeweler can suggest someone for you if a clockmaker won't do the work.

BASEBOARD

Pulling Away from the Wall. Renail to the studs with small-headed, cement-coated nails. (See Section II, WORKING WITH NAILS, SCREWS, AND FASTENERS, p. 236.)

Molding on Baseboard Loose. Renail the molding on the top of the baseboard. If molding is not flush against the wall after you do this, fill the gap with patching plaster. Renail molding at the bottom of the baseboard with finishing nails, driving the nail at a slight angle through the molding and into the floor.

BASEMENT

Like coal mines and subways, basements come by most of their problems through the surrounding earth. Some basements are part way underground, some are all the way. Lack of sunlight, poor ventilation, moisture seepage are common causes of trouble. Coping with the effects of these is the basic business of basement repair. But because the basement also happens to be the *base* (or support) for your house, many repairs downstairs will require the attention of an expert. You can help the expert—and, probably your bank account, too—by learning to diagnose your basement's ills.

Below are some minor maladies and their cures, a list of symptoms to alert you to serious ills, and some tips on what to do till the basement-doctor comes!

Basement or Outside Cellar Door—Metal Rusting. If the bulkhead or door is metal (and most are), check it for peeling paint and rust. Rub small rusted areas with steel wool until marks disappear, wipe the surface clean, then paint these spots (or the entire surface, if you're interested in the looks of the door) with two coats of metal paint from the hardware or paint store. Be sure to tell the dealer that you want an *outdoor* paint. Follow directions on the paint can. If the paint has an oil base, remember not to work with it in damp weather.

Basement or Outside Cellar Door—Wood Rotting. If the damage is minor and merely unsightly, sandpaper the wood, then prime the surface; finish with two coats of outdoor paint. (See Section II, PAINTING/OUTDOOR, p. 298.) If the damage is severe (the door is hard to manage and the wood is giving way), don't fuss with repairs. *Replace* the door mith a new metal one. A building contractor or a carpenter can handle the job for you.

Foundation Around Basement or Outside Cellar Door—Cement Crumbling. Check the area where the door or bulkhead frame nears the ground; examine the cement and masonry work. Cracks and crumbles do get worse with weather. Repair them before they're large enough to let rain, snow, insects, and rodents into the basement. Clean the crack, then undercut it with a hammer and cold chisel (see diagram). Wet the old cement, then apply a cement mix available at the hardware store. Or buy a sealant (the polysulfide type). Be sure to follow directions on the container. You should apply a primer first, to get the best results. Apply both primer and sealant carefully, then allow the sealant to cure. Some sealants dry in two days, some need as much as two months for complete curing.

If the mortar is crumbling, it should be *pointed.* To do that, carefully scrape out the old mortar, dust off any little particles that are loose, and wet the surface to be repaired. Apply new mortar with a trowel (or even a plastic butter-spreader, if you have nothing better). For details on how to point bricks and mortar, see Section II, BRICKS AND MORTAR, p. 273.

Basement Windows and Light Wells—Clogged with Leaves and Debris. Leaves and twigs brought by wind and weather not only prevent daylight from entering the basement; the dampness they hold also causes wooden window frames to rot. Check windows in spring and fall and clear away accumulated debris. If the windows need repair, see WINDOW.

Ceilings—Plaster Loose. Replaster the ceiling. See CEILING.

Ceilings—How to Check for Dry Rot. First, don't be misled by the term *dry rot.* It doesn't result from air that's too *dry.* If you discover it in your ceilings, you've had enough dampness at some time or other to encourage a wood-eating fungus that destroys the fibers of the timbers. Even so, you won't notice dampness at the site. The only way you can discover the creeping menace inside the beams, sills, and joists that support your house is to poke around with an ice pick. Poke them every few feet with the pick. If you can poke the pick an inch or more into any part of the wood—if the wood is *that* soft and spongy—your house has dry rot, and woe betide you, for dry rot means trouble.

At this point, call a building contractor and have him examine the work to be done. The decaying wood must be replaced—a job for a professional. Be sure the new wood is decay-resistant or specially treated to withstand moisture and dry rot. The work should be done soon, before the rot spreads, or before the weight supported is too great for the weakened supports. *Note:* Don't fail to track down the source of dampness that gave rise to the fungus that ate the beams. Often it can be wood in contact with earth (a wooden porch, for instance).

Ceilings, Walls, Floors—How to Check for Termites and Carpenter Ants. (See Section II, PEST CONTROL, p. 307.)

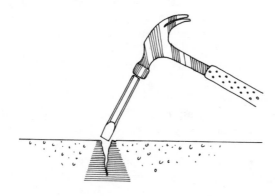

Basement Floors and Walls—Small Cracks. Sooner or later, water will find its way through cracks, so it's best to patch them right way. First, undercut the crack with a hammer and cold chisel. (To undercut, consult the diagram above.) This shaping is important, because it makes your patch stronger, helping it to resist possible water pressure behind it in the floor or wall. (For details on wet basements, see below.) Brush away any loose particles or vacuum them off. Mix a batch of hydraulic cement (from the hardware or paint store). Be sure to follow the manufacturer's directions. Pack the mix firmly into the wedge-shaped crack, smooth off the surface, and allow to cure before you paint the area.

Cracks in Floor Only—Mostly Around Hot-Water Heater and Other Appliances. Take a closer look at your floor. If the cracks in it radiate out from around your furnace, hot-water heater, or other heavy appliances, their weight is too great for the cement floor. The floor should be repaired by a professional (a mason). Be sure to specify that the new layer of cement is at least one-and-a-half inches thick and extra-strong (it should not have more than three parts sand to one of cement).

Large Cracks in Walls and Floors. If you have only one or two of these, patch as above, with hydraulic cement. Large cracks throughout your floor and walls indicate a major repair job. At this point, you should think in terms of professional help, but should also try to diagnose the case from the following indications:

Wet Basements. The great basement bugaboo is water. If water flows through cracks in your basement's walls and floor, you need help. Even a little dampness is unhealthy for your house and belongings, and may foretell future seepage. Any of these conditions requires your attention, and some will require professional waterproofing. As you will see, the remedy varies with the malady. From least to most, here are the sources for the moisture and water that find their way into your basement.

1. Condensation. Moisture in the air, especially in humid weather, forms as water on cold surfaces (water pipes and cement floors). It's the same thing that happens when the outside of your iced-tea glass sweats.

2. Storm Flooding. Water flows into the basement after a sudden severe storm. Sometimes this happens when your gutters and downspouts are not working properly, and sometimes (rarely) it's backflow from city drains that are too full.

3. Seepage. Moisture or water from outside the house enters through cracks in the walls or floor, especially through old and porous foundations.

4. Hydrostatic Pressure. As the seasonal level of water rises through the earth in the area where you live, water forces its way up through the floor or through the walls. The pressure against the walls and floor of your basement increases like the pressure of rising flood waters against a dam, sometimes buckling the floor and opening cracks there and in the walls.

Below are tests to determine these conditions and ways to cope with them.

Basement Floor—Cement Damp Because of Condensation. To test for condensation, place heavy-duty aluminum foil on the floor for twenty-four hours. Weight it down with a rock. If your finger becomes wet or moist when you run it over the topside of the foil, condensation is present. If the underside of the foil feels wet, see below.

The solution is clear: You must dry out the air. Open the windows on dry, fair days. Place a fan on the floor and direct it toward a window. Wrap sweating water pipes in insulating tape. If you still have a clammy basement, buy a secondhand dehumidifier; it costs less than an air conditioner and is cheaper to run. Double-check to be sure that your clothes washer (if it's in the basement) is vented to the outdoors. (The plumber can do this for you if it isn't.)

Basement Floor—Damp or Wet After a Storm. If your house's gutters and downspouts are clogged, or if the downspouts don't direct the water far enough away from the house, a sudden heavy storm can bring water into your basement. Experts say downspout runoffs should extend eight to ten feet away from the building, and should direct water into a dry well or into a storm drain. Clean the gutters and add piping or plastic tubing to extend the downspout runoffs.

If backflow from city drains after a storm is the cause of your trouble, ask a contractor or plumber about installing a threaded standpipe for the floor drain.

Basement Floor—Cement Is Damp or Wet from Seepage. Tough though your cement floor seems, underfoot it may still be soaking up moisture from the ground beneath (the way a blotter soaks up ink). Experts call this *capillary action.* Test for it with heavy-duty aluminum foil (as above). This time the moisture will be on the *underside* of the foil.

To cure the ailment, ask your hardware or paint dealer for a sealer or for a masonry paint. Follow the directions on the container in applying. After the seal is dry, you can add another moisture barrier—cover the floor with asphalt tile. First, apply mastic, then lay the tiles. (See TILE.)

Basement Floor and Walls Cracked—Floor Puddly Due to Seepage. Sometimes if the cement and plaster work in your basement is old or of poor quality, it will be porous. Water is bound to find its way to and through such material. To remedy, contact a waterproofing firm. What you need is a new layer of cement on the floor and waterproofing on the walls. Be sure that the cement is at least one-and-a-half inches thick, or water will force its way through the floor again.

Water Spurts Through Cracks in Your Walls and Floor. If water gushes, dribbles, or spurts through openings in the floor and walls in the spring or fall (or other times when the underground water level rises) hydrostatic pressure is acting on your basement, and you have a serious problem. But there are ways to solve it. Because these are costly operations, we suggest that you double-check on the possibility that your basement's ills are the result of a rising water table. Consult the phone book, and call or write the regional or municipal water department. Its engineers can tell you if the water table is on the rise where you live. (If it isn't, consult the earlier portions of this section; *porous* walls and floor are probably the culprits.)

If the diagnosis *is* hydrostatic pressure, contact a reliable waterproofing company to bring in the required basement "doctoring."

There are several types of cures, but the Good Housekeeping Institute recommends that if you hire a professional waterproofer, be sure, first, that he understands that you will not pay for the work if the treatment is not successful.

These are the treatments available:

1. Digging a trench or trough around the inside line of the foundation, and laying special "weeping" tiles in it. These tiles channel the water to

a pump (called a sump pump). The pump works automatically (when needed) to send the water to storm drains outside.

2. Installing special waterproofing materials outside your foundation. Doing this means digging down to the base of your house (the footing).

3. Treating the problem by injecting a special compound into the places where leaks have sprung.

Remember, after you've decided which treatment is best, you must also have the interior walls and floor repaired. Again, be sure a new layer of cement on the floor is at least one-and-a-half inches thick.

BASIN

Faucet Leak or Drip. See FAUCET.
Stained, Nicked, etc. See SINK.
Clogged. See DRAIN.

BASKET

Baskets come in all sorts of shapes and sizes and materials, and they hold all sorts of things—babies, laundry, bread, wine, picnics, sewing, wastepaper, and wood. To find the correct repair for a broken basket (because there are so many varieties), determine what it is made of. Then follow the appropriate suggestion below.

Leather Basket—Leather Discolored, Dirty. *Note:* Never use furniture oils or furniture polish on leather; chemicals in these may damage the finish on your leather. Your best bet for proper care and cleaning is to ask your shoe repairman for a good commercial leather cleaner. But even without this, you can do the job, if you're careful. First, brush off dirt with a soft brush or clean rag. Wet a clean sponge, then make a fluffy lather with saddle soap (your shoe repairman has this too, if you can't get it elsewhere). Rub the lather into the leather, wipe it off, and repeat the process. Let the second coat dry, then polish the surface with a soft cloth (cotton flannel is good). To give extra protection to the surface, and to prevent it from cracking, rub in a small amount of castor oil (sold at the drugstore). Let the basket dry in a warm place for an hour and a half, then polish the treated surface with a soft cloth. If you prefer, you can use a matching-color shoe polish for this postcleaning operation.

Leather Torn. Buy a matching leather remnant at your local arts and crafts supplier (or filch a scrap from a worn-out leather glove). Cut a slender patch, just a little wider and longer than the tear. Thin the leather (on the reverse side) around the edges with a razor blade, small sharp paring knife, or leather tool (a *skife* is what you ask the arts and crafts shop for). Coat the damaged area with rubber cement, and apply a thin coat to the reverse side of the patch. Let these two surfaces dry until the shine evaporates, then carefully stick the patch down on the torn spot and smooth it out with a soft cloth. If the tear is a large one, cover the leather with padding made with folded cloth, then clamp or bind the area until the cement cures. (For more on this, see Section II, GLUING AND CLAMPING, p. 248.)

Baskets Woven of Reed, Rattan, Wood—Soiled or Spotted. First, try washing off the grime with a sudsy brush or cloth. Rinse quickly (you can do this in the shower, or outdoors with a garden hose). Wipe dry, and stand the basket on cloth or paper towels in the sun to finish drying. (If spots remain, see treatments for BAMBOO.)

Strands or Slats of Weaving Coming Loose or Broken. Select the appropriate glue for the job (consult Section II, GLUING AND CLAMPING, p. 248), then apply pressure to the glued surfaces to be sure the bond is a strong one. You can clamp the work (see Section II as cited above, p. 253), or you can improvise a tourniquet: tie a strand of twine around the basket over the spot you've just glued, then, with a pencil or a metal rod, twist the twine until it is tight.

Bottom Falling Out. Use strapping tape to give the woven bottom added strength. Strapping tape is available at hardware and stationery stores. Crisscross the sticky tape on the inside of the basket bottom and bring it partway up the sides. Or reinforce the bottom by cutting a piece of ¼-inch plywood just a little smaller. Nail or staple the broken wicker, reed, rattan, or woven-wood strands to the plywood insert, from the *underside*.

Handles Coming Off. Clip or saw off the remaining strands of the handles. Sandpaper the rough edges smooth and unsplintery. Buy canvas or leather strips, or use a canvas or leather belt, cut in half, for each handle. Or, to be really fancy, buy leather handbag handles from an arts and crafts supplier (look in the yellow pages of your phone directory). Directions for attaching come with the handles. If you're just using the strips, thread these through the basketry where the handles used to be, then staple, sew, or rivet them together. (For more on rivets and riveting, see Section II, BOLTING AND RIVETING, p. 245.) *Note:* If the basket weaving is close and tight, cut the ends of the belt into ¼-inch strands an inch or more long, and weave these through the basketry. Then join each of these ¼-inch tabs to the inside of the basket by sewing or riveting them.

Metal Baskets (such as Silver Breadbaskets or Metal Wastepaper Baskets)—Tarnished. (See BRASS, COPPER, SILVER.)

Sides Dented. If the dent is on the outside, place the basket, dent-side down, on a wooden workbench or chopping block, then gently hammer from the inside of the basket until the dent disappears. *Note:* The hammerhead should be wrapped in a soft cloth. If the dent is on the *inside* of the basket, place a wood block against it and hammer gently on the *outside* (the bulging portion of the dent). Consult the diagrams for ALUMINUM POT AND PAN.

Mirror Baskets—Segments of Glass Coming Loose. Remove the loose mirror tiles and coat the backs with the appropriate glue. (See Section II, GLUING AND CLAMPING, p. 248.) Also spread glue on the damaged area of the basket, then press the mirror segments in place, cover with a soft cloth, and wind a tourniquet around the basket to make a tight bond.

Bottom Falling Out. Use strapping tape as described above, in "Baskets Woven of Reed, Rattan, Wood—Bottom Falling Out." Or reinforce by gluing canvas or any strong fabric to the inside bottom half of the basket. First, make a pattern from paper: push the paper into the basket, fold or pleat it to conform to the basket's sides, then take it out, slash the folds, and use it to cut a fabric pattern. Apply glue to the bottom and sides of the basket and apply the fabric reinforcement. Allow the glue to cure before you use the basket.

BATHMAT | terry, tufted, or chenille

Terry Mats—Edge Tattered, Frayed. Inspect your favorite mats before a frayed selvage edge turns into a big repair job. If the selvage border is wide enough, turn the edge under, as you would to make a hem, baste it, then finish. You can:

1. Blanket-Stitch It. Go around the entire edge by hand. Use cotton yarn or embroidery floss and a tapestry needle. Make the edge more decorative by stitching with a contrasting color.

2. Machine-Stitch It. Use several rows of stitches to reinforce the frayed area. In this case, choose a matching cotton thread that will be almost invisible when the mend is complete. To achieve this, *pick a shade slightly darker than the mat;* thread tends to look lighter when it's in the fabric.

3. Sew-on or Press-on Cotton-Tape Bindings. Notions counters carry both types of tapes. And there are press-on tapes that have decorative designs to make your work look attractive and less like a mending job. (For details on sewing, see Section II, MENDING BY SEWING, p. 276.)

Tufted or Chenille Mats—Rips in the Center. Rips often can be made invisible by mending with a simple overhand stitch. The nap or tufts on both sides of the mend will disguise the repair work. But if the area looks "bald" after the mending, use matching cotton yarn or embroidery floss and make new tufts. (For details see Section II, MENDING BY SEWING, p. 287.)

BATHROOM

Perhaps you think that the best thing to do about moisture in the bathroom is to live with it. But, unfortunately, water vapor from the bathroom can spread to other rooms. Eventually, excessive moisture can affect the walls and even the exterior of your house.

Walls and Ceiling Damp. The remedy is to dry the air, and the easiest way is to open a window. Tell your family to open windows after showers and tub baths. If moisture continues to accumulate, consult your electrician about installing an exhaust fan. For details, see FAN, EXHAUST.

Paint Peeling from Walls and Ceiling. The cause is probably moisture. After you've dried the air as suggested above, you'll want to repaint. Ask your paint dealer for a waterproof enamel or latex paint, and follow the directions on the container for preparing the surface and applying the paint. You'll probably want to use two coats to make a good, thick seal that will prevent the moisture from seeping into your walls.

Toilet Tank Sweats. If your bathroom is well-ventilated but dampness accumulates on the toilet tank and drips onto the floor, your moisture problem is condensation. In other words, the moisture in the air turns into water when it hits the cold surface of the toilet tank, just the way the outside of a glass of iced tea sweats. For four ways to solve this problem, see TOILET.

BATHROOM ACCESSORIES | shower and window curtains

Fabric Mildew-Stained. Before tackling the stains, examine the fabric to see if the material has actually rotted away. If so, discard the curtain.

If the fabric is intact, soak the curtain in the bathtub, using detergent or soap. Scrub the stained area briskly with a brush and rinse in clear water. If the stain persists through washing, fill the tub again and let the curtain soak in water to which you've added a diluted solution of chlorine bleach (one-half to one cup of bleach in a gallon of water). Soak until the stain disappears, then rinse the curtain thoroughly and hang it outdoors, or from the shower rod.

Fabric Torn. Patch the tear with a piece of the same material. Cut it from the hem if you can't buy a scrap of matching fabric. (See Section II, MENDING BY SEWING, p. 284.) Or, buy press-on patches at the notions counter of your department store and iron these onto the wrong side of the shower curtain. Be sure to follow the directions on the package when you apply the patches.

Plastic Curtain Shows Black Mildew Spots. Wash with soap or detergent, then scrub the area with a brush, as above.

Plastic Torn. Mend with a matching piece of plastic, preferably taken from the hem of the curtain. Be sure to cut the patch a little larger than the tear. Place the curtain, wrong side up, on a flat surface. Apply the appropriate glue to the area and to the patch and bring them together. Then weight the work down until the glue cures. (For the correct glue, see Section II, GLUE CHART, under GLUING AND CLAMPING, p. 248.)

BATHROOM ACCESSORIES | shower rod, soap dish, etc.

If your shower rod and soap dish mountings keep coming loose, no matter how often you tighten the little screws that hold them to the wall, the problem lies *behind* the surface of the wall. What's there will dictate what type of fastener you should use to mount the accessories securely, *once and for all!* Make this test:

Tap the wall right around the area where the dish or rod is mounted. If you hear a dull, thumping sound when you tap, the wall is solid. If so, the fastener you need is called a *Molly* (or expansion fastener).

If, when you tap, the sound reverberates slightly, your wall is hollow, with empty spaces between the studs, or vertical wood supports. That hollow sound indicates that you should use special fasteners. Ask the hardware man for spring-wing or butterfly toggle bolts. Be sure the toggle bolt is the same *diameter* as the old screws you're replacing. The bolt must be able to go through the holes in the mounting for the rod or dish.

Shower Rod—Coming Loose from Solid Wall. Remove the screw and rod holder. Let the rod rest on your shoulder as you work. Push a Molly into each screw hole in the wall. Place the rod mounting over this, and drive the screws through it and into the Mollies. Unscrew the mounting at the other end of the pole, slip the mounting and rod aside so that you can push the Mollies into the plaster, then repeat the above process.

Shower Rod—Coming Loose from Hollow Wall. Remove the old screws and mounting. First, insert spring-wing or butterfly bolts through the hole in the mounting, then through the hole in the wall (made by the old screw). The wings of the bolt will open out *behind* the wall as you tighten the bolt. When the wings are spread-eagled, the mounting is firmly in place. At the *other* end, take out the old screws, insert the winged bolts, and drive them in as above.

Towel Rod—Coming Loose. See above, "Shower Rod."

Soap Dish—Coming Loose. See above, "Shower Rod."

Paper Holder—Coming Loose. See above, "Shower Rod."

Shower or Towel Rod—Corroded or Rusty. The simplest and most attractive way to cope with this problem is to cover the entire surface of the rod with plastic, self-stick wall covering. First, measure the length and thickness (circumference) of the rod. Be sure to allow at least ½ inch extra for overlapping around the pole's circumference because this type of plastic covering shrinks with time.

Buy the material at your hardware store in a roll, and in a color that enhances your bathroom. Wipe the rod or pole, then cut a long strip of the plastic, and, following the directions that come with it, apply it to the length of the rod. Rotate the rod or pole when you're finished so that the overlapping seam is on the inside of the shower (or the wall side of the towel rod). *Note:* You can apply self-stick plastic wall covering with the pole or rod in place. Or, if you prefer, remove the mountings, apply the plastic, then refasten the mountings as discussed above ("Shower Rod— Coming Loose.")

BATHROOM CABINET

Shelves Stained. Wipe the shelves with detergent or scouring powder and water, rinse and dry. Measure the area, then buy self-stick plastic wall covering for each shelf. Follow the directions on the back of the covering, making sure to allow at least ½ inch more than you measured when you cut the pieces because this material eventually shrinks a little.

If you prefer paint to a plastic covering, scrape the surface and rub it with sandpaper until it is smooth. Vacuum off sand and paint particles, wipe with a damp rag and allow to dry. Ask your hardware or paint dealer for a waterproof paint—you can use either an oil- or water-base paint, as you choose. *Note:* You might want to try the glossy, extra-durable paint that is used for spray-painting or touching up refrigerators and freezers. Be sure to follow the directions on the container.

Exterior Chipped and Stained—Paint. See above, 'Shelves Stained."

BATHROOM FAN

See FAN/EXHAUST.

BATHROOM FIXTURE

See FAUCET, DRAIN, SHOWER HEAD, TOILET, SINK, etc.

BATHROOM LINEN

Torn. See Section II, MENDING BY SEWING, p. 276.

BATHTUB

Loud Hammering, Banging Sounds When Water Is Turned On. See PIPE.

Large Cracks Between Wall Tile and Tub Rim. Get rid of the crumbling tile cement or loose caulking compound. Start pulling this off with a beer can opener or a screwdriver. Then brush or vacuum the section free of any lumps or grit. At your hardware store, buy some mildew-resistant tub caulking compound (it usually comes in a handy squeeze-tube) and poke the nozzle into the crack. Fill the crack, then smooth down the compound with your finger or, if you're finicky, a small, flat stick. (A doctor's tongue depressor or a manicurist's orange-wood stick is good for the job.)

If you've recently caulked this crack and it keeps opening (which it will do if your house is settling or the earth beneath it quakes a little), there's a better way to conceal this recurring unsightliness. At your paint, plumbing, or department store, you can buy a kit which contains little "edging" tiles (tile men call them *quarter-round* tiles because they are just one-quarter of a circle). With the tiles comes the adhesive to apply them to the tub rim. Apply adhesive to all but the bottom edge of the tile and to the crack, too. Then hold the tile in place until the adhesive takes. Apply the next, and the next, until you've masked the crack with a tile overhang. Your house may continue to settle, but the tub will still be nicely bordered.

Tub Surface Stained. See SINK.

Tub Surface Scarred. See SINK.

Tub Won't Empty—Drain Sluggish or Clogged. See DRAIN.

BATTERY

See FLASHLIGHT.

BEAM

Sagging. If you can, inspect the beam. Examine it and test it for dry rot (see BASEMENT—CEILINGS, HOW TO CHECK FOR DRY ROT), termites or carpenter ants (see Section II, PEST CONTROL, p. 307). Perhaps the beam is bearing more weight than it should—have you just rearranged the room and added a grand piano or other heavy object? In any case, *your* contribution to this repair job is to detect as much of the cause of the trouble as you can. As soon as possible, have a building contractor or carpenter look the situation over. He may decide to jack up the floor above a floor beam with a jack post. He may need to replace a portion of a rotten beam. Because beams are part of the support system for your house, all repairs to them are tricky work and require the skills of an expert.

BED

It's been said that if you live to be seventy-five, you'll spend twenty-five years of your life sleeping or trying to. The bed that makes drowsing a pleasure should be sturdy, with good springs and a high-quality mattress to aid relaxed slumber. We don't, therefore, suggest that you try to repair sagging bedsprings or lumpy mattresses. They should be replaced as soon as possible. Below are various tips to help you take proper care of your bed.

Squeaks and Creaks. These can keep you awake, and there's no reason to suffer them. If the bedstead is metal, get out your oilcan and go to work. First, you'll need to remove or prop up the mattress. Squirt just a small drop of oil on the places where any two metal parts touch or rub. Don't slurp the oil. If you prefer, use the lemon-scented furniture polish for this purpose. Protect the mattress from oil stains by wiping off excess oil, then covering the bedsprings with an old clean sheet or cotton flannel blanket.

If the bedstead is wood, melt some paraffin or a delicately scented candle (a bayberry one is nice), and pour a little of the paraffin into small cracks in the wood frame.

CAUTION: *When you melt the paraffin, do it in a double boiler over hot water because paraffin is flammable and can ignite if it's in a saucepan over flame.*

Slats Loose. Take up the mattress and look at the slats. If the bed is old or poorly made, the slats may be too small for the bed. Measure for the correct size, remove one of the loose slats, take it to the lumberyard or ask a carpenter to cut as many longer ones as you need. You can leave the wood raw, but it's a better idea to give the slats one coat of a wood sealer to keep the wood from drying out or warping. (For details on wood finishing see Section II, REFINISHING WOOD, p. 301.) When the sealer is dry, insert the new slats.

Casters Frozen. Moving the bed around in order to clean becomes difficult if the casters freeze. Check each of the casters to see if string or thread has entwined itself around the wheels. If some has, clip it and pull all of it off. If there is no string there and the caster still won't move, squirt some oil into the bearing, near the axle of the wheel. Then work the lubricant into the part by moving the caster back and forth until it rolls readily.

Caster Loose. If the caster is attached to the bed leg with screws and now is loose, driving the screw into the leg again will not solve this problem. We suggest you take the screws out and start all over again. First, prop the bed up so that the leg is slightly off the ground. Take the screws out and the caster off. Now, mix up some plastic wood. CAUTION: *Plastic wood is highly flammable. Don't work near any flame—pilot light and cigarettes included!* Fill the screw holes with plastic wood and allow the glue to cure according to the instructions on the container. Then, put the caster back on the leg with the screws.

If the caster *fits into a socket* on the bed leg, prop this corner of the bed up and remove the caster. You can wrap some sticky-tape around the caster shank to make the fit snug, or you can spread glue on the caster shank and on the inside of the socket. (For the correct glue, see Section II, GLUING AND CLAMPING, p. 248.) Replace the caster and allow the glue to cure before you move the bed.

Side Rail of Wooden Bedstead Broken at Joint. Take out the mattress and take a look at the damage. The pieces of wood in most beds are held together with glue and a mortise-and-tenon joint, which looks something like your ten fingers interlaced. If only two or three of the wood "fingers" are broken, you can probably reglue the side rail. First, apply vinegar to the inside of the joint, then work the pieces free. Clean out all traces of old glue with a rag dipped in vinegar. Save the broken pieces. When the joint is dry, apply glue, very sparingly, to the broken piece and the rail. Clamp them tightly together, and allow the mend to dry for at least forty-eight hours. Next, apply a thin coat of glue to both surfaces of the joint. Bring them together, clamp them firmly, and allow the mend to cure for another forty-eight hours. Remove the clamping, clean off the wood, and make the bed!

If the joint has been so badly broken that the pieces will not interlace, buy some metal braces or angle irons from the hardware store, and attach these to the bottom side of the rail and to the bedstead. (They are strong enough to take the place of a mortise-and-tenon joint, but antique dealers say they decrease the value of collector's items.)

If you just can't handle the repair, a cabinetmaker is the professional to consult.

Antique Bed—Finial Broken off Bedpost. The decorative, carved knob that sits atop the bedpost can break off with rough handling, but restoring it is a simple repair.

First, examine the parts. Usually, the finial will have a small wooden peg at its base, called a dowel, which is inserted into the bedpost. It's the dowel that usually breaks. If it has, remove it from the hole in the top of the bedpost and take it to your lumberyard. You can buy a new dowel there, cut to size. Brush the inside of the hole in the bedpost with vinegar to remove any traces of glue. Allow this to dry. Sand the bottom of the finial to remove the remnants of the broken dowel. Now, glue the new dowel to the bottom of the finial, clamp it or weight it so that the two parts are tightly held together, and let the glue cure for a least forty-eight hours. (For details on glue and clamps, see Section II, GLUING AND CLAMPING, p. 248.) Unclamp your mending job and insert the dowel into the top of the post. *Do not glue these parts together.* Remember that if you're moving the bed, you can take the finials off and pop them back in place after the bed has arrived at its new home.

If the finial is a carved but continuous part of the bedpost, and this top part has been broken off, glue both pieces and clamp them together for at least forty-eight hours.

If you don't have the time or the patience for either of these repairs, a cabinetmaker or carpenter can do it for you.

Mattress. See MATTRESS.

BED | hideaway

See SOFA BED/CONVERTIBLE.

BEDDING

See BLANKET, and BLANKET/ELECTRIC.

BEDSPREAD | chenille or tufted

Rips and Tears. You can often make these invisible by mending the tear with a simple overhand stitch. The nap or tufts on both sides of the mend will disguise the repair work. But if the mended area looks bald or the mend shows, camouflage it by making new tufting. Take some tufting from a corner or along the hems (you may have to make a new hem when you do). Anchor the tufting threads with thread of the same color, bringing your needle from the wrong side of the spread, and stitching through the tuft. (For details on sewing and stitches, see Section II, MENDING BY SEWING, p. 276.) If you can't spare material from around the hem, buy some tufting yarn or embroidery floss of the same color as the tufts (pull one strand out and take it to the notions counter of your department store). Make new tufts of the yarn or floss: fold the floss over four or eight times to make the new tufts thick enough. Cut them and anchor them with thread and needle, as above.

Holes. If you can't steal some material for a patch from the hem or a corner of the spread, buy a scrap of matching material and set in a patch. (See Section II, MENDING BY SEWING, p. 284.) Cover the patch with new tufting, as described above.

Hem Coming Out. Hem the spread by hand or machine. With thick tufted spreads, you may prefer to do the work by hand. If you hate to sew, use press-on tape, securing the hem that way. Follow the instructions that are given with the tape.

BEDSPREAD | crochet

Handmade crochet spreads in lacy patterns are expensive (they are valued at several hundred dollars), and are true collector's items. If you have one—made, perhaps, by an ancestor—handle it with care. Inspect the spread every so often. Sometimes you'll find a small loop that is loose, and this can became a large ravel. Be sure you check for any unraveling before you wash the spread, and when you do wash it, use mild soap and rinse thoroughly. (You can send it the the dry cleaner or use a coin-operated dry-cleaning machine, if you prefer.)

Blocks or Squares of Crochet in Spread Coming Apart. Most crochet spreads are assembled from small crocheted squares or several-sided crocheted blocks. These are then sewn or crocheted together into rows, and the rows are then attached, row after row, to make the spread. Examine the work between the squares. If you recognize the work as sewing, then use matching yarn, or thread, and sew the squares together on the wrong side of the spread. Be sure to slip your needle through the tops of the little loops, so that your stitches are invisible on the right side.

If the blocks are joined by a crochet stitch, get a small crochet hook and join the blocks with crochet stitches.

If you can't crochet and you hate sewing, take the spread to a shop that specializes in needlework, and have the repair done by an expert. You can find such shops by looking in the yellow pages of your phone directory.

Stitches in Squares or Blocks Unraveling. Unless you are happy with a crochet hook in your hand, have an expert do this mending. But first, anchor the unraveled loop with a safety pin. If you enjoy crocheting, duplicate the pattern of the block.

BEDSPREAD | patchwork quilts

Patches Wearing Thin. Try to duplicate the color and design of the patch, and appliqué the new patch over the worn one. Be sure your thread and stitches match those of the original used in the quilt. (For details on this, see Section II, MENDING BY SEWING, p. 286.)

Edges Tattered. Buy an attractive binding—it can be cotton, silk, or velvet ribbon—and bind the edges of the quilt. (For details, see section as cited above, p. 287.)

BEDSPREAD | woven fabrics

See AFGHAN AND THROW/WOVEN FABRICS.

BELL

See DOORBELL.

BINDINGS

Book—Fixing Fine Leather Bindings. See BOOK.
Fabric—Cotton, Satin, Velvet, and Other, Used to Replace Worn Blanket Bindings. See BLANKET.

BLANKET

Bindings Coming Off. Restitch these. First, tack down the end of the loose thread, then duplicate the size of the stitches and the color of the thread already used. If you stitch by hand, use a very small backstitch to match the machine-stitching that is still intact. (See Section II, MENDING BY SEWING, p. 278.)

Bindings Worn, Ragged. If the blanket is in good condition except for the binding, rebind it. You can use any wide ribbon binding for this, but if you'd like to "fancy up" the blanket, you can use a flowered satin ribbon or a velvet ribbon. Be sure that the ribbon you buy is wide enough to make a border about an inch and a half deep on *both* sides of the blanket edge. The selvage edge of the ribbon means that you will not have to turn the edge under when you sew the ribbon to the blanket.

Take the old binding off, being careful not to damage the blanket. Iron the blanket edge flat (it will be easier to work with). Wash the new ribbon to avoid shrinkage later. Fold the binding in half *lengthwise* and press a crease at the fold, then pin it on the blanket, with the fold at the top edge of the blanket. Sew the binding to the blanket. You can use little running stitches, or, if you want to give an added decorative touch, catch-stitch it with embroidery floss. Fold the cut ends of the binding under and pin these, then sew together with invisible stitches. (For details on types of stitches suggested, see section cited above, pp. 277, 280.)

If you don't want to use ribbon binding, finish the blanket edge with several rows of running stitches (or several rows of machine-stitching) to keep the blanket from raveling, then, with bright yarn or floss, do a border of blanket-stitching. (See section cited above, p. 280.)

Holes in Blanket. If you really want to keep it despite the holes, darn them with matching yarn. (See section cited above, p. 281.) Or, you can slip the blanket into a cotton blanket cover. Tack the corners of the blanket to the cover so that the blanket won't slide around inside.

BLANKET, ELECTRIC

The wiring in your electric blanket is more vulnerable than that of other electrical appliances. Your steam iron's internal wiring, for example, is encased in rigid steel, but your blanket's wiring is sewn into flexible fabric coverings. Further, you probably toss and turn when asleep, tugging and moving the blanket when you do. So blanket wirings are much more apt to be bent than the wires of other appliances, and since you sleep *under* this appliance, the problem is one of safety rather than repair. The Good Housekeeping Institute and the National Fire Protection Association recommend that you buy only electric blankets which have the Underwriters' Laboratories (UL) seal. The seal means that the blanket, including its wiring and controls, has been tested for safe use. In addition, we suggest you follow these rules for using and handling:

- *Don't* store the blanket in a bag or box that contains camphor mothballs. The chemical can damage the insulation around the wires and thus expose you to shock or fire when you next use the blanket.
- *Don't* dry-clean the blanket. (Some manufacturers indicate that certain dry-cleaning fluids will not hurt the insulation around the wires, but you probably can't check which fluid is used.) Launder the blanket with mild soap, and follow instructions for washing that come with the blanket.
- *Don't* fold the blanket often—if at all. It is best left open and flat on the bed, where the wires will not be bent.
- *Don't* attach the blanket to the bed with pins: These are conductors of electric current. (Don't stick needles in it, either.)
- *Don't* tuck the blanket under the mattress; doing so bends the wires and builds up heat under the edge of the mattress.
- *Don't* sleep on top of the blanket. (Don't sit on it, either.)
- *Don't* ever use an electric blanket on your baby's crib or bed: bedwetting can cause shock and short-circuiting because urine is acid and a conductor of electrical current.
- *Do* check the cord. Is it frayed? Is it coming loose from the control box? (Don't use the blanket.)
- *Do* check the control box. Be sure it is not cracked or coming apart. (Don't use the blanket.)

Blanket Is Stone Cold. The fault may lie with your power company. Maybe for miles around, all the electric blankets are stone cold.

Follow these points in checking for a power failure. First of all, reach over to your bedside light and turn it on. If all remains dark, get up and find another light, preferably in another room. If this and still others you try don't go on, you can figure it's a power failure—in your house, the area around it, or the whole region. (It's a good idea to have a flashlight and battery radios for just such somber moments.)

If the bedside light goes on, look at the dial setting for your blanket. Is the control switch at the right setting?

If the setting is correct and you're still cold, the trouble may be with the cord plug and the wall outlet. While you're up, double-check. Is the plug really secure in the outlet? Wiggle it to be sure the prongs are as far in as they'll go. If you still get no comfort from the blanket, *unplug* it. Go back to bed, but in the morning, look over the cord for fraying and loose wires. If wiring *outside* the blanket is the problem, a serviceman (authorized by the manufacturer) can probably fix it. If the trouble is internal, *get rid* of the blanket and buy a new, UL-seal-bearing one.

Blanket Heats Up But Control Box Makes a Noise. If you hear a buzzing sound in the box that holds the switch and thermostat, turn off the blanket immediately, unplug the cord from the wall outlet. Take the blanket to an authorized serviceman.

Blanket Overheats. Follow instructions above, "Blanket Heats Up But Control Box Makes a Noise."

Cold *and* Warm (or Hot) Spots. Follow instructions above, "Blanket Heats Up But Control Box Makes a Noise."

Noticeably Discolored. Follow instructions above, "Blanket Heats Up But Control Box Makes a Noise."

Takes Too Long to Reach Proper Warmth. Follow instructions above, "Blanket Heats Up But Control Box Makes a Noise."

BLENDER, ELECTRIC

CAUTION: *Handling any electrical appliance requires care. It's imperative that you follow all safety precautions given in Section II,* ELECTRICITY AND WIRING, *p. 257, before you try to investigate trouble with your electrical equipment.*

Blender Labors or Groans When Switched from *Off* to *Low*. Switch the machine off. Food may be too tightly jammed into the jar for the blades to turn, or the food may be too coarse or tough for the machine. Take a look. If you think this is a possibility, remove some or all of the food to a bowl, then turn the switch to *Low* again. If it works now, you know the problem is not electrical. Mash or chop the food up a bit, then try it in the blender. (Consult your owner's manual on just what to feed your blender.)

If the blender still groans when the jar is empty, try switching from *Off* to *High, then* to *Low*. Sometimes the machine resists low speed because the packing around the stem (which turns the blades) is extra-tight. If so, experts say you might as well give in to the machine and run the blender from *Off* to *High* to *Low*—the packing will loosen up in time. (You're better off not fiddling with the packing yourself. This is what keeps the liquid in the container from oozing into the works below, and possibly short-circuiting them.)

Won't Run. Is the plug securely set in the wall outlet? Take a look, then wiggle it. If you notice that the plug is loose, take it out and examine the prongs that fit into the outlet. You can try to spread them apart, just a little, to make the plug fit more firmly in the outlet. Do this and switch the blender to *Low* again.

If it doesn't run this time (and you've tried *High* too), try the lights in the house. If they're all out, it's possible there is a local power failure.

If the lights in the house work, then test the outlet you're using for the blender. Plug in a lamp. If it lights, the trouble is in the blender. If it doesn't, the trouble is in the *outlet* or in the circuit that feeds this outlet. Now check the fuses for this part of your electrical current to be sure they have not blown. (You can change the fuse, if need be, but consult Section II, ELECTRICITY AND WIRING, p. 257, before you do.)

If you know, by running these checks, that the blender is the trouble spot, don't fool around with it. Take it to a licensed service center for repair.

Blades Need Sharpening. Don't try to take the blades out. Because of the delicate construction here, it's simpler for you to have a professional repairman sharpen the blades. Some experts even suggest that you buy a new jar, complete with blades, especially if the glass jar is chipped and the blades are bent or out of whack. The service center can do the work or sell you a new jar; it is listed in the yellow pages of the phone directory.

BEE | carpenter or borer

See Section II, PEST CONTROL, p. 307.

BLIND, ROLLER

Blind Doesn't Roll Up Far Enough. If your blind is rather tired and sluggish, and rolls up only partway (and does *that* slowly), the remedy is simple. First, take a look to be sure that the little brackets (the metal holders that attach to the window) are not rubbing against the roller and holding it back. (If they are, see below, "Brackets Bent.")

If the brackets are not rubbing, you can almost always bring a little zing back into the blind's performance in a few seconds. Pull the shade partway down, slip it out of the brackets, then roll it by hand. *But be sure that you only roll the fabric of the blind around twice* (or, as the experts say, "two complete revolutions"). Replace the blind, try it, and repeat the process, if necessary, until the blind responds properly to your touch. *Note:* Never roll the shade halfway up by hand. You can wreck the spring mechanism if you do.

Blind Flies Up When You Barely Touch It. Roll the shade up to the top, slip it out of the brackets that hold it, and *unroll two* (*no more, no less*) *complete revolutions worth of fabric.* Next, slip the blind back into its brackets, roll it up again. If the shade still moves too quickly for you, repeat the routine until you get the roller-spring to the right tension.

Blind Won't Catch When You Roll It Up or Down. If the blind doesn't catch and hold, check the brackets to be sure that the shade doesn't rub against them. (The roller should have $\frac{1}{16}$ to $\frac{1}{18}$ inch clearance on each side. Measure to see if there is this much room between it and the bracket.) Next, be sure that the little flat end that sticks out from one end of the roller rests *straight up and down* (*vertically*) in the slot of the bracket, and that it doesn't turn when you raise or lower the blind. *Note:* Never oil the mechanism in your roller, and don't take the cap off the mechanism, either! If you do, you'll ruin the workings of the spring mechanism.

Shade Falls Out of Brackets. Take a closer look at the way the brackets are mounted. Are they loose? If so, you probably need a longer bracket-fastener. Remove the nails or screws that hold the brackets, and take the bracket to the hardware store. The screwhead and shank you buy will then be the correct size for the bracket hole. Drive the screws in with a screwdriver, but use the old holes for the mounting.

Brackets Bent. If the brackets are old and bent, take them down and mount new ones. Follow directions on the package, and be sure to allow $\frac{1}{16}$ to $\frac{1}{18}$ inch clearance for each end of the roller. *Note:* Be sure that when you fasten the brackets to the window frame they are level. Use a carpenter's spirit level to check this. (See Section II, GLOSSARY OF TOOLS, p. 226.)

Fabric or Plastic Torn. You can make small mends with thin, sticky mending tape, but if the rips or tears are large and unsightly, take the roller out of the brackets and have a new blind cut to size at the department store, dime store, or window-shade shop. If the roller and spring mechanism are still in good shape, the new fabric can be stapled to the old roller.

Roller Broken. If you've had an expensive blind made, with fabric laminated onto a plastic blind, replace the roller. Your fabric can be taken off the old one and stapled to the new. A department store or window-shape shop can do this for you.

BLIND, VENETIAN

When Venetian blinds are in good working order, they lend style and a sense of order to their surroundings, but when they're the least bit damaged, they can make a room look chaotic and disreputable. Below are some suggestions to help you keep your blinds in good shape.

Cord Won't Hitch Up Blind. The trouble is in the little catch mechanism, and the solution is some sort of lubricant. Take the blind down and check to see that the cords are running over the pulleys. Spray the catch and the pulleys with a silicone spray (buy it at the hardware store). Rehang the blind.

Cord Frayed or Broken. Check the cords on your blinds, and when they're frayed or broken, replace them: Untie the knots under the bottom board of the blind, then pull the cord up through the slats, over the pulleys and finally through the catch. In threading the new cord into the blinds, start with the catch and go through the pulleys, down through the slats, finish by tying the cord under the bottom board or bar. Buy the new cord at a department or specialty (or even hardware) store. If you hate working on a ladder, take the blind down and thread the cord through it while the blind is flat on a bed or table.

Slats Broken, Bent. The simplest thing to do is remove the broken or bent slat and throw it away. But you can only do this if your blind won't look odd with a lost inch or so of length. Untie the knotted cord under the bottom board, pull the cord through the slats (*up to and including the broken slat*), and slip the slat out through the tapes. Now, take the lowest slat in the blind out, and replace the discarded slat with it. Rethread the cord through the slats and knot them under the bottom board or bar. *Note:* You'll have some extra tape dangling near the bottom of the blind. Cut the last segment of the tape off. Staple or tack this to the bottom board, or, if the blind is metal, use the appropriate glue and clamp the tapes until the glue cures. (See Section II, GLUING AND CLAMPING, p. 248, for details.)

If you need the length, have a new slat cut to fit, and slide it in place. Your department store's window-shade and blind section can do this for you.

Tapes Damaged, Stained. The small cross tapes on which the slats rest can be sewn back to the large, vertical tape, but if many of them are loose, this is tedious and finicky work. Save yourself the eyestrain and buy a new set of tapes at your department store. You might even want tapes in a new, zingy color to make the blinds themselves look new.

Replace the tapes by taking the blind down. Put it on a flat surface (a table or bed), untie the cords, and slip them through the slats. Slip the tapes off or cut them off. Slip the new tapes over the slats, secure them at top and bottom (tack them or clamp them), and rethread the cords back into the slats.

BLOCK, CHOPPING | also, butcher board

Chopping blocks and butcher boards—popular work surfaces in kitchens these days—are made of seasoned hardwoods and are tough enough to take rough treatment from all sorts of knives and cleavers. Remember, though, that any wood is porous, and too much water will cause it to swell and warp. Clean these surfaces quickly, with warm water and suds, or, if you've been chopping meat, a quick wiping of chlorine bleach diluted with water. Then wipe with a wet rag, and dry the surface. Below are suggestions for care and repair.

Chopping Block Surface Badly Stained. Follow the grain of the wood and rub the surface with a soapy, steel-wool pad. Rinse the surface with clear water. Dry it thoroughly.

Surface Has Lost Its Lustrous Finish, Looks Tacky. If looks matter to you, you can restore the satiny finish. (But the board will be perfectly usable without it.) To do this, rub the surface with a mixture of one tablespoon of mineral oil and one-half tablespoon of powdered pumice. Keep rubbing till the wood feels smooth to the touch. Let the board dry for twenty-four hours, then repeat the process until the surface has the sheen you want. Wipe clean with a damp cloth.

Surface Badly Scarred. Remove the scars with sandpaper or with a wood scraper. Vacuum off the dust, then finish as described above.

BOARD

Loose, Split, Warped, etc. See FLOOR and SIDING.

BOILER

See FURNACE.

BOLSTER

See PILLOW.

BOOK

Old books and first editions of your favorite writers are treasures to enjoy, but they also need tender loving care. Keep them clean and away from moisture. If you have a set of classics in fine leather bindings, you may want to have any damage done them repaired by an expert (look under "Book Binders" in the yellow pages of your phone directory). Minor repairs that can be made on less valuable books are outlined below.

Dirty Fingermarks on Pages. First, try removing the marks with an art gum eraser. If the marks are greasy, sprinkle a little talcum powder on them and rub gently over the area. Dust the powder off. If the marks persist, put metal foil or plastic kitchen wrap under the page, then moisten a wad of cotton or a cotton-tipped stick with cigarette lighter fluid, and dab this lightly on the spot. Blot up the fluid with blotting paper or towel. If none of these does the trick, rub a little chalk onto the fingermarks and camouflage the damage as best you can. (And give that dirty-fingered culprit a pair of gloves to wear the next time he gets near your books!)

Mildew Damage on Pages and Cover. First, figure out how the mildew got there. Is the room musty or damp? If so, all the books there will be affected. Dry out the room with a fan or electric heater, or open the windows to let in sunlight and air. Be sure the bookshelves are dry, too. Wipe them off. Then start on the books.

Wipe the mildewed areas with a soft, dry cloth, then with a cloth moistened with a little alcohol. Prop each book open and let sunlight dry it. CAUTION: *Remember, alcohol is flammable. Don't work near flame—or even a lighted cigarette!*

Book Badly Warped. Wrap the book in a soft cloth, then put it on the floor and weight it down with something heavy. (A typewriter in its case or a suitcase filled with books should do the trick in a few days.)

Binding Loose. Coat the underside of the loose binding and the surface beneath it with contact cement, then roll a clean paint roller on them to join the surfaces. Cover the book with a cloth, then weight the work. (Or, snap some rubber bands around the mend until the cement cures. See Section II, GLUE CHART, p. 249 under GLUING AND CLAMPING.

Page Torn. Cover the tear with a thin strip of one of the new non-yellowing plastic tapes. Use a tape that has a dull surface and you'll hardly notice the mend. (If you prize the book, take it to an expert repairer. See first paragraph of entry, above.)

Leather Bindings Dry, Shabby Looking. Fine tooled bindings should be treated to a yearly oiling. Use a soft cloth or chamois, and rub in either castor oil or neat's-foot oil. (Castor oil will give you a glossy finish, to match the leather, neat's-foot oil will give you a dull one.) Or, you can rub on saddle-soap lather, then polish the surface when the lather dries. Repeat the process with any one of these treatments until the leather is restored.

BOOKCASE | free-standing

Wall-mounted units are so popular nowadays that old, free-standing (self-supporting) bookcases seem in danger of neglect. Even so, lots of us still have them. Because these types of bookcases don't depend on the wall for support, they're usually sturdy and can carry a load of books without trouble. If they're not quite up to the job, you'll find some tips on how to fix them below. (For wall-mounted units, see BOOKSHELF.)

Shelf Tilted. Take out the books and see how the shelf is supported. Is the wood cleat or strip under the end of the *shelf* loose? If so, drive additional screws along the strip. Be sure the screws you use are not so long that they burst through the sides of the bookcase. Drill holes at regular intervals along the strip, then drive the screws in with a screwdriver. For looks, you can countersink flatheaded screws into the wood, then cover these indents with plastic wood. (If you're using stain to match the finish of the bookcase, mix some stain with the plastic wood, and spread the mixture over the screwhead. Or, you can stain the filled indents before the plastic wood has hardened.) CAUTION: *Plastic wood is extremely flammable. Follow instructions on container and do not work near flame—including lighted cigarettes!*

If your shelf is supported by little metal clips that are pushed into holes drilled on the inside of the case, take out the books, then look at the clips. Are they loose? The weight of the shelf can sometimes enlarge the holes in which the clips are placed. You can move the clips to a new hole, or you can reinforce the wood around the worn hole. Take the clip out, build up the hole with plastic wood, put the clip back in before the plastic wood dries. Use sticky-tape to keep the repair firm, and remove the tape when the filler dries.

You may want to add support to your sagging shelves another way. Nail or screw a piece of wood to the entire back of the bookcase, then drive nails or screws through this into the back of the shelves.

Bookcase Tilts Forward. Insert wood wedges (shims) under the front and sides of the base until the unit stands up straight.

BOOKSHELF | wall-mounted

Perhaps your newly self-installed, wall-mounted bookshelf unit, loaded with books, has just collapsed and you are somewhat shaken by the experience. Take heart—the problem is simply one of matching the fastener for the unit to the type of wall you're fastening it to. Before your pride of workmanship suffers again, make these tests.

Tap the wall where the metal or wood upright strips (standards) are to be mounted. If you hear only a dull, thumping sound when you tap, you have a *solid* wall, and the fastener you should use is a plug anchor. (To find out what it looks like, and how this and other fasteners work, see Section II, WORKING WITH NAILS, SCREWS, AND FASTENERS, p. 241.)

If, on the other hand, when you tap the wall, the sound reverberates slightly, you have a *hollow* wall. This means there are empty spaces behind the wall, between what are called *studs*. (Studs are a part of the supporting structure of the wall and they're almost always spaced or *centered* every sixteen inches.) Locate the studs by more tapping. You'll come upon a spot where the sound is muffled, dull. Mark this, and tap or measure sixteen inches from this spot to find the next stud. Studs are the best support for your bookshelf. Mount the standards on the studs by drilling a hole, then driving long screws through the standard and into the stud. (Be sure the hole you drill is smaller than the shank of the screw.)

If you know that your wall is hollow but you don't want to mount the standards on the studs, use a toggle bolt as a fastener. (See Section II, WORKING WITH NAILS, SCREWS, AND FASTENERS, p. 236, for varieties of toggle bolts.) Toggle bolts have metal, movable "wings" that lie flat when you push the bolt through the wall. The wings open up like a bird's in flight when you drive the bolt into place. Outspread, against the back of the wall, the wings hold the bolt securely.

Below are ways to cope with bookshelf units that utilize these fasteners.

Shelves Tilting Down. This is a warning sign that the fasteners that are there now are not good enough for the job. The whole bookshelf unit is beginning to give way under the weight of the books. Take the books out, and take the shelves off the brackets. Look at the standards. Are they loose and pulling away from the wall? Is the plaster crumbling around the holes in the wall? Pull out the old nails or screws and insert long stud screws, toggle bolts, or plug anchors. (See Section II, WORKING WITH NAILS, SCREWS, AND FASTENERS, p. 236.) Depending on the type of wall you have, you can:

1. Mount the Standard with Anchor Fasteners. Drill a series of holes up the wall to match the mounting holes in the standard. Push the anchors into these, then place the standard against the wall. Now drive the new screws through the holes in the standard and into the anchors. (Be sure to use a spirit level to keep your standards even with one another.)

2. Mount the Standard with Long Screws into the Stud. Drill holes through the wall and into the stud. Place the standard against the wall, then slip the screw into the standard and *through* the hole and drive the screw in tightly. (Make sure your standards are level.)

3. Mount the Standard with Toggle Bolts. Drill holes in the hollow wall. Inserting the bolt is a one-time thing: *Do not try to slip the bolts into the holes until you have the standard in place. Otherwise the wings of the toggle bolts will fly off and fall down behind the wall when you unscrew the shank of the bolt.* The next operation is a bit tricky. Put the bolt (without wings) through the mounting hole of the standard. Then attach the little wing nuts. Now push the whole thing through the wall—that is, bolt with flattened wings. Then tighten the bolt with a screwdriver. The wings will open behind the wall as you do this, and the standard will be firmly in place.

Shelves Sagging. This indicates that the weight of the books is too great for the shelf. Take the shelf down and add a standard. Mount the standard midway between the other standards, using the appropriate fastener (see above). Turn the shelf over, put it back in place, then put the books back.

Their weight will flatten the shelf, and the new standard should prevent further sagging.

BOWL

See BRASS, CHINAWARE, CRYSTAL, SILVER, etc.

BRACKET

See BOOKSHELF, and see also Section II, GLOSSARY OF TERMS, p. 230.

BRAIDED RUG

See RUG/BRAIDED.

BRASS

Tarnished. Apply brass polish with a soft cloth. Wash the polish off with soap and water. Dry the object and buff it with a clean cloth.

Lacquer Coming Off. Remove the rest of it. (You can use nail polish remover; it's cheaper, though, to buy a commercial paint remover from the hardware store. Be sure to follow directions on the container.) Then polish, as above. You can apply new lacquer by just painting or spraying it on. (But spray out of doors and away from people, pets, and flowers. Again, be sure to follow directions on container—for safe handling.)

Dented. See ALUMINUM POT AND PAN/SIDES . . . DENTED.

Badly Broken. Take it to a metal workshop. Consult the yellow pages of your phone directory.

BRICK

See Section II, BRICK AND MORTAR: CLEANING, REPAIRING, AND REPOINTING, p. 273.

BROILER | electric

See RANGE/ELECTRIC.

BROILER | gas

See RANGE/GAS.

BROILER | portable electric

See ROTISSERIE.

BRONZE

See BRASS.

BURNER

See FURNACE, and RANGE/GAS.

CAFE CURTAIN

See CURTAIN.

CANDELABRA

See CANDLESTICK.

CANDLE

Bent. Straighten a bent candle by putting it in hot water for a minute. When you take it out, it will be soft enough to mold with your hands.

CANDLESTICK

If your candlestick is damaged or broken and you're still using it, you may be playing with fire—literally. With the range of materials, cements, and techniques available, repairs are usually simple and the results often first-rate.

Broken Straight Across. This is the simplest mend to tackle, and finished it should be almost invisible.

1. Ceramic. Be sure the two sections to be joined are clean. Take a careful look at the parts so that you match them exactly. Apply the thinnest possible coat of contact cement (or clear cement) to both surfaces, and

bring them together accurately. Apply pressure until the glue cures. (You can weight the mend by putting a small sandbag, a sack of beans, or even an ice bag filled with water on top of the candlestick. For details, see Section II, GLUING AND CLAMPING, p. 248.) Touch up the design with artist's enamel from an art supply shop.

2. Crystal. If the piece is valuable, have it mended by a professional. An antique dealer can refer you to one. To repair the piece yourself, follow instructions for "Ceramic," above, using epoxy or clear cement.

3. Metal: Brass, Copper, Iron, Pewter, or Silver. Take the piece to the ironmonger or metalsmith for soldering or other repair work. If the candlestick is an antique, consult an antique dealer.

4. Wood. See above "Ceramic." Refinish. See Section II, REFINISHING WOOD, p. 301.

Split or Broken Lengthwise. This is a slightly tricky operation. The two pieces to be mended are prepared as above (see "Ceramic"), joined, then splinted. Use a pair of wooden chopsticks as splints—place them on either side of the candlestick. Wrap the chopsticks and candlestick tightly, or bind them in place with wire. Keep the splints on until the glue cures. (For details, see Section II, GLUING AND CLAMPING, p. 248.)

Loose at Joints. The base and branches of metal candlesticks (or candelabra) are often joined by being screwed together. If you notice that the candlestick is tilted or wobbly, unscrew the parts. Are the threads of the screw worn? If so, insert a small sliver of sticky-tape over the threads, then screw the two parts together. Trim away excess tape, if it shows, with a razor blade.

Candlestick Bottoms Scratchy. You can protect your fine furniture finishes from the candlestick's scratchy base by applying moleskin with an adhesive backing to the bottom of the candlestick.

CAN OPENER | electric

CAUTION: *Handling any electrical appliance requires care and savoir faire. It's imperative, therefore, that you follow all the safety precautions given in Section II,* ELECTRICITY AND WIRING, *p. 257, before you start to investigate the trouble with your balky appliance.*

Won't Run at All. Make the preliminary checks for all electrical appliances. Is the cord plug set securely in the wall outlet? Take a look at it and wiggle it slightly. If you notice that the plug is loose, take it out and examine the prongs. Are they working loose from the plug, or are they damaged in any way that you can see? If so, *don't* put the plug back in the socket. (You can repair or replace the plug; to do this, see section as cited above, p. 266.)

If the plug is in good repair, try spreading the prongs—just a little—with your fingers. This may make for a tighter connection when you push the plug into the outlet. Now try the can opener.

If it still doesn't work, check the lights and other appliances in your house. If they're out or not running, there may be either a local or regional power failure. (Check with your neighbors, or turn on a battery radio to find out.)

If the lights in the house work, test the outlet you're using for the can opener. Plug a working lamp into it. If it lights, the trouble is in the can opener.

If the lamp doesn't go on, the trouble is either in the outlet you're using or in the circuit that feeds the outlet. Now check the fuses for this part of the kitchen to be sure they haven't been blown. You can change the fuse, if need be, but be sure to consult Section II, ELECTRICITY AND WIRING, p. 257 before you do.

If the fuse hasn't blown, you know the trouble is with the outlet. For now, move the can opener to a working outlet, and open the canned goods you need. (*Have an electrician repair the outlet.*)

Cutting Wheel Is Sticky with Food. Old food, stuck to the cutting wheel or blade that opens your cans, is not good for you and yours, and it will hinder the operation of the can opener. Manufacturers and other experts recommend frequent cleaning of these surfaces. If yours has a removable cutting wheel or blade your chore is simple. Following your owner's manual, remove the part, scrub it in soapy water, rinse and replace it on the appliance. If the cutter is screwed into the machine, first remove the magnetic lid-lifter (just pull it down and off), then, with a small screwdriver, remove the cutter's screw. Take the cutter off, scrub it in soapy water, rinse, dry, and screw it back on the appliance. (Since there are minor variations among makes of openers, be sure to follow your owner's manual in this operation.)

Machine Runs but Can Keeps Slipping Off. You are not feeding the can to the machine properly. Be sure to hold the can *level* and the machine should perform as advertised.

Machine Runs, then Stalls. The can may be badly dented. *Note:* Be sure the dented can is not actually broken before you attempt to open it. If it is, throw it away; its contents are contaminated! Wash your hands, too. If the dents are superficial, put the can in the opener, and help the opener by merely turning the can clockwise a little. This gets the cutter past the bump or irregularity, and speeds it on its way.

Machine Makes a Racket When Run. If you hear an unusual grinding noise when you run the opener, it's possible that the gears that drive the opener need lubrication. But before you do anything drastic, unplug the cord from the wall outlet, then stand the opener upside down under a warm light or in a bright patch of sunlight. The grease that helps the gears run smoothly and quietly may have run down to the bottom, inside the case. When you stand the opener on its head in a warm place, you are probably doing a "lube job" without even taking the works apart!

If the opener continues to make a noise, take the appliance to the authorized service center for repair.

Cutting Wheel or Blade Edge Is Dull. If this happens (and you're sure that encrusted food is not covering the blade), take the unit to the authorized service center and have a new cutter installed.

Motor Works but Can Won't Revolve. If you know the motor is working (you can usually hear it), but the can won't budge, the trouble is probably not the *can* but the mechanism! The little engaging wheel that pushes the can up and into the sharp cutter is bent or damaged. Put the unopened can aside for the time being, and take a look at the works. Locate the damaged wheel. If you're handy and want to save time and money, do this repair yourself. Unplug the unit from the outlet and unscrew the case. Then from *inside* the case, unscrew the engaging wheel mounting. Take the damaged wheel to your local machine shop or electrical supply store, buy a new wheel of the same size and type, and screw this onto the opener. If you find this too complicated, take the unit to your authorized service center for repair. (And keep a hand-operated can opener in the kitchen, just in case any of these problems occur.)

CAN OPENER | mechanical

New designs in mechanical can openers make them easy to operate, whether they're wall-mounted or portable. Since the important features of these are similar, we treat them together, below.

Hard to Work. Take a look at the cutting wheel and at the gears on the wheel below it. If food is sticking to these surfaces, the unit won't work well, and sometimes will not work at all. If the opener is wall-mounted, slip it out of the mounting. Scrub the food off with a stiff brush and soapy water, rinse, dry and replace the opener.

If the opener is clean but is hard to work, drop a smidgen of salad oil onto the moving parts (the wheels), work them, add a little more oil and test the device again, until it responds easily.

Cutting Wheel Won't Bite into Can. If the wheels move without difficulty but the opener doesn't hold the can in place, or fails to cut into the top of the can, the space between the cutting wheel and the gear wheel below it is too big. Bring the cutting wheel nearer to the gear, using a small wrench or pliers, and tighten the bolt in the center of the cutting wheel.

If the opener is still out of whack, don't fuss with it. Treat yourself to a new one. For a few dollars you can buy an opener that carries a five-year guarantee!

CANVAS | awning, chair, cushion

Ripped, Torn. Make the repair on the wrong side of the awning or chair. If you can, find or buy a matching piece of canvas (use denim, if you can't find canvas). Cut a strip at least ½ inch longer and wider than the tear. At the hardware or department store, buy one of the new silicone caulks. You may want to buy the colorless, translucent variety or to select one that is a close match to the color of your damaged canvas. Spread the silicone caulk on the patch and apply a thin coating around the wrong side of the tear. Bring the surfaces together, and let the caulk cure. (It takes about an hour for the caulk to lose its stickiness, and about ten days for a full cure, so don't use the item during that time.) You'll find that when the caulk is dry, the mend will be as flexible as the undamaged canvas, and will also be waterproof.

Colors Faded, Drab-Looking. Paint and department stores carry special paint to give new life to canvas furniture or awnings. First, be sure the canvas has *not* been waterproofed. Then check to see if it's clean. If not, scrub it with soap or detergent and water. Put it in the sun to dry. After it's dry, apply the paint according to the directions on the container, and be sure to keep your brushstrokes in line with the weave of the material. Don't hang the awnings or use the furniture until the paint is bone dry.

If you'd rather dye than paint, canvas takes to such color-renewing readily. Choose a color a shade *darker* than your canvas. Follow directions given on the dye package.

Awning Needs Waterproofing. You can make your own waterproofing mixture and put this on your awnings. A good time to do it is after you've restored their color with dye or paint. Be sure the canvas is dry, then stretch it really taut. Apply a homemade mix of beeswax and turpentine. Melt the wax by putting the whole container into hot water. Add the melted wax to a bucket of warmed turpentine. (Warm the turpentine the same way.) CAUTION: *Wax and turpentine are flammable and should not be heated in containers placed over direct flame!* Use about a pound of wax to a gallon of turpentine. Apply this mixture to your canvas awnings and let them dry thoroughly before rolling them up. If you don't want to fuss with homemade mixtures, buy a special waterproofing compound to spray onto your canvas furnishings and accessories.

CARD TABLE | folding

Legs Stuck. Use a silicone spray (buy it at the hardware store), on the metal hinges so that the legs will open and close with ease.

Legs Wobbly. Turn the card table over and examine the screws that hold the legs and supports to the table. Tighten any loose screws.

Top Damaged. If the surface is plastic fabric, replace this with new covering. First, unscrew the screws that hold the top to the frame. You'll find them along the underside of the frame, between the leg braces. Take the top off the frame, remove the old, damaged plastic, and use this as your pattern in buying and cutting a new covering. Anchor the new fabric onto the top with sticky-tape (this is temporary), then insert the top in the frame and screw it in place. Remove the tape.

CARPET

Soiled. No matter how conscientious you are about daily vacuuming, eventually your wall-to-wall or room-size carpet will need a good shampooing. Although all carpet fibers can be home-shampooed, don't risk ruining your precious area rugs and Orientals by cleaning them yourself. These are special pieces, and they should be cared for by experts. (See RUG.)

Before you begin to shampoo, vacuum up all the loose dirt and dust, and if possible, move the furniture into another room. You will do the most efficient job by using a shampoo machine, either hand-operated or electric. (See RUG SHAMPOOER and FLOOR SCRUBBER-POLISHER.) You may be able to rent a heavy-duty electric shampooer from the hardware store or supermarket. Both electric and mechanical devices have pushbutton dispensers to regulate the amount of cleaner that goes onto the carpet—important, because this will prevent you from oversoaking the surface. A carpet that absorbs too much water could stretch and ripple, or, if it is wool, shrink.

Use only specially marked cleaner for your carpet shampooing. (We have found that rug shampoo with foam-cleaning action is preferable. Mix it with water according to the instructions on the package, and fill the machine.)

Make overlapping strokes with the applicator, as you travel across the carpet. When the suds disappear and the carpet dries, vacuum away the dirt that the foam has brought to the surface. When you're certain that the fibers have dried completely, put the furniture back in place. (If it's necessary to put the furniture back in place sooner, place squares of aluminum foil under each leg or pedestal of the chairs, sofas, and tables, to prevent possible rust stains on the carpet.)

Stained. If you can catch most stains before they set, you can usually wipe them away with a little mild detergent and water on a sponge, cloth, or paper towel. Wipe inward, and you'll avoid leaving a ring. If the stain is stubborn, and is one of those listed below, try using these cleaning tips:

1. Animal Stain. Mix one cup of water and a teaspoon of white vinegar. The solution should be applied and allowed to remain on the stain for

fifteen minutes. Then sponge the stain with warm, soapy water and rinse with a clean sponge. Blot up any moisture with absorbent cloth or paper towels.

2. Blood Stain. Apply cold water or an ice cube, and then wash with warm, soapy water. Rinse and blot dry.

3. Grease. First, try warm, soapy water, but if the spot is resistant, use any of the available all-purpose liquid cleaners.

4. Nail Polish. If you catch the spill quickly, nail polish can be wiped away with mild detergent and water. But don't use nail polish remover; if there are polyester fibers in the carpet, it will dissolve them, and you will be left with a bare spot. Better send the carpet to an expert rug cleaner.

In all cases, if you've tried everything and stains still linger, let a professional rug cleaner take over.

Frayed Edges and Worn Spots. An edge that is unraveling can be trimmed back and bound. (See Section II, MENDING BY SEWING, p. 276.) But if you don't like to sew, remove the old binding and iron press-on carpet binding along the torn border.

Trouble in the center is more difficult to fix. When the threads in the body of the carpet are worn down and almost threadbare, roll the carpet up and look for cracks or ridges in the floor. Sand the jagged spots and fill in the cracks to level the floor as best you can to prevent further wear on your carpet. Then put a good carpet pad underneath your carpet for protection.

Worn-away carpet fibers are usually not worth replacing. If your carpet is not tacked down, rotate it, and cover the worn areas with furniture or a small rug.

Rippling. A wavy carpet has to be smoothed out by a professional installer with a specially made, pronged tool. (The repairman will work out the ripples and retack the carpet for less than the cost of installation. The effect is worth the relatively small charge.)

If your carpet is not tacked, try to straighten it out yourself before you call in the expert. Dampen the rippling area and cover it with a clean rag or sheet. Pile books, heavy flat objects, or weighted boards on the area. When you remove these, the ripple more than likely will have disappeared.

Insect Damage. (See Section II, PEST CONTROL, p. 307.)

CARPET SWEEPER | electric

Won't Work. See VACUUM CLEANER.

CARPET SWEEPER | mechanical

Brushes Don't Sweep. If your carpet sweeper seems balky and it's not sweeping up the lint and dust on the carpet, a tangle of threads, cat fur, or hair may be the cause. Turn the case over and take a look at the brush. With scissors, cut between the rows of bristles on the brush or brushes. Be careful not to damage the brush itself when you do this. Then pull off dust and lint that may have become impacted at either end of the brush.

Lint Drops Back onto Carpet. If it's winter and the air in your room is extra-dry (because you have the heat on), the fault lies not with your carpet sweeper, but with the atmosphere. You're generating static electricity like mad by walking across the carpet, and you make even more of it by running the sweeper back and forth across the carpet. (The condition is not dangerous, and will cease with a change in the weather.) The small electrical charges tend to make the carpet attract the fuzz you're trying to sweep up. To cope with the problem, cool off the room and make the air moist. Open some windows before you sweep, and keep several bowls of water in the room (you can disguise these by putting flowers in them).

Brush or Brushes Worn. If you've looked at your sweeper and find that the brushes look bald, snap the brush or brushes out of the clamps that hold them in place on the underside of the case. Take them to your local carpet-sweeper dealer and replace them with new brushes.

Handle Coming Loose. After rough handling and long use, the handle on the sweeper may be working loose. The threads at the base of the handle that screw into the top of the case are probably stripped (worn away). Buy a new handle to fit into your sweeper's case at the local dealer. Take the old handle with you to be sure you duplicate it.

CART | tea or serving

Casters Frozen or Loose. See CASTER.

Cart Rolls Away from You. See CASTER.

Marble Surfaces Damaged. See MARBLE.

Wood Finish Marred or Burned. See Section II, REFINISHING WOOD, p. 301.

CASTER

Won't Move. If the caster is frozen, check to see if string, thread, or dust is the cause. These can wrap around the wheel and the bearing, and prevent them from rolling. Clip the thread or pull the dust off, then roll the caster back and forth to be sure it moves easily.

If there's no string or dirt impeding movement, spray a silicone lubricant into the bearing. Aim this at the place where the axle joins the wheel. Then, work the lubricant into the part by moving the caster back and forth until it rolls steadily.

Caster Loose. If the caster is attached to the piece of furniture with screws and now is loose, driving the screws into the furniture leg will not solve the problem. We suggest you take the screws out and start all over again. First, prop the furniture up so that you can get at the leg (you can use a bench or sawhorse). Take the screws out and the caster off. Now mix up some plastic wood to the right consistency for the job. Fill the screw holes with plastic wood, and allow the plastic wood to harden according to the instructions on the container. CAUTION: *Plastic wood is extremely flammable. Do not work near flame—including pilot light and lighted cigarettes.* Drill new holes, smaller than the screws, then insert and drive screws through caster-mounting and into wood of the furniture.

If the caster fits into a socket on the piece of furniture, prop the item up (as suggested above), then remove the caster. You can wrap some sticky-tape around the caster shank to make the fit snug, or you can spread glue on the caster shank and on the inside of the socket. (For the correct glue, see Section II, GLUING AND CLAMPING, p. 248.) Remove the caster and allow the glue to cure before you move the furniture on its casters.

Caster Keeps Rolling—Furniture Attached to It Won't Stay Put. If your tea cart starts rolling away, immobilize the casters. If you feel comfortable working with a drill, drill a small hole through the yoke that holds the caster. Insert a screw in the hole; it will act as a locking pin to keep the furniture where you want it. Remove the screw when you want to move the furniture.

If you hate handling drills, buy a set of four casters, two of them equipped with brakes. Remove the old casters as described above, and attach the new ones. Follow directions that come with the package.

CAULKING

See Section II, CAULKING, p. 271.
See also BATHTUB, and SIDING.

CEILING | plaster

Cracks and Small Holes. When the plaster ceiling in your home begins to crack, it's time to do some patching. Usually, thin cracks that show up when a house is settling are not serious problems or difficult repair jobs. Spackling compound, a white powder that turns into paste when water is added, is easy to apply.

Use a pointed beer-can opener or sharp chisel to widen the crack or hole, and moisten the fresh opening with a wet paintbrush (or, if there are children and toys in your household, borrow a water pistol to squirt water into the crack). If possible, *undercut* the crack, making it wider on the underside. Force in spackle with a putty knife, a small trowel, or your finger, and then smooth the surface. When the mend is completely dry, you can sand off any bumps or rough edges and ready the patch for painting. (See Section II, APPLYING THE PAINT under PAINTING/INDOOR, p. 294.)

Large Holes. Holes up to a foot in diameter can be fixed with patching plaster (plaster of Paris), but a larger hole is a job for a professional plasterer.

For the job you *can* tackle, remove all the loose plaster with a putty knife until you reach the lath, the network of wooden strips or metal grillwork nailed across the beams. If the lath is intact, you are ready to patch; if not, back the hole with ¼-inch mesh screen or a piece of metal lath. (Make the screen larger than the hole and force it in so that the edges are wedged against the sides of the plaster around the hole. If you loop a piece of string through the mesh at the center and pull down on it, the mesh will come toward you, making the area relatively shallow. Apply the first layer of plaster; let it dry. Cut the string, and finish the job.)

To insure a good bond, dampen the edge of the hole before you apply the plaster. (A deep hole will need at least two layers—the first should be only a bottom or half-layer.) Since plaster hardens rapidly, be careful not to mix more than you can use in ten minutes. Follow the mixing instructions on the package, and if the plaster does start to set while you're working, add a combination of one-half water and one-half vinegar to loosen its consistency.

After the first coat is completely dry, wet down the surface and pack in the final layer. (A square-edged trowel will make it easier for you to smooth out the new surface.)

After drying, the plaster can be finely smoothed with sandpaper to ready it for painting. (See Section II, as cited above, p. 294.)

Bulges. A bulging ceiling may be a sign of water leaks. Check for faulty plumbing (see PIPE), and roof leaks (see ROOF) to find the source of the problem. After the leak has been sealed, take a hammer and chisel and chop out all the plaster from the bulge area. Then follow the directions above for filling large holes.

Loose Plaster and Stains. These are also signs of water damage. As with bulges, check for faulty plumbing (see PIPE), and roof leaks (see ROOF.) You can brush away any loose plaster flakes and smooth out the pitted surface with spackling compound (see "Cracks and Small Holes," above).

For stains, prepare and paint the surface. (See Section II, as cited above, p. 294.)

CEILING TILE

See ACOUSTICAL TILE.

CEMENT AND CONCRETE

Surface Scarred or Uneven. You can free your cement walk from scars or depressions that hold puddles after a rain storm with a mixture from the building-supply or hardware store. This extra-strong adhesive cement contains latex or vinyl, and it's simple to handle. You don't even have to soak the damaged surface with water. Just spread the latex cement on, the way you'd spread icing on a cake. Smooth it over rough spots, and build up the low areas. Use a square-edged trowel. Follow the directions on the package, and be sure to let the patch cure before you set foot on the walk.

Holes and Cracks. See BASEMENT—FLOORS AND WALLS, SMALL CRACKS.

Stains. Because cement is porous, oil, paint and rust stains sink into it, and when they do, removing them is a chore. Remember this and wipe up drips and spills as soon as you can—the sooner, the cleaner the cement! Here are the particulars for the stains that you don't get to right away:

1. Oil Stains. Scrub the stained area with a steel brush and a solvent (benzine, for instance). CAUTION: *Be sure there is good ventilation, and remember, such solvents are flammable. Don't use them near flames or running motors.*

2. Rust Stains. Buy a commercial rust remover from your hardware store, and follow the directions on the container.

3. Paint Stains. Buy a water-soluble paint remover, follow the directions on the container, and scrape the softened paint off. Then hose off the residue.

Note: If you scrubbed or rubbed off the oil or wet paint, and still find the cement discolored, make a mixture of strong detergent and chlorine bleach, and brush this on the area. Rinse area with water. (CAUTION: *Never mix any solutions that contain ammonia with any that contain chlorine. The chemical reaction you thus start is toxic and can be lethal.*)

CERAMIC

For objects made of ceramic (dishes, etc.), see CHINAWARE; for tile, see CERAMIC TILE.

CERAMIC TILE | decorative

See also FLOOR/TILE.

Spaces Between Tiles Are Dingy, Dirty. The shiny, glazed surfaces on ceramic tiles used on counter tops, tables, walls, makes them easy to clean. Sooner or later, though, the little spaces between the tiles will become dingy. These little divisions are filled with a substance called *grout*. Cleaning grout is a breeze if you have a typewriter eraser handy. Just erase over the spaces, and you erase the dirt.

Individual Tile Broken. If the tile is one you treasure and one you wash frequently, the best mend is made with superstrong epoxy. (See Section II, GLUING AND CLAMPING, p. 248, for details.) Be sure the two surfaces you're joining are clean, and remember that the *thinnest coat of glue makes the finest bond*. Press the broken parts together so that the design on the surface of the tile is continuous (or appears to be). Then put pressure on the two joined parts with clamps or strong rubber bands and weights on the flat surface. The epoxy takes from half an hour to eight hours to cure completely. Play safe and don't move the tile for a day.

Wall or Counter Tile Loose. Pry the tile up, but be careful not to break it when you do. (A dull-edged knife or a chisel is handy for this operation.) Scrape the crumbling tile cement or adhesive from the back of the tile, or scrub it off with steel wool. Scrape the cement adhesive from the wall or counter top, too. Use a tile adhesive from the hardware store to reglue the tile. Apply the adhesive to the back of the tile and "butter" the wall or counter top with a thin coat of it. Then score both surfaces with a fork or comb (this roughened, tacky surface makes the tile stick more firmly). Hold the tile in place until it takes (a few minutes will do), or weight it down with books. When the adhesive is dry, trim off any excess that may have squeezed up around the edges of the tile. Fill the join with tile grout or mildew-resistant plastic grout (buy both at the hardware store).

Wall or Counter Tile Cracked. Remove it, buy a replacement, and apply as above.

CESSPOOL

See SEPTIC TANK.

CHAIR | side or armchair: wood

If your favorite chair wobbles when you sit on it and squeaks whenever it's moved, the time has come for repairs. These and several other chair ailments are curable, but if they're done by a cabinetmaker, they're costly, too. If you tackle the work yourself, fixing the furniture may help satisfy a craving for creativity, and it certainly will give your bank account a break. *Note:* This sort of work requires care and precision. Study the techniques, and begin your training by learning the do's and don'ts, below.

- *Don't* try to repair an expensive antique (or any valuable heirloom) unless you are sure your techniques and materials are those of a professional. Otherwise you can decrease the market value of the chair you may someday want to sell. Do practice on something inexpensive and unimportant, first.

• *Don't* use nails and metal bracing if you're repairing antiques. Experts frown on the use of these—again, because they "spoil" a chair that is typically put together with glue. Do use the glue and clamping techniques given in Section II, GLUING AND CLAMPING, p. 248. Save the nails and braces for less valuable furniture.

• *Do* protect the surfaces of your chair when you begin a repair job. Use wax paper, clean, soft rags, or blanket scraps to cover the finish, especially when you're working with clamps and glue.

• *Do* remember that wood responds to temperature and moisture. Do your repair work where the chair will be protected from cold and damp, and at the proper temperatures for the glues to bond. (See Section II, as cited above, p. 248.)

• *Do* study carefully whatever you take apart. You'll discover the special quirks of your chair this way, even if it's one of a mass-produced series.

• *Do* play it safe when you work with glues. Some of them give off vapors that are dangerous to inhale; others are flammable. *Work in a well-ventilated room with no flame (including pilot light or lighted cigarettes)!* Read the instructions on the containers, and follow these to the letter.

Small Scratches on the Surface. See Section II, REFINISHING WOOD, p. 301.

Dents on the Surface. See Section II, as cited above, p. 301.

Surface Is Chipped or Gouged. See Section II, as cited above, p. 301.

Chair Wobbly. Turn the chair upside down and examine it. Are the rungs loose? If so, try the easy way to take the shakes out of your chair. Wedge some toothpicks or shaved wood matchsticks into the loose, wobbly joints to make them tight. Clip off the ends of these small wedges so that they're flush with the surface around the joint.

If small wedges don't solve the problem, you'll need to reglue the loose rung—a more complicated repair—and you'll need to allow time for the project. (Experts say you should plan to complete a glue job once you've started it.) These are the steps for the repair:

1. Turn the chair upside down on a *padded* workbench or table, and remove the rung from the legs. Do this with a "soft" hammer (a regular hammer wrapped in rags to protect the wood surfaces from the metal hammerhead). Gently knock the legs outward until the rung comes free. Clean the ends of the rung and the sockets (joints) into which they fit. First, scrape or sandpaper off the old glue. Then pour one or two tablespoons of warm vinegar on these surfaces (to soak the old glue out of the wood pores). Wash the residue off, then wipe the surfaces bone dry.

2. Mix up a batch of plastic resin glue, such as Weldwood (it should be

the consistency of soft butter or whipped cream). Apply the glue with a small stiff-bristled brush, covering both surfaces to be joined. Use a thin coating of glue and allow it to seep into the pores of the wood for five minutes or so.

3. Insert the rung in the legs, wipe off the excess glue, then pad and clamp the joints (using a band-clamp or a tourniquet) to keep the proper pressure on the repair. (See Section II, GLUING AND CLAMPING, p. 248.) Allow the job to dry overnight before you move the chair.

4. Remove the clamps and padding. Sandpaper off any residues of glue. Touch up the joints to match the finish. (See Section II, REFINISHING WOOD, p. 301.)

Arm Loose. If your rocker's arms are rickety, you can repair them in a jiffy. First, check to see if the joints (connecting the arm to the frame) are held by screws. (If there are round wood plugs in the arm or in the back of the frame where the arm connects with it, you know *beneath these* lies a screw. The plug is purely decorative.)

1. Take the plug out with a drill that is slightly smaller than the plug. Be careful, when you do this, *not to gouge the wood around it.* Cut out the rest of the plug with a small chisel or knife.

2. Under the plug is the screw. Unscrew it almost all the way (or at least far enough so that you can squeeze some white glue into the joint). Tighten the screw, and wipe off any excess glue.

3. Glue a new plug over the screwhead. You can buy these at hardware stores and some arts and crafts supply shops. Color the plug to match the finish of the arm. (See Section II, as cited above, p. 302.) If the arm joints are held by glue, follow the procedure given above, "Chair Wobbly."

(If the foregoing process is impractical or too much trouble, you can probably strengthen the arm by driving a screw into the arm and frame from the back of the chair. To protect the wood, drill a small hole to take the screw, then drive the screw in with a screwdriver. You might want to disguise *this* screwhead with a wood plug, and if you do, see above.)

Arm Broken. Remove the arm ends from the frame. Clean out the joints, as outlined above under "Chair Wobbly." Mend the two pieces of the arm. Glue them together, then clamp or weight these. After the glue has dried, attach the repaired arm to the chair. Use screws if the arm was previously joined this way. (See above, "Arm Loose.") Use glue if the arm had been glued to the frame. (See above, "Chair Wobbly.")

Rung Broken. Unless this chair belongs in a museum, don't try to mend the old rung with glue. (It will break again, soon after you mend it, if the chair is one that's used much.) Take the old rung to the lumberyard and buy a dowel of the same diameter and length. Whittle this down so it looks just like the old rung. Clean the joints as outlined above. Apply glue to the joints, insert the rung and, over some protective padding, apply a tourniquet or a band-clamp. (See Section II, GLUING AND CLAMPING, p. 248.)

When the glue is dry, refinish the dowel to match the rest of the chair. (See Section II, REFINISHING WOOD, p. 301.)

Leg Broken. Turn the chair upside down, remove the unbroken part of the leg (if glued, tap it out with a "soft" hammer; if screwed, unscrew it). Clean the surfaces to be joined, as described above under "Chair Wobbly." Glue and clamp, as indicated. When the glue in this mend is dry, prepare the joints that connect the leg to the frame. (Clean them as outlined above.) Insert the glue in these, clamp, and let the glue dry. Refinish the mend to match the rest of the chair. (See Section II, as cited above, p. 301.)

Chair Falling Apart. Take it to a cabinetmaker for repair, unless you feel you want to tackle this job. (One tip: all of the gluing should be done in one sitting. Don't glue some joints of the chair, then wait a week and do the rest. The joints will be *set,* and you won't be able to adjust the chair to be sure it's symmetrically mended and level for use.)

CHAIR | cane seat and/or back

Cane Seat Sags. You can take the middle-aged sag out of the woven cane seat of your chair with just plain old water! Protect the chair frame-edge, around the seat, with plastic kitchen wrap or any waterproof material you happen to have. Wet an old, clean towel, squeeze out excess water, then fold it so that it is about the size of the sag in the seat. Leave the damp towel on the seat for an hour or so, or until the cane is thoroughly moistened. Remove the towel and let the cane dry. As it does, it shrinks and the cane is tightened. When the seat is bone dry, apply a coat of clear lacquer or shellac to the caning—to prevent it from sagging again.

Woven Cane Broken. If two or three strands of cane are broken, mend the seat or back with additional strands of cane. You can buy small bundles of cane from an arts and crafts shop, or you can buy a large bundle (a hank) from cane supply stores, or shops that restore and reweave caned furniture. (Find these stores in the yellow pages of your phone directory.) Soak the strands of cane in water to make them soft and supple. Study the weave of the broken strands, clip these out, one by one, and replace them with new strands, copying the weaving. Glue the cane ends down under the chair frame, and clamp or tape the ends of the new strands in place until the glue dries.

Cane Seat Badly Damaged. If most of the strands are broken, the chair will need to be recaned. If you're a putterer, you can teach yourself to do the weaving for the seat. Buy a hank of cane, and follow our instructions on the weaving. (See Section II, CANING, p. 289.)

If you don't feel like spending the long winter evenings weaving a cane seat, buy prewoven caning for the chair and install the new seat yourself. These are the steps to follow:

1. Measure the seat. Most prewoven caning is wide enough for most ordinary cane-seated chairs. Take the measurements or an outline of the seat with you when you go to the woven cane shop. (Find the shop by consulting the yellow pages of your phone directory.) Woven cane retails for under two dollars per square foot. Buy some extra strands of *loose* cane while you're there for the finishing touches on this repair.

2. Cut out the old seat, and clean out the holes through which the original caning was attached to the frame. Wash or wipe the chair, and do any refinishing the chair frame may need. (See Section II, REFINISHING WOOD, p. 301.)

3. Have on hand plastic electrical cord or heavy plastic-coated clothesline to go around the edge of the seat. You'll also need a small sharp knife, a squeeze-bottle of white glue, and at least six C or bar clamps. The lumberyard can supply you with four pieces of wood (one inch thick) to fit the chair frame and to be used with the clamps. (See Section II, GLUING AND CLAMPING, p. 248 for details on these supplies and tools.)

4. Squeeze a thin line of glue around the chair frame, *between the inner edge and the line of holes that held the old cane.* (See diagram below.)

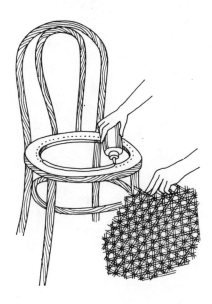

5. Before the glue hardens, put your piece of prewoven cane over the chair opening. Be sure the rows of the weave pattern are straight in relation to the chair frame. (See diagram above.) Keep the caning flat and tight, and press it into the glued edge.

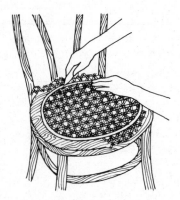

6. Now make a ring of the clothesline or electric cord which just fits the frame groove where the cane holes are. Put the ring on top of the cane. (See diagram above.)

7. Cover the frame with the boards and clamp them to the chair frame, thus pressing down the cord. Leave the clamps there, in place, until the glue dries. (See diagram below.)

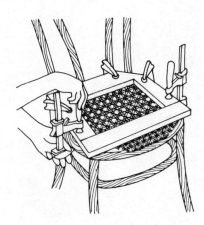

8. Remove the clamps and boards. Using the cord as a guide, *very carefully* cut the woven cane around the seat—outside the cord ring.

9. Gently loosen the cord and pull it free. The cane is firmly glued to the frame, but needs a finishing border of cane for a neat, trim look.

10. Lay a strand of cane over the edge of the cane seat and, with a second, wet strand, "sew" this binding to the chair frame by pushing the flexible, wet strand up through the holes around the rim, over the cane binding, and down through the hole again. (See diagram below.) (This, by

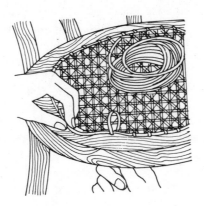

the way, is the method by which regular stitches are made by your sewing machine. You may recognize the similarity.) Glue the ends of the binding together, masking this join at one of the cane loops. (If you can't face this project, have your chair recaned by a professional. Find him listed under "Caning, Furniture," in the yellow pages of your phone directory.)

CHAIR | upholstered

Like Gaul, your upholstered chair is divided into three parts. The structural part is the skeleton of wood or metal, called the frame. This is made comfortable and soft with various paddings and springs. To keep the bounce or softness in shape, attached to the framework there are several coverings, the last being the *decorative* fabric (or leather or plastic). Each of these parts can be damaged, and below we treat some typical upholstery problems, working from the simpler to the more complex, starting with types of damaged trimmings.

Decorative Trimming Coming Loose. The trim is apt to be a braid made of cotton, silk, leather, or plastic called *gimp*. Also popular as a finishing for upholstered pieces is a single or double ridge of binding, often made of the same material as the covering, called *welting*. If the trim is coming loose from the edge of the upholstery, examine the way it was applied to the frame. If glue was used, spread a thin layer of white glue on the edge of the fabric and press the gimp or welt down over this. Drive in a small tack to hold the trim until the glue hardens.

If the gimp has been tacked to the frame with decorative upholstery nails, duplicate the nail at the hardware or upholstery supply store. Be sure, when you drive the nail in, that you've spaced it correctly in relation to its neighbor. Measure the distance between two other nails, and use this measurement in spacing the new nails. (Measurement is made from the center of one nailhead to the center of the next.)

Decorative Trim Tattered. Replace the gimp or welting with new gimp or welting. Gimp is a standard item. (You can probably duplicate gimp that's worn, but you may want to change the style and color. Department stores and upholstery or fabric shops usually carry a wide assortment of styles in many colors.) Be sure to get enough for the job and some to spare—the best repairer can sometimes make mistakes that need redoing. Glue it to the frame as described above, "Decorative Trimming Coming Loose."

Ready-made welting is sold by the same suppliers, but if you have trouble finding the right color or fabric, buy matching material by the yard and have an upholsterer or seamstress make enough welting for your chair. *Double welting* (two rows, side by side, around the frame, and between the covering and the wood) is *glued on* the way you glue gimp. *Single* welting is sewn to the fabric cover, then tacked with the smallest of upholsterer's nails. (It's easier to use the double than the single row—something you should plan for if you decide on new welting.)

Decorative Nails Popping Out. If your chair's been redone many times, and the frame into which the nails are driven is full of nail holes, your chair may develop a severe case of nail-popping. Even so, nail trim may be what you want. Take out the nails and fill the holes with plastic wood. CAUTION: *Plastic wood is extremely flammable. Don't work near a pilot light or even a lighted cigarette!* You can do it the stopgap way now—filling just the holes from which the nails have popped. (But you may have to go over the whole frame sooner or later.) Remove the decorative nails with a tack remover, but *gently*. After the plastic wood is dry, drive the nails back into the frame with a tack hammer. (See Section II, GLOSSARY OF TOOLS, p. 226.)

Experts suggest that with a well-worn frame, you should use nails one size larger than those that have worked loose. Remember this if all of the nails are popping out (or seem insecure).

If you hate the idea of filling all those holes, remove the nails (with a tack remover). At this point, check the small upholstery tacks that hold the cover to the frame, and be sure *these* tacks are secure. If not, replace them with new upholsterer's tacks from the hardware or upholstery supply store. Drive them in with a tack hammer. Buy some attractive gimp and glue this to the frame as described above (see "Decorative Trimming Coming Loose").

Dust Cover on Underside of Seat in Tatters. If the chair's dust cover is showing, it's time you took a look at what goes on under your chair. Pad a table or bench with cloth or blankets, then have someone help you turn the chair upside down on it. If the black dust cover is loose and/or shredded, lift the tacks up with a ripping tool or small chisel (be careful not to gouge the frame when you do this). Buy some black cambric (it's a stiff glazed cotton made especially for upholsterers) at your department or fabric store, and cut a new cover from it. Turn the edges under and drive three or four tacks around the bottom of the frame just partway in. They'll hold the cover while you stretch it tight and tack it permanently.

Webbing Loose. If you notice when you remove the dust cover that the crisscrossed jute webbing under the chair is sagging, tighten the webbing.

First, with a flashlight, check to see that the springs are still tied with twine. Poke the flashlight up through the webbing. If you see that *all* the coiled springs are tied at the *top* with twine, you can finish the webbing repair. Experts say that the best way to do this is to apply bands of steel webbing *over* the old jute webbing: the steel will not sag later the way jute does, and it's simpler to leave the jute webbing in place while you do the repair. Follow these steps, illustrated in diagrams on p. 74:

1. Measure the jute webbing on the bottom of the chair and add two or three feet extra to the total length—just in case! Buy steel webbing at the upholstery shop, either corrugated or flat ribbons.

2. While you're at the upholstery shop, get a webbing stretcher (you can use pliers for the same purpose if you want to save money).

3. Get about two dozen 1½-inch ring-type nails to fasten the steel webbing.

4. At the lumberyard, buy two one-by-two-inch wood strips, and be sure that they're several inches longer than the opening of the chair frame. (See diagram.) Drill holes through these strips, and drill small holes in the bottom of the seat frame.

5. Attach these wood strips to the bottom of the frame. They're only temporary, and they're there to prop up the webbing and hold it in place while you're applying the tight steel bands across the bottom of the chair.

6. Start to add the new webbing at the center of the chair. (See diagram.) First, nail the webbing to the front of the frame between the wood strips (see diagram). Pull this across the chair to the back of the frame, cut the webbing about an inch longer than the chair frame and, with the pliers, pull the webbing tight. Then nail webbing in place. *Note:* Protect the wood finish by taping some cardboard over the edge of the frame. (See diagram.) Cut the steel webbing by sawing it near the nail, then file a groove in it (see diagram), and bend the webbing back and forth until it snaps off at the groove. (*Then* you can fasten the edge down with tacks as shown in the diagram.)

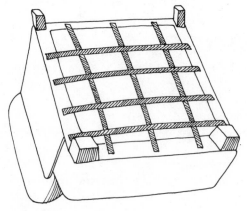

7. Continue the front-to-back webbing, and when the bottom is covered remove the wood strips. Then, work from side to side, interweaving the webbing strips (just the way the jute strips interweave). See diagram.

8. Tack on the dust cover.

Arms Need Padding. If the fabric cover still looks good but the arms seem lumpy or uncomfortable, repad the arms. Remove the trim (gimp or welting), and put it aside. Then carefully remove the fabric covering; put it aside, too. Under this you'll find a muslin cover, which you also remove and save. Finally, you come to the cotton felt, a material specially made to pad upholstery. If it has been packed down into hard layers or has wadded into lumps, buy new cotton at the upholsterer's. Be sure, when you use it, that you *tear* it. Cutting this material gives it a hard edge. Don't fold it or wad it, either, but put the torn pieces on the arm and let the muslin cover give the cotton the final contour. (Tack down the muslin cover and over it, the fabric; and finish the arm with its trimming.)

Note: Remember that if your upholstered piece is worn and stained beyond redemption, you can cover it with a slipcover. Consult the *Good Housekeeping Complete Book of Needlecraft* on how to make one. Or you can call a department store and have one of its experts measure and cut a cover at your home.

Arm Loose or Broken. Remove the trimming, the decorative cover, the muslin cover, and the padding. Set these aside and repair the damaged wood frame. Follow the procedures given in CHAIR/SIDE OR ARMCHAIR: WOOD. When the wood mend is made and the joints thoroughly dry, cover the arm with padding, muslin cover, outer cover, and trimming. Be sure to consult earlier repairs, above. Refinish the "show" wood if it's been damaged. (See Section II, REFINISHING WOOD, p. 301.)

Chair Falling Apart. Have an upholsterer repair it unless you think you have enough know-how by now to do the job yourself.

CHANDELIER

CAUTION: *Repairing electrical fixtures can be dangerous: It is imperative, therefore, that you follow all the safety precautions given in Section II,* ELECTRICITY AND WIRING, p. 257, *before you tinker with a piece of electrical equipment.*

Doesn't Light. Check the bulbs to make sure that they are tightly screwed in their holders. If the chandelier lights still don't go on, try other lights and some appliances in the house; if they're not workable, you probably have a power failure. (Ask your neighbors, or turn on a battery-operated radio to find out.)

It's likely, though, that the problem is with the fuses. Check the fuses for the room that you are in, to make certain that they haven't blown.

(See Section II, as cited above, p. 257, before you change the fuse.) If the fuse is all right, then the switch or outlet is definitely the culprit. *Have an electrician repair the switch or outlet.*

Broken Parts. If a small fragment or a decorative part of the chandelier breaks off, repair it according to the type of material it is:

1. Wooden. Secure it with epoxy glue. (For details, see Section II, GLUING AND CLAMPING, p. 248.) The glue will hold permanently if the repair is minor. But if the branch of a chandelier comes loose or breaks off, you will probably not be able to join it securely enough to support a light again. If the fixture is removable, take it to a repairman, or call an electrician to remove it.

2. Metal. Repair wrought iron, pewter, brass, or copper pieces with plastic metal glue. (See Section II, as cited above, p. 248.) If the broken part is in a *weight-bearing* portion in the chandelier, take the fixture to a qualified metal craftsman for soldering or welding.

3. Crystal. Secure a cracked prism on a crystal chandelier by wrapping fine wire around the damaged part and fastening the wire to the fixture. (This is just a temporary measure, because the prism must be replaced. You can buy a new prism from an antique dealer or manufacturer of lighting fixtures.)

Make regular inspections of the small wire hooks that hold the prisms. If you see any of them opening up, squeeze them tighter with narrow-nosed pliers. (If the little hook opens too far, the prism may fall, hitting someone on the head or shattering to pieces on the floor.)

Ceiling Attachment Loose. The weight of your chandelier pulls on the ceiling attachment and in time may loosen the fasteners holding the whole thing up. To repair the attachment fasteners, first take down all the removable parts of the chandelier (the prisms and ornaments). Then *tighten* the screws holding the attachment to the ceiling (or replace the screws—one at a time—with *larger* ones). If the attachment is held by a center turn bolt or large lag screw, turn them *clockwise* to tighten.

If the attachment is dangling, detached from the ceiling, and the wiring is exposed, call in an electrician immediately! Remove the fuse for the fixture circuit—as a safety precaution.

CHEST

Hinges Loose. Blanket and toy chests that get constant use often suffer from hinge troubles. If yours does, you can insert toothpicks into the holes that hold the screws for the hinges. These small wedges will tighten the screws.

If the hinges are about to come off, remove the loose screws and buy larger or longer screws at the hardware store. Screw these in the old holes; they will give the hinges greater support.

Top or Sides Cracked. Use a wide strip of self-adhesive cloth tape to cover the crack *inside* the chest. On the outside, fill with plastic wood. CAUTION: *Plastic wood is extremely flammable. Don't work near pilot light or lighted cigarette.* Refinish or paint the mend to match the rest of the chest. (See Section II, REFINISHING WOOD, p. 301, and PAINTING/INDOORS p. 294.)

Lid Won't Close. See if the hinges are loose. If so, fix as above. If the top misfit is caused by moisture (swelling of the wood), sandpaper or shave the fitted edge of the top until it drops into place with ease when you shut the chest. After a spell of dry weather (or when the heat has been turned on for awhile in the winter), shellac or varnish the whole inside surface of the lid. Do the inside edges where the sides touch the lid, too. *Note:* Do not shellac or varnish the entire inside of a cedar chest if you count on the wood's odors and resins to protect woolens from pest or insect damage.

CHEST OF DRAWERS

Drawer Sticks. Try silicone spray lubricant on the runners in the *chest,* and on the bottoms of the *drawers. Note:* If the drawers stick during damp weather *only,* the wood is swelling with moisture. When dry weather comes, and the drawers shrink (and stop sticking), shellac or varnish the *inside* and the *outside* of the drawer-sides. (This treatment will keep the drawer from swelling again in humid weather.)

If the runners are so worn that the bottom front of the drawer catches on the frame of the chest, *raise the runners* by sticking a row of thumbtacks along the bottom of the drawer slides. Drive the tacks all the way in. (The heads will make the extra little difference you need.)

Drawer Wobbles. The honest-to-goodness way to cope with a wobbly drawer is to take it *completely* apart. Knock the sides off from the back and front pieces with a "soft" hammer. (Make the hammer soft by wrapping the head in a clean scrap of cloth. This protects the wood finish.) Soak off any residue of old glue on the joints with warm vinegar. Brush or wipe it on, then wipe the surface dry. Reglue and nail the parts. You can use white glue for the job. (Put the parts together, reversing the way you took them apart.) Pad the finished surfaces, then apply a tourniquet around the drawer and leave this in place until the glue cures. (For details, see Section II, GLUING AND CLAMPING, p. 248.)

You can give additional strength to the drawer by bracing the inside corners with ¼-inch-round molding. (Buy it at the lumberyard, and have it cut to the proper length.) Glue the *angular* sides of the molding into the corners; the molding should run from top to bottom of the drawer. Clamp the work until the glue cures. (For details, see Section II as cited above.)

Bottom Cracked. Does it bother you that your earrings or his cuff links, or whatever, keep falling through to the drawer below? If so, fix the crack. Use self-sticking, cloth tape on the underside of the bottom of the drawer, then fill the upper side with plastic wood. CAUTION: *Plastic wood is extremely flammable. Don't work near a pilot light or a lighted cigarette!* When the filler is dry, sandpaper the mend till it's smooth. Refinish.

Or, if you'd rather, you can cover a piece of cardboard, cut to fit the bottom of the drawer, with self-stick wall or shelf covering. Glue the covered cardboard to the bottom of the drawer at the corners. (For details, see Section II, as cited above, p. 248.)

Knobs or Handles Loose. Open the drawer. If you see a metal fitting (the head of a screw or the end of a bolt) on the inside of the drawer, tighten it with a screwdriver or wrench. Forewarned is forearmed: if you keep the bolts and screws tightened, you won't lose bolts, screws, or even handles and knobs. (Finding replacements is a chore. If you can't duplicate one of them you may have to replace *all* of them to have a matching set.)

CHIMNEY

CAUTION: *If your chimney gives off showers of sparks, if you see smoke leaking between the bricks and mortar, or if you hear a roaring sound in the chimney when you have a fire in the fireplace, douse the fire immediately. A couple of boxes of table salt (or rock salt) will help, then you can wet down the smoldering fire or remove the logs with fire tongs. But if you have a roaring chimney fire, get your family out of the house, then call for help. You need the fire department if you have a real chimney fire. Don't use the chimney or fireplace until chimney and fireplace have been cleaned and/or repaired. Hire a professional.* (See below.)

For safe operation (and kindness to your repair budget), your chimney should be inspected regularly. Experts suggest you do this *at least* once a year, especially if you live in an area where the winters are severe and the summers are steamy. Extremes of temperatures affect most things, and the bricks, mortar, and lining of your chimney are no exceptions. Any crevices between bricks that catch rain will be enlarged when the rain turns to ice. If you're agile, follow the inspection routine outlined below; if not, hire professionals. The work to be done may involve your contractor, a mason, and a chimney cleaner. You'll know which, as you read, below.

Cracks in Chimney Cap. If you've started at the top (on the roof), inspect the *top of the chimney!* Check the cement covering that goes from the brick to the inside lining of the chimney. (It's called the *cap.*) Are there any cracks in the cement or the mortar? If they are large, don't use the chimney (or fireplace or stove that leads into it) until you have a mason repair the job. If small, repair with cement. (See Section II, BRICKS AND MORTAR: CLEANING, REPAIRING, AND REPOINTING, p. 273.)

Masonry Hood over Cap Broken. Some chimneys have bonnets over their caps. If yours has a masonry hood, and this is cracked, or if parts of it are broken, shine a flashlight down the chimney to be sure no chunks of the broken hood have gotten stuck inside your chimney. If they have, call a contractor or mason *forthwith!* (The broken piece lodged in the chimney will block it, so don't try to use the chimney before the chunks are dislodged, and the hood is repaired.)

Flashing around Chimney (on Roof) Has Come Loose. Metal strips are applied around the chimney where it meets the roof, and these (called *flashing*) seal the joint between the roof and the chimney. Check to be sure the flashing is firmly stuck in place. If it isn't, water will get in under it. (You'll soon have leaks on your upstairs or attic ceiling and water damage around the mortar joints of your chimney.) Fix the flashing by using asphalt roofing compound to make the seal watertight. Buy it at the hardware store. (For details, see Section II, CAULKING, p. 271.) If you don't trust yourself with this chore, a carpenter, roofer, or mason will do the job for you.

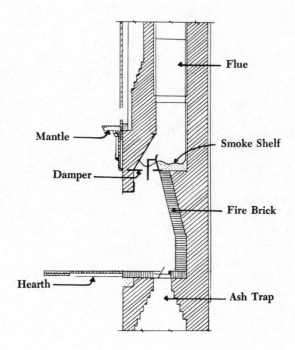

**Chimney and Fireplace
Cross Section**

From *Consumer's All*, U.S.D.A., United States Government Printing Office, Washington, D.C., 1965.

Sooty Chimney. While you're up there inspecting, shine a light down the chimney to check on the sooty insides. If the interior is heavily caked with soot, don't use the chimney until you or someone else cleans it. (For more on this, see below, "Fireplace Smokes, Chimney Is Sooty.")

Cracks in Bricks and Mortar of Chimney. It's important to check the bricks and mortar of the chimney, *outside* and *inside* the house. If the mortar is crumbly in one or two places, you can make the repair yourself. But if you spot an area where many bricks are cracked, it means the foundation beneath the house is shifting. You need a professional for this job. Have your building contractor handle it; the chimney and its foundation will have to be rebuilt.

Chimney Bricks, Inside House, Have Small Cracks. If you see one or two tiny hairline cracks on the chimney *indoors*, don't let them fret you. The condition is not serious, just unsightly, and the repair is simple. (For details on how to do this and other minor repairs to mortar, see Section II, BRICK AND MORTAR, CLEANING, REPAIRING, AND REPOINTING, p. 273.)

Cracks in Large Area or in a Line of Bricks, Inside House. As with the *outside* of the house, this damage is a warning that the chimney foundation is shifting. Call in your building contractor for basic repairs. (See above.)

Chimney Flue Cracked. (You won't be able to see cracks in the flue, but you *can* see their effects. Smoke will leak through the bricks and mortar.) To *test* your chimney and flue for this potential fire hazard, light a *small, quick-burning paper fire* in the fireplace or stove. If you see smoke leaking out of the joints between the bricks, or through the bricks themselves (*or* if you ever see smoke in upstairs rooms when you are using the stove or fireplace downstairs), you know your chimney is a *menace*. Put out the fire immediately and don't use the chimney until it is repaired or rebuilt.

Fireplace Smokes, Chimney Is Sooty. The time has come for a cleaning. CAUTION: *Remember, don't use the chimney until you do this. Heavily encrusted soot can ignite and explode into a roaring chimney fire, and the sudden blast and heat can crack your chimney open and set fire to your house.* Cleaning the chimney is not as ghastly as it sounds. It's a chore you can *share*, with one of you on the roof and the other down below, preparing the fireplace or chimney opening. Here are the steps to follow:

1. Be sure there's no fire in the fireplace or stove.

2. Choose your cleaning device. You can make a broom out of a burlap bag. Fill it with leaves, weight it with stones, and tie it to a long, sturdy rope. Or, if it's easier, you can cover a brick with some old carpeting, and tie this to a long, strong rope. Or, you can just tie a tire skid chain (from your car) to a long, heavy rope. (This last is least popular with the experts because it may chip the chimney lining.)

3. Seal off the fireplace or chimney opening. (Do this with care, otherwise you'll have soot flying all over the room!) If you have a large piece

of plywood, hardboard, or a sheet of metal, put it over the opening, then seal the opening tight with a wide band of sticky-tape—masking tape is good. If you don't have wood or metal sheeting handy, wrap an old window screen with a wet blanket or heavy paper, and seal this shield, as above. Then, secure this cover by propping a chair or bench against it.

4. Give the go-ahead signal to your partner on the roof, and let the cleaning begin! The cleaning device should be moved, *carefully,* up and down the inside of the chimney. The caked soot will cascade into the fireplace or stove, and when the job is done, the sweeper device (pulled back up the chimney to the roof) will be covered with soot. Have a large plastic trash bag handy up there to dump the chimney-sweeper in. (Tie the bag tightly and dispose of it.)

5. Allow several hours for the soot to settle in the fireplace before you take the seal and cover off. When you do, sprinkle some water on the soot. Have the vacuum cleaner nearby and ready to go. Vacuum the shield or cover, and take it outside. Remove the soot. (If your fireplace has an ash dump, open it, and dump the soot. If it doesn't, shovel the soot into something you can close quickly—a garbage bag in a pail will do.)

6. Put a bucket or pail in the fireplace under the *flue opening* and clean the smoke shelf. You may have to scrape some soot off with a small hoe. Clean soot off the damper with your vacuum cleaner. Be sure there's not much soot in the bottom of the fireplace when you've finished your cleanup. (Soot, as we've said, is a fire hazard.)

If you can't stand doing this chore, hire a professional chimney cleaner. Your fuel dealer can probably find an experienced professional for you. (This expert will clean your chimney with a vacuum-cleaner-type device.)

Note: There are various chemical cleaners on the market that can be added to the fire in your fireplace to lessen the buildup of soot. Experts don't agree on the effectiveness of these cleaners, but they *do agree* that mechanical cleaning is the surefire way to do the job! CAUTION: *Don't fall for the suggestion that you chemically clean your chimney by throwing an old flashlight battery into the fire. The resulting chemicals are noxious, and can poison food if you barbecue in the fireplace.*

Bricks Smoke-Stained, Dirty. See Section II, as cited above, p. 273.

Fireplace Doesn't Work. See FIREPLACE.

CHINAWARE | dish, vase, knickknack

Many of us have gone through the small agony of seeing some treasured keepsake smashed. Probably you've gotten hardened to these little hurts and abandoned the treasure, assuming that once it was broken it couldn't be properly fixed. But some sophistication about mending techniques *can* help you if you want to restore your precious china bowl or favorite piece of pottery. With this know-how—if you're patient and careful—you should be able to make most mends almost invisible. But if you don't trust yourself to put together a badly broken and valuable antique, take it to a skilled restorer, some of whose "magical" methods we indicate. Whether you do the repair, or the restorer does it, the job always involves these four processes: 1. cleaning; 2. gluing; 3. accurate joining; 4. exerting proper pressure. Below, we tackle some typical breaks and give you some tips on what can be done about the more tortuous. (Types of mends are given according to the *shape of the object* to be repaired.)

Flat Plate (or Any Flat, Symmetrical Piece)—Broken in Half. Use a magnifying glass to study the broken edges: You must later make them fit together perfectly. Then start the repair.

1. Clean the Parts. Use warm, soapy water or a mild detergent. Rinse and dry thoroughly. (If someone's attempted a mend before, you'll have to pull off the old glue; you may possibly have to soak it off. If water and soap don't work, try warm vinegar, and if this fails, apply alcohol or nail polish remover to the glue residue.)

Make a dry run: fit the parts together (on a wood work-surface). Drive four nails into this surface. The nails should be placed (as in the diagram)

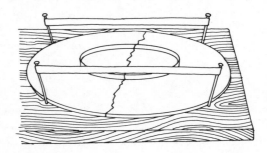

just touching the rim of the plate, with each pair in line. The nails should be on a slant (as shown).

2. Glue the Parts. Choose your glue: If the plate is used and washed frequently, epoxy should be your choice. It will withstand high temperatures, and is dishwasherproof and ovenproof. (Otherwise, use the less expensive contact cement. For details on each, see Section II, GLUING AND CLAMPING, p. 248.) *Apply the thinnest possible coating of glue along both edges to be joined.* Remember that the *least* amount of glue between the pieces makes the *best* bond (and makes the mend less visible.)

3. Join the Parts. Bring the pieces together, carefully, so that any design on the surface looks almost continuous, and so that the pieces interlock. Insert the plate between the four nails.

4. Exert Pressure on the Mend. Slip heavy rubber bands over the nail-heads. (See diagram.) *Note that the pressure on the plates is always at right angles to the break.* (If you don't use pressure at this angle, you may force the pieces askew.) Leave the plate in place for twenty-four hours or longer, until the glue cures.

Flat Plate—Chunk Broken Out. Prepare as indicated above. To exert pressure: use spring clothespins or stationer's clamps (buy them at the stationery store).

Bowl or Vase—Broken Lengthwise. Prepare as above. To exert pressure: stretch rubber bands around the vessel, or make tourniquets with strings and pencils.

Handle Broken Off Pitcher or Cup. Prepare as above. (Use epoxy.) To exert pressure: when the parts are joined, sink the pitcher or cup into a bed of sand. (You can even use a box filled with dried beans or peas.) When the pitcher is securely embedded, bring pressure on the mend by using a sling made of string and two small sandbags. (You can substitute marbles, lead shot, beans, or beads.) The weight of the two small sandbags on the string should be applied at right angles to the break. (See diagram.)

In this case, test the mend after the glue has cured, to be sure it is strong enough for ordinary use. Don't fill the pitcher with, say, hot chocolate, and run the risk of having the handle come off or fall apart in your hands! (If the joint seems weak when you fill the pitcher with water, throw the water *out,* but save the pitcher for display.)

Flat Plate Broken in Three or Four Pieces. Prepare as above. The smaller pieces should be fitted to the larger one and all glued at the same time. To exert pressure, add another pair of nails and crisscross the rubber bands.

Design on Plate Marred by Break. Follow steps as above. When the glue has cured, touch up the design. Use artist's enamel (paint) and a fine brush. Mix the colors until you have an exact match, then, using a magnifying glass to see the work, paint the small damaged spots to follow the rest of the pattern. Allow paint to dry (according to instructions on the tube).

Fine Pieces Broken. Take these to a restorer of antiques (or an artisan who specializes in mending china and glass). A museum can recommend someone to do the work if you don't find one listed in the yellow pages of your phone directory.

The expert uses many techniques not usually associated with china and glass. Bowls, handles, and lids can be *riveted* together with rivets as small as a straight pin. Knobs on lids can be secured with metal *dowels,* a superstrong, invisible mend. Bases or footings of vases can be *bolted* in place. Metal sleeves called *ferrules* cover the damage and hold the stems of broken stemware together. (They are visible, but are finished to look like a decoration, and some are made of silver.) New spouts and handles can be *cast* or *molded* and fitted to the original piece. And any of these can be finished with appropriate enamel, or even with glaze.

CIRCUIT BREAKER

See Section II, ELECTRICITY AND WIRING, p. 257.

CLAPBOARD

See SIDING.

CLOCK | antique, mechanical

Too Slow or Too Fast. A windup pendulum clock is a treasure if it keeps time but annoying if it doesn't. Should your clock lose time, loosen the nut that keeps the pendulum bob (the round weight at the base of the pendulum) in place. Move the bob up the rod slightly, and secure it at a higher level. This should make the clock go faster.

If the clock is already running fast, loosen the nut and slide the bob down the rod.

If you've lowered or raised the bob as far as it will go in either direction, and the clock *still* is not keeping accurate time, you'll have to take the clock to a repair shop—you may need a different bob.

Chimes Not Synchronized with Time. This happens when your clock has not been wound regularly. (It's a good idea to wind an eight-day clock every Sunday night, as a weekly ritual, or a twenty-four-hour clock at a set hour each day.)

When the chimes on a clock are not synchronized with the hour, you may hear, for example, seven bongs at three o'clock, eight bongs at four o'clock, and nine bongs at five o'clock. A simple readjustment is all your clock needs.

With your thumb and forefinger, carefully take the short (hour) hand and move it *clockwise* to the number that corresponds to the number of strikes you just heard (in *this* case, nine o'clock). Now, you have coordinated the chimes and the hour. To reset the clock, move the minute hand *clockwise* around the dial until it reaches the proper time, letting the clock bong away at each hour and half-hour strike.

If your chimes strike without *sequence* (for example, seven times at three o'clock and nine times at four o'clock), then the trouble is within the striking mechanism. This is a tricky problem and should be handled by a qualified clockmaker or repairman.

Clocks made before 1900 have the above synchronization quirk, but they may *also* strike the hour on the *half*-hour! (Clocks made during this century do not do this.) If, for example, you hear one bong at three o'clock and three bongs at 3:30, the problem is not in your mind but in the works. Solve it by resetting the hands. As with the above example, when the clock strikes once at four o'clock, take the long, minute hand, and rotate it (without stopping at the half-hour) clockwise to five o'clock. You will now hear four bongs for five o'clock! Reset the clock, as above, by moving the minute hand *clockwise* around the dial until it reaches the proper time. *Note:* Never turn the hands counterclockwise. This will injure the delicate works of the clock.

Hands Broken. Check the yellow pages of your phone directory for the nearest supplier or manufacturer of clock parts. If one of the hands has been broken off, gently pull out the center tubing that holds the hands (by grasping the base of the hands). Measure the radius of the dial to make sure that the replacement will be the proper length. The short hand should *just touch* the *beginning* of a number, and the long hand should just reach the *minute dots* or the *outside* of the number.

Bring the tubing and clock hand measurements with you to the supply house, and you'll have no trouble finding new hands that will fit your clock.

Glass Broken. Mechanical clocks under ten inches in diameter usually have glass doors with rounded (convex) or flat glass. If the glass is broken, remove the door by unscrewing or taking the pins out of the hinges. Then rest a piece of flat board on the center post that is in the face of the clock. If the hands touch the wood, you should buy convex glass. If the hands cannot reach the wood, flat glass is what you want.

Take the door to the manufacturer or supplier of clock parts and have him install a new glass. If the clock is *over* ten inches in diameter, you will have to go to a glass cutter or a mirror company for a larger piece.

Lost Key. Clock keys are usually numbered, and a master key in the shape of a star, with five different types of numbered keys on it, can be bought for about two dollars from a supplier of clock parts. (Odd numbers are most frequently used for old clocks.)

Take a star master key home and see which number key fits your clock. If, for instance, on an odd-number master key, *five* is too loose and number *seven* is too tight, take the master key back to the supply house and buy a number *six*.

CLOCK | battery

Stops Running. The battery is probably worn out. You can replace it with a new one, but be careful to face the positive and negative ends in the proper directions. See FLASHLIGHT.

To save repeating the job too often, buy a long-life mercury battery to keep your clock running.

Glass Broken. See CLOCK/ELECTRIC.

CLOCK | electric

CAUTION: *Handling any electrical appliance requires care: It's imperative, therefore, that you follow all the safety precautions given in Section II,* ELECTRICITY AND WIRING, p. 257.

Stopped Running. Make the preliminary checks for all electrical appliances: Is the cord plug set securely in the wall outlet? Take a look at it and wiggle it slightly. If you notice that the plug is loose, take it out and examine the prongs. Are they coming out of the plug, or are they damaged in any way that you can see? If so, don't put the plug back in the socket. (You *can* repair or replace the plug; to do this, see Section II, as cited above, p. 266.)

If there is nothing wrong with the plug, spread the prongs a little with your fingers. This should give you a tighter connection when you plug the clock cord into the wall outlet again.

If your clock still doesn't work, try the lights and other appliances in the house; if they're out, you probably have a power failure. (Check with your neighbors, or turn on a battery-operated radio to find out.)

It's possible, however, that the particular outlet you're using doesn't work. To find out, try a lamp in that outlet. If it lights up, the trouble is inside the clock. If it doesn't light, either the outlet or the circuit that feeds the outlet is the source of the trouble. Now, check the fuses for the room that you're in to make certain that they haven't blown. (See Section II, as cited above, p. 257, before you change the fuse.) If the fuse hasn't blown, then the problem is definitely with the outlet. *Have an electrician repair the outlet.*

Once you have ruled out other possibilities of electrical trouble, you may find that the clock isn't running because the lubricant has settled inside the bottom of the clock case. If the clock had been making small whining sounds before it finally conked out, the little gears need more lubrication than they're getting now. (Usually the lubricant lumps up because the clock hasn't been moved in a long time.) Turn your clock upside down to move the lubricant and very likely the clock will soon run.

Too Fast or Too Slow. Again, the problem may be that the lubricant has settled in the bottom of the case. If turning the clock upside down doesn't help, take the clock to a repair shop.

Glass Broken. Flat glass can be replaced by removing the broken pieces and putting in a new glass that has been cut to the proper size (or you can have it replaced by a professional clockmaker).

Case Broken. A plastic case that is broken or cracked can be mended with plastic cement. (See Section II, GLUING AND CLAMPING, p. 250.)

CLOSET

Bent Clothing Rod. Replace your bent or breaking clothes rod before you find your wardrobe on the closet floor. Take out the old rod and insert a strong metal one in its place. (See BATHROOM ACCESSORIES—SHOWER ROD COMING LOOSE.)

You can also support the present rod. Put a screw eye into the ceiling or shelf above the rod. Then, fasten a heavy wire around the sagging rod and up through the eye. (Twist the wire to make it tight.)

Splintered Clothing Rod. If you're having trouble sliding hangers along the wooden clothes rod in your closet, you'll want to smooth away the splinters. This can be done by sanding and painting, but it's easier to cover the surface with plastic self-stick wall or shelf covering. Apply the covering as indicated in BATHROOM ACCESSORIES—SHOWER OR TOWEL ROD, CORRODED OR RUSTY.

Sagging Shelf. To support a sagging shelf, screw or nail a wooden cleat to the wall studs under the shelf at the back of the closet. Metal brackets can also be screwed to the wall and shelf for extra support.

Door Sticks. See DOOR/HINGED.

Door Jammed. See DOOR/SLIDING.

Mildew. The reaches of a damp, dark, warm closet offer a perfect home for mildew growth. If you don't get rid of it, your closet will begin to get the musty smell of an old pair of sneakers.

Scrub the mildewed area with chlorine bleach and water, and spray the corners and walls of the closet with mildew retardant that comes in an aerosol spray can.

To keep mildew from returning, you'll have to change the inside environment. You can install a baseboard dehumidifier in the closet that will remove the moisture from the air, or you can buy chemicals such as *silica gel, activated alumina* and *calcium chloride*. These materials can be put into small packets that hang from the clothing rod. Follow the package directions.

COCKROACH

See Section II, PEST CONTROL, p. 307.

COFFEE MAKER | electric

Before you blame your coffee maker for bad-tasting coffee, check the manufacturer's instructions for the proportion and the blend of coffee that you should be using. It may be that the problem is not with the appliance at all. (Also, a long extension cord, not adequate for the current needed, contributes to poor performance. It's best to plug the pot directly into a wall outlet using only the cord that came with the pot.)

CAUTION: *Handling any electrical appliance requires care. It is imperative, therefore, that you follow all the safety precautions given in Section II,* ELECTRICITY AND WIRING, p. 257, *before you attempt to repair electrical appliances and equipment.*

Doesn't Work. Is the cord plug set securely in the wall outlet? Take a look at it and wiggle it slightly. If you notice that the plug is loose, take it out and examine the prongs. Are they coming out of the plug, or are they damaged in any way that you can see? Also, check the female plug that sets into the coffee maker. Is the plug casing loose or broken? Do the screws need tightening and is the cord intact where it enters the plug?

If something is wrong with either connection, don't put the plug into the socket or the wall outlet. You *can* repair or replace a plug (see Section II, as cited above).

If all the above items check out, and the appliance isn't working, take the cord plug, spread the prongs with your fingers just a little, and plug the coffee maker into the wall outlet. If you're still left with cold water instead of coffee, check the lights and other appliances in the house. If they're out, you probably have a power failure. (Ask your neighbors, or turn on a battery-operated radio to find out.)

It's possible, however, that the particular outlet you're using doesn't work. Plug in a lamp. If it lights up, the trouble is *inside the coffee maker,* and you'll have to take your pot to a dealer for repair.

If the lamp doesn't light, either the outlet or the circuit that feeds the outlet is the source of the problem. Now, check the fuses for the room that you are in to make certain that they haven't blown. (See Section II, as cited above, p. 257, before you change the fuse.) If the fuse is all right, then the trouble is in the outlet. *Have an electrician repair the outlet.*

Stained. When coffee oils accumulate and leave dark stains on the inside of the coffee maker, get rid of them by scouring, or buy a coffee-stain remover. (It should be used according to the manufacturer's directions.) *Note:* Do not immerse the entire pot when you clean it. Water will seep into the heating chamber and, in many electric pots, the heating element can be damaged. There are a few coffee makers that are completely immersible and these are usually labeled as such.

Percolator Top Broken. See COFFEE MAKER/MECHANICAL.

Percolator Stem Clogged. See COFFEE MAKER/MECHANICAL.

Coffee Maker Dented. See ALUMINUM POT AND PAN—SIDES . . . DENTED.

COFFEE MAKER | mechanical

Percolator Top Broken. With rough handling, the glass top of your percolator may be chipped at the point where it fits into the metal cover. More than likely, as it jiggles around when the coffee perks, the coffee will squirt out and down the sides of the pot. Replace the top with a new one from the hardware store, but note the manufacturer and model of your coffee maker before you shop, or take the old one with you to match it.

Percolator Stem Clogged. When the hollow stem inside your coffee maker clogs up with grounds, clean it out with a pipe cleaner, then wash and rinse.

Drip Coffee Maker Leaks. Sometimes, while it is being brewed, coffee will leak from the center of your drip coffee maker. This indicates that the sievelike holes in the basket are clogged. Flush them out with water and *brush* them clean before using.

Coffee Maker Dented. See ALUMINUM POT AND PAN—SIDES . . . DENTED.

COMFORTER

Soiled. All comforters, whether they are filled with wool, acrylic, or fluffy down, should be dry-cleaned and *never* laundered. Although the tag on a new comforter may be marked "washable," don't take chances with laundering. (Rarely will a quilt fall apart in dry-cleaning, but in laundering, you run the risk of damaging your favorite quilt forever.)

Tattered Edges and Tears. Buy an attractive binding of cotton, silk, or velvet ribbon. Bind the border of the quilt with it. (For details, see BLANKET, and Section II, MENDING BY SEWING, p. 276.)

Once you see that the border is beginning to become frayed, be on guard! Shredding edges foretell the quilt's demise. If you notice small tears, they can be restitched, and worn patches on a patchwork quilt can easily be replaced. (For details on this, see Section II, as cited above, p. 276.)

Stuffing Needs Replacing. Down and feather comforters are expensive. If you have one that is close to you, it can be refeathered and refurbished! Though the sheen is gone and the quilt flat and torn, a quiltmaker will be able to help you. You will find him in the yellow pages of your phone directory. The quiltmaker-repairer has the skill *and the machinery* to refill your comforter and to repair the quilting. When you get the quilt back, it will look and feel like new.

CONCRETE

See CEMENT AND CONCRETE.

CONDENSATION

Dampness in your house can be there for a variety of reasons, but the common cause throughout the house is condensation. This simply means that the warm, moisture-laden air in the house hits a cold surface. Sometimes, in summer, it hits your iced tea glass and causes the glass to "sweat." Other times, in winter, warm air will hit the colder surfaces of a windowpane or an attic roof that isn't insulated. You'll notice beads of water or dampness on these surfaces. Moisture of this sort, though, is not healthy for your house; eventually it will rot beams and they will give way. In the meantime, your rooms are apt to be happy spawning grounds for mildew. Below, we tackle some of the problems of condensation, and refer you to the sections of the book that treat other aspects of the problem.

Attic Damp. Attics, like basements, are damp-prone. But unlike the lower reaches of the house, attic moisture occurs only two ways. Either your roof has sprung a leak, or the moisture comes from condensation. (*Note:* Be on guard for leaks; for more on this, see ROOF.)

If the roof isn't leaking and your attic is damp, the condensation there very likely is due to lack of insulation upstairs. In winter, the warm air from the house travels upstairs and hits the cold surfaces of the walls or roof and turns into little droplets of water.

The simplest and cheapest way to cope with this condition is to keep the attic *cold*. Keep the doors closed during the winter months.

If you'd rather be able to come from and go to the attic in winter, ask your contractor to insulate the attic. (Get an estimate from him before you have the job done.)

In summer, any moisture problems you may have in the attic can be minimized by more ventilation. (See FAN/ATTIC for details.)

Basement Damp. See BASEMENT.

Bathroom Damp. See BATHROOM.

Closet Damp. See CLOSET.

Single Window Steams Up. If you don't use storm windows in winter (and don't have the new double panes for insulation), your window will steam up when the warm, moist air inside the house hits the cold of the outdoors, transmitted by the window glass. Solve the problem by applying thin-gauge, transparent vinyl to the window. Buy it at the hardware store in large sheets or rolls. (The 9-foot by 12-foot sheets range from under a dollar a piece to under two dollars, depending on the thickness of the material.) Put this on the window the way wallpaper is put on a wall: cut a panel the size of the window, cover the vinyl with clear glue—brush it on evenly. Place the vinyl on the window, and smooth it out with a wallpapering brush or squeegee. Go over the entire surface to work out bubbles (if necessary, poke a pin through any air bubbles).

Double Windows Steamed Up. If it's winter and the storm windows are up, you may find steaming on the storm window or on the inside window. If the moisture is on the *inside* window, this tells you that your *storm window* is not weathertight: cold air is hitting the *inside* windowpanes. Open the inside window and caulk the edges of the storm windows with rolled caulking cord. (It's called Mortite, and is bought at the hardware store; it can be peeled off in the spring.)

If you see steaming on the *storm* window, that tells you that the *inside* window is not tight: it's letting warm air into the space between the two. Check the *inside* window: have you really closed it tight? Is it latched? If you've closed the window correctly and still have the problem, you can use caulking cord around the *inside* window. (It'll be weatherproofed this way, but not very attractive-looking.)

COOKING UTENSILS

See ALUMINUM POT AND PAN, COPPER, and POT AND POT COVER.

COPPER

CAUTION: *Copper contamination, generated by acid substances of various foods, is poisonous. Thus, cooking utensils made with copper should be tin-lined.* Inspect your copper cookware regularly. Check the inside of every copper pot before you use it, and if you see an area where the tin lining has worn away, put the pot back on the shelf. When you get a chance, take the utensil to a department store with a reconditioning service, or consult the yellow pages of your phone directory for "Cooking Utensils—Reconditioning." These experts will reline it and make it safe for cooking.

Tarnished. See BRASS—TARNISHED.

Lacquer Coming Off. See BRASS—LACQUER COMING OFF.

Dented. See ALUMINUM POT AND PAN—SIDES . . . DENTED.

Handle Broken. This repair requires the skill of a metal craftsman. Look for one in the yellow pages of the phone directory; he will know how to rivet the handle to the pan so that it will be secure. (If you tackle this job yourself with bolts, the handle that you have rebolted may come loose when you are holding a kettle of boiling water.)

CORD, ELECTRIC

See Section II, ELECTRICITY AND WIRING, p. 257.

CORK TILE

See FLOOR/TILE.

COUNTER TOP

Ceramic. See CERAMIC TILE.

Plastic Laminated Top—Stained. Be cautious with this elegant, shiny surface. First, try rubbing the stained area with a cloth soaked in liquid detergent. If the stain is stubborn, take the next step: try a household liquid cleanser. Rinse off the cleaner. *Note:* Abrasive cleaners (scouring powders) and scouring pads will leave permanent scratches on this surface, and you will rue the day you used them. Scouring can sometimes make the stain look much worse, and it will ruin the shiny finish you paid for.

Plastic Laminated Top—Knife-Scarred. The damage is permanent. Avoid more of the same by *prevention*. Have cutting boards handy, and train your family and friends (even if you have to speak gruffly) to cut on cutting boards, and not on your shiny counter!

Plastic Laminated Top—Corners and Edge Coming Loose. The corner or edging of your counter can curl up if the adhesive that glued it there dries up. Sometimes this will happen if the counter (Melamine or Formica) has been laid above a heat-giving appliance (clothes- or dishwashers). To re-lay corner: first, lift it up further—very *gently*, because the material is brittle. Scrape the undersides, using a sharp knife, to remove as much of the old adhesive from both surfaces as possible. Vacuum up the dust with the radiator attachment of your cleaner. Next, spread counter-top adhesive on both surfaces with a spatula or a plastic (picnic-type) butter spreader. (Buy the special adhesive from the hardware store or from a building supply house. Be sure to follow the directions on the container.)

Let the adhesive dry until it no longer is tacky to touch. Now, with a rolling pin, work over the surface from center to corner, rolling the laminated top down into the adhesive. Cover the surface with wax paper or clean rags, then cover these with a board. Weight the board with books, pots and pans, or rocks.

If edging is involved in this repair, put pressure on it by placing a small board against the edge, then tilting a heavy chair against the board. (The weight of the chair holds the board in place while the glue cures. Keep up the pressure overnight.)

Tile Counter. See CERAMIC TILE.

Wood Counter. See BLOCK, CHOPPING.

CRYSTAL

Grubby, Soiled. The glinting facets of cut crystal are targets for dust and grime. Clean crystal bowls, goblets, vases, and other crystal pieces with a mixture of vinegar and uncooked white rice. Put a few tablespoons of each into the crystal piece and more of the same into a large pan or tub, then swish the mixture around the inside and the outside of the piece. Rinse and dry. If the crystal still has a milky haze, fill it with warm water, mild detergent, a little vinegar, and soak it overnight. (Let it stand in the same solution in a pan.) Rinse the crystal in the morning. Repeat this treatment until the crystal shimmers.

Decanter Looks Filmy. Crystal decanters used for wine or vinegar can develop a filmy residue that will disappear with the proper treatment. Make a solution of two tablespoons of ammonia and one quart of water. Pour this into the decanter and let it stand for an hour. Rinse *extra-thoroughly*. Polish the exterior.

Cracked or Broken. It's usually possible to mend broken crystal with one of the many types of cements and glues on the market. (For details, see CHINAWARE, and Section II, GLUING AND CLAMPING, p. 248.) Valuable pieces of crystal should be repaired by a professional; to find the right person for the job, ask an antiques dealer.

CUPBOARD

Latches Won't Work. There are many types of latches on cupboards. Sad to say, each has its problems. Below we give some hints for coping with different types.

1. Magnetic Latches. In these devices, the magnet is attached to the

cabinet, but it needs a metal plate to attract it to the door. So, if your cupboard door won't stay closed, check to see if this metal plate has slipped down below the magnet connection or has fallen off. Put the plate back where it belongs and screw it to the door.

If the magnet part of the latch has come loose or fallen off, rescrew it or replace it. (The hardware store can sell you the part.)

2. Push-Ball Type Latch. The small round spring ball (which is used in many bathroom cabinets) can go awry. It may keep the door from closing. Painters sometimes paint over the steel ball, rendering it immobile. To remedy this: use some paint remover to free the ball. Then clean the area and spray it with silicone lubricant.

On the other hand, the door may have been painted so that the ball can't reach the socket. If so, sandpaper or scrape the inside edge of the door. (This allows it to close so that the ball reaches the socket.)

3. Latches and Handles. Paint may have jammed up the fastener on your cupboards. (Before the next paint job, you might want to take the latch and handles off.) To remove the paint on the latch *after* the damage is done, dab a bit of paint remover on the latch with a small brush. Be careful not to let the remover run down over the rest of the cupboard. If you don't make progress this way, take the latches off and soak them in paint remover. And if you don't want to fuss with paint remover, buy a bright, shiny new set of latches at the hardware store and screw them in place.

Doors Sagging. Your cupboard doors, most likely, are opened and closed more times than others in the house. Sometimes you may even slam them shut or yank them open—when you're rushing to get a meal on the table.

Such treatment puts a strain on the hinges. Before the door sags even more, or before it falls off, fix the hinges. *They* control the sag or lack of it. Check the top hinge. Has it come loose? If so, prop the door all the way open, then rig up some sort of support that will take the weight off the hinges. (You can tie a cord to the doorknob and hitch this to a hook above the cabinet, or you can stack books under the door, but be sure the stack is steady.) Now, tighten the screws. If the screws still can be turned by your screwdriver when their heads are driven flush with the hinge, you have these options: wedge toothpicks into the screw holes to make the screws fit tighter, or buy screws one size larger in diameter. Drive these into the old screw holes.

CURTAIN

Curtain Ring Coming Loose. Curtains (especially café curtains) that hang on curtain rods from decorative rings lose their charm and looks when the ring and the curtain part company. Bringing them together again can be done in a jiffy. Take the curtain off the rod (and slip the ring off, too); then, on the wrong side of the top hem, sew the ring back on. Do this with plain, old-fashioned overcasting. Use matching-color thread, and secure the stitches. (For details, see Section II, MENDING BY SEWING, p. 276.)

If you hate to sew, clip off all of the rings and buy the new no-sew clip-on curtain rings. They're sold in most department stores and come in many styles and in several sizes to suit your rod.

Hems Coming Out. Use an invisible stitch to put up a hem that is falling out. (You take the curtain off the rod to do the sewing, and remember to use matching-color thread for the work. For details, see Section II, as cited above, p. 276.)

If the curtain weights fell off and got lost when the hem came down, buy new ones at the department store. Tack them inside the hem, in the bottom corners. Follow the instructions on the package when you do this. (If your curtains tend to billow at the hem, sew on lead taping along the wrong side of the hem. You'll find the curtain will hang more evenly.)

Rips or worn spots along the hem can be disguised by stitching on an embroidered border or braid. You'll find a large assortment at fabric shops and drapery counters.

Pinch Pleats Coming Undone. Laundering and ironing can open up the tacking that holds pinch pleats together. To fix them, study the depth of the neighboring pleats, fold the loose pleats likewise on the right side of the curtain, and tack through these folds.

Tears in Fabric. Mends are made to suit particular fabrics; below we cover various types.

1. Cotton, Silk, Synthetics. Vertical tears in lined cotton, silk, or synthetic curtains are relatively easy to mend. Bring the two sides of the rip together by reinforcing the material on the wrong side of the curtain. Use matching material for this, even if you have to snitch some from a seam. Tiny stitches in matching thread will help to disguise the repair.

If the curtain is translucent and unlined, make the smallest, narrowest of seams, using tiny stitches, and hope that the folds of fabric will keep the mend from view. (For details on stitches, see Section II, as cited above, p. 276.)

2. Woolens and Loose Weaves. A tear in wool curtains or any loosely woven material can be repaired with a rewoven patch. You can do this yourself or, if the work is too finicky for you and you dote on the curtain, take it to your cleaner and tailor. He will usually know where expert reweaving is done. (If you do the work, consult Section II, as cited above, p. 276.)

3. Lace or Net. Unravel a remnant or take out a strand from the seams, thread it through your needle and weave across the tear. Use a matching

thread if you can't pull some from the curtain. Reinforce fragile laces by stitching matching net or tulle to the wrong side of the mend. (For details on mending lace, see Section II, as cited above, p. 287.)

Lining Worn Out. You can make a new lining yourself by using the old one as a pattern. If you can't face the chore, take it to a professional seamstress or drapery shop.

CURTAIN, BEADED

String Broken. Collect the scattered beads before they get lost. Take a look at one of the strands and, starting with the bottom bead, restring them in the same manner. If you have no guide and have to restring the whole curtain, follow these simple steps:

1. Borrow some fishing line from your husband, or buy some at a sporting goods store. Or, at an arts and crafts shop, buy special waxed thread made for this purpose.

2. Cut the line or thread twice the length of the *finished* beaded curtain.

3. String the bottom bead on the thread, and slip it to the middle. Grasp the two cut ends of the thread, twist them and slip both through the second bead. The first bead acts as the anchor for the rest of the beads you string.

4. Continue stringing until strand is the length you want, then knot the two ends of thread to a metal ring, or sew them to a tape at the top of the strand. (The tape corresponds to the top of a curtain. The ring corresponds to a curtain ring, through which you slip the curtain rod.)

CURTAIN ROD

See DRAPERY HARDWARE.

CUTLERY

See KNIFE.

CUTTING BOARD

See BLOCK, CHOPPING.

DAMPNESS

See BASEMENT, BATHROOM, CLOSET, CONDENSATION.

DECK

Protruding Nails. Guard against this menace by inspecting the deck regularly. Hammer down and countersink the protruding nails.

Rotten or Defective Plank. Pry out a sagging, rotten wooden plank before it gives way and causes serious injury. Cover the space where the board was with a larger board, or place a bucket or a piece of outdoor furniture upside down there (to keep traffic away).

Then, take the plank's measurements to the lumberyard. If your deck planks are all the same length, buy several of them and save the extras for future repairs.

Before renailing the replacement, waterproof the edges of the crosspieces (they are called *stringers*) with building paper. Cap the paper around *each stringer section* and staple it to the sides of the stringers. Coat the underside of the new plank with a wood preservative, such as Woodlife. (It's a good idea to treat the whole deck by brushing on a wood preservative. This will save deck planks from weather damage—and you from having to replace them).

Splintered Planks. Locate splintering area and sand lightly by hand. Put a coat of wood preservative (to which a quarter as much boiled linseed oil has been added) over this and other splintering areas (to keep splinters from developing).

Sagging Deck. A sagging deck is dangerous and needs immediate attention. Rent or borrow a steel house-jack from a lumber dealer or hardware store, and jack the deck up to the proper level. Then call in a professional contractor to put in a new pier or support.

DESK

See CHEST OF DRAWERS, TABLE, and Section II, REFINISHING WOOD, p. 301.

DISHWASHER | electric

CAUTION: *Handling any electrical appliance requires care: Protect yourself by consulting the safety rules given in Section II, ELECTRICITY AND WIRING, p. 257, before you start to investigate the trouble. Remember: If the dishwasher makes loud or unusual noises or gives off strange odors while it's running, you should stop it immediately. The trouble may be corrected through some of the suggestions below. If not, you may need professional help.*

Won't Run. If you've loaded the dishwasher and pressed the starting button, and *nothing* happens, there are several items to check before you blame the machine:

1. Are you sure that the lid or door is able to close properly? Take another look at the way you've loaded the china, and be sure that nothing keeps the door or lid from closing.

2. Is the latch on the lid or door stiff or damaged? Work it while the lid is open to test it. If you can't get the latch to close, call the repairman.

3. *Portable Only.* Are you sure that the appliance plug is firmly set in the electrical wall outlet? If it is, and the machine doesn't run, check the outlet. (Test it with a lamp that works. For details, see Section II, as cited above, p. 257.) If the prongs on the plug allow it to wobble, spread them open just a little.

4. Has the fuse in the circuit for the dishwasher blown? If not, check your other appliances and your lights. Is the refrigerator off? Are the lights working? There may be a power blackout in your neighborhood or in the region. Consult your neighbors or turn on a battery-powered radio, to find out.

Note: If the fuse has blown, you can change the fuse, but this may not be the end of your troubles. The new fuse may also blow. (Remember to play safe: before changing any fuse, consult Section II, ELECTRICITY AND WIRING, p. 257.) Next, send for the repairman or an electrician. Your circuit may be overloaded, or your dishwasher may be short-circuiting.

Dishes Come Out Dirty or Spotted. There are various reasons your dishwasher may not be cleaning the dishes, but none involves actual *repair*. We include them here so that you can cope with the difficulty yourself. (You save money by not sending for the repairman, and some simple adjustment may mean you can use the machine without waiting for outside help.)

1. You may be loading the dishes improperly. Water jets must reach all the surfaces of the china and flatware you put in the machine. A large bowl on the lower rack, for example, will keep water from reaching glassware on the upper rack. Follow the loading instructions that are given in your owner's manual.

2. Experiment with another *dishwasher detergent.* (*But remember to use only those sold for dishwashers.* These are extra-strong chemically, and are low in suds. The regular detergent you use for washing by hand would suds up and overflow your machine.)

3. Your water may not be hot enough to do the job. The Good Housekeeping Institute recommends that the water temperature be between 150 and 160 degrees Fahrenheit. Check the thermostat on your hot-water heater, turn it up to at least 150 degrees, and test the dishwasher with a load of dishes, including those from the last, unsatisfactory run. If you live in an upstairs apartment, it's possible that the hot water from the basement heater takes too long to reach your dishwasher. Run the tap water until you get hot water, *then* switch on your dishwater.

4. The water pressure may be low. Experts say that you need pressure

of fifteen to twenty pounds per square inch to get the best results from your machine. If, suddenly, your dishwasher doesn't operate properly, there may be a water main break in your neighborhood, or some momentary drain on the supply—either in your house or your neighborhood. Check your house first, then consult your neighbors. If your tap water continues to run feebly, call your water supply company or the plumber. (You can be supplied with adequate pressure, but this may require alterations or repairs to your piping system.)

5. The detergent cup may be jammed closed. Check to be sure that in your last run the cup has opened and dispensed the detergent. If the cup doesn't open automatically, open it by hand, and run the machine through a complete cycle. When you've emptied the machine, take a closer look at the cup: is it encrusted with salt or minerals? Sometimes, hard water (water with too much calcium content) will cause this. Scrape the cup clean, snap it open and closed until it works easily.

(If the cup *still* jams, sprinkle the detergent in the next load by hand. That is, open the machine when it reaches the *wash* settings on the dial, add detergent to the machine, close it and resume the cycle. Then, call your repairman and have him repair or replace the cup.)

Hums But Won't Wash. Open the door (to switch the machine off), and lift up the flatware basket. Is a fork handle dangling from the bottom of the basket? If so, this has prevented the impeller in the bottom of the dishwasher from rotating. Double-check to be sure that, for instance, a spoon hasn't slipped clean through the flatware basket and down into the bottom, jamming the impeller. (Slide the lower rack out to do this.)

Banging Sounds During Wash and Rinse Operation. We've all probably heard these warning sounds. Usually they mean that a fork (or something else slender) has slipped out of the flatware basket and is hitting against the twirling impeller. Unlatch the door, wait a few seconds for the water to drip down into the bottom of the machine, then open the door all the way. Slide the lower rack out; then, with rubber gloves, snatch the fork or other impediment out of the hot water. Close the door and resume the cycle.

Front-Loading Machine—Small Leaks. If you see a tiny puddle on the floor (less than a teaspoon of water) when your machine is running, it's possible that the seal around the door is defective. At the end of the complete cycle, open the door and check the rubber or plastic rim around the inside edge of the door. Is it loose or damaged? If it's loose, glue it back in place with a dab of epoxy. Allow the glue to cure. (For details, see Section II, GLUING AND CLAMPING, p. 248.)

Front-Loading Machine—Larger Leaks. Your pumping mechanism may not be operating properly (or at all). Whatever the cause, the situation is serious. Turn off the machine and call the serviceman. (Water leaks can sometimes reach the motor of the dishwasher and cause a short circuit there, and this usually is a repair that calls for the removal of the motor and the installation of a new one.)

Any Style Dishwasher—Water Overflows. The pump may have failed (see above), or the waste line may be clogged. Turn off the dishwasher immediately, and call the repairman. All you can do till he comes is mop up!

Machine Starts, Then Stops. Open the door to the dishwasher to disconnect it. Then check the fuse box for a blown fuse on the dishwasher circuit. If the fuse is blown, there are two possible causes: 1. another appliance on the same circuit has been running (your circuit is overloaded). 2. The motor in the dishwasher is short-circuiting. In the latter case, call the repairman. *Note:* You can usually detect a motor burnout; you can smell an acrid odor when it occurs. But don't just trust your nose. Get help from the expert.

DISPOSER | electric

CAUTION: *Handling any electrical appliance requires care: protect yourself by consulting the safety rules given in Section II,* ELECTRICITY AND WIRING, *p. 257, before you start to investigate. Remember: If your disposer makes* unusual *noises while it's running, you should stop its operation immediately. Remember, too:* Never *put your hands into the disposer.*

Below, we give you some additional dos and don'ts for disposers, tell you how to cope with minor disposer malfunctions, and, figuratively speaking, hold your hand till the repairman comes to fix the machine's major maladies.

SPECIAL CAUTION: *Your garbage disposer is made to handle food you'd otherwise put in the garbage pail. Don't grind metals, glass, plastics, ceramics, leather, cloth, string, paper cartons, newspaper, or rubber.* All of these, though the machine is tough enough to grind and shred them, will clog your sanitary sewer or septic tank, and sooner or later you'll have serious plumbing problems. For the same reason, the experts tell you, *don't feed seafood shells, artichokes, or corn husks to your disposer.*

Disposer Area Gives Off Faint Odor of Garbage. In normal operation, the disposer cleans itself when you feed it meat bones or fruit pits—these actually scour the works the way you scour your pots and pans. But if you detect an unpleasant, garbage-y odor, feed your machine some lemon rinds and ice cubes! The Good Housekeeping Institute also suggests that you give the disposer half a cup of sink cleanser—to clean it and dissipate any odors.

Hums But Won't Start. There are two reasons why this happens—both of them having to do with what you've fed the disposer.

1. Food wastes are packed into the disposer too tightly. This can make it impossible for the machinery to work. Turn off the control switch and the cold water from the faucet. With tongs or a large spoon, loosen the

waste material in the disposer. (Take some out for the time being.) Now, flip the switch on, run the cold water, and resume normal operations.

2. A fork or other item on the forbidden list (see above) is jamming the works. Turn the machine and the water off, and remove the fork (or other impediment) with tongs. Replace food wastes in disposer, turn on both the machine and the water. If the machine still hums but won't run, switch it off again, turn off the water, and use a barbecue fork or long, sturdy tool to nudge the rotating wheel down in the disposer. Move the wheel back and forth until it turns readily. Then, repack wastes into unit, turn water and machine on. If it still will not work, make a note of its model and serial numbers, call your dealer or service center, and give the repairman the necessary information. (Turn the machine off until the repairman comes to fix it.)

Makes Loud Noises While Running, Then Stops. This tells you that you have fed the disposer something—a knife or fork, for instance—that you shouldn't have. Turn unit off and retrieve the obstacle, as above.

Won't Work. If you have double-checked to be sure that you have not packed the wastes into the disposer too tightly (see above), *and* you've turned the control switch on again, and the machine *still doesn't operate,* make the routine electrical checks:

1. Look at the fuse for the disposer circuit: is it blown? If so, replace it with another. Because safety is involved in this operation, consult Section II, ELECTRICITY AND WIRING, p. 257, before you change the fuse.

2. If the fuse has not blown, check the other appliances and lights in your house. It's possible there's been a power failure in your area.

Sink Flange Corroded. Call the repairman. Your dealer or service center will install a new flange. First, though, consult your owner's manual; you may have a warranty that covers the cost of the part.

Hopper Corroded. Call the repairman, as above.

Drain Elbow Corroded. Call the repairman, as above.

DOOR | hinged

If your door squeaks like the creaky doors in a Hitchcock movie, or if it sticks and refuses to budge until you hurl yourself against it, you'll need the help of our door-repair clinic. Some of the treatments are simple, but others require a bit of brawn and some carpenter's brain power. (If any of the instruments required in this segment seem unfamiliar, consult our GLOSSARY OF TOOLS in Section II.)

Lock Stiff, Won't Unlock. See LOCK/DOOR.

Lock Broken. See LOCK/DOOR.

Hinges Squeak When Door Moves. Spray the hinges with a silicone lubricating compound. It comes in a spray can at the hardware store. Aim the spray so that the compound reaches into all the hinge parts. If the squeak continues after this treatment, you'll have to take the hinges apart and clean them, then spray them, as follows:

1. Open the door. Put a wedge of wood under the door on the *latch side* (this takes the weight off the hinges).

2. Take the pins out of the hinges. Do this, starting with the bottom hinge, by gently knocking the pins upward, to loosen them. Use a hammer and a small piece of wood. (Put the wood, like a wedge, under the head of the pin and tap the head up by hammering on the wood wedge. The wood wedge protects the hinge from dents.)

3. Clean the bottom hinge and the pin. Rub them with a soapy steel-wool pad, rinse, then wipe the parts dry. (You can swab the inside of the hinges with a cotton-tipped swab.) Spray with silicone lubricating compound. Replace the pin, and repeat this treatment for the top hinge.

Air Leaks in Around Edges of Door. Use rubber, metal, felt, or plastic weather stripping. See WEATHER STRIPPING.

Door Sticks. If you're lucky, you can remedy this simply by tightening the hinge screws. When they're loose and the hinges sag, the door will rub against some part of the door frame (door jamb). To correct the situation, first examine all those screws in the hinges. (Remember that a hinge has two leaves, like the front and back covers of a book. All the screws in both these leaves should be tightened.) You'll need a really hefty screwdriver for this job; for such a tool, consult Section II, GLOSSARY OF TOOLS, p. 229.

Door Still Sticks—Hinges Can't Be Tightened. If you've tried the method above to unstick your door, and the hinge screws twirl around in the wood but won't tighten, you'll need to resort to more drastic treatment. The trouble is with the wood in which the screws are set. It has been so chewed up that the screws will not hold. You'll have to take the door off, and if it's a heavy one, you'll probably need help in this maneuver. Here's the procedure:

1. Close the door as best you can (even though it's askew). Stick a small wedge under the door on the latch side—that is, the corner *opposite* the bottom hinge.

2. With hammer and wood wedge, knock the hinge pins up and out of the hinges (see above, "Hinges Squeak" for how to do this). Save the hinge pins.

3. Have your assistant help you handle the door after you move it from the unpinned hinges. Lean the door against the wall or put it flat on a couch or on padded sawhorses.

4. Where you've spotted the trouble, remove the screws. (They may be holding the hinge leaves of the jamb or they may be holding the leaves on the door.) Save these.

5. Dip matchsticks or wood slivers in glue, then force these into the old, chewed-up hinge holes. Let the glue set. (For details on glues, see Section II, GLUING AND CLAMPING, p. 248.)

6. Replace the hinge leaves and drive the screws into the wood you've doctored. They should now take firm hold.

7. Lift the door (use a helper for this). Put the door in proper position, and reinsert the hinge pins—top hinge first, then bottom. The door should open and close without sticking after this treatment.

Door Won't Close Because Top Corner (on Latch Side) Strikes Door Jamb. If the door won't close properly, and you notice that the *top corner* strikes the jamb, the problem lies with the *setting* of the hinges. Because they are not exactly aligned, the door hangs crookedly and hits a part of the door frame. In this case, the *bottom hinge* is at fault, and to fix the door you need to shim up the bottom hinge as follows:

1. Take the door off (see above, "Hinges Squeak.")

2. Unscrew the bottom hinge from the jamb.

3. Cut a piece of cardboard just a bit smaller than the hinge leaf. (This will be your shim.) Place the shim exactly where the leaf was, on the jamb (see diagram). Put the leaf over it and screw both the cardboard and leaf into the jamb. (Just the extra thickness of the cardboard will push

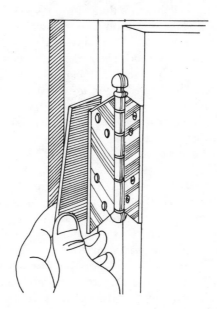

the bottom hinge out a fraction so that the door hangs correctly, that is, with top and bottom hinges in a straight line.) Add another shim if your first one isn't thick enough to do the job.

Door Strikes Jamb on Bottom Portion (on Latch Side). The reverse of the above problem, this means you must shim up the *top hinge*. Repeat the procedure above, treating top hinge leaf on door jamb.

Door Swollen. If the door has seen a lot of humid weather and has become swollen with moisture, you'll have to give the door a "slenderizing" treatment by taking wood off the hinge edge. Here's the procedure:

1. Close the door as far as it will go, then take a look at how much the door overlaps the door jamb. Measure this overlap. (For example, the overlap may be ¼ inch.)

2. Measure in ¼ inch (or whatever the overlap was that *you* measured) from the *hinge* side of the door and draw a line from top to bottom of the door on the hinge side.

3. Knock the hinge pins out of the hinges and move the door to a work area.

4. Prop the door up against a heavy piece of furniture with one end against the wall. The door should rest so that the latch edge is on the floor, and the hinge edge is up, facing you.

5. With a wood plane, slice off very thin shavings of the surface. Start at one end and work to the middle, then turn the door around and work from the other end to the middle. Shave just to the line you've drawn, *no further!*

6. When you've finished this, you'll have to make new little shallow beds for the hinge leaves. These are called *mortises*. You simply deepen the previous mortise with a chisel. Cover the raw wood (the part you've planed and the new mortises) with a wood sealer such as linseed oil or primer paint.

7. Screw the hinge leaves in place and rehang the door.

Latch Won't Catch. The latch tongue must reach and fit into the strike plate to be securely closed. If you've readjusted the door by shimming the hinges, the new alignment may call for adjustment of the strike plate. To make the repair *precise*, you need an impression of the trouble. Make this just the way the dentist does when he tests your bite. Coat the strike plate on the jamb with something that will be marked by the latch when you close the door. Rub carbon paper on the strike plate, or use lipstick, chalk, crayons, or stove black. Now close the door, then open it and look for latch marks on the strike plate. Are the marks too high for the latch to fit into the strike plate hole? Too low? The remedy is as follows:

1. Unscrew the strike plate from the jamb.

2. If the marks tell you that the latch was just a wee bit off, say less than ¼ inch, use a file to enlarge the strike plate opening. This is all the adjustment you'll need. Rescrew the strike plate to the jamb.

If the marks on the strike plate tell you that the latch and plate are more than a little out of kilter (or more than ¼ inch off), unscrew the strike plate. Move it around to the spot where it catches the latch tongue. Make pencil marks here. Fill the old screw holes with plastic wood. CAUTION: *Plastic wood is extremely flammable—don't work near a pilot light or even a lighted cigarette!* Then, enlarge the mortise that the strike plate sits in (use a chisel to do this). Drill new holes for the screws. If any of the old mortise shows on the jamb when you've reset the plate, fill *this* with plastic wood, too! Screw the strike plate to the jamb.

Door Swings Free—Latch Doesn't Reach Strike Plate. The door may have shrunk. There are three cures for this condition:

1. Shim up the hinges. (See above, "Door Won't Close.")
2. Using the same technique, shim up the strike plate.
3. Shim up both the strike plate and the hinges.

Door Rattles and Shakes. If the noise gets on your nerves, the temporary remedy is to ram a rubber wedge under the door to immobilize it. But the true cure calls for some door surgery.

You should understand *why* you have the rattle, and how the surgery stops it. If there's too much space between what the carpenter calls the *doorstop,* that strip of wood that runs down the jamb, and the latch, your door will flap back and forth between them every time there's a puff of wind. The idea is to *narrow the space* between these two, to make the door secure. (See diagram.) Do this as follows:

1. Remove the strike plate (as discussed above, "Latch Won't Catch"). Move it back (closer to the doorstop). Make a new mortise. Drill holes for the screws in the new mortise and screw the plate to the jamb. (Fill the old mortise with plastic wood. CAUTION: *Plastic wood is extremely flammable. Don't work near a pilot light or even a lighted cigarette!*)

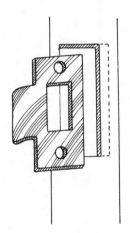

2. Pry up the doorstop. Use a chisel and pry it up very gently, so as not to damage the wood. Nail it closer to the strike plate, and touch up the jamb and any other repaired surfaces with paint or other wood sealer.

Note: On exterior doors, rubber or plastic weather stripping that fills in this gap will stop the rattle. For details, see WEATHER STRIPPING.

DOOR | screen

Screening Torn. Small holes or tears in any type of screening—copper, aluminum, glass fiber, or plastic—can be mended by gluing a patch or strip of the same material over the hole or tear with epoxy. Be sure the patches overlap at least an inch beyond the damaged area. Cut the screen patch with tin snips. (See Section II, GLOSSARY OF TOOLS, p. 229.) Buy both the screening and the tin snips at the hardware store.

Door Sags or Sticks. Check the hinges (see DOOR/HINGED). If the hinges are *not* loose, the door may have ailments elsewhere that make it sag. The door may be coming apart at the corners. Take a look at them. If the joints are loose you can choose your cure. Reinforce with wood strips or with a metal brace:

1. Buy two strips of wood at the lumberyard. (Lathe or batten is what you ask for.) These strips should be 1½ inches wide, ¼-inch thick, and about ½ inch shorter than the width of the door.

2. Take the door off its hinges (see DOOR/HINGED). Place it on a flat surface (a large table or several sawhorses). Now, nail one batten across the top rail (the wood frame on the door). Allow ¼ inch on each side, centering the batten on the rail. Nail the second batten on the bottom rail of the door. You should use ¾-inch finishing nails for the job. (See Section II, WORKING WITH NAILS, SCREWS, AND FASTENERS, p. 236.) Space the nails at random (not in a straight line) to keep the batten from being split by the nails.

You may prefer the second method, with wire and turnbuckle brace:

1. Measure the length of the door, diagonally—that is, measure the distance from hinge side, top, to latch side, bottom.

2. Buy wire this length, and get two screws eyes and a turnbuckle. (See Section II, GLOSSARY OF TERMS, p. 230.) You can find the items at the hardware store or at a marine supply shop. (Marine supply houses carry stainless steel wire and turnbuckles, and though they are more expensive than the ordinary variety, they'll not rust. The additional expense is worthwhile in the long run.)

3. Set the screw eyes at the hinge side, top, and latchside, bottom. Cut the wire in half. Attach one half-length of the wire to the top screw eye and to one end of the turnbuckle. Attach the other length of wire to the other screw eye, and to the other side of the turnbuckle. Now, tighten the turnbuckle by turning it with a screwdriver inserted through the open turnbuckle shaft. (See diagram opposite.) As you tighten the turnbuckle, you will pull the sagging corners toward each other until, finally, you have lifted the sag right out of your door.

Door Rails Split or Cracked. If the split or crack is on the hinge side (and this can happen when the door is slammed to and fro all day long), make the repair with some little metal mending plates. These are made

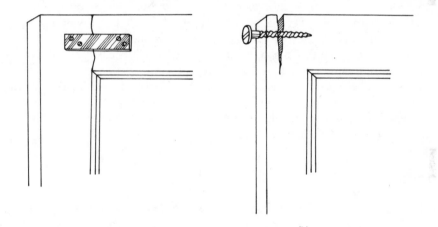

of iron, with four screw holes, two on each end of the plate. Screw these plates on the inside and outside of the door, across the split. (See diagram above, left.)

If the split is close to the edge of the door, drill holes in the edge of the door, and drive long, thin screws *across* the split. (Countersink the screws, and be sure that they reach at least an inch beyond the split. See diagram above, right.)

Door Slams or Blows Open All the Time. If your screen door flaps in the breeze, it's because the springs and door checks have gotten loose from wear and tear. Constant banging and slamming is hard on the door and harder on your nerves. Stop the slamming this way:

1. Pneumatic Door Check. These are metal cylinders you attach to the door and door jamb. Air pressure in the cylinder works the device and keeps the door from slamming. If your pneumatic door check has been overworked, the air pressure in the tube will be low. Adjust the pressure by turning the knob or fastener on the device. Do this, back and forth, while swinging the door open and closed. When the air pressure builds up to the point that suits your door and you, *and* lets the door close at the right speed, stop turning the knob.

2. If your screen door uses on old-fashioned, nonpneumatic coil spring to keep it from swinging to and fro with the breeze, don't fuss with repairs. The old spring is probably stretched (like an old elastic) past the point of endurance. Buy a new spring at the hardware store. (Remember, though, the *new* spring is apt to close the door with a bang unless you hand-close it. You may want to buy a pneumatic door check instead.)

DOOR | sliding

Sticks in Track. Push the door all the way open, then clean out the track along the floor. Scrape off any drops of dried paint you may find there. Then, smooth the bottom and sides of the metal track with silicone lubricating compound. This will make the door slide easily. Buy the lubricating compound at the hardware store.

Won't Budge. Call the repairman (a carpenter). Have him rehang the door.

Keeps Leaving the Track. Call the repairman and have him do the job. New wheels and a new track are called for.

DOOR | swinging

Stands Ajar or Sticks. Dust or rust may be jamming the spring device. In full-length swinging doors you'll find this device in the floor, under the bottom hinge. To bring back the swing to the door, unscrew the plates on either side of the spring covering. Vacuum carefully, to get rid of the dirt and dust. Scrape off any rust you see, then vacuum again. Spray the spring and the pivot with a silicone lubricating compound. Rescrew the plates and swing your doors!

DOORBELL | battery-powered

Bell Won't Work. See DOORBELL/ELECTRIC.

Batteries Dead. If you've made the tests given in the above-cited section, and you suspect that the batteries are at fault, test them. Do this by placing a wood-handled knife blade across the battery terminals—the small metal points around which the bell system wires are wound. If the batteries still have "juice" you'll see and hear sparks when you make this blade test. *Note:* The test is not dangerous. Replace the batteries with new ones if the batteries are dead. Remember to buy the same size and types as the old ones, and be sure the connections are secure.

DOORBELL | electric

Doorbell, buzzer, chime—whatever goes wrong with these, you can usually make right again with a small scrap of sandpaper, a dab of persistence, and an ordinary screwdriver. Although bell or buzzer systems work on electricity, the amount they use is so low that you run no risk of shock when you do *most* of this work. (The two danger spots are noted below.)

Bell, Buzzer, Chime—Won't Work. The system is connected to the house electricity, so, first, check the fuse in the fuse box to see if the doorbell circuit is working. (It should be labeled "doorbell.") If the fuse has blown, change it. (*Note:* To change this or any fuse, consult Section II, ELECTRICITY AND WIRING, p. 257.) Test the bell. If it still won't ring, start with the repair routine below:

1. The Bell Pushbutton at the Front Door. This is the easiest part of the whole hookup to get at. It's literally at your fingertips (beside the door). Take out the screws that hold the casing (see diagram). Then, pull the

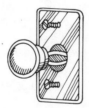

unit away from the door frame or exterior wall. (If the casing has been painted over, you may have to pry it loose with the screwdriver.) Now, check the contact points—where the wires are connected to the button "works." Tighten the screws or bolts you find here. The point that makes the electrical connection may be dirty or corroded. (You can locate this easily enough by just pressing down on the button.) Sand or scrape the connection, using sandpaper or a knife.

Next, check over the wiring around the button. Look for any fraying or breaks in it. If you find a break, twist the two ends of the wire together tightly. If the covering on the wire is frayed, cut it, then twist the ends together. (Use needle-nose pliers for this operation. See GLOSSARY OF TOOLS, p. 227.) Try the bell. If it rings, reinstall the unit. If it doesn't, make this test: place your wood-handled knife *blade* across the terminals (the little

metal screws around which the electric wires are hooked); see diagram above. If the bell rings, the trouble is in the little button part itself. Buy a new one at the hardware store and replace the defective one. If the bell *fails to ring* when you make the knife-blade test, the trouble lies elsewhere in the system. Check it out, as follows:

2. The Bell or Chimes or Buzzer Inside the Home. Your bell or chimes may be housed near the ceiling inside your home. If so, you'll need a ladder for this phase of the repair. (If you're not used to ladders, consult Section II, LADDER SAFETY RULES, p. 312.) Remove the cover or housing for the bell or chimes. Now, check the terminals. Are they loose? Tighten them. Dust the inside works with a soft-bristled, clean paintbrush. Scrape or sandpaper the contact points indicated in the diagram. At this phase of the work, send some member of your household to ring the bell for you. (That is, have someone press the *outdoor pushbutton*, while you observe the inner workings of the bell.) Does the bell ring? If it does, replace the housing. If it doesn't, take a closer look at what's happening when the button is pushed. Does the bell clapper or hammer *vibrate* but *not strike* the gong? If so, bend the arm of the hammer just a little, so that it almost (but not quite) touches the gong. Ask your bell ringer to push the button once more. It should now strike the gong. (If you have chimes, check the terminals, as above, then clean the small metal rods that strike the chimes.)

If these steps fail to make the bell ring, or the chimes to ching, you'll need to move to the next area of operations.

3. Transformer Near Fuse Box (Probably in Your Basement). *Note:* This part of your bell system bring you to an area where you should observe all the safety procedures given in Section II, ELECTRICITY AND WIRING, p. 257. The transformer is usually mounted near the fuse box for your house. On one of its sides, the transformer is fed by the 110-115-volt house-current wires. *Shocks from these can be dangerous.* The transformer turns this high voltage into safe, low voltage. Its other side holds these "safe" wires, which

run the entire doorbell system (the volts are usually 6 or 8). Make these checks in the transformer area:

Have your doorbell ringer stay on the job, and have him press the push-button—outside the front door. (If you have to do the whole thing alone, go to the front door and stick a pin in the button the way trick-or-treaters do on Halloween.) Now, at the transformer, listen carefully. Does the transformer hum? If so, you know that all is well down here, but that you have trouble in the *bell mechanism* itself. Replace the bell with a new one from the hardware store. (Be sure that you take the old bell to the store with you so that you will get one of the same voltage; install it as directed.)

If the transformer *doesn't hum* when the pushbutton is pressed, turn off the house current (see Section II, as cited above, p. 257). Now, tighten the wire connections on each side of the transformer box. (See diagram.)

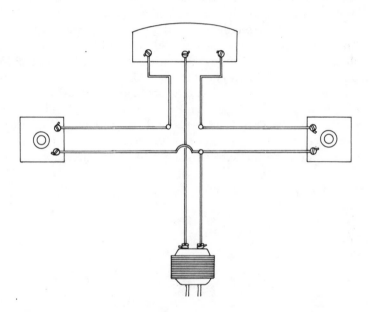

Turn on the current and test the bell again. If there's still no ring and there's still no hum (in the transformer) send for the repairman. It takes a professional electrician to do this work. The transformer may be burned out and may need to be replaced—not a job for an amateur. Or, the wiring in the system that you can't check may need fixing or replacing.

Doorbell or Buzzer Won't Stop. Take the pushbutton out of its casing (see above, item 1). Disconnect one of the wires at the terminals shown in the diagram. The ringing will cease immediately!

To get the bell back into regular operation again, replace the button with a new one.

Buzzer Upstairs to Open Downstairs Door Doesn't Work. Sometimes your doorbell will ring, but the buzzer upstairs won't function. When this happens, follow the routine given above, in item 1, to repair the upstairs buzzer.

DOORKNOB

Loose or Falling Off. If you've ever been imprisoned in a room because the doorknob came off in your hand, you know it's ignominious and possibly even dangerous to be marooned alone this way. So attend to your doorknobs. When they're slightly loose, tighten them. There are three ways knobs are set in doors. Each requires its own repair, as follows:

1. Knob on Flat Spindle. Use a screwdriver to tighten the screws that hold the knob in place. Move the knob slightly as you do this—so that you feel the screw hitting the flat part of the spindle.

2. Knob on Threaded Spindle. Twist the knob to tighten it, until there's just enough clearance between knob and door plate (so the knob can *turn*). Then, with a screwdriver, tighten the screws that hold the knob.

3. Glass Knob Glued To Metal Ferrule (Sleeve), Attached to Spindle. If the knob has a metal sleeve that attaches it to the spindle, and if knob and ferrule have parted company, take the whole works off the spindle. Pour some sand in between the ferrule and the knob to fill up the space between them. Next, drip glue into the two pieces to be rejoined. Let the glue cure. To put some pressure on the mend, stand the knob and ferrule upside down, in a small sandbox. Put a small weight (a stone will do) on the knob to bring pressure where it's needed.

DOWNSPOUT

See GUTTER.

DRAIN

Although no one likes to fix sluggish or clogged drains, coping with them *early* saves facing more unpleasant problems *later*.

All drains in your kitchen, bath, and laundry are connected to your sewer or septic tank by pipes, and each of these pipes has what the plumber calls a *trap*. Often this is the site of the trouble and the place to apply the remedy. So, get to know the various traps in your house. Usually, they're goosenecked or U in shape. (See diagrams opposite.) Each trap holds water in it that prevents sewer gas from rising up through the pipes and polluting the air you breathe at home. But, though the

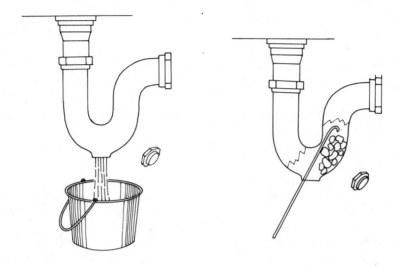

trap blocks gas seepage, it's apt to be a collecting place for debris—lint, grease, food, and other clogger-uppers. Below, we indicate ways to unclog your drains.

Kitchen Sink Drain Sluggish. If you notice that the water doesn't drain out of the sink as quickly as it should, try the simplest remedy first. Place a large saucepan or stewpot over the sink drain opening and fill it with the hottest water you have. Then let hot water run into the sink around the pot. Lift the pot and dump the water into the sink *quickly*. The pressure of all this very hot water going down the drain will often clean your pipes and carry some possible refuse out of the trap. Repeat the treatment if you get some slight improvement with the first try. Keep at it till the sink drains freely.

Kitchen Sink Drain Clogged—Water Stands in Sink and Won't Drain Out. *Note:* Don't resort to chemical drain cleaners at this stage. (If you do, and the chemical doesn't work, you're just making a messy job danger-ous. The sink will be full of a powerful chemical which can burn your skin or make holes in your clothes, and you or the plumber will be forced to do the rest of the repair with this liquid hindrance.)

Do reach for a force cup or plunger, called a "plumber's helper." (If your sink is the type that has on overflow slot or opening, stuff this slot with a wet cloth: you need all the pressure you can get for this operation and don't want to dissipate it by having the slot open.) Take out the sink strainer (or perforated plate over the drain opening). Put the force cup down over the drain opening, and pump up and down, vigorously, several times. Then, after one strong downward stroke, pull the plunger up—with all you've got. This should work out whatever obstruction is there. When it does, water will flow down the drain again. But keep trying if your first pumpings aren't successful. If you've done about fifty pumping operations, and nothing's changed, see below.

Kitchen Sink Drain Continues Clogged After Workout with Plunger. Now is the time to open the trap beneath the sink. First, get yourself a large, deep pan or bucket, and put this under the bottom part of the U-shaped trap. Next, take an old wire coat-hanger, open it up, and bend one end into a small hook. Open the trap either by:

1. Unscrewing the plug at the bottom of the trap with a monkey wrench; or

2. Removing a section of the U, if there is no plug.

Push the wire, hook-end first, into each side of the trap, fish around for the obstruction, and see if you can hook it and pull it out. Dump the lump into the bucket. Wait for the water to empty out of the sink and the pipe. Close the trap. Be sure it's snug. Throw out the water and obstruction. *Note:* Be sure you don't throw it down the toilet! You don't want to clog up another drain!

Kitchen Sink Pipes Clogged After Trap Is Worked On. If the obstruction is beyond the U of the trap and you can't reach it with your coat-hanger device (as above), you'll need a plumber's snake or auger. (You've probably seen them demonstrated on television commercial cartoons.) Buy the snake at a hardware or plumbing supply store. They come in various lengths, but the one you want is 5½ feet long.

Open the trap, as described above. Insert the head of the snake into the portion of the pipe that leads away from the sink. Now, crank the handle of the auger so that the tip is rotated and travels deeper into the pipe. Suddenly, you may feel the crank is harder to turn. This means that you've met the enemy, but he's not yours *yet!* To capture the obstruction, keep twisting the auger, and push and pull it back and forth in the pipe. *Note:* When you've caught the obstruction and you start to pull the auger out of the pipe, be sure to continue to turn the crank in the same direction you started. This way the cloth or paper or whatever will stay impaled on the tip (and not get lost in the pipe again).

Now, get rid of the clogger-upper. Reconnect the pipe (the trap sections), and run hot water down the drain. Then, *really wash* that snake in hot water and a strong household cleaner. Wash your hands and then give yourself a pat on the back. You've saved the day, cleared the drain, and learned to plumb!

Bathroom Basin Drain Sluggish. See above, "Kitchen Sink Drain Sluggish."

Bathroom Basin Drain Clogged—Water Won't Drain Out. See above, "Kitchen Sink Drain Clogged."

Bathroom Drain Continues Clogged After Workout with Plunger. See above, "Kitchen Sink Drain Continues Clogged."

Bathroom Sink Pipes Clogged After Trap Is Worked On. See above, "Kitchen Sink Pipes Clogged."

Bathtub or Laundry Drain Sluggish. See above, "Kitchen Sink Drain Sluggish."

Bathtub or Laundry Drain Continues Clogged After Workout with Plunger. See above, "Kitchen Sink Drain Continues Clogged."

Bathtub or Laundry Pipes Clogged After Trap Is Worked On. See above, "Kitchen Sink Pipes Clogged."

Toilet Drains Slowly. See above, "Kitchen Sink Drain Clogged." For this operation, you should use a plumber's helper (plunger) that has at least a 2-foot handle. (It's best to use this plunger only for the toilet. Wash it thoroughly after you use it.)

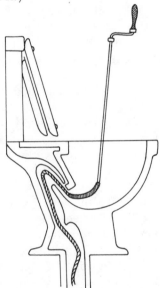

Toilet Continues Clogged After Workout with Plunger. You'll need the special toilet auger. It's 5½ feet long, but some of those sold for other types of drains are shorter, so double-check when you go to the hardware store. (Be sure you wash the snake *thoroughly* after you've used it.) Follow the procedure given in "Kitchen Sink Pipes Clogged." See diagram above.

DRAPERY

Hems Coming Out. See CURTAIN—HEMS COMING OUT.

Pinch Pleats Coming Undone. See CURTAIN—PINCH PLEATS COMING UNDONE.

Tears in Fabric. See CURTAIN—TEARS IN FABRIC.
Tears in Valance. See CURTAIN—TEARS IN FABRIC.
Lining Worn Out. See CURTAIN—LINING WORN OUT.

DRAPERY HARDWARE

Elegant and expensive though they may be, your draperies (and the room they're in) will look frowzy if they're improperly hung from their mountings.

Mounting Looks Loose. There are two reasons the mountings for your draperies work loose.

1. The Brackets Are Not Mated to the Rod. Each type of rod—extension, traverse, or just simple café—requires its own special type of bracket. Usually, you buy them together. But if you haven't done that, check the drapery hardware displays at your department store, hardware store, or sewing center. Discover if you've *mismated* your rod and bracket. Buy new brackets or rods, according to the type of draperies you have, and install them. (See below.)

2. The Fasteners Are Wrong for the Rod. Rods can be mounted almost anywhere around the window—on window casings, on the adjacent wall, and even on the ceiling above the window. But if the screw or bolt is not equal to the job, your draperies are bound to droop or fall. Check your fasteners. For instance, have you used *wood screws* to mount the brackets on wood? Or, perish the thought, have you used wood screws to hold your brackets to a plaster wall? If you have, the screws will be pulled loose and the draperies will come down in a big whoosh someday.

If your curtains or draperies are sheer (and thus lightweight) you can use *plaster screws* to mount the brackets on a plaster wall. But if you're hoping to hang heavy velvet draperies with these, you're in for a sudden disappointment. What you need in this case is a strong expansion fastener, Molly bolt, or toggle bolt. These bolts have parts that spread out behind the wall or ceiling (like a parachute opening up). Anchoring devices that expand in or behind the wall firm up the bolt and make it able to carry more weight than nails or screws can. For details, see Section II, WORKING WITH NAILS, SCREWS, AND FASTENERS, p. 236. *Note:* Ceiling mountings always call for toggle or Molly bolts. If you haven't used them for installation, take the rod down and reinstall it with these bolts.

Mounting Not Level, Draperies Slant Downhill. If your room seems out of kilter because your curtains or draperies are working on one horizontal line and your floor and ceiling are on another, it's a case of hardware maladjustment. More than likely, the mountings for the draperies are not aligned. The simple way to fix this is with your own, homemade T-square. Find yourself a sturdy piece of cardboard (your husband's shirt

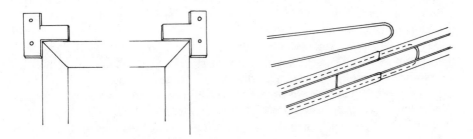

board is dandy for this) and cut it into a true T. Make holes in it where the bracket screws go into the wall on the side of the window. (See diagram above, left.) Now, set this T-square on the other side of the window. (You have to flip it over to fit it to the opposite corner of the window.) Are the screws in line with the holes in your T-square? No? Then remove them. Make the necessary marks, drive the screws into the wood or wall, and enjoy all those parallel lines! (It's best to take the draperies down when you work on the mountings.)

Extension Rod Sags. Check the brackets. If they're loose, remount the rod with longer screws. Does the rod still sag—generally around the middle? Make a splint for it. Bend a clothes hanger into a hairpin shape, and slide the "hairpin" into the back of the hollow rod. (See diagram above, right.) If this is not suitable for your rod, you can install a bracket or a supporting hook at the exact center point of the rod. Your hardware store or drapery department will supply the correct bracket or hook and the proper fasteners for it.

Traverse Rod Doesn't Work. If the curtains won't close when you pull the cord for the traverse rod, double-check the cord and pulleys. Has the cord slipped out of one of them? If so, loop it over the guide or pulley, and pull the curtains closed.

Note: If you're having difficulty hanging draperies on various unusually shaped windows, single curved rods, double bay rods, and single bay rods are available in most department stores. With these come directions for mounting and the instructions for special fasteners.

DRAWER

See CHEST OF DRAWERS.

DRESSER

See CHEST OF DRAWERS.

DRIVEWAY | asphalt

Holes and Cracks. When time and weather have turned your driveway into a maze of cracks and crevices, repair it with a bag of ready-to-use blacktop asphalt.

Buy bags of patching asphalt at the lumberyard or an industrial supply house (where it's cheaper than at hardware stores). Read the manufacturer's instructions carefully. The blacktop will fall from the bag in lumps, and you will have to rake it into fine particles as you fill in the hole or crack. While you're raking, also mound the new surface about ½ inch higher over the crack or hole than the surrounding drive. Next, level the patch with a lawn roller. (If you don't have a roller, fashion a homemade tamper to pound down the paving. Take a 12-inch by 12-inch flat piece of ¼-inch iron or steel and have a pipe welded to the middle of it for a handle.)

Note: If you do your patching in hot weather, cover the new surface with boards until it hardens completely. During the day, the sun will soften the asphalt. If the board is not in place, your bicycling youngster (or someone else's) may sink his front bike wheel into the new paving. (Hard on *his* bike and on *your* repair.)

Also, remember to wear old shoes for this job, and take them off before you go into the house (or there will be black footprints across the living room rug).

DRIVEWAY | concrete

See CEMENT AND CONCRETE.

DRYER, CLOTHES | electric

CAUTION: *Handling any electrical appliance requires care: Protect yourself by consulting the safety rules given in Section II,* ELECTRICITY AND WIRING, *p. 257, before you start to investigate the dryer's trouble. Remember, if your dryer makes unusual noises while it's running, if it gives off strange odors, or if it scorches your laundry, you should disconnect it immediately. Remember, too: never put foam-rubber-filled pillows, or any foam rubber, in the machine. This substance is combustible in the high temperatures of a dryer, and you're likely to have a dryer-fire.*

Won't Start. There are several checks to make before you call the repairman. First, consult your owner's manual and be sure the dial is set correctly. Have you pressed the right button (made the correct dial setting)? If you've passed *this* test, then make the usual checks with the electrical connections and the fuse or circuit breaker, as follows:

1. Check the plug. Is it snug in the wall outlet? Is the plug case damaged

in any way? If so, don't use the machine until the repairman fixes the plug.

2. Is the fuse for the dryer circuit blown? (Or, has the circuit breaker been tripped?) You can change the fuse (or close the circuit breaker) but we urge you to consult the safety rules in Section II cited above, p. 257, first. If the fuse blows again, after you've changed it and turned the dryer on, disconnect the dryer and call the authorized serviceman. Your circuit may be overloaded (too many appliances working on the same source of electric current). The Good Housekeeping Institute recommends that you use a separate circuit for the appliance. Have the electrician do this electrical work before you use the dryer again. Or, your dryer may have internal trouble; it may be short-circuiting. If so, call the authorized service center; an expert should handle the repair.

Machine Makes Loud or Unusual Noise While Running. First, turn the machine off. Then make these checks:

1. Have you loaded the dryer correctly? Or have you stuffed it too full? Is a belt buckle or a pebble in your son's jeans hitting the inside of the dryer? Reload and start the machine again.

2. Take a careful look at the way the machine stands on the floor. Is it level? Use a carpenter's spirit level to find out. If the machine is not level, call the repairman and have him do the job.

Note: Sometimes the belt that turns the tub will wear out. The noise you hear may be a result of this condition. If you've made the checks above, don't use the machine until the repairman gives it a going-over. A worn belt can be replaced, but let an expert do it.

Machine Dries Too Slowly. First, be sure you've set the dial correctly (consult your owner's manual for this). If the machine *still* dries too slowly, disconnect the machine and make these checks:

1. Is the lint trap clogged? Experts say that in many models the lint trap should be *cleaned after every operation*. If it *is* clogged, remove it and clean it, then start the machine again.

2. Is the exhaust vent blocked? Look at the hose that vents the dryer and, if necessary, poke a long wire down it to dislodge any accumulated lint.

Machine Scorches Your Clothes. Disconnect it and call the repairman. Usually the reason for this is a malfunction in the thermostat. When the temperature-controller won't respond, the machine continues to generate heat. (*Now,* if you have nothing *else* to do till the repairman comes, get out your owner's instruction booklet and find out if you have a guarantee that covers the replacement of the thermostat and any other repairs!)

DRYER, CLOTHES | gas

Gas-heated clothes dryers are made and work like electric dryers, except that heat for the drying process comes from gas (bottled or from the gas main). Be sure to check the owner's manual if the pilot light for the dryer goes out, and call your authorized service center for repairs on the machine. For all other malfunctions, see DRYER/CLOTHES: ELECTRIC.

DRYER, HAIR | electric

CAUTION: *Handling any electrical appliance requires care. Before you investigate the whys and wherefores of your hair dryer's failure, consult the safety procedures in Section II,* ELECTRICITY AND WIRING, *p. 257.*

Hood Torn. Replace the hood with a new one bought through the manufacturer's representative. If you've "inherited" the dryer, note the model, then find the local representative in the yellow pages of your phone directory. You'll need the model number when you buy any replacements.

Hose Damaged. Replace, as above.

Won't Work. Before you blame the appliance, make the basic electrical checks.

1. Is the plug firmly set in the wall outlet? If it's loose, take it out and examine it. The prongs may be wobbly or damaged. If they are, and if the wiring leading in and out of the plug is damaged, don't insert the plug in the outlet. Repair or replace the plug, but first consult the section cited above. If this repair is too complicated for you, have the repairman do it. An appliance repair shop or the service center will do the job.

2. If there's nothing wrong with the prongs of the dryer cord plug, spread the prongs a little with your fingers. This should give you a better connection when you insert the plug into the wall outlet.

3. If the dryer still doesn't work, check the fuses for this circuit, and test the wall outlet. The fuse may have blown or the outlet may be defective. (Again, consult Section II, as cited above, p. 257.) You can change the fuse, but don't try to repair the outlet! This is a job for an electrician.

4. If all the above checks have been made, and if you're sure there's no power failure in the area that accounts for the dryer's breakdown, take the appliance to the service repair center for overhauling.

DRY ROT

See BASEMENT.

DUCT

See AIR DUCT.

EARTHENWARE

See CHINAWARE.

EGG BEATER | electric

See FOOD MIXER.

ELECTRICAL | appliance, fixture, outlet

See Section II, ELECTRICITY AND WIRING, p. 257, or see specific items, e.g., DISHWASHER, DRYER, HEATER, etc.

ENAMEL

See Section II, PAINTING, INDOOR.

EXHAUST FAN

See FAN/EXHAUST.

EXTENSION CORD

See Section II, ELECTRICITY AND WIRING.

EXTERIOR WALL

See SIDING.

FABRIC

See specific items: BEDSPREAD, CURTAIN, etc. Also see Section II, MENDING BY SEWING, p. 276

FAN | attic

CAUTION: *When you handle any electrical appliance be sure to follow the safety procedures outlined in Section II,* ELECTRICITY AND WIRING, *p. 257.* Don't tackle the job until you know the rules.

Won't Work. Check the fuse for this part of the house. It's in your fuse box, and should be labeled. Replace the fuse if it has blown, as outlined in the section cited above. Now try the fan. *If the fuse blows a second time, turn the fan off, and disconnect it if it's plugged into a wall outlet. There is a short circuit in the fan wiring or in its motor, and this condition calls for the work of a professional.* (If the fan framework can be unscrewed from the wall, take the unit down. Perhaps your husband will help with this chore. Then take the fan to the repairman. You'll save money if you bring the unit to him. If you can't figure out how to remove the unit, call the electrician and have him do the repair at your home or in his shop.)

Motor Hums But Blades Won't Turn. Turn the switch off. Put a few drops of machine oil in the hole marked "oil." Turn the blades around by hand several times (to work the oil in). Turn the fan on again. *If it still hums and the blades still don't turn, switch the fan off, then disconnect it.* (This way you're sure no one else will come along and flip the switch.) At this stage, you should go to (or send for) the repairman. The humming you've heard in the fan indicates that something is really out of order in the motor.

Shakes, Shimmies, Vibrates. Turn the fan off. Tighten the screws or bolts that hold the fan mounting (framework) to the wall. Turn the fan on again. If the machine *still* vibrates, again turn the unit off. The blades may be loose—a job that calls for expert repair. Call the electrician or take the fan to his shop.

FAN | floor or tabletop

CAUTION: *When you handle any electrical appliance be sure to follow the safety procedures outlined in Section II,* ELECTRICITY AND WIRING, p. 257. *Don't tackle the job until you know the rules.*

Won't Work. Be sure the fuse hasn't blown, and check to see that the electricity is on. (Consult Section II, ELECTRICITY AND WIRING, p. 257, for procedures and details.) Next, examine the plug. Are its prongs loose? Are they bent? You can spread the prongs, a little, with your fingers; and the next time you insert the plug in the outlet, you may get a *good* electrical connection. (If the prongs are loose, replace the plug as outlined in the section cited, above.)

Plug Cracked, Damaged. Replace the plug (do this by following the procedures given in Section II, ELECTRICITY AND WIRING, p. 257).

Blades Don't Turn Readily, Tend to Jam. Turn the fan off. Test the blades: are they hard to turn when you rotate them by hand? If so, put a couple of drops of machine oil in the oil hole or on the shaft. Turn the blades by hand again, to work the oil into the fan parts. Wipe off any excess oil. Switch the fan on. If you still have problems with the unit after this treatment, take the fan to a repairman. (Most models are portable and easy to carry.)

FAN | exhaust

CAUTION: *When you handle any electrical appliance be sure to follow the safety procedures outlined in Section II,* ELECTRICITY AND WIRING, *p. 257. Don't tackle the job until you know the rules.*

Won't Work. See FAN/ATTIC.

Sluggish, Doesn't Ventilate. Bathroom and kitchen exhaust fans have louvers (like Venetian blinds) which open when the fan is on. You'll find the louvers either on the fan case (housing) or on the outside of the house (in the air duct). Check to see if the louvers are stuck. If they don't open up, old paint or corroding metal may be the cause. Scrape off the paint around the little hinge that swings the louvers open. If metal corrosion is jamming the louvers, rub them with steel wool, then oil them.

Kitchen Exhaust Fan Clogged with Grease. If you use your stove often for greasy frying, your fan may be covered with old grease and dirt. *Note:* Be sure fan is off first. Then take off the grille that covers the fan. Scrub the housing (or case) and the fan blades with a heavy-duty household liquid cleaner. Wipe dry. Put a drop of machine oil into the oil hole. Wash the grille, dry it, and put it back over the fan.

FAUCET

The steady drip-drip-drop of a leaky faucet is as annoying as it is wasteful. So, learn some foolproof faucet-fixing. First, though, you should find out what kind of faucet you *have*. Here we treat only the most common—the one the plumber calls the *compression* type. (The ultra-new, fancy faucets (including the single-lever varieties) are complex mechanisms and are best left in the plumber's capable hands.) If yours is the ordinary compression faucet, study the diagram to get to know its parts. You'll see that the flow of water through the faucet is controlled by a washer which is pushed against (or pulled away from) a seat. The process is somewhat like corking and uncorking a bottle of wine. But, instead of a corkscrew, what you need for this work is a wrench and screwdriver. (Consult Section II, GLOSSARY OF TOOLS, p. 229, if you're unfamiliar with these.)

Drips. No amount of turning the faucet handle will shut off a leak, if the washer or valve seat is damaged or worn out. To cope with the drip, follow these steps.

1. Shut off the water supply. (There's a gate valve under the sink or basin. It's really just another sort of faucet, and when it's turned off, no

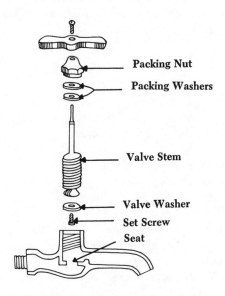

Packing Nut

Packing Washers

Valve Stem

Valve Washer

Set Screw

Seat

water will flow into the faucet you're working on. If you can't find this valve, you will probably be able to find the main water supply valve for your house. Turn *this* valve off.)

2. Take up the monkey wrench, and wrap its jaws with adhesive tape, so as not to scar the faucet's fine satiny finish.

3. Consult the diagram, then unloosen the packing nut so that it's free from the faucet. (If the packing nut is round, you'll need a pipe wrench for the work. It has curved jaws to grab a rounded surface. See Section II, as cited above, p. 229.)

4. To unscrew the faucet stem, turn it counterclockwise. Remove the stem from the fixture, and you will find the washer at the base of the stem.

5. Remove the set screw that holds the washer. (See diagram.) Now, pry out the old washer—you may need a knife to get it out of its socket.

6. Scrape the socket clean. Replace the old washer with a new one of the same size. (Ask your hardware dealer which kind of washer is best for cold or hot water: buy the one designed for the faucet you're fixing.)

7. If the old washer is in good shape, the problem may be a chip or cut in the brass seat. To find out, poke your finger down in the fixture (or look into it with a flashlight). Is the seat smooth? If it's chipped or scarred, you can *grind* it smooth again. You use a tool that screws into the faucet in place of the valve stem. The tool is available at hardware and plumbing-supply stores, and it's not expensive. (If the seat is *cracked* or if the chips on it are too deep, you'll have to have the faucet replaced; this is a job for your plumber, not for you.)

8. With the washer replaced and/or the seat smoothed, rescrew the stem, *clockwise,* back into the fixture. Tighten the packing nut, run the water, wash out the sink *and* your hands!

Leaks from Stem. Try tightening the packing nut. If it is as tight as it can be, the faucet needs new packing to keep the water from traveling up the stem. This graphite-impregnated fibrous stuff comes in different forms. The easiest kind to use is shaped like a sleeve which fits over the stem. (Graphite-impregnated strands also can be purchased at hardware and plumbing-supply stores.) To replace the packing, remove the stem as above. Then slip on a new sleeve-type packing the same size as the old one, or wind packing strands around the stem. Put the stem back in the fixture and press the packing washers down on the packing material. Tighten the packing nut until the stem leak stops. (*Note:* If you tighten it too much beyond this point the faucet will be hard to turn on and off.)

FIGURINE

See CHINAWARE, MARBLE, etc.

FIREPLACE | built-in

CAUTION: *If your chimney gives off showers of sparks when you have a fire in the fireplace, if you see smoke leaking between the bricks and mortar (or metal chimney-piece connections) douse the fire immediately! A couple of boxes of table salt or rock salt will help, then you can wet down the smoldering logs or remove them with fire tongs. But if you have a roaring chimney fire, get your family out of the house, then call for help. You need the fire department if you have a real chimney fire. Don't use the chimney or fireplace until these have been cleaned and/or repaired. Hire a professional. (See below, and see also,* CHIMNEY *for text and diagram.)*

There's nothing cheerier than a brightly burning fire on the hearth, and nothing drearier (*and* tearier) than a fireplace that doesn't work, or one that smokes up your house. Fireplace failures range from minor to major, and though many of them are corrected without too much fuss, the major failures are serious and should be attended to quickly, by a professional. Below we offer help to keep your hearth a happy cozy one, and advice to keep you alert to some hearthside hazards.

Bricks—Smoke-Stained, Dirty. See Section II, BRICK AND MORTAR: CLEANING, REPAIRING, AND REPOINTING, p. 273.

Small Cracks in Bricks or Mortar. If these are thin cracks on the surface (occurring at random), you can continue to use the fireplace. The repair is simple; for it, consult the section cited above. Large cracks are a danger (see CHIMNEY—CRACKS IN LARGE AREA OR IN A LINE OF BRICKS . . .).

Damper in Fireplace Sticks, Won't Open or Close Easily. The metal may be corroded or caked with soot. Shine a flashlight on the damper to check its condition. If the metal is rusty and soot-encrusted, use a long-handled wire brush to scrape the rust off. (You may want to cover your nose and mouth with a Western-style bandanna to protect your lungs from soot and rust while you do this.) Now, wiggle the damper catch, then open and close the damper until it works with ease. If you can't budge the damper, call your mason or building contractor, and have the job done by an expert. *Note:* Don't light a fire with the damper stuck closed!

Fireplace Smokes. This *may* happen with a well-made fireplace, but it's *bound* to happen with a poorly made one. The various causes for both types follow:

1. The Draft Is Poor. Well- or ill-made, if your fireplace is in a super-sealed room, it will have difficulty drawing. A draft (*wind,* that is) must waft itself *through the room and up the chimney* to send the smoke up there, too. Solve the problem by opening a window or door.

2. Obstructions Above the Chimney. Trees or other obstructions can change the air current, and prevent the fire in the fireplace from drawing properly. Solve the problem by inspecting the area above and around the chimney. When the fire is out, remove the obstructions, or have the tree limbs cut down. (If you're not sure, consult a mason or your building contractor about this.) See CHIMNEY—MASONRY HOOD OVER CAP BROKEN.

3. The Proportions of Your Fireplace Opening Are Wrong for the Size of the Chimney. Obviously, this is a structural problem, and one you may have inherited with the house. Although we don't suggest that you do the actual repair, we *do* think you ought to know how to test for the condition. And you need to know some of the ways a professional corrects the disproportions; because some are apt to be costly and others are relatively inexpensive. To get down to cases, the U.S. Department of Agriculture says *the size of the opening of a lined flue ". . . 22 feet high should be at least one-twelfth of the area of the fireplace opening. The area of the opening of an unlined flue or a flue less than 22 feet high should be one-tenth of the area of the fireplace opening."* This may sound like government gobbledygook to you, but the point is that there's only one set of magic numbers in the relations between fireplace opening and chimney size that will keep a fireplace from smoking. If you're a whiz at numbers, measure yours and compare it with the table, below.

If you're not great at math, there's a easier way to find out what size your fireplace opening should be to keep it from smoking. Light a fire, then hold a piece of sheet metal or asbestos board across the top of the opening. Move this hood slowly down across the opening. At some point you'll find that the fire stops smoking and draws beautifully! Mark this point

RECOMMENDED DIMENSIONS FOR FIREPLACE
AND SIZE OF FLUE LINING REQUIRED

| Size of Fireplace Opening | | | Size of Flue Lining Required | |
Width	Height	Depth	Standard Rectangular (Outside Dimensions)	Standard Round (Inside Diameter)
Inches	Inches	Inches	Inches	Inches
24	24	16–18	8½ x 8½	10
28	24	16–18	8½ x 8½	10
30	28–30	16–18	8½ x 13	10
36	28–30	16–18	8½ x 13	12
42	28–32	16–18	13 x 13	12
48	32	18–20	13 x 13	15
54	36	18–20	13 x 18	15
60	36	18–20	13 x 18	15
54	40	20–22	13 x 18	15
60	40	20–22	18 x 18	18
66	40	20–22	18 x 18	18
72	40	22–28	18 x 18	18

From *Consumer's All,* USDA, United States Government Printing Office, Washington, D.C., 1965.

on your fireplace frame. Now, you can measure the area used by your makeshift hood, add two inches for overlap, and order an iron hood made to that size. The ironmonger or metal shop will make one that can be bolted to the top of the fireplace opening. Have someone from the shop or a mason bolt this in place.

Note: The area of the opening can also be reduced by raising the *bottom* of the fireplace with one or two layers of brick. Measure for this as above, but lay the fire bricks below, not above! You can also have a chimney expert (a mason) reduce the size of the opening by applying firebrick to the *sides* of the fireplace. Whatever course you choose, the table given above is your guide to the ultimate area of the opening. Also, for other reasons, your chimney repairman may decide that the best solution is to raise the *height of the chimney,* by adding more bricks and a cap to it.

Chimney Sooty. Clean it; if you don't you run the risk of a chimney fire, which can set your house on fire. See CHIMNEY, for detailed instructions on how to clean the chimney and fireplace.

Note: There are chemical cleaners on the market that you can add to your fire to clean the chimney. But first see note under CHIMNEY.

Hearth Sagging. If the bricks on the hearth or any of the firebricks *inside* the fireplace start to sag, send for the mason or building contractor at once! Don't use the fireplace until the repair is made. There's danger that the bricks may give way and spread fire to the basement or parts of the house adjacent to the fireplace.

Flue Cracked. Another hazardous condition. Though you can't see the flue or the crack, you can discover the condition by its results; when you do, have it repaired immediately. See CHIMNEY—CHIMNEY FLUE CRACKED.

Metal Firebox (in Prefabricated Unit) Cracked. You *can* see this damage. Don't use the fireplace until you've had the mason or metal repairer seal the cracks.

FIREPLACE | freestanding

See STOVE/WOOD OR COAL BURNING.

FLASHLIGHT

One of the handier small appliances you have is your flashlight. If you learn the do's and don'ts of flashlight care and repair, you'll know how to handle any small appliance or device that runs on batteries. Follow these rules, below:

Don't just insert new batteries in the flashlight and expect light. You must put batteries in with the positive (+) end forward so that an electric current will come out of them and reach the little light bulb. *Study diagram for the correct positioning of each battery.*

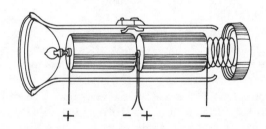

Don't leave a flashlight out in the cold all winter and expect it to light up. Cold is hard on batteries. (Warmth, indoors, however, will often bring a battery back to life.)

Don't expect a flashlight to keep burning the way your regular lamp, plugged into house current, does. Batteries are short-lived power plants. Save your flashlight for emergency use.

Do use the ordinary battery unless you have a special need for the longer-lasting, rechargeable (but more expensive) battery.

Flickering Light. The problem is usually a poor connection. Open the case. Then, using the diagram as your guide to the parts, clean and stretch the spring in the cap. Use sandpaper or steel wool. Take out the batteries and rub the little metal contact points on these with steel wool. Wipe them clean. Do the same with the bottom of the bulb. It pushes through the reflector and touches one of the batteries. Now reassemble the flashlight and switch it on.

Faint Light. The batteries or bulb may be at fault, so check them first. Buy new ones at the hardware store if they're old. If the light is *still* faint, clean all the parts as indicated above. Reassemble.

Batteries Leaking Gooey Substance. Get rid of the batteries, clean the innards as described above, and insert new batteries in the case.

Switch Won't Work. Take the flashlight to a repairman. The hardware store or local appliance shop can fix it for you.

FLOOR | brick and stone

See Section II, BRICK AND MORTAR: CLEANING, REPAIRING, AND REPOINTING, p. 273.

FLOOR | cement

See BASEMENT—BASEMENT FLOORS AND WALLS, SMALL CRACKS, etc., and CEMENT AND CONCRETE.

FLOOR | tile

Once upon a time, if you had a tile floor you had only one thing: tiles made of clay, strengthened by the fire of a kiln. Now if you have "tile" floors, you may have one of several different substances. Maybe you have the original ceramic tile. Or maybe you have one of the newfangled types: vinyl tile or asphalt, or even a combination: vinyl-asbestos. Whatever you have, your tile will sooner or later wear down in the places where there's most traffic—in front of the sink, in doorways and passageways, and in front of the refrigerator. You need not rip up the whole floor if you want to fix these worn spots. But you *do* have to know what you have, and you have to buy tile to match. Color, size, and thickness are as important in this selection as finding tile of the same material. You should also know that each type of tile has its own special adhesive and, depending upon whether it is rigid or pliable, its own method of setting and removal. For details on ceramic tile, see CERAMIC TILE.

Cracked or Worn. Get to know the tile and the source: department stores and flooring supply shops carry a wide variety. Then go to work, as follows:

1. Asphalt or Vinyl-Asbestos Tiles, which are rigid, are taken up by, first, breaking or cracking them. Whack the tile in the center with a hammer. Then, with chisel and hammer, work from the center to the edges of each tile. (Do this so as not to damage the neighboring tile's edge.) Remove as many as necessary, then scrape away the old adhesive (mastic) still on the floor. Get the floor surface clean and smooth.

Warm the new asphalt or vinyl-asbestos tiles: you can set them out in the sun, or put them in a low-heat oven for a few minutes, or you can shine an infrared heat lamp on them. Cover the floor area with the proper adhesive, press the tiles down, one by one, then apply more heat to the tiles, so that they melt into place as they set.

2. Vinyl Tiles, which are pliable, can be cut down the center with a knife or chisel, then peeled up to the edges. Scrape up adhesive residue from the floor. Spread a thin coat of adhesive over the area, then set the vinyl tiles in place. Wipe up any excess adhesive around the seams. Then, roll the tiles flat with your rolling pin. Weight them down with stones or heavy furniture, but put these on top of a board so that the new tiles aren't dented.

Edges or Corners Curled Up. With both the rigid and pliable types of tile, you can usually squeeze a little dab of the proper adhesive under the corner, then reset the tile. Here are details:

1. Asphalt or Vinyl-Asbestos Tile: Rigid. If you can't get the adhesive under the curled corner, don't make the mistake of trying to force the corner up—you may crack it *off*. Instead, warm the tile with an iron or an infrared heat lamp. (If you use an iron, put aluminum foil down first to protect the iron's clean surface.) If the tile won't budge, replace the entire tile (see above).

2. Vinyl Tile: Pliable. Peel up the corner to get the adhesive under the tile. Roll flat with rolling pin and weight down, as described above.

FLOOR | wood

Refinishing Floor Surface. See Section II, REFINISHING WOOD, p. 304.

Stains. If you wax and polish your floor frequently, or if your floor is protected with a synthetic sealer or varnish, stains are easy enough for you to take up. Just wipe them with a little detergent and warm water, wipe off, and dry.

Stains on exposed wood (where the finish has worn off) tend to work into the grain of the wood, so that getting them out takes stronger solution than detergent and water, and more elbow grease. These are the steps:

1. Begin with detergent and water, as above.

2. If this fails, try denatured alcohol or benzene (buy it at your hardware store and be sure to follow the directions on the container—it's flammable).

3. If the stain's still there, try bleaching (with a household laundry bleach). Rub it on with a clean rag (you'll need gloves if you use the bleach full strength). Rinse the area, wipe dry, then refinish the spot as indicated in the section cited above, p. 304.

4. If you'd rather, you can rub the spot with steel wool. And if you've rubbed extra-hard and made a small "valley" in the floorboard, fix this, first, by applying an oil stain that matches the rest of your floor. Then, over this, fill in the valley by coating it with several layers of varnish. (Follow the directions on the containers. Be sure to allow the right amount of drying time between finish coats.)

Squeaky Floor. Your floor will squeak and creak when you walk on it if two or more floorboards are loose. You can stop small creaks by just forcing some powdered graphite into the crack between the boards. Buy graphite in a handy squeeze tube from the hardware store. (Use a putty knife to push the powder into the cracks between the floorboards.) You can also squirt some liquid soap into the crack: when it dries it will "de-squeak" the floor. (Wipe up any excess soap while it's still liquid.) If the boards are very loose, nail them down with 1½-inch finishing nails. Countersink these with a special tool called a *nail set*. Then, fill these little holes (over the nailheads) with plastic wood or with wood putty.

CAUTION: *Plastic wood is extremely flammable—don't work near a pilot light or even a lighted cigarette!* Sandpaper the filler when dry, and color the putty with a crayon that matches the floor. Finish the repair with a coat of shellac.

Boards Split or Cracked. This usually occurs because the wood for the floorboards was either damp or "green" when it was put down. As the wood dries out it tends to shrink—especially with the dry, warm atmosphere created by artificial heat. Fill the splits with plastic wood or wood putty, sandpaper the filler when it's dry. Color the repaired area with a crayon that matches the rest of the floor. Coat the repair with shellac.

Warped Floor. If some of your floorboards are warped it means that they're getting moisture (from *somewhere*) on their undersides. (The basement may be damp at times, and some of this moisture may seep through to the other side of your floor. If so, you should dry out your basement. (See BASEMENT.) You can take the warp out of the floorboards by simply giving the *topside* some moisture. Spread a wet towel over the board. When the board flattens out enough, nail it down. Drive 1½-inch finishing nails along the *edge* of the board, but not in a straight line. Countersink the nails with a nail set, then fill these little holes with plastic wood or wood putty.

CAUTION: *Plastic wood is extremely flammable—don't work near a pilot light or even a lighted cigarette!* Touch up the repair to match the rest of the floor (see "Squeaky Floor," above). If *all* the boards in your floor curl up at the edges, you can rent a sanding machine, and sand down the bumpy areas. (Hire a professional floor finisher if you're not up to the job: consult the yellow pages of your phone directory.) If *you* do the work, finish the floor as outlined in Section II, REFINISHING WOOD, p. 304.

Sagging Floor. If the furniture in your room seems to slant at crazy angles, your flooring is not even. Sagging floors should alert you to problems *beneath* the floor. For instance, a joist (or beam) which supports your floor may be rotting away (see BASEMENT—CEILINGS, HOW TO CHECK FOR DRY ROT). Or one of the joists may be split. Sometimes the posts that hold up the joists can settle (which, in plain, everyday terms means they're sinking down into the earth). Whatever the case, you should find the cause quickly, and have repairs made by a contractor. While you're waiting for the repairman to come, you can rent a jack post from a building supply store, and jack up the sagging floor until the repair is made. Use the jack just the way you use a car jack. *But take care, when you do use it: Better to jack the floor up too little than too much. If you try pushing up the sag too fast and too high, you can crack plaster and damage plumbing connections.*

FLOOR SCRUBBER-POLISHER | electric

Note: Some of these come with special attachments that convert your machine into a rug or carpet shampooer. See also RUG SHAMPOOER.

CAUTION: *Handling any electrical appliance requires care. Before you investigate the whys and wherefores of your floor polisher's failure, consult the safety procedures in Section II,* ELECTRICITY AND WIRING, p. 257.

Won't Work. Before you blame the machine, make the basic electrical checks.

1. Is the plug firmly set in the wall outlet? If it's loose, take it out and examine it. The prongs may be wobbly or damaged. If they are, and if the wiring leading in and out of the plug is damaged, don't reinsert the plug in the outlet. Repair or replace the plug, but first consult the section cited above. If this wiring repair is too complicated for you, have someone from an appliance shop or service center do the job.

2. If there's nothing wrong with the prongs of the polisher cord plug, spread the prongs a little with your fingers. This should give you a better connection when you insert the plug in the wall outlet.

3. If the polisher still doesn't work, check the fuses for this circuit, and test the wall outlet. The fuse may have blown or the outlet may be defective. (Again, consult the section cited above.) You can change the fuse, but don't try to repair the outlet—this is a job for an electrician.

4. If all the above checks have been made, and if you're sure there's no power failure in the area that accounts for the polisher's breakdown, take the appliance to the service repair center for an overhauling. Loose

connections inside the machine may be the problem, or your polisher may have motor trouble. Both conditions call for repair work by an expert.

Handle Comes Loose. Take a careful look at the handle. You'll discover that there are screws that *normally* keep it attached to the base. Are they loose? Tighten them with a screwdriver. If the handle is made in two metal sections, tighten the screws that hold these parts together. If you can't tighten the screws, don't be downcast. Drill a hole of the same diameter on the opposite side of the handle. Insert a bolt through both holes, and tighten the bolt. You can buy a hand-operated drill at the hardware store, and there you can also buy the proper size bolts and nuts for the repair.

Polishing Pads and Brushes Are Gummy or Grimy. Soak them in hot water and strong detergent or liquid household cleaner. Rinse and dry.

Wax Doesn't Feed from Canister to Pads or Floor. Take a look at the small plastic hose that carries the liquid wax from the dispenser down to the pads or floor. Is it clogged with old wax? If so, remove it, run hot water through it until the wax dissolves. If the valve (or opening) at the bottom of the canister is stuck tight with wax, clean it with denatured alcohol or benzene. Be sure to follow directions on the containers. Then, flush the valve with hot water. And next time you use the polisher, empty the wax dispenser, then clean it with hot water and a detergent. Rinse it with clear hot water.

Pads or Brushes Worn Out. Replace them with new ones from a local dealer or hardware store.

FOOD MIXER

CAUTION: *Handling any electrical appliance requires care. Play safe: before you investigate the whys and wherefores of your food mixer's failure, consult the procedures in Section II,* ELECTRICITY AND WIRING, p. 257.

Bowl Won't Turn. The batter is in the bowl, the motor purrs, but the bowl on the turntable of your mixer won't budge. Before you reach for your trusty old mixing spoon, check these items:

1. Look at the Beaters. They're different: one has a button on its tip and the other doesn't. The beater with the button should be on the outside of the track. If it isn't there, this may keep the bowl from rotating. Reverse the positions of your two beaters, then flip the switch to *on*. Your troubles may be over. If not, make the next check.

2. Put the Batter in the Refrigerator. Then get at your turntable. It may be stuck because it's gummy with food from previous mixings. Remove the turntable by unscrewing the nut under the stand. Clean the platform. In the platform's center, as shown, you'll find a built-in ball bearing. Oil this lightly with 3-in-1 oil. Reassemble the turntable, flip

the switch. The bowl should spin, and your batter beating should begin. If not, take the unit to the repairman.

Beater Bent. If the beaters are badly bent, you can buy new ones. Look up the dealer's representative in the yellow pages of your phone directory.

Doesn't Work. Before you blame the appliance, make the basic electrical checks:

1. Is the plug firmly set in the wall outlet? If it's loose, take it out and examine it. The prongs may be wobbly or damaged. If they are, and if the wiring leading in and out of the plug is damaged, don't insert the plug in the outlet. Repair or replace the plug, but first consult the section cited above. If this repair is too complicated for you, have an appliance repair shop or service center do the job.

2. If there is nothing wrong with the prongs of the mixer's cord plug, spread the prongs a little with your fingers. This should give you a better electrical connection when you insert the plug into the wall outlet.

3. If the mixer *still* doesn't work, check the fuses for this circuit, and test the wall outlet. The fuse may have blown or the outlet may be defective. (Again, consult the section cited above.) You can change the fuse, but don't try to *repair* the outlet—this is a job for an electrician.

4. If all the above checks have been made, and if you're sure there's no power failure in the area that accounts for the mixer's breakdown, take the appliance to the service repair center for an overhauling. The problem, no doubt, lies either in the motor—it may have short-circuited—or in loose wiring *inside* that you can't get at. In any case, this is a job for an expert.

FRY PAN | electric

CAUTION: *Handling any electrical appliance requires care. Play safe: Before you try to figure out the whys and wherefores of your fry pan's failure, consult the procedures in Section II, ELECTRICITY AND WIRING, p. 257.*

Handle Loose. *Don't use the fry pan until the handle is fixed.* A panful of hot bacon fat or bubbling oil can give you a terrible burn, and you run this risk if you use the pan when the handle is not securely attached to the pan. Take the fry pan to the repairman. Look up listings for appliance service centers in the yellow pages of your phone directory: most manufacturers have such local service shops.

Handle Cracked or Broken. See above.

Doesn't Heat Up. Save yourself possible expense and embarrassment by making some elementary electrical checks before you take the fry pan to the repairman. Follow this procedure:

1. Check the plug in the electrical (wall) outlet. Is it firmly set? If it's loose and wobbly, take the plug out and look at it. Are the prongs in the plug damaged? If they are, and if the wiring leading in and out of the

plug is frayed or coming loose, don't reinsert the plug in the outlet. Repair or replace the plug, but first consult Section II, as cited above. (If this repair is too complicated for you, have the repairman do it. Find him at the service center or appliance repair shop.)

2. If there's nothing wrong with the prongs in the cord plug, spread the prongs a little with your fingers. This should give you a better electrical connection when you insert the plug into the wall outlet.

3. Take the handle of the fry pan off. Clean the set of prongs you find here (they're called *terminal pins* by the repairman). Use steel wool to rub them, then wipe them clean and attach the handle. Doing this may be all that's needed to give you a good electrical connection.

4. If the fry pan *still* doesn't work, check the fuses in the fuse box for this circuit. (Usually, the fuse box is in the basement, and each circuit is labeled.) The fuse may have blown. You can replace it if it has, but be sure to consult Section II, as cited above, before you do.

5. If the fry pan *still* doesn't work, test the wall outlet you're using. (Test the outlet by plugging a working lamp into it. If the lamp doesn't go on, don't try to repair the outlet: This is a job for the electrician.) The outlet may be defective. If it is, plug your fry pan into another outlet that *is* in working order.

6. If you've made all these checks, and if you're sure there's no power failure in the area, take your balky fry pan to the repairman. The trouble is probably inside the appliance, and this is work only the expert should handle. Find the local dealer or service center in the yellow pages of your phone directory.

FURNACE | steam, hot water, warm air systems

The care and feeding of the furnace is usually—and properly—left to the professional. Often he's a repairman whose services are supplied by the fuel dealer, but you may also contact a furnace repairman through your heating contractor, or through a listing for furnace and heating repairs in the yellow pages of your phone directory. Wherever you find him, this invaluable helper cleans and inspects the furnace and flue in the warmer months of the year, so that you'll be all set with a cozy, heated home when colder weather comes. Some fuel oil dealers recommend that chemicals be added to your fuel to reduce the accumulation of soot in the furnace and flue. We suggest, however, that you let your supplier advise you on this and on other methods of soot control. You should know, too, that chimney care is also part of furnace maintenance: soot or obstructions in your chimney will hinder the operation of your furnace, and if they are not quickly removed, endanger your home. For more information on related subjects, see AIR DUCT and CHIMNEY.

CAUTION: *Remember that unusual noises and smoke warn you of faulty furnace operation. When either occurs, switch off your furnace, then put in a call to the repairman.*

Heat Stops. Furnace Is Off. Call the repairman, and be sure he's coming as soon as possible. Then, read on! Here we outline routines to follow *until the repairman comes.* (You should follow these routines if you've tried and failed to reach the repairman—if, say, the furnace goes off in the middle of the night, and you're up and not too sleepy to investigate the heating system.)

All Systems.

1. Check to be sure you have electrical power (and that the furnace's failure is not due to a power blackout). Switch on some lights. If none of your lights or appliances work, you can assume there's a power failure, and that as soon as you have power your furnace will be able to function again.

2. Next, take a look at the fuse that controls the furnace circuit. (You may need a flashlight for this.) If the fuse has blown, put a new fuse of the same wattage in its place (but be sure you consult Section II, ELECTRICITY AND WIRING, p. 257, before you do this, even if the hour is late and you're shivering. Better to be cold than shocked by a jolt of voltage). If the fuse seems to be intact, try tightening it a little by turning it in its socket. Street and house vibrations can jiggle fuses loose from their connections.

3. If you *still* don't have heat, check the switches that control the electricity for the furnace. Usually, there's one by the furnace, and often another (*emergency* switch) installed at the head of your basement stairs. Either of these may have been turned off by mistake. Your repair may be as simple as flipping one of these switches to *on.*

4. If you have one, take a look at the thermostat. Maybe it's been turned way down—again, by mistake. Test the thermostat by moving the setting at least 5 degrees *above* the reading on the thermometer next to it. Listen till you hear the sound of the furnace starting up. (*Note:* If yours is the automatic day-night thermostat, move *both levers* on the thermostat up above room temperature. It's possible, too, that the day-night cycle may have been reversed, and this way, at least, you'll find out if the furnace goes on.) While you're here, remove the cover of the thermostat. Dust on the contact points (the working parts that automatically turn your heat on) may be keeping the device from doing its job. Blow on these to remove the dust. Replace the cover.

5. If you still don't have heat or hope of getting the repairman soon, there are additional checks to make for each type of furnace, as follows:

Oil Burner. Check your oil supply. It's just possible that the oil gauge on the tank is stuck and that it indicates you have oil when actually the tank is empty. Test for this by tapping the gauge. The needle should move. If it doesn't, and if the tank has a cap, unscrew this and measure the level of the oil inside by dipping a long stick or straight wire down into the tank. Tell your oil burner man if your tank is *less than one-fourth full.*

Gas Furnace. Check to see if the pilot light is burning. If it's out and if you're comfortable doing it, you may want to light the pilot. Read the directions for this on the metal plate attached to your furnace. CAUTION: *Be sure to follow all the procedures exactly.* Never try to light the main burner by hand; the burner can flare up, causing serious burns. Let the pilot light do the work. That's why it's there.

Steam Heat. Check the boiler gauge. If it tells you that the level of the water is low, you've found the reason for your furnace's shutdown. *Note:* If the boiler is hot, let it cool for awhile, first. Filling it with cold water at this point may crack the metal. When you do fill the boiler, the furnace should turn on automatically as the water level in the boiler rises. And when your serviceman *does* come, have him find out why the boiler went dry and do the necessary repairs forthwith.

Furnace Doesn't Give Enough Heat. Your furnace may be roaring away (or, at least purring, gently), yet some or most of the rooms in your house are chilly. To find out why, check, first the radiators or warm-air ducts. Is the heat actually coming from them? If not, there are some adjustments that you may be able to make before the repairman comes. Find your particular type of heating system and check the items, as follows:

Steam Radiator Systems. Radiator Filled with Water. This will block the flow of steam that heats the radiator. There are two causes for this condition:

1. The *shutoff valve* (that is, the thing you turn the radiator off with) may not be open all the way. Open it completely if it isn't. If the radiator slants (because the floor does) the valve can be affected and may act as if it were partly closed. Wedge some wood blocks under the radiator legs to level the radiator. Now perhaps you'll hear the happy sound of steam on its way up.

2. The *air valve* may not be working. Remove the valve and clean it (wash it by hand), then reinstall it. If you still have trouble with the air valve, buy a new one from the plumbing or heating supply store. You may want to get yourself one with an adjustable air-opening. This lets you regulate the pressure of steam in the radiator to suit various temperature needs.

Hot Water Radiator Systems. One Radiator Cooler than Others. The radiator may have what's called an air block. The air, in this case, collects from time to time and must be vented out of the radiator to let the hot water *in.* Open the air valve and let the air escape. Do this until water starts oozing out, then close the vent. (Some systems have special venting keys. Get one of these from the heating contractor who installed your system, or from a plumbing or heating supply store. Unlock the vent as described, let air out, then lock it closed.)

Forced Warm Air Systems. Air Filters Clogged. If these are not cleaned and/or replaced regularly (three times a year in normal operation, and every month during peak use of the heating plant in winter) the air can't flow into the room. Proper cleaning or replacement is essential. Have the repairman clean the filters, and try to learn *how* from him. You can then do it yourself later in the season, if necessary.

FURNITURE

See specific items: BED, CHAIR, etc.

FUSE

See Section II, ELECTRICITY AND WIRING, p. 257.

GARBAGE CAN

Plastic Can Cracked. If you've been washing the can out with strong bleach and very hot water, the can will get cracks and holes. Small ones can be patched with similar plastic which is cut just an inch larger than the damaged area. Roughen the surfaces a little, and glue together with plastic cement. For details, see Section II, GLUING AND CLAMPING, p. 248.

Metal Can Has Hole in It. Rub the area to be mended with a steel wool pad. Cut a patch (just an inch larger than the hole) from a piece of galvanized iron with a pair of tin snips. Glue this over the damaged area with plastic steel. Clamp the mend until the glue cures. Buy the plastic steel, tin snips, and iron patch at the hardware store.

Metal Can Rusting. Rub the rusted areas with steel wool until the marks disappear, wipe the surface clean, then paint the entire can (or just the rusted spots, if you're pressed for time), with two coats of metal paint (from the hardware or paint store). Be sure to tell the dealer that you want an *outdoor* paint. Follow directions on the paint can. If the paint has an oil base, remember not to work with it outdoors in damp weather.

GARDEN HOSE

See HOSE, GARDEN.

GAS RANGE

See RANGE/GAS.

GLASS

Cracked or Broken. It's usually possible to mend broken glass with one of the many types of cements and glues on the market. (For details, see CHINAWARE, and Section II, GLUING AND CLAMPING, p. 248.) Valuable glass objects should be repaired by a professional. To find the right person for the job, ask an antiques dealer or write to a nearby art museum.

GUTTER

See also BASEMENT, and ROOF.

Leaks. Your metal gutters and downspouts may rust and corrode with the onslaught of weather, or winter's ice may open up their seams. And that's not all. Drips from these leaks in your downspouts and gutters can spot the windows, leave rust stains on the siding of the house, or bring unwanted dampness to the foundation and basement. Fortunately, you can make simple repairs and rid yourself of all these drippy problems.

1. Small Holes, Leaks in Seams. These areas and the places where gutter sections and downspout elbows are joined can be mended with plastic steel. It is sold in hardware stores in a squeeze tube. Clean the damaged areas by rubbing them with steel wool, wipe, then squeeze on the plastic steel. It hardens quickly. Paint over this (with an outdoor paint) if you want your gutters to look trim and unpatchy.

2. Series of Holes, Long Cracks. Patch these. You work from the *inside* of the gutter and the *outside* of the downspout. Cut patches from the heavy-duty aluminum foil you use in the kitchen, or, if you have it, use heavy insulating (tar) paper or strips of fiber glass. First, spread a layer of roof cement over the area. Then, press the patch into the gutter or wrap it around the downspout. Next, spread another layer of roof cement over the patch. The cement as well as kits containing fiber glass for patching, adhesive, and detailed directions on how to use them, can be bought from the hardware store.

Note: To forestall the problem of leaks in both metal and wooden gutters, spread a layer of roof cement in the trough of the gutter. Save yourself money and work by adding to your gutters' life.

Won't Drain. If the gutters overflow, there's probably something in them that shouldn't be there: too many leaves will clog them and, all too often, tennis or other small balls will land in the gutter and jam it up. Scrape out the leaves, then hose the downspout with a stream of water. (If the downspout runs into a sewer or dry well, disconnect the bottom section before trying to flush the downspout clean.) If the downspout is *still* clogged, try dislodging the leaves and other obstructions with a long stick.

(The handle of a broom is handy for the job.) *Note:* To keep leaves or anything else from lodging in them, cover the gutters with a heavy wire mesh made especially for this purpose. Buy it at the hardware or building supply store. Directions for installation are included.

Gutter Sags—Fasteners Broken. If the gutter sags in places, it can't do the job it was meant to do. It may, in fact, overflow, and send rainwater cascading down the side of the house. Here are various ways to take the sag out of gutters:

1. Gutter Straps Broken. If they've come away, renail the straps to the roof. And if the roof strap pulls away from the strap around the gutter, drill a small hole through both of them (where they're supposed to join). Slip a small machine bolt through this hole (see Section II, BOLTING AND RIVETING, p. 245) and fasten it.

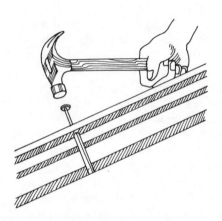

2. Gutter Held by Spikes and Ferrule. If the gutter sags because the spike is not long enough, buy a longer spike and drive it through the ferrule (or tube) and deeper into the rafter-end. Or, install a new spike and ferrule at the point where the gutter sags. Be sure to install it at the rafter-end (see diagram).

Note: If spending your time patching and repatching the gutters and downspouts is not your idea of fun, think in terms of replacing them. Once a gutter starts to split, even if you patch it up several times, it'll probably spring a leak soon again. The investment in new gutters may be worth it.

HAIR DRYER | electric

See DRYER, HAIR/ELECTRIC.

HAMPER | laundry

Metal-Bin-Type, Rusting. Rust marks inside the laundry hamper will stain your clothes and linens, so get rid of them as soon as they appear. Rub the rusted areas with steel wool until the marks disappear. Wipe the surface clean, then paint the inside of the bin with two coats of high-quality enamel paint or refrigerator enamel. Follow the directions on the paint can. If the paint has an oil base, remember not to work with it outdoors in damp weather.

Woven Reed, Rattan. See BASKET—WOVEN OF REED, RATTAN, WOOD.

HANDBAG

Catch Doesn't Work. If you're pink with embarrassment and fury because your purse has just popped open and dumped everything in it all over the sidewalk, don't get even with the handbag by tossing it out with the trash. There are ways of fixing the catch so that you'll be proof against a repeat of the purse-popping. Handbag catches are mostly of two types, and repairs to both of them are easy.

1. Twist-Catch Doesn't Work. Fix the twist catch by wrapping a cloth around the prongs of the catch and squeezing them together. The prongs should be near enough for the catch to close, and not give you difficulty when you want to open it. If the catch is hard to open, wrap the cloth around the prongs again and pull them a little away from each other.

2. Spring Catch Doesn't Shut. The catch may not be meeting the prong that will keep it closed. Bend one side of the frame *in* a little and see if the bag does not shut tightly from then on.

Strap Broken. Replace a broken leather strap with a piece of chain from a chain belt, or part of a canvas or leather belt. At arts and crafts stores you can buy canvas or leather strips, or actual leather handbag handles. Directions for attaching them come with the handles. For the *leather* and *canvas strips:* Staple, sew, or rivet the handles on. (See BASKET—HANDLES COMING OFF, and Section II, BOLTING AND RIVETING, p. 245.)

Lining Coming Out. Bend the inside of the frame with a screwdriver, and slide the lining under the frame. With pliers (pad them so you won't scar any part of your handbag), press the frame back into place.

Leather Stained or Torn. (See BASKET—LEATHER DISCOLORED, DIRTY, and BASKET—LEATHER TORN.)

Straw Bag Soiled or Broken. (See BASKET—WOVEN OF REED, RATTAN, WOOD, SOILED OR SPOTTED, and BASKET—STRANDS OR SLATS OF WEAVING COMING LOOSE OR BROKEN.)

Cloth Bag Torn. Sew colorful patches over the rips and tears and make a virtue of necessity. If the rip is in the seam or close to it, stitch the seam together (include the ripped portion if you can). See Section II, MENDING BY SEWING, p. 276.

Zipper Jammed or Broken. See ZIPPER.

Note: If your favorite leather handbag is badly ripped or damaged, take it to a handbag repairer or your shoemaker. Look under "Handbags–Repairing", in the yellow pages of your phone directory.

HEATER | electric

CAUTION: *Handling any electrical appliance requires care. Before you investigate the whys and wherefores of your heater's failure, consult the safety procedures in Section II,* ELECTRICITY AND WIRING, *p. 257.*

Doesn't Turn On. First, check the cord and plug. If the cord is frayed around the plug or the plug is broken and the prongs loose, replace the plug (see Section II, as cited above). Then check the fuse for that circuit and replace it if it has blown. (Electric heaters take a lot of current—at this point, the circuit may be overloaded, so if you want to use the heater, turn off other appliances on this circuit.) If neither of the above problems exist, test the wall outlet with a working lamp. If the lamp fails to light, it is the wall outlet that's at fault; call the electrician.

When none of the above steps makes the heater glow, take it to a repairman. A defective heater is a hazard no one needs.

HEATING PAD

See BLANKET/ELECTRIC.

HINGE

See DOOR.

HOSE, GARDEN

If you treat the hose properly you'll save yourself money *and* the work of repairing. Buy a curved hose hanger. Use this for storing the hose—instead of hanging it across a rusty old nail!

Leaks. Cracked or Broken Parts. If the rest of the hose is in good shape, repair the damaged area: Cut out the cracked or broken section with a sharp knife. Then join the two pieces of hose together with what the expert calls a *clinch-type couple* (it looks like a small bracelet and it clamps the two ends together). Buy the couple at the hardware or garden supply store. Take the piece you've cut out so that you can buy a couple that fits the hose.

Leaks at Faucet or Nozzle Connection. Try replacing the washer, or, if need be, put in *two* washers. If two new washers won't stop the leak, replace the coupling on the *end of the hose.* (When you buy the coupling you should know what kind to ask for. The kind you attach the nozzle *to* is called a *male coupling.* The device that you attach to a faucet is called a *female coupling.*)

HOT PLATE | electric

CAUTION: *Handling any electrical appliance requires care. Before you investigate the whys and wherefores of your hot plate's failure, consult the safety procedures in Section II,* ELECTRICITY AND WIRING, p. 257.

Won't Work. If the hot plate doesn't heat up, make the routine electrical checks. Take the plug out of the wall outlet and examine it. The case, wires, and prongs should all be in good condition. If wires are exposed or if the prongs are loose, don't use the hot plate. (Have the plug repaired at the local appliance shop or buy a new cord.)

Test the outlet to see if it works (plug in a working lamp), and check the fuse to be sure it hasn't blown. Be sure to consult Section II, as cited above, before you change the fuse. If all is well when you've made these checks, the trouble is in the hot-plate wiring. Have it repaired by a professional (or throw out the hot plate and get a new one). Don't try to be an amateur repairman with this gadget.

INSECT

Ants, cockroaches, termites, etc., see Section II, PEST CONTROL, p. 307.

INSULATION

See WEATHER STRIPPING.

IRON | electric

CAUTION: *Handling any electrical appliance requires care. Play safe. Before you try to figure out the whys and wherefores of your iron's failure, consult the procedures in Section II,* ELECTRICITY AND WIRING, p. 257.

All Types—Sole Plate Sticky. If your iron doesn't glide smoothly and freely over the clothes you're pressing, you've probably got starch from other washings and pressings on the sole plate (the bottom of the iron). Let the iron cool a bit. Then, run it over ordinary kitchen aluminum foil onto which you've sprinkled a little damp table salt. Do this several times. Wipe the iron clean with a damp cloth by just ironing the cloth several times. Or use a commercial "hot iron" cleaner. Then go back to ironing your clothes.

All Types—Sole Plate Surface Rough, Scratched. This can happen to the best of irons. You may not be able to feel the tiny scratches with your fingers (when the iron is *cold!*), but you'll notice a difference in the iron's performance. It will not slip and slide easily across the clothes you're ironing. The repair is simple. Rub the scratched sole plate with some clean, crumpled brown paper onto which is sprinkled some slightly damp table salt. But be sure the iron is at least *coolish*—or you'll have a wad of very hot paper to cope with.

Steam and Steam-Spray—Doesn't Give Enough Steam. If the water used to fill your iron happens to be hard (it has more than the usual amount of mineral material, like calcium, in it), the tiny holes that the steam comes out of will get clogged. To fix the iron, first turn off and disconnect it. Then, when the iron's cool enough to handle, clean the little ports by sticking a long tapestry or other needle into them and working the mineral substance out. Finally, flush out the inside of the steam iron with a mild solution, in equal proportions, of distilled white vinegar and water. Pour this into the water hole, then plug the iron in and let all of this mixture vaporize right out of the clean ports. *And next time,* if you can, *use distilled water* for the iron, bought from the auto supply or hardware store.

Steam and Steam-Spray—Puffs of Steam at Irregular Intervals. If your steam iron pants and puffs and the jets of steam come in uneven bursts, you will have trouble getting the ironing dampened evenly. The problem here is with the thermostat adjustment. Check to be sure you're using the correct setting for the fabric. If you are, and the iron still doesn't work well, unplug it. Let it cool, then take it to the local appliance repair shop and have the thermostat mended or replaced.

All Types—Won't Stop Heating. Unplug the iron and take it to the repairman. The problem is serious and can be dangerous.

All Types—Won't Heat Up. Save yourself possible expense and embarrassment by making some elementary electrical checks before you take the iron to the repairman. Follow this procedure:

1. Check the plug in the electrical wall outlet. Is it firmly set? If it's loose and wobbly, take the plug out and look at it. Are the prongs in the plug damaged? If they are, and if the wiring leading in and out of the plug is frayed or coming loose, don't reinsert the plug in the outlet. Repair or replace the plug (see Section II, ELECTRICITY AND WIRING, p. 257) or have your repair shop do it.

2. If there's nothing wrong with the iron's plug, spread the prongs a little with your fingers. This should give you a better electrical connection when you insert the plug into the wall outlet.

3. If the iron *still* doesn't work, check the fuses in the fuse box for this circuit. The fuse may have blown. You can replace it if it has, but first be sure to consult Section II, as cited above, before you do.

4. If the iron *still* doesn't work, test the outlet you're using. The outlet may be defective; if it is, plug the iron into another outlet that is in working order. (Test the outlet by plugging a working lamp into it. If the lamp *goes on,* you know the trouble is in the *iron.*) At this point, take your iron to an expert for repairs. And by the way, if the lamp *doesn't* work in the outlet you tested, have an electrician repair the *outlet.*

IRON COOKWARE

Cast-Iron Kettle or Dutch Oven—Rust Marks. Rub the rust marks off with steel wool, wipe the surface clean. To protect against further rusting, wipe with a clean cloth dipped in a smidgen of salad oil and place in a 250°–300° F. oven for several hours.

IRON FURNITURE

Pitted Surface. Rub the surface with steel wool to smooth it out. Wipe the surface clean, then paint the repair with a flat (nonglossy) black paint (if you want to keep the wrought-iron look). Follow instructions on the paint can. *Note:* If the furniture is used outdoors, ask the paint dealer for a paint like *asphaltum* which will withstand the rigors of weather.

Rusted. Liquid rust-removers are sold in hardware stores, but you should know that they're poisonous and must be handled carefully. If the rust spots are small, remove them by steel-wooling, as above. When the rust is rubbed off, touch up the surface with paint (see above).

Piece Broken. If the break involves a leg or arm, take it to an ironmonger to be welded back into place. Consult the yellow pages of your phone directory. Small, ornamental pieces that have been broken off the furniture can be glued back with plastic steel, which can be gotten from the hardware store. It comes in a handy squeeze tube. When you've finished the repair, and the mend is dry, touch up the area with paint (see above).

IRONING BOARD

Stiff When Opened and Closed. If you and the ironing board have a tussle every time you open or close it, spray the joints of the folding legs and the works underneath the board with a silicone lubricant. Buy this at the hardware store. Slide the legs back and forth until they work easily.

Board Seems Unsteady. Inspect it and look for loose bolts near the feet and where the legs are attached to the board. Tighten these with a small wrench.

Catch Doesn't Hold—Board Collapses on You. Get to know where the catch is and how it works.

1. Metal Board. The catch is usually a spring-type device, and hard to get at. Spray the spring-catch with silicone lubricant (a few jets will do), so that it works easily. If the spring is broken, take the board to the hardware store or to the local handyman to have it replaced.

2. Wood Board. The catch is usually a clip-device. If this is bent out of shape, try to straighten it with pliers. (Turn the board upside down to do this.) If you can't make the catch work, it's probably time to get a new board.

IVORY

Carved ivory figurines, handcrafted from elephant or walrus tusks, usually can't be duplicated in color or texture. If the one you have breaks, treat it as you would fine china. By cleaning, gluing, joining, and putting pressure on the broken parts, you may be able to restore the treasured object. Of course, if the breaks are many and intricate, you may have to turn to an expert mender for help (see below). Clean ivory and repair simple breaks yourself as follows:

Stains or Yellowed Ivory. Dip soiled ivory in alcohol for several minutes and let it dry in the sun. (If the carving is too large to dip, wipe it with cotton balls soaked in alcohol.) Dust and soil marks should disappear, and the ivory will gleam. *Note:* If the carved ivory's yellowed with age, the color, at least, will testify to its "antiquity."

Broken Ivory Object. First clean the parts with warm, soapy water, rinse and dry thoroughly. If the carving has been mended before, remove all traces of the old glue with warm vinegar or a little alcohol. When the joints are perfectly clean, you are ready to fit them together.

A strong, clear cement is the right glue for this job—it is inexpensive and gives a bond that is practically invisible. (See Section II, GLUING AND CLAMPING, p. 248, for more about clear cement.)

Put a very thin coat of glue on the edges of both joints, and match the parts as evenly and carefully as possible. Then hold the mended pieces together for about twenty seconds.

In ten minutes, the glue will begin to harden. Allow two days for the cement to set permanently before handling the object.

Delicate Pieces Broken. The skills of an expert are needed here, since restoration of ivory is difficult. An antique restorer, or a craftsman who mends china and glass, will know how to work on ivory. (See CHINAWARE—FINE PIECES BROKEN, for the way to locate an artisan, and an explanation of the techniques he may use on your piece.)

KITCHEN RANGE

See RANGE/ELECTRIC, RANGE/GAS, and STOVE/WOOD OR COAL BURNING.

KITCHEN UTENSIL

See ALUMINUM POT AND PAN, COPPER, IRON COOKWARE, and KNIFE.

KNIFE

Dull, Won't Cut. Several methods are used to sharpen dull knives and to keep them sharp. Each method has its own technique:

1. An electric knife sharpener is a quick and convenient way to sharpen the kitchen cutlery, but draw the knife blade through it *gently*. Several passes through the grinder with light pressure are better than bearing down for a heavy grind.

2. A whetstone with a coarse side and a fine grinding side is a traditional method for keeping knives sharp. If the knife is very dull, start on the coarse surface until a good bevel has been made on both sides of the knife's cutting edge. Then finish off on the fine surface. If you want to touch up an already fairly sharp knife, use the fine side.

3. A steel shaft with ridges on it—a part of many carving sets—is used to put a fine-ground sharp edge on an already sharpened knife. Draw the blade along the steel toward the cutting edge, not away from it.

Handle Loose. Misuse is usually the cause of a loose knife handle. Wooden-, bone-, and ceramic-handled knives should *not* be put in the dishwasher, or left to soak in the sink. Various ways to repair handles are given below:

1. If you can pull a loose handle off the knife shaft, you can then pour epoxy glue into the hollow well of the handle. Reglue the shaft into it. (This repair is good for bone and ceramic handles. For metal and honest-to-goodness silverware, see below.) Be sure to keep the blade and handle straight until the glue sets. (Do this by lashing the blade and handle together with masking tape.) See also BAMBOO-HANDLED UTENSIL.

2. You can save your favorite kitchen knife with plastic wood! If the wood handle has split down the middle, fill the split with plastic wood, then sand the handle smooth. CAUTION: *Plastic wood is extremely flammable. Don't work near a pilot light or a lighted cigarette.* Paint the whole handle with waterproof varnish. (This will keep moisture from splitting the wood again.) If the handle is beyond redemption, have it replaced; it should be riveted to the shaft. Ask the hardware dealer if he can do this for you, and if he can't, ask him if he knows of a tinker who can.

3. Good metal or silverware handles that come loose should be taken to a metal- or silversmith for repair.

KNIFE SHARPENER | electric

See CAN OPENER/ELECTRIC.

KNITTED ACCESSORY

See AFGHAN AND THROW (knit); also Section II, MENDING BY SEWING, p. 276.

LACE

Tears. Tears in tablecloths or dresser scarves can be mended in a way that isn't at all noticeable. Pull a strand from one of the seams or buy a matching thread, and use it to weave the rip closed. (For details, see Section II, MENDING BY SEWING, p. 287.)

Holes. Weave, as indicated, above. Or patch a hole with a matching piece of lace, if you have it, if not, buy new lace that is similar to the damaged piece. Stitch the patch onto the underside of the hole and trim away the excess lace from the right side.

To strengthen the repair, back the patch with net or tulle reinforcement.

LACQUER WARE

CAUTION: *Whether you're the proud possessor of a hand-painted, lacquered Japanese bowl or a commercially lacquered dish, don't try to clean your lacquer ware in hot water. Use lukewarm water and a mild soap or detergent. (If you do otherwise, the finish will be ruined.) Wipe the lacquerware piece dry immediately! And do it thoroughly!*

Chipped or Cracked. Buy a high-grade lacquer (paint) from your paint or hardware dealer. Be sure you select one that will *exactly* match the piece. (It's a good idea to take the piece with you when you buy the lacquer.) Use a fine touch-up brush (and a magnifying glass, if needed) when you apply the lacquer to the damaged area. Fill in the hairline cracks and chipped portions. Do all this in a dust-free room (if you can find one), and do it carefully and delicately. If you do, your lacquer finish may look as good as new.

Broken. You can mend broken lacquer ware by applying matching lacquer. Apply it in very thin coats to the edges of the broken pieces, then join these. But if the bowl or dish or whatever is likely to be handled a lot, use epoxy glue. It's less traditional, but it *is* strong. (For details on how to mend a broken bowl, plate, or cup, see CHINAWARE.) After the epoxy glue has been given time to set properly, relacquer the mend by the method given above.

Fine Object Broken. Finish Badly Damaged. If your valuable lacquerware is lusterless, broken, or otherwise losing its looks, turn to a museum or consult the yellow pages of your phone directory to find an antiques restorer or skilled craftsman who mends fine china, crystal, and other objects. After he's put the pieces in place, he'll relayer the surface with new coats of lacquer. And if you have *carved lacquer,* this expert may even use sealing wax! He'll match the color, then heat and flow on sealing wax over the damaged part. He then carves this with little heated tools.

LADDER

See Section II, LADDER SAFETY RULES, p. 312.

LAMP | electric

See also Section II, ELECTRICITY AND WIRING, p. 257.

CAUTION: *Handling any electrical appliance, even* including *your lamp, requires care. To be safe, consult the procedures in Section II,* as cited above, p. 257.

Lamp Base Loose. If there's a felt covering glued to the bottom of the lamp to protect the table from being scratched by the base, pull the covering off. Try not to tear it. Now, tighten the nut you see here. (It is attached to a metal tube or spindle; this runs up to the light socket.) Wiggle the base as you tighten the nut to get the best fit. After you've done this, reglue the felt pad to the bottom of the lamp with contact cement.

Socket Wobbles. Again, the problem is mechanical, not electrical. Tighten the nut at the base. If the socket screws onto the spindle at the top, tighten it. If you find what's called a set screw on the side, tighten this, too.

Doesn't Light. First, try a new bulb! Then, save yourself possible expense and embarrassment by making some elementary electrical checks before you take the lamp to the repairman. Follow this procedure:

1. Check the plug in the electrical wall outlet. Is it firmly set? If it's loose and wobbly, take the plug out and look at it. Are the prongs in the plug damaged? If they are, and if the wiring leading in and out of the plug is frayed or coming loose, don't reinsert the plug in the outlet. Repair or replace the plug (see Section II, as cited above, for details), or have the repairman do it.

2. If there's nothing wrong with the lamp's plug, spread the prongs a little with your fingers. This should make a better electrical connection when you insert the plug into the wall outlet.

3. If the lamp still won't light, check the fuses in the fuse box for this circuit. The fuse may have blown. You can replace the fuse, but first, be sure to consult Section II, as cited above.

4. If the lamp still doesn't work, test the outlet you're using. The outlet may be defective, and if it is, try the lamp on another outlet that *is* in working order. (To test the regular outlet for your lamp, try another lamp

that *does* light in it. If the second lamp goes on, you know that the trouble is in the wiring of the lamp you're puttering with. At this point, unless you're a whiz at wiring, take the lamp to the repairman.)

LAMP | kerosene

Smokes When Lighted. First, lower the wick to keep the flame down (turn the little wheel on the rod beside the wick). If this doesn't stop the lamp from smoking, blow the lamp out. When it's cool enough, trim the wick: pinch off the charred part if the wick is charred *evenly all around*. If it's not even, use sharp scissors to trim off the charred section to make the wick even. Then, pinch the fibers of the wick *together* with your fingers. (This keeps loose fibers from flaming up later.) When you relight the lamp, keep the flame low to begin with. The flame will creep up when the wick gets warmer, because the kerosene will seep upward into it with heat. Adjust the flame to your liking.

Wick Too Short. If the wick doesn't dangle down in the kerosene fount far enough to touch bottom, replace the wick. You can buy another at the hardware or camping supply store. Be sure it's the same width. Thread one end of the wick through the metal wick holder, and turn the wick winder while you do this. If the wick doesn't feed into the holder easily, or if it jams up, get a needle and thread and *tack* each end of the wick, leaving some thread at both ends. Now, thread the wick holder with these pieces. Just let the threads dangle through the upsidedown wick holder. Pull the threads and turn the winder and see the wick go through!

When the wick is where it should be, clip off the threads, and trim off the wick (if need be) with your scissors. Remember to pinch the wick with your fingers if you must cut it with scissors.

LAMPSHADE

Tears or Holes. You can find a lampshade in almost any material—paper, fabric, glass—and usually, if your shade gets holes or tears, it's easy to replace it with a new one. However, you may have a favorite shade or cherished antique that you want to repair and keep. Here is how to fix it:

1. Fabric Shade. Select a new fabric to use for recovering the shade. Remove the binding and detach the damaged material from the shade's wire frame. Examine the way the fabric is attached (and remember or take notes on the way you take it apart). Use the original shade cover as a pattern when you cut a new one. Some shades, supported by vertical wires, are seamed vertically, while others are only stitched around the top and bottom of the wire frame. Attach a new shade by following the same sewing method used for the old one.

After you have secured the new covering to the frame, glue on a binding made from the same material. Or, be creative: pick a band of fabric that contrasts and use that. Polyvinyl resin glue, or white glue, is nonflammable, and will hold the binding in place with no trouble. (See Section II, GLUING AND CLAMPING, p. 252 for how to use white glue.)

2. Glass. Glue a glass chip back in place with epoxy. However, if the break is larger, and the shade is in two or more pieces, you may have to replace it.

Wire Frame and Shade Separated. When the binding loosens, the wire rim that supports the shade breaks away and the shade droops. Fit the shade and wire together and glue on a new binding to hold the frame in place. Use white, polyvinyl acetate glue. (See above section, "Tears or Holes, Fabric Shade.") If you don't like to fuss, use self-stick binding tape for the job.

Some shades have holes punched at the top and bottom and are laced to the rims with leather thongs (like shoelaces). If the leather has come undone, buy new thongs at an arts and crafts shop. Whipstitch the shade back onto the rims.

Wire Broken. This is not a job for you. Take the broken shade to a metal shop and have an expert solder the wire frame together.

LEATHER | furniture, leather-covered items

See also BOOK.

The enemy of leather is the sort of dry atmosphere most of us have in our homes—especially in winter. Protect your leather treasures by using the proper conditioners on them. Leather experts suggest you do this at least twice a year. *Never use furniture oils or furniture polish on leather. Chemicals in these may damage the finish on leather.*

Pay special attention to folds and corners of your leather-bound or leather-covered pieces—cracks usually start there. The conditioner you use will depend on the type of surface you're treating: if the leather is smooth, use one of the commercial conditioners, or use castor oil or neat's-foot oil. If the leather has a suede finish, be sure to use one of the special *suede* conditioners. For details on aspects of leather care, see below.

Smooth Leather Surface—Discolored, Dirty. You can ask the shoe repairman to suggest a good commercial cleaner, or use that tried-and-true cleaner, saddle soap. First, flick off the dirt with a clean rag or brush. Wet a sponge and make a fluffy lather with saddle soap. Rub the lather into the leather, wipe it off and repeat the process. Let the second coat dry; when it does, polish the surface with a soft cloth (cotton flannel is good). To give extra protection to the surface, rub in castor oil. Let the leather piece dry in a warm place for an hour and a half, then polish the treated surface with a soft cloth.

Finely Tooled, Gilded Leather—Dry, Shabby-Looking. Rub in castor oil (for a *glossy* finish) or neat's-foot oil (for a *dull* finish). For details see BOOK—LEATHER BINDINGS DRY. . . .

Leather Torn. Buy a matching leather remnant at the local arts and crafts supplier (or filch a good scrap from a torn leather glove). Cut a slender patch just a little wider and longer than the tear. Thin the leather, on the reverse side, around the edges. Use a razor blade, a small sharp paring knife, or a leather tool called a *skife*. (Arts and crafts stores have skifes and other leather tools.) Coat the damaged area with rubber cement, and apply a thin layer on the reverse side of the patch. Let the two surfaces dry until the shine evaporates. Then, carefully, stick the patch down on the torn spot. Smooth it out with a soft cloth. If the tear is a large one, cover the leather with a folded cloth, then clamp or bind the area until the cement cures.

Soft, pliable leather-covered items (like cushions) can be mended with needle and thread if the stitches in the seam are coming out.

LIGHT | electric

See Section II, ELECTRICITY AND WIRING, p. 257.

LIGHT | fluorescent

CAUTION: *If the tube of your fluorescent light breaks, handle it with gloves or by the unbroken ends. The interior coatings of these lights are poisonous. Sweep up broken shards and put these and the rest of the tube in a plastic bag or box you can seal. Finally, vacuum the area where the damage occurred.*

Note: Switch off the fluorescent light before you make the repairs below.

Blinks When You Turn It On. This is normal performance for a fluorescent light (but the blinking should stop in a few seconds).

Blinks All The Time. An indication of trouble. Try to find the cause, because this sort of fluttering of the light will wear out the tube quickly. Usually, there are two reasons the tube does this:

1. Tube Doesn't Fit Securely into Fixture. The light is held in the light fixture by pins at either end of the tube (see diagram opposite) which are pushed into the sockets (at right angles to the fixture). After the pins are put into the sockets, turn the whole tube *one-quarter* of the way around to make the fit *snug*. If the light flickers *all the time,* try turning the tube

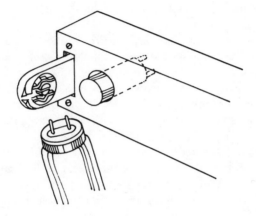

to make the connection better. If the tube *still* flickers after you do this, turn off the light, take the tube out and look at the sockets. Are they wobbly? If so, tighten the screws that hold them to the fixture with a screwdriver (consult the diagram).

2. The Tube Is Wearing Out. Blinking and flickering in the fluorescent can be a warning that the tube's life is waning. (If you've made the checks above and the tube *still* flickers, have a replacement tube handy.) Take the old one out by turning it in the opposite direction from that given above. Take it to the hardware or electrical supply store and buy a new one the same size and power. Insert the new tube as indicated above. If the new tube blinks, then there's trouble in the fixture *itself*. For this repair, call your electrician.

LIGHT FIXTURE | electric

See CHANDELIER, and Section II, ELECTRICITY AND WIRING, p. 257.

LINOLEUM | sheet

See also FLOOR/TILE, for ways to handle linoleum tile floors.

Stained. When food stains and furniture marks mar the linoleum floor-covering you can usually sponge up the damage with a mild cleaner. Rinse quickly; water is hard on linoleum and can cause it to bulge and warp.

If the stain is a tough one (e.g., nail polish or paint) take it up by scouring very lightly with fine steel wool. Rinse and wipe dry. Then, to protect the surface from more spills and drips, apply wax and buff this. Be sure to use the type of wax recommended for linoleum. *Note:* Don't ever use harsh floor cleaners that contain strong chemicals on the linoleum—unless you want to ruin it!

Bulges. At some time or another, the linoleum floor-covering probably was cleaned with too much water, and too often. First the linoleum will warp, then bulges will show up here and there. Cope with these unsightly bumps simply by slitting them open. Buy a linoleum knife from the hardware store, or use any small, sharp knife. If the bulge is smallish, the slit edges will meet each other when you've finished the repair. *Test to see that they don't overlap each other.* Just flatten the edges on the floor. Then, with a spatula or wood tongue depressor, spread linoleum paste on the back of the linoleum, under the slits. Press the mend down, and wipe off any paste that oozes up. Weight the repair down with a heavy cutting board or heavy box. (Cover the spot with wax paper to protect the cutting board!) Leave the weights in place until the paste dries.

If the bulge is sizable, the linoleum has been stretched like a blown-up balloon. Slit the bulge straight down the middle, then make two more slits at the ends—at right angles to the main one. Now, test to see how far the slit edges overlap when you flatten all the slit parts down to the floor. Trim off the excess with a linoleum knife by cutting down the middle of the overlapping pieces, *through both layers of linoleum.* Pull off the trimmings. The two trimmed edges should now just *exactly* meet. Spread paste on the back of the mend, then weight the area down with flat boards, as above. (A suitcase filled with books is good for this if you have nothing else handy.)

Torn. Use a putty knife to spread linoleum paste on the underside of the tear. Weight the mend down, as above.

Worn Spot or Large Hole. Sooner or later, the linoleum floor-covering will show the effects of wear and tear, usually in front of the refrigerator or the stove. Remember, small holes that grow larger with neglect are a hazard in the kitchen: you run the risk of being tripped by one of them, and that's not fun if you're carrying a large pot of hot soup.

If you're lucky, you'll be forearmed for this repair with some linoleum scraps (leftovers from when the linoleum was installed). Use these for patches. But if you have no scraps, plan on patching the holes with a new piece of linoleum in contrasting colors. Make a design out of the old and new, and a virtue out of necessity! These are the steps to follow in the repair:

1. If you need to buy new linoleum for the patch, make a paper pattern of the damage (so that you'll know your minimum requirements when you buy new material). Then, pull or cut out a smidgen of the old linoleum from the edge of the worn spot or hole. This will help you to select new linoleum for the mend. Remember that the new must be of the *same thickness* as the old. Buy enough so that you have at least an inch to spare all around the worn spot you're about to patch.

2. Place the new material over the worn area. Kneel on it, and press it down, or nail it. With a linoleum knife, *cut through both the old and the new linoleum at the same time* to insure that the insert and hole will be exactly the same. (Follow the general shape of the hole but cut pieces about a half inch larger than the hole.) (See diagram.)

3. Pull up any slivers of the old linoleum you've trimmed off. Take up old paste that may be on the floor.

4. Spread the area with linoleum paste, and insert the patch. Weight it down with a flat board or a suitcase filled with books. Leave the weight there until the paste is dry.

5. If the patch isn't *flush* after the paste has dried, hammer down the edge of the patch. Use a soft hammer (a hammer with cloth wrapped around the head). Then, sandpaper the edges so that the seam around the patch is smooth. Wipe, and wax and buff the area.

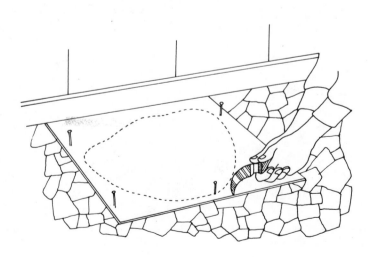

LOCK | door

See also DOOR/HINGED—LATCH WON'T CATCH.

For locks on windows, see WINDOW.

Stiff or Won't Work. Sticky locks are always a bore, and all the more so if you're in a rush to come or go. Happily, most of these can be made to function smoothly again. After you've got your lock in working order, give it tender, loving care. But first, follow this procedure:

1. Take the key out of the keyhole, then blow a little powdered graphite into the keyhole. (Graphite is the same thing that's used for pencil lead. The powdered form can be bought at the hardware store.) Rub some graphite on the latch bolt. Or, use silicone lubricant (in a spray can) for both areas.

2. Work the key back and forth in the keyhole. Work the latch bolt back and forth, too. This spreads the graphite or silicone over the balky parts.

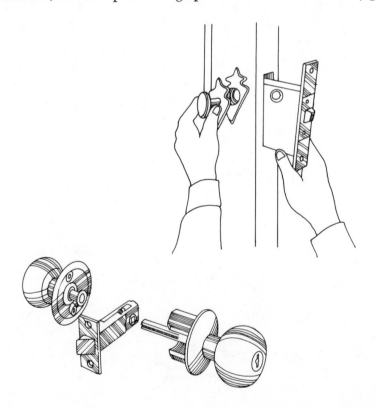

3. If neither treatment works, your lock may have internal troubles. What to do about them depends on the type you have:

- Separate Lock, Screwed onto the Inside of the Door. Remove it by taking out the screws. Inspect the lock parts for broken springs or broken metal parts. If nothing is broken, just clean the parts in a solvent—alcohol, kerosene, or turpentine. (Be careful—all are flammable.) This will remove grease and grime that may have impeded the lock's works. Lightly oil the movable parts. Wipe off any excess. Put the lock back together and put it back on the door.
- Lock in Doorplate or in Knob (see diagrams opposite). If the lock is in the plate above or below the knob, or in the knob itself, remove the knob, the doorplate, and the latch plate. Use a screwdriver to take out the screws. Start with the knob: loosen the set screw and then pull it out or unscrew it. Next, unscrew the doorplate. Now pull out the spindle (which turns the latch). Do this from the *outside* of the door. Finally, remove the latch plate from the edge of the door by taking out the screws that hold it, and by removing the latch bolt. Inspect all these parts for broken springs and broken metal parts. If no parts appear to be broken, proceed (as above) to clean with a solvent. Oil, as above. Reassemble the parts and put them back on the door.

4. If any of the parts are *broken* (after you've disassembled them), or if the lock doesn't work when you've put it back on the door, either take the whole thing to the locksmith or have him come and fix the lock for you.

Note: If you have a new key made for the front door, don't always blame the lock if the key doesn't work. If you can, try the *original* key. If *it* turns in the lock, the new key obviously hasn't been cut properly. Take the new key back to the locksmith with the old one, and have him file it and make a more exact copy of the old key.

LUGGAGE

Handle Loose. When the handle of your suitcase feels as if it might fall off any second (and you're far from home and handy tools), head for the nearest shoe repair store. The shoe repairman can at least make temporary repairs right away, and you can continue your journey without losing control of the luggage. If you're home, inspect the handle. See if the metal hooks that hold the handle to the case are opening up. Squeeze the hook that's gaping open with a pair of pliers until it is closed. Reinforce here by wrapping a thin wire tightly around the hook.

If the leather covering on the handle is coming apart, coat the underside of the leather handles with rubber cement or contact cement. Let the glue get tacky before you press the two parts together. Bind the leather handle tightly until the glue cures. (See Section II, GLUING AND CLAMPING, p. 248.)

Leather Binding Coming Off. Use rubber or contact cement to glue it back into place. (See section cited above for details.) If the leather is worn and tired-looking, cut off the loose portion. Replace this part with a new piece of leather; glue it as indicated above.

Plastic Binding Loose. Use clear cement on the binding. Coat both surfaces to be joined, then bring them together. Remember to allow two days for this glue to cure after you've applied it. (See section cited above for details.)

Leather Torn. Patch the rips on your leather case with a matching piece of leather. Buy a remnant at the arts and crafts shop, or cut up an old leather glove that matches. For details about patching leather, see LEATHER.

Fabric Case Torn. Mend canvas or other types of fabric on luggage with matching material. If the tear is not too conspicuous, mend by gluing a reinforcement on the inside of the case. Be sure to bring the edges of the rip as close together as possible (baste them in place before you apply the patch of material on the other side of the bag). Take out the basting stitches before the glue dries. If the rip is very noticeable, cover it with a patch. Sew on the material if the fabric is lightweight and pliable, or glue on a patch over the rip if fabric is stiff and heavy. Since the patch will be visible, make the most of it. Use a contrasting color and pink the edges (with pinking shears), or buy decorative patches at the sewing counter of the department store. For details on gluing, see CANVAS—RIPPED, TORN, and Section II, GLUING AND CLAMPING, p. 248. For details on sewing, see Section II, MENDING BY SEWING, p. 276

MARBLE

Though much of the glory that was Greece and the grandeur that was Rome were made of marble, its glossy, veined substance is vulnerable to more than the etchings of time. If you have marble tabletops, mantels, figurines, or carvings, you'll need to know the inside story of marble care and repair. And what is true for marble is true for its "cousin," alabaster. Below, we give you tips on handling types of marble trouble.

CAUTION: *Never use acid or oily cleaners on marble.*

Marble Surface Dull, Dusty. You may be tempted to use liquid detergent to clean the surface, but the Good Housekeeping Institute advises you to invest in a marble-care kit that you can buy at the department store. It contains a polish that is made especially for marble. Dust the surface, then simply rub on a dab of the polish and buff the surface lighty. The virtue of this polish is that it gives marble a protective coating *and* a handsome, shiny finish.

Surface Etched by Food and Drink Spills. In the marble-care kit (see above), there is a restorer. Rub this on the marble top, over the etch marks made by acids from, say, a glass of lemonade or a tomato juice cocktail. The Good Housekeeping Institute advises "rubbing in all directions to obtain a smooth finish." When the etch marks disappear (and they will without too much effort on your part), polish the surface with a soft cloth.

Surface Badly Stained. Butter, oil, and other fat stains tend to seep down into marble because it is porous and, normally, these stains are hard to remove. But, according to the Good Housekeeping Institute, if you use the stain remover that comes in the special marble-care kit (see above), you'll be able to lift off those unsightly discolorations. Spread the stain remover on a foil disk (the disk comes with the kit), place the disk upside down on the stain, and leave this in place overnight. The chemicals in the stain remover act like a poultice, to draw out the grease and fat globules. If your first try is not completely successful, repeat the treatment. Then rinse the marble with cold water, wipe dry, and polish with the marble polish.

Stubborn Stains. If the above treatment doesn't take care of the stain, the Institute suggests you make up and apply a special mix: Combine ¼ cup of hydrogen peroxide with 8 drops of household ammonia. Drip this remover-mixture onto the stain with an eyedropper. Let the liquid stand on the stain overnight. Rinse off and polish, as above.

Surface Lightly Scratched. Use fine-grade sandpaper and sand the spots lightly. Wipe clean, then apply polish, as above.

Surface Deeply Scratched. Fixing this is difficult for an amateur. Consult a marble finisher or dealer. He can probably do the job for you.

Marble Carving Broken. Use contact cement, and be sure to exert pressure on the mend until the glue cures. For details, see CHINAWARE and Section II, GLUING AND CLAMPING.

Parts of Art Object Broken or Missing. Choice marble objects and collector's items (and carvings that simply have great sentimental value) can be restored by an expert. He uses several techniques, depending on the damage. Mixtures of beeswax and carnauba wax can be molded to replace the missing pieces. Plaster of paris, tinted with paint and given texture by the addition of wax, can be cast in the shape of the missing curlicue or toe. The restorer also uses dowels and sunken rivets if the damage calls for it. The nearest art museum can recommend a restorer for your treasure.

MATTRESS

Buttons Loose or Off. If your mattress is popping its buttons, or if they're loose and you can feel them through the bedding, the remedy is simple. Arm yourself with an upholsterer's needle (buy it at an upholstery supply store, a department store, or the arts and crafts shop) and some thin but strong twine. Nylon is durable, but upholsterer's twine is good, too. Make a loop through the button, push the *long upholstery needle* through the mattress, and catch the button on the under side. Pull the twine tight, knot several times.

Holes. The simplest way to cope with this is to iron down one of the press-on patches you can buy at the sewing counter of your department store. Or cut a patch from mattress ticking or any heavy cotton (like denim), pin the patch down, then sew it in place with a *curved upholstery needle.* For details see Section II, MENDING BY SEWING, p. 276.

Lumps. Live with the mattress for the moment, but replace it as soon as you can.

METAL FURNITURE

See ALUMINUM FURNITURE, IRON FURNITURE, and STEEL FURNITURE.

MIRROR

Framed Mirror—Wood Frame Separating. If your antique wood mirror frame is in good condition, but is coming unglued at the corners, use contact cement to fasten the joints together again. See Section II, GLUING AND CLAMPING, p. 248.) *Note:* Sand and refinish before the repair is made. (For details, see Section II, REFINISHING WOOD, p. 301.)

Frameless Mirror—Mountings Coming Loose. An unframed mirror should be mounted with plastic or metal edge clips along the top, bottom, and sides. If the clips are loosening, you may not be using the proper *fasteners.* Clips on a mirror hung on a *hollow* wall should be secured with toggle bolts. *Solid* walls require expansion fasteners and screws. (For descriptions of these fasteners and how to use them, see Section II, WORKING WITH NAILS, SCREWS, AND FASTENERS, p. 236.) If the mirror is hung on a wood wall, use wood screws.

Glass Broken. Tradition has it that broken mirrors bring bad luck! Replace the glass.

Plating Coming Off Glass. The spots you see are signs that the silver-plating on the back is flaking off. Tape aluminum foil to the peeling areas. *Note:* This is just a temporary measure. Some day take the mirror to be resilvered by a professional. (Find him in the yellow pages under "Mirrors," or call an antique dealer.)

MIXER | electric

See FOOD MIXER.

NAIL

See Section II, WORKING WITH NAILS, SCREWS, AND FASTENERS.

NEEDLEWORK | crewel embroidery, needlepoint

If you're the owner of fine needlework pieces, and you're all thumbs when you pick up a needle and thread, don't despair. Contact an expert to repair your damaged treasures. Whether it's needlepoint, crewel embroidery, or any other decorative stitchery, these skilled specialists do the salvage work for you. Some of them, listed in the pages of decorating and women's magazines, do business by mail. Others, who can *consult* with you, are listed in the yellow pages of your phone directory under "Art Needlework," or "Needlepoint." If you enjoy sewing and mending, do the simpler repairs yourself. Below, we pass on a few pointers on needlepoint care.

Crewelwork Bedspread, Curtain, or Pillow—Soiled. You may be tempted to wash these with mild soap, but don't! *All crewel-embroidered pieces should be dry-cleaned.* The reason: the embroidery is done with special yarns (usually wool), on linen, cotton, and other fabrics. The fabric and the yarn respond differently to water—the *embroidery* tends to tighten up, puckering the fabric.

Stitches Coming Loose. If the yarn is not damaged, pull out a few more stitches—enough so that you can thread the yarn through the eye of a needle. Use a tapestry needle (see Section II, MENDING BY SEWING, p. 276), or any needle with a large eye. Copy the stitching, then secure the yarn on the reverse side of the work. (For details, see section cited above.)

Needlework Moth-Damaged. Crewel and needlepoint are worked in high-quality wool yarn, which makes the pieces vulnerable to moths. If some stitches of your needlework have been chewed by moths, pull out the damaged bits of yarn. Match the color and the *ply* (the number of strands) of the yarn. (The needlework counter of a department store in your area should be able to duplicate the yarn.) Work the damaged area with the new yarn, using the appropriate stitches. (For details on types of stitches, see Section II, MENDING BY SEWING, p. 276, and for a comprehensive guide to needlework consult the *Good Housekeeping New Complete Book of Needlecraft*, by Vera P. Guild.)

Piece Is Warped. If your needlework pillow is out of shape (and diagonal when it should be square), it should be reblocked and remounted. Get instructions from a needlework shop, or have a professional block and mount the piece for you.

PAINT

See Section II, PAINTING/INDOOR, and PAINTING/OUTDOOR.

PAINT | drip or splatter

See Section II, PAINTING/INDOOR, p. 294, and PAINTING/OUTDOOR, p. 298.

PAINT BLISTERS

See also Section II, PAINTING/INDOOR, p. 294, and PAINTING/OUTDOOR, p. 298.

Large Blisters. Blisters sometimes appear even on a new paint job—perhaps several months after the wall has been painted. Experts tell us the cause is either dampness in the wall, or a water leak coming through or down the wall from somewhere. To get rid of the blisters, first attack the cause. Find the leak or the source of dampness. (See ATTIC and ROOF, for details on these problems.) Then, attack the blisters on the wall. There are two ways to accomplish this:

1. If you have some matching paint left over from the time the wall was painted, scrape off the blister, sand to a bevel the edges around it, and touch up the bare spot. However, paint from the same batch will tend to look newer and fresher. The patch will probably be visible. A better way, if you're careful, is method 2.

2. Slit the blister with a sharp razor blade. Squeeze a clear glue (see Section II, GLUING AND CLAMPING, p. 248) into the slit so that it is forced back under both halves of the blister. Press these smooth and wipe off the excess glue. Cover a piece of stiff cardboard with wax paper, attach the top to the wall with masking tape, and lean a board or broom handle against the cardboard to keep some pressure on the blister while the glue dries.

Small Blisters All Over. A series of small blisters over the whole paint job usually means you have painted with oil paint on a damp wall, or that the surface was greasy or dirty when the paint was applied. The only thing to do in this case is start afresh. *This time prepare the wall thoroughly!* Scrape the blisters off with a scraper (from the hardware store). Sand the rough edges where the blisters *were*. Put on *two* coats of good-quality paint. *Note:* Some of the heavier paints, like latex, will hide blister marks better than a thin coat of the old-fashioned variety of paint. For details, see Section II, PAINTING/INDOOR, p. 294, and PAINTING/OUTDOOR, p. 298.

PAINTBRUSH

See Section II, PAINTING/INDOOR, p. 294, and PAINTING/OUTDOOR, p. 298.

PAINTING AND DRAWING

If you're lucky enough to own original paintings and drawings, you probably know that giving them gentle and correct care *now* can preclude costly repair *later*.

We've consulted an internationally renowned art conservator (as they're known in the art world) for advice on care and repair of your cherished paintings and sketches. Properly treated, this expert says, they can live for centuries. So treat your art properly and give pleasure to generations yet unborn!

First, here are some general do's and don'ts:

- *Don't* let anyone talk you into home remedies for cleaning oil paintings. Some books suggest that you rub the surface of your painting with a slice of raw onion or a piece of bread. Don't! These items of food can cause the painting's surface to mildew. Onion juice will also stain the painting.
- *Don't* wipe the surface of your painting with a dustcloth of any sort. (Many art works are damaged by this "care.") If you must dust, be sure the duster is a feather one, and even with *this* duster be sparing. Twice a year is probably good enough!
- *Don't* clean the glass over a charcoal or pastel drawing with a dry cloth or with paper. You generate static electricity when you do, and you'll transfer the drawing to the inside of the glass, and off of the paper. Do use a damp cloth to clean the glass.
- *Don't ever* store your paintings in the attic or cellar: they can be damaged by the extremes of heat and cold in either place. Dry atmosphere can crack paint and dampness can bring mildew to it.
- *Don't* expose paintings (or any artifacts, for that matter) to abrupt changes of temperature and humidity. If you want your art work to last and look good, don't hang it near a fireplace (where it will get too warm) or next to an outside door or wall (where it will get too cold).
- *Do* invest in a *humidifier* if you live in a home that's heated in winter. (You can also keep the air from being too dry in your home in winter if you just put some bowls of water on top of your radiators. This adds moisture to the atmosphere, and that's not only good for your *paintings,* it's better for *you* and your *furniture,* too!)
- *Do* invest in a *dehumidifier* if you live in a warm, wet climate. This device prevents mildew damage to your paintings *and* your other belongings.
- *Do* inspect your paintings and drawings regularly. Be on the watch for the particular danger signals we indicate, below.

Art Work: Oil Painting—Preparation for Inspection. If you can't afford to have an art expert inspect your painting, do it yourself. *Note:* If there's a picture light on your painting, be sure to disconnect it, *first,* before you take the painting down! To prepare for inspection, you'll need:

1. Good Light. If possible, you should have daylight from a large window *and* artificial light from a high-intensity lamp.

2. A Large Table. (It should be larger than the painting.)

3. Help. If the painting is unwieldy and large, someone should be there to help you take it down and to replace it on the wall after inspection.

4. Old Bankets. Cover the table you'll work on with several layers of these. (The top one, or a sheet on it, should be *clean!*)

Inspection Routine. After you take the painting off the wall, examine the picture hook attached to the wall. Be sure it's secure. (Our expert says that most paintings are damaged when the wall fastening or frame gives way and the painting falls to the floor. If it's not secure, consult Section II, WORKING WITH NAILS, SCREWS, AND FASTENERS, p. 236. *Note:* If your painting is large and heavy, it may need better or stronger wall fasteners, or several picture hooks to hold it. Place the painting face up on the table. Now, proceed with the inspection.

1. Frame. Your painting should not be *squeezed* by the frame: the frame should hold it just loosely enough to allow for some very slight movement of the canvas or panel. (Of course, the frame must hold the painting so it doesn't *fall out* of the frame.) Take a look at your painting and frame to be sure the frame is not pressing against any part of the canvas. If it is, take it to the picture framer for the proper adjustment.

2. Backing. Turn the painting over. Is there a protective covering here? If not, cut one from cardboard or brown wrapping paper, and tape it to the back of the frame. The covering will minimize the effects of heat or moisture on the canvas, prevent dirt from falling between the stretcher and the canvas, and keep it more securely moored to the frame.

3. Warped Canvas. Turn the painting right side up and check to see that the canvas is absolutely flat and even—with no slight dips in its center, no warping or folds of canvas across the surface or in the corners. If you notice any of these signs, do as the expert does: insert wooden wedges in the corners of the stretcher (turn the painting wrong side up to get at these). The technique is called *keying out* the painting. Buy the small wedges (several dozen for less than a dollar) at the art supply store. Insert these keys in the stretcher corners. Drive them in gently, until you feel the stretcher has expanded slightly. Alternate the positions of the wedges as you go from corner to corner of the canvas. *Note:* If you have any doubts about the frame, the stretcher, and your ability to insert the keys, take the painting to a reputable framer or to an art expert to have the work done. (You find art conservators through a fine arts museum. Conservators usually don't charge for the small service of keying a canvas.) CAUTION: *Some frames can't be keyed-out this simply, and others are completely "fixed." Don't try to force wedges in if there is no place for them. Also, don't try to key out the painting if the stretcher or canvas is fragile or*

damaged. Take your painting to an expert to have the stretcher fixed or the painting remounted.

4. Bumps and Lumps on Bottom of Canvas. Dirt, nails and the keys (wedges) may have fallen down here. Remove these. The bumps from them can cause the paint to flake or can make small perforations in the canvas.

5. Blisters or Loose Paint on Canvas. If the paint is coming off the canvas, put the painting back on the wall and call an expert. He can advise you on the necessary treatment, give you an estimate, and do the work if you decide it's worth doing.

6. Canvas Brittle. Rolled Away from Frame. Again, you need the help of a professional. (See above.)

7. New Painting, Surface Unvarnished. Modern paintings are usually not varnished when they're sold. (But check with the art dealer to be sure.) All oil paintings, however, need a coat of varnish to protect their surfaces from the ravages of air pollution. A new painting should be so treated not more than a year after it's been completed, but not earlier than six months from completion. The framer or art conservator can do this for you, or tell you if it has already been done. The charge for this service is minimal.

8. Old Varnish on Surface Is Dirty. It's reassuring to know that a coat of old varnish can be removed by an art conservator. (Don't think that because you're a whiz at refinishing furniture, you can remove the varnish from your oil painting. You may destroy it if you try to.) Put in a call to the expert and let him look over the job and give you an estimate. (By the way, putting glass over oil paintings is not recommended by art experts. Glass is only, and *rarely*, used when there's danger that the painting may be fingered by careless "appreciators.")

Oil Painting on Wood—Cracks in Panel. If you notice small cracks, call in the expert as soon as possible. The repair is not difficult, but if the painting is not attended to, the wood panel will split and the painting will be seriously, if not irreparably, damaged.

Paintings or Sketches on Paper—Watercolors, Pastels, Charcoal Sketches, etc. Again, the best repair is constant care: inspect the work for several conditions:

1. Matting Dirty. If the matting is dirty, the painting is likely to get that way, too. Have the painting rematted. (But continue the inspection before you do.)

2. Glass over the Painting. Paintings or art works that aren't given the protection of a coat of varnish should be covered with glass, but be sure to check the *glass itself*. There should be enough space between the surface of your art work and the glass over it to hold a cushion of air. If the glass *touches* the work's surface, have the painting reframed.

3. Backing. Acid-free or "neutral Ph" cardboard and an acid-free paper should be sealed over the back of your art work to protect it. If you don't

have these covers, or if there are breaks in the backing, you'll soon have discoloration on the surface of your painting. If you have doubts about the backing, or if it's damaged, take your painting to a good frame shop for a proper backing. An art supply store can sell you acid-free paper if you want to apply the backing yourself. *Neutral library paste* is the correct glue for the job, and you can find that at the art supply store.

4. Strong Light on Watercolor, etc. This is hard for any art work to endure, and if yours hangs so that the light falls on only a portion of it, you may discover that this part is beginning to bleach. Rehang the painting where the light will be kinder to it. Nothing can be done about the bleaching, sad to say!

PERCOLATOR | coffee

See COFFEE MAKER.

PHOTOGRAPH

Torn. A torn photograph can never be really *right* again, but it can, unlike Humpty Dumpty, be put *together* again. Join the pieces (work on the wrong side of the photo) with invisible plastic mending tape. *Don't use glue for the repair. Eventually whatever type of glue you use will discolor and show through the photograph's surface.*

The best, and usually the simplest, thing to do when a photograph is torn is to have another print made from the negative. But if the negative is lost, take the damaged photograph to a professional photo lab or studio, and have the photograph copied. Find a copier near you in the yellow pages of your phone directory. This professional will seal the photograph together, retouch it, then make a negative from the original. What you will receive from him will be an almost unblemished, new print.

Curling Around the Edges. If you have a photograph that hasn't been framed or mounted, sooner or later it will ripple or curl up at the corners. But you *can* treat the malady. Put the picture in a pan of room-temperature water. Take the photograph out after a few minutes. Shake the water droplets off it, then gently insert it in a folded paper towel. Put this flat packet on your ironing board. Cover the picture-side with more clean, white paper toweling. *Note:* Do not use a decorated towel! If you do, you'll transfer the design to your photograph. Set your *dry* iron at a low temperature, then iron across the towel. Now, take the towel off. Lo and behold! A flat, ready-to-frame photograph!

Mounted Photograph Coming Off Cardboard Backing. If the cardboard mounting and the photograph are parting company, the mounting was not done well in the first place. To remedy this, use wallpaper paste to stick the two together again. (Most other glues, say the photo experts, will stain the picture. So be forewarned. And see Section II, GLUING AND CLAMPING, p. 248, for details.)

The best and most lasting way of backing a photograph is a technique the photo people call *dry mounting*. The expert puts a waxed tissue between the photograph and the backing. Then he tops these three layers with a protective paper. He slips the whole package into a *dry mount press*. (It's sort of like a sandwich grill.) The press is closed, turned on, and, you guessed it, the wax tissue melts and seals the photograph to its cardboard or paper backing.

You can adapt this technique and do your own dry-mounting. Buy some mounting cardboard and some special waxed mounting tissue at a camera or photo supply store. Cut them to the size of the photograph. Set your *dry* iron at a low temperature, then touch the tip of the iron to the top two corners of the tissue-photo-sandwich. Next, flip the photograph over on its back and onto the cardboard. Lift the bottom of the photograph up, then use your iron to tack the loose corners of the tissue to the bottom corners of the cardboard backing. Now you've got the three layers of your photo-sandwich in place! Cover the front of the photograph with a cotton or linen tea towel (be sure it's *clean*), and iron over the whole surface! The photograph is now dry-mounted.

Aging Photograph Needs Restoring. You can't do this yourself. Check the yellow pages of your phone directory under listings for "Photographs Copied and Restored." A skilled copyist will do the job for you.

PIANO

Keys Discolored. Try washing them with mild soap and water. Be careful not to let too much moisture run down the sides of the keys. If this doesn't do the trick, try cleaning with alcohol (see IVORY). The keys will yellow with age, so don't hasten the process by using furniture polish or other oily substances on them.

Needs Frequent Tuning. Move the piano to an inside wall (away from window and outside wall temperature changes). Keep the room at an even temperature, if possible.

Finish Scratched or Marred. See Section II, REFINISHING WOOD, p. 301.

PICTURE FRAME

Wood. If the frame is coming apart at the corners, buy small metal mending plates at the hardware store, and screw these on the wrong side of the frame.

Gilded Frame—Looks Dirty. *Note:* Art experts warn you to be careful about cleaning old gold-leafed frames. Whereas you and I might want to clean and polish that frame and make it all shiny and new-looking, the art expert says that the old "look" adds value to the frame and to the painting it holds. That slightly dirty look is a "patina," and to be left undisturbed. The expert suggests that you apply a little butcher's wax to the frame (using a small, soft paintbrush). After this, rub *gently* with a soft cloth or soft brush to bring out the glowing, burnished finish.

Pieces Broken Off. Usually these frames are made of wood covered with a substance called *gesso*—a mix of plaster of paris and various types of glue. You can buy the materials to make gesso at the art supply store. (Or make your own mix with plaster of paris and ordinary brown glue.) Mold the gesso in the shape (roughly) of the missing piece, glue it to the frame with casein glue, and allow it to dry in place. When the gesso and the joint are dry, sandpaper the repair and give it a coat of shellac. (Thin the shellac with alcohol, and be careful—alcohol is extremely flammable. Don't work near a pilot light or a lighted cigarette.) After this paint the mend with oil paint or tempera—to match the rest of the frame. Gild it with gold leaf from the art supply store, or use gold paint to touch up the surface. Ask your art supplier for instructions on *leafing*.

Antique Frame. If you have any doubts about your ability to restore a treasured antique frame, consult an antique dealer. Or, ask the fine arts museum near you for help in finding a craftsman who'll do the work. Don't ruin the frame by frantic fixing.

PILLOW

Bed Pillow—Feathers and Down Working Through Cover. Make a second cover from an old but clean pillowcase. Sew the case closed by overcasting. (See Section II, MENDING BY SEWING, p. 276.) Or buy yourself a new pillow cover in the bedding section of a department store. Some covers have zippers to close them, others snap together, and some are meant to be stitched together.

Hole in Fabric. Patch this with cotton scraps. (See section cited above.) Put a cover over the whole pillow when you're finished patching (see above). It's neater, cleaner and will keep the patch from showing through your pillowcase.

Bolster—Holes in Fabric. Use the old covering as a pattern to make a new bolster cover.

Cushion—Holes in Fabric. If the couch or sofa cushions are wearing thin or are torn, and you can't duplicate the material to make new covers, cover them with contrasting fabric. Use the old cover for your pattern. For details on sewing, see Section II, MENDING BY SEWING, p. 276.

Decorative Pillows: Needlework (Needlepoint or Crewel-Embroidered and Others.) See NEEDLEWORK.

All Types—Zipper Stuck. See ZIPPER.

PIPE | gas

See RANGE/GAS.

PIPE | water

See also DRAIN, SEPTIC TANK, and TOILET.

Noisy Pipes. The rattle and knock in your water pipes will not only disturb your family's nighttime sleep and daytime peace and quiet, these unseemly goings-on can also loosen pipe fittings and cause leaks in the system.

One of the easiest pipe rattles to fix is the noise made by a faucet when you turn it on. Usually, this is caused by a loose washer or screw at the base of the valve stem. To get rid of the noise, replace the washer and tighten the screw. (See FAUCET, for details on how to do this.)

Louder knockings are almost always caused by *water hammers* (the plumber's name for them). They occur when the faucet is suddenly closed. Doing this brings on water vibrations in the pipe. The banging sounds as if you were bonging with a wooden mallet on a large kettle. You may be able to stop this racket by draining the water from the pipes. Do this at the lowest outlet you can find in your pipe system (by following the pipes downward). Then *close* the faucets and turn on the water supply. Enough air may *now* remain in the pipes to act as a cushion when the water is turned on—and to keep the pipes from banging. But this is *not* a permanent cure: eventually the air will work itself out of the pipes—and you'll have the noise again. So, at *this* point, call the plumber, who can install a stand-pipe air chamber just ahead of the faucet. This will give the water in the pipes a built-in cushion, and the noises will fade to a mere whisper.

Sweating. Exposed cold water pipes (either in the basement ceiling or as lead-ins to the bathroom and kitchen sinks) collect moisture from the air—especially when your house is heated. The condensation, as you probably already know, drips onto the floor and causes damage. But there's an easy way to solve the problem. Wrap those pipes in an insulating material. Fiber glass, which you can buy at the hardware store or building supply shop, is ideal for this. Ask for the kind that is waterproof (or has a waterproof outside cover). With this only one wrapping is made around the pipes. With the nonwaterproof type, you would need to add a moisture-proof wrapping on top of the insulation.

Leaks. Leaky pipes are something you wouldn't wish on your worst enemy: if you have them you know what havoc they can wreak. The damage from leaky pipes will be in the walls where the pipe is hidden, or in exposed pipes. First, turn off the water. Then, call the plumber. And if he can't come—because it's midnight or the middle of a holiday weekend—here's what you can do in the meantime:

Exposed Pipe Is Leaking.

1. When you turn off the water and the leak stops leaking, dry the pipe thoroughly with a towel. Then wrap the leaky part with several layers of gummed, plastic tape—like electrician's tape. Turn on the water and go back to normal usage of the water system. But keep an eye on your pipe patch job, until the plumber comes.

2. Dab the new, quick-drying epoxy glue on the leaky portion of the pipe. But first, clean that section of pipe and dry it. This type of epoxy will be hard in five minutes, and after that you'll be able to turn on the water again. But do keep checking your temporary repair till the plumber does a permanent job of fixing your pipe.

3. You can also improvise with a clamp and some rubber you cut from an inner tube, a drainboard mat, or the rubber ring inside the top of a glass jar. Use the rubber strip as a gasket. Put it over the pipe-leak, then tighten the clamp on the pipe until the rubber closes off the drip. (See diagram.) Turn on the water and resume near-to-normal living, but do keep an eye on that repair till the plumber comes!

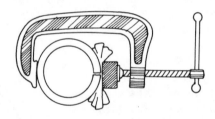

Pipe Hidden in the Wall Leaks. This is a different and more complex problem. If you know exactly where the leak is, be brave and chop into the wall. Then, use one of the methods outlined above to stop the leak. *Note:* Cutting into the wall is a drastic step, so be sure you know that the leak is behind the piece of wall you've hacked up—and not ten feet away! If you're really not sure where it is, and the plumber is coming soon, let him be the one to hack at the wall. He's had more experience at this sort of thing, and may be able to zero in on the leak.

Frozen Pipe. When your water runs very slowly or not at all in winter, start to worry about the possibility that the pipe is freezing. (A pipe far enough away from the source of heat will do this in cold winter weather.) Act quickly when you notice that the faucet is sending out little or no water. If you don't, the pipes can burst—*water expands when it freezes!* (If that happens, you'll need to have the pipes replaced by the plumber, and that's inconvenient, and these days, not inexpensive!) When you've taken charge of the emergency in the ways indicated *below,* do some sleuthing and find out *why* the pipe gets cold enough to freeze. Has a crawl space vent beneath the floor been left uncovered? (If so, the weather will get in and get at the pipes.) Is there a basement window part way open? (The weather can come in this way, too.) Now, for the home remedies that'll keep you busy till the repairman comes.

1. Pipe Is Easy to Get At. Wrap the pipe in rags and pour hot water on them from a teakettle. Be sure to leave the faucet open. Start the hot water treatment from the faucet-end of the pipe so that when the thaw comes, the water can run out the faucet.

2. Pipe Not Easy to Get at. If you have an infrared heat lamp, aim it in the direction of the pipe. Start at the faucet-end, as above, and leave the faucet open to let the thawing water run out.

3. Pipes Often Start to Freeze Up. For longer term remedies, it's wise to buy an electric heating cable at the hardware or building supply store. The cable is wrapped around the pipe and is connected to electric current. Install it to thaw out a pipe, and leave it there, turned on, until the weather no longer threatens the water system.

CAUTION: *Never try to unfreeze pipes by using a flame torch. You may set the house on fire. Also, the pipe can get so hot where you're applying the flame that the ice will turn to steam and burst the pipe—and possibly scald you, too.*

PLASTER AND PLASTERBOARD

See CEILING WALL.

PLASTIC

See also, COUNTER TOP—PLASTIC LAMINATED TOP.

Cracked or Broken. The knobs, handles, and trimming on many small accessories for appliances and home furnishings are made of various plastic materials. Most of these plastics can be glued *readily,* but there are some that resist it. No matter how much pressure you use, the cracked or broken pieces won't stick together. Before you replace the piece, try these techniques:

1. Force plastic cement into the crack. Clamp the sides of the crack together. (See Section II, GLUING AND CLAMPING, p. 248.) If the plastic is so rigid that the two sides of the crack can't be pressed together, just fill the crack with plastic cement and wipe off the excess cement.

2. If the piece is broken in two, coat each side with plastic cement or contact cement. (If you use contact cement, let it dry on the plastic pieces until it's tacky.) Bring the pieces together—try to do it accurately—and clamp, if need be. (*Note:* When you use contact cement and let it get tacky, you won't need to clamp the mend.)

PLUG | electric

See Section II, ELECTRICITY AND WIRING.

PLUMBING

See specific items: DRAIN, TOILET, etc.

PORCELAIN

See CHINAWARE.

POT AND POT COVER

See ALUMINUM POT AND PAN, COPPER, and IRON COOKWARE.

PRINT

See PAINTING AND DRAWING, PICTURE FRAME, and PHOTOGRAPH.

QUILT

See BEDSPREAD/PATCHWORK QUILT, and COMFORTER.

RADIATOR

See FURNACE—STEAM RADIATOR SYSTEMS and FURNACE—HOT WATER RADIATOR SYSTEMS.

RADIO | battery operated

Case Cracked. Try to force some plastic cement into the crack. Wipe off any excess, then exert pressure on the mend by binding the case tightly with masking tape until the cement cures. (For details, see Section II,

GLUING AND CLAMPING, p. 248.) If the crack keeps opening up, do a patch job: bind the case with colored cloth adhesive tape. Be sure to wrap the tape *tightly* around the case. Make a design with the tape and your mend won't seem so tacky.

Won't Work. Check to see that the batteries are firmly set in position. Scrape the contact points at both ends of *each* battery with a knife, or rub them with steel wool. Do the same for the contact points in the battery holders. If the radio still doesn't play after this treatment, get new batteries. But be sure that you insert the batteries *correctly* (see also FLASHLIGHT). If new batteries won't bring the little box alive with sweet music, take it to a radio repairman. (The trouble may be minor, but the works are hard to get at and delicate.)

RADIO | electric

CAUTION: *Handling any electrical appliance requires care. Play safe and consult Section II,* ELECTRICITY AND WIRING, *before you try to fix your radio.* Remember: Always unplug the radio before you inspect it. Never poke around the insides of your radio while it's on with a screwdriver or your fingers. You'll get quite a shock if you do.

Case Cracked (Plastic). See above. RADIO/BATTERY OPERATED—CASE CRACKED.

Wooden Cabinet Scratched or Marred. See Section II, REFINISHING WOOD, p. 301.

Won't Work. If the dials light up and you hear a hum, the cord and plug that carry the electricity to the radio are functioning. You can assume, then, that the fault lies somewhere in the tubes or the circuitry (the electrical works inside the radio). These are complex repairs to tackle, so take the set to the radio repairman.

If the dials *don't light up* when you turn the set on, there are other possibilities to consider. The radio obviously isn't getting electrical current, and without it the radio can't function. First, inspect the cord and plug to see if the cord is frayed, or if the plug is cracked, broken, or has loose prongs. Replace the plug if it *is* broken (see Section II, ELECTRICITY AND WIRING, p. 257). If the prongs are not broken, spread slightly to get a better connection in the wall outlet. Next, test the wall outlet with a working lamp. Plug the lamp into the outlet, and if it doesn't light, you know the outlet needs repair. Fixing the outlet is a job for an electrician: don't try it. At this point, switch the radio to another outlet. If the radio *still* doesn't go on, take it to the radio shop or radio section of a department store for repairs. Or call a radio repairman and have him do the work at your home.

Tubes May Not Be Working. If yours is the type of radio that uses tubes, and if the cabinet is large and unwieldy, don't give up hope. Take the tubes out of the radio and have them tested at the radio section of a department store, or at a local radio repair shop. Most radios have diagrams on the inside of the cabinet or case that show where each tube goes. If the diagram is missing, *make* one. Get yourself a piece of paper and make a map of the radio's tube emplacements. Just draw a circle for each tube. Then, take the tubes out, one by one. Look for the number printed on the tube. Note this number on your map, in the circle that corresponds to the tube's place in the set. This way, you'll know which tube goes where when you bring the tubes back from the radio shop. If the old tubes don't test out, buy new ones. The replacement tube will bear the same number its predecessor bore. Keep the map with other appliance manuals.

RANGE | electric

CAUTION: *Most, if not all, electric ranges use 220- to 240-volt electric current, and—just a reminder—this is twice as powerful as the usual household current. Some models, with self-cleaning ovens, will bake an oven clean with superhigh temperatures (between 850 and 1050 degrees Fahrenheit). There are various safety controls on electric ranges, but remember: when you tinker with an electrical appliance, you should be protected with basic know-how. Consult the procedures in Section II,* ELECTRICITY AND WIRING, *p. 257. Learn the particulars of your range by studying the operating instructions that come with it. Don't forget that strange noises and fitful performance are indications of trouble. If you have any doubt about your dexterity, turn the stove off and turn the problem over to an expert.*

Porcelain Enamel Finish Chipped or Scratched. You can make repairs to the damaged areas that will look almost as good as new. Use a special porcelain enamel or epoxy resin paint. Sand the areas smooth when the paint is dry. Be sure to use very fine sandpaper, and buy it when you buy the paint from the paint or hardware store. (These paints, by the way, are also good for touchups on other appliances finished in porcelain. Save some for the refrigerator or whatever.) And from now on, be gentle when you heft your pots and pans to the stove! Use warm water and detergent when you clean the porcelain surface. Avoid, like the plague, any abrasive cleaning powders or pads. They'll wear down that lovely, glossy look.

Oven and Top of Stove Lights Out. If the range goes on but the lights don't, the problem is local. That is, the bulbs themselves are probably dead. Replace them with new ones, but be sure to use the same kind of light bulbs. See APPLIANCE LIGHT, and consult your owner's manual for details.

Foods in Oven Overcooked. If your cakes come out charred on top and bottom, but just right in the middle, something may be wrong with the oven —or you've failed to place the cake in the right portion of the oven. Go back to your owner's manual and check the instructions. Usually, the center of the oven (with the rack halfway up the oven) is the place for baking.

Foods in Oven Undercooked. The problem may look different but, as with the item above, you've probably put the cake or the soufflé in the wrong place. Check your owner's manual, as indicated, above.

Burners or Ovens Smoke When You Turn Them On. Usually the cause is spilled food. This will burn off the heating coils—sooner or later—but who wants to cook in a smoky kitchen? Put your food in the refrigerator, turn off the surface unit (burner) or the oven, let this cool, then go to work. Use warm water and detergent for the job, or a special oven cleaner. Don't use the spray-on oven cleaners: these can be harmful to your eyes and lungs. Do use the cleaner you spread on with a brush, and be sure to follow the instructions on its container. Wipe off with water and vinegar solution, rinse, then dry.

Note: If yours is a self-cleaning oven, clean it as instructed (follow directions in the owner's manual).

Units On Top of Range Work but Oven Doesn't Go On. Check the automatic timer. If you've just used the timer, it's probably not back to the manual position, and the oven won't heat until it is. Turn the timer to *off*. Then turn on the oven. If it still doesn't work, turn the controls to *off* again, then inspect the heating unit in the oven. If it's the detachable type, it may be slightly loose. *Be sure the heating element fits tightly into its connections. Push it in if it seems loose.* Then, turn the oven on again. If you still have a cold oven, send for the repairman. The unit is probably burnt out, but he can replace it for you. (When you call him, tell him you've made the above checks.) If your oven doesn't have a detachable element, call the repairman.

Single Unit on Top of Range Won't Work. If the units are the detachable type, inspect to be sure that the unit is securely connected. See above. If yours are not detachable, call the repairman.

Lights Won't Work, No Units Work, Clock Not Running. Whatever the cause, the range is not getting any electric current. Before you send for the repairman, turn the oven and top of stove units off, then run down this checklist:

1. Locate the fuse in the range (there's usually one there, and the owner's manual will show you where it is). Has it blown? If you don't know how to read a fuse, consult Section II, ELECTRICITY AND WIRING, p. 257. *Be sure that you replace this fuse with one exactly the same size (the same number of amps).* Now see if the range works. If the new fuse blows, turn off the range and call the repairman. Someplace inside, there's a defect that's causing the appliance to short circuit. The repair should be handled by a professional.

2. If the fuse inside the range is working, but the range isn't, check the fuse for this circuit, which is in your fuse box. It should be labeled. *Be sure to read the section on electricity cited above before you do this, and before you replace this fuse.* If you've replaced the fuse, go back to the range and see if it works. If it doesn't, there may be trouble in the wiring

leading from the range to the fuse box. Turn the unit off and call the electrician.

3. Check your other appliances and lights. They may be off, too. If so, you can assume there's a power failure in your area. Get out the flashlight, candles, and the chafing dish, and make the best of the breakdown!

RANGE | gas

CAUTION: *If you notice a strong odor of gas in your kitchen, get your family and yourself out of the house, then call the police. If the odor is distinct but not overpowering, follow these procedures.*

- *Don't* light a match or candle.
- *Don't* turn on electrical appliances or lights.
- *Do* open the windows here and in other rooms, *wide!*
- *Do* put in a call for emergency help. The utility company has emergency crews to handle this problem. Or you may want to call your handyman or superintendent or the repairman who services your range. (Remember, though, the *repair* must be done by a licensed professional.)
- *Do* turn off the stopcock, the faucetlike handle in your range or on the gas pipe leading to it.

Note: If the leak is a small one, the odor will quickly dissipate when you air out the room. If you're handy, test for this small leak while you're waiting for the repairman to come. We tell you how at the end of this section.

Porcelain Enamel Finish, Chipped or Scratched. See RANGE/ELECTRIC.

Foods in Oven Overcooked. See RANGE/ELECTRIC.

Foods in Oven Undercooked. See RANGE/ELECTRIC.

Oven and Top-of-Stove Lights Out. If the other lights in the house are working, and if the *clock-timer built into the gas range is working*, then the trouble with the range lights is local. That is, the light bulbs are probably dead. Replace them with new ones but be sure to use the same type of light bulb. See APPLIANCE LIGHT, and consult the owner's manual for details.

If the clock-timer has stopped, too, but your house lights and appliances are working, it's time to do a more thorough check of the gas range. First, check to see if the electric cord that connects the range lights and timers to the house current is plugged into the wall outlet. (Usually this is behind the stove.) If the plug is firmly set in the outlet, check the fuse for this particular circuit in the fuse box. It should be labeled. Has the fuse blown? If you don't know how to read a fuse, consult Section II, ELECTRICITY AND WIRING, p. 257. *Be sure that you replace this fuse with one exactly the same size (the same number of amps).* Now see if the clock-timer and range lights work. If they don't, the wiring inside the range or leading to it is at fault. Call the electrician and let him do the repair.

Burners or Ovens Smoke When You Turn Them On. See RANGE/ELECTRIC.

Burners Work But Oven or Broiler Won't Light. If the oven or broiler are lit by pilot lights (not a hand-held match), check the pilot light. First, turn off the oven or broiler controls. Then, open the oven door. Is the pilot flame still burning? If not, light it with a kitchen match (you may have to hold it near the pilot tube for a few seconds, so a small book match is not the thing to use). If the pilot doesn't catch after two or three tries, do the following:

1. Clean the Pilot Burner Tip. (Consult the owner's manual if you're not sure where it is.) Clean off any caked food or carbon from the tip with a needle or a pin. There's a tiny hole in this tip that must be opened up to supply the gas for the pilot.

2. Check the Gas Supply to the Pilot. If food and carbon are not blocking the pilot tip, then it's possible too small a supply of gas to the pilot is the problem. The owner's manual will show you where there's a little screw valve on the pilot supply line. This valve controls the amount of gas that flows into the pilot light. Use a screwdriver, and turn this screw valve counterclockwise (that is, to the left). More gas should now feed into the pilot, so light a match and try to light the pilot again. If the flame goes high, turn the screw valve back down—that is, clockwise—until you've adjusted the pilot flame to its proper height.

Note: When a gas oven or broiler pilot is relighted, it may take several minutes before the oven or broiler burner lights up. *This is because the pilot has to have time to heat up a metal bar that leads to the oven or broiler burners.* When the metal bar is warm, the gas flows along it, and the oven goes on. So don't fret or call the repairman the minute you've lit the pilot, and the oven doesn't seem to "work." Wait. Let the pilot do its job. Then turn the oven controls on.

3. Check the Electrical Connections and the Fuse. In the new gas ranges the gas feed to the oven, including the pilot, is reguated electrically. If you have no electric power, you can't make the oven work. First, see if the clock-timer is still running. If it's stopped, check as above, "Oven and Top-of-Stove Lights Out."

Burners on Top of Stove Won't Work. Check the pilot light, or lights, on the top of the stove. If the pilot is out, try to light it with a match. A gust of wind can sometimes blow the pilot out. To do this lift up the top of the stove, then hold the lighted match to the top of the pilot light burner. If the pilot still won't light, follow the procedure given in lighting the oven or broiler pilot light: items 1 and 2 above.

If the pilot light works but the burners still won't light, check the small openings (they're called the lighter ports) in the burners to see if they're clogged with spilled food. Open these ports or windows with a hairpin or a small wire.

Note: Some burners are easily removed (so that you can clean them in the sink). Others are bolted down. If yours are bolted to the range, scrub them clean right there. But don't get the top of the range and the gas tubes slurpy with soap and water. The ports will become clogged if you do.

Gas Odor Around Stove. See CAUTION note above. If you have ventilated the room, and the leak is so minor that you don't get woozy working around the range, *and if you really want to locate the leak yourself,* this is the way to do it: make a mix of soap and water (make it a very thick sort of wet paste). Spread this (you can use your fingers) on the gas pipe *joints* of the range. If you see any bubbles coming up through the soap mix you've found the leak. The gas blows soap bubbles where the pipe is damaged or open. Don't use the range until you have the leak repaired. Do turn off the gas supply to the range (as indicated in the CAUTION note above). Get out your hot plate, or, better yet, go *out* to dinner!

RECORD PLAYER | electric

CAUTION: *Record players, like any appliance run by electricity, require careful handling. If you're planning to inspect or repair your player—or the amplifier it's attached to—play safe.* Always unplug the record player from the power source—that is, remove the plug from the wall outlet. (This caution doesn't apply to the wires that run from the needle cartridge, along the arm and into the player. These sound-giving wires have only a tiny amount of electric current in them.)

Needle Sounds Scratchy or Music Fades. The needle probably needs to be replaced. Inspect the needle and the cartridge that holds it. If you find that you can take the needle *out* of the cartridge, or if you can *remove the cartridge* from the rest of the player, take the needle or the cartridge unit to the record or radio shop. Get a new needle to match the one that's worn out. (Replace the cartridge or insert the needle.)

If the whole operation looks too tricky (if, for instance the sound wires are soldered to the cartridge), don't try taking *anything* apart. Just take the player itself into the shop and have the needle changed by a professional.

Record Revolves But No Sound Comes from Machine. Check the connections between the record player and its amplifier. Sometimes the pronglike connecting plugs are pulled out or are loose. Push them in, *tight.* If you've done this and still get no sound, take the machine to the repair shop or have the repairman come to you.

Machine Won't Run. Check over the cord and the plug that fits into the wall outlet. Are the prongs loose? Is the plug cracked or broken? You can replace the plug, but first, consult Section II, ELECTRICITY AND WIRING, p. 257, to learn the technique. If the plug and cord are in good condition, check the outlet by plugging a working lamp into it. If the lamp lights, the trouble is in the machine. Take it to the repairman. (If the lamp *doesn't* light, then the trouble is in the outlet. Let the electrician do this repair. In the meantime, plug your record player into another, working outlet.)

REFRIGERATOR, REFRIGERATOR-FREEZER | electric

CAUTION: *Handling any electrical appliance requires care. Play safe and consult Section II,* ELECTRICITY AND WIRING, p. 257, before you investigate your refrigerator's malfunctionings.

Note: Be sure that the refrigerator operates on its own electrical circuit (that is, there are no other lights and appliances on this particular line.)

Be sure, also, that the electrician who installs your refrigerator grounds it—to keep you from getting possible shocks when you touch the machine's surface. If you've been jolted when you've opened the door, turn the refrigerator off, then inspect the cord plug that's set in the wall outlet. Most refrigerators come with a three-prong plug (whereas your lamps and small appliances have two-prong plugs). This third prong is the ground. To do its job, this plug must fit into a three-slot outlet. (For details on ways to ground appliances, see Section II, as cited above.) Put in a call to the electrician right away and have him ground the refrigerator before your food gets too warm in there.

Machine Works But Light Inside Refrigerator Is Off. Reach in under the light's cover, if it has one. Touch the bulb. Is it loose in its socket? Most, but not all, refrigerator lights are screwed into their sockets the way ordinary lamp bulbs are. If the bulb is loose, tighten it by turning it clockwise. If it still doesn't go on, unscrew it and test it in a working lamp. (Just screw it into the lamp socket and switch the lamp on.) If the bulb is dead take it to the hardware store and get another, matching bulb. (Most refrigerators use 15 watt bulbs.) Screw the new bulb into the refrigerator socket. (If the *new* bulb doesn't light, see below.)

Some refrigerators use snap-in bulbs, like the ones in the high-intensity table lamps. If yours is one of these, press the bulb into the socket, then twist it counterclockwise until it's released from the socket. Have it tested at the hardware store, and if it's dead, buy another. Insert the new bulb by pressing it into the socket, then turning the bulb *clockwise* until it snaps into place.

If you've replaced the bulb and the light *still* doesn't go on, the trouble is either in the automatic light switch that works when the door is opened, or in the interior wiring. Call the serviceman and have him fix the light. Until he comes you can use a flashlight to survey the insides of the refrigerator.

Porcelain Enamel Finish, Chipped or Scratched. Repair with a special epoxy resin paint. See RANGE/ELECTRIC—PORCELAIN . . . SCRATCHED.

Unpleasant Odors in Food Compartment. Put the food in the freezer compartment or in an insulated bag, then take out the refrigerator's various drawers and bins. Wash these and the rest of the interior surfaces with a mixture of water and baking soda. Rinse and wipe dry.

If the refrigerator is the frost-free type (it defrosts automatically) the odor may be coming from the *drain tube* or evaporation pan. Flush out the tube with the water and soda solution until the odor vanishes. The pan can be thoroughly washed in the sink.

Plastic Shelf Cracked. See PLASTIC—CRACKED OR BROKEN.

Bin or Drawer Badly Damaged. Replace the item. Go to your dealer and buy it from him.

Single-Door Refrigerator-Freezer—Interior Freezer Door Broken. Call your serviceman and have him install a new one.

Machine Keeps Foods Cool But Makes Annoying Noises. Your slanty floor may be the cause of this unseemly racket. But you can level the appliance and compensate for the tilt underneath it. Consult the owner's manual, and find the leveling screws. These are at both corners of the machine underneath the front panel (they're where the front legs would otherwise be). Try turning these levelers up or down, depending on the slant of the floor. (If the job is too much for you, call the repairman and have him level the machine for you.)

Frost-Free Model Only: It may rattle if it's askew. If the floor is level, and the machine makes unusual noises, check the evaporating pan to be sure it's set properly.

If you've done all this and the refrigerator still makes a racket, send for the repairman.

Runs But Doesn't Keep Foods Cool, Doesn't Make Ice. To retard spoilage of your food, temperatures in the food compartment of your refrigerator should be between 34 and 38 degrees Fahrenheit. Freezers should be 0 degrees for proper conservation of frozen foods. (In the one-door model refrigerator—which has only a small *interior* door to the freezer, the temperature in the freezer should be between 10 and 20 degrees Fahrenheit.)

You can test the temperature in each compartment: just slip your outdoor thermometer in there and give it time to register. Take a reading, then turn the control dial of the refrigerator to a colder setting. See if the mercury falls to its proper chilly level. If it doesn't, inspect the seal around the door. Does it look gummy? Wash it with warm water and soap or detergent. Is it damaged? If so, call the repairman and have him fix or replace the gasket (the rubbery seal inside the door).

Hot Air Coming Out of Machine. Give the machine a chance to breathe by providing plenty of circulating air *around* it. Look at the owner's manual. If your machine vents from the back (that is, the hot air is exhausted there), pull the machine out from the wall a little, and *be sure you don't have pots and pans or a bread box blocking the air circulation above the machine.* If your machine vents from the front, take off the metal grille. Scrub it in the sink, then vacuum around the bottom of the machine. Replace the grille. If the air around the refrigerator stays too tropical, call the repairman.

Nothing Works. Food Is Warming Up! Take a look at the temperature control dial. Is it set at *off?* (Stranger things have happened!) Don't blow a gasket, just twirl the dial to its proper setting. (Clean out the refrigerator as soon as you can. *Be sure to dispose of any frozen food packages that are swollen or thawed. Get rid of meat that has gone from ripe to impossible!*) Clean the machine's surfaces, as described above.

If you turn the dial to its proper setting and *still* nothing happens to bring life back to the refrigerator, make the routine electrical checks before you call the repairman:

Is the cord plug firmly set in the wall outlet? If it isn't, plug it in and consider your refrigerator *repaired!* If the plug *is* in place, inspect the fuse in the fuse box. (It should be labeled.) If it's blown, you can replace it, but not before you consult Section II, ELECTRICITY AND WIRING, p. 257. If the fuse is intact, and your other appliances and lights work, it's time for you to put in a call to the repairman.

ROOF | shingled and metal

A leaky roof can do more than dampen your spirits. If you don't stop the leak, the walls, ceilings, and even the furnishings will suffer, sooner or later. So, the best roof care is early *repair!*

What you need to know, though, is that finding the leak may be more time-consuming than stopping it. If you're eager to avoid high repair bills, you can take on *this* part of the chore and leave the actual *repairs* to the roofer. And if you dread the steep view outside from the peaks of your house, be aware that leak-detecting doesn't necessarily require you to go aloft—up the ladder and loping all over the roof-tops. You can often spot a leak, after careful hunting, from inside the house. Below, we give you tips on tracking down leaks, and routines for rudimentary roof repairs.

Locating Leaks. Your chore will be much easier if the attic is "unfinished"—that is, if the rafters aren't enclosed by plaster or board ceilings. From easy to not-so-easy, work this way:

1. Unfinished Attic. Take a flashlight and inspect the rafters under the roof during a rain or snowstorm. If you see a rafter or crossbeam that is wet, follow the wet course with the flashlight beam, going up toward the peak of the roof. *Note:* Sometimes the roof leak will be far from the place where it stains. Water often runs down the rafters and across the beams (or other crosspieces in the roof structure). When you're lucky enough to find a hole (at the end of the water trail) push a thin wire through the hole. (Colored ties that come with plastic garbage bags are good for this.) Use the wire as a little flag to tell the roof repairman just *where*, on the map of your roof, the leak starts.

2. Finished Attic (Rafters Enclosed). If stains appear on the ceiling, note the *highest* point of the stain. Then, measure up to this point from the top of your wall. Next, measure again—this time at a right angle to

the above—to the nearest outside wall of the peak. These measurements will be at least a *rough guide* for your roofer in hunting for the leak. He can make the same measurements on the outside of the roof. Then he can concentrate on that territory in his search for the hole.

Temporary Repairs. If you're up to the chore of handling a ladder and clambering around the roof, there are repairs you can make that will protect the house while you're waiting for the roofer to come to do a *complete* job. First, buy some plastic roofing cement that contains asphalt and asbestos fibers. It comes in a gallon can at the hardware or building supply store. While you're there, buy a small, pointed trowel—use this to apply the roofing cement. And get out the ladder, but consult our LADDER SAFETY RULES, p. 312, in Section II, before you do.

1. Asphalt Shingles Slipped Out of Line. Take the roofing cement, the trowel, some zinc-coated, flatheaded roofing nails, and a hammer, and go up the ladder to the roof. (Buy the nails at the hardware store.) Raise the shingle above the one you're about to fix, but do it very gently. Then, push the loose shingle back into position. Nail it there. Nail at the *top* of the shingle, under the flap of the shingle above. (There's an overlap here.) Next, dab some roofing cement on the nailheads, and dab some more roofing cement on the underside of the overlaps: both the shingle you've nailed and the one above it. Press the shingles down and let the cement take hold.

2. Asphalt Shingles Broken, Cracked. Fill the cracks with roofing cement. If the shingle is badly broken, replace it. Pry up the nails that hold part of the broken shingle, using a long screwdriver. Nail the new shingle in place, then finish the repair with roofing cement, as above.

3. Wooden, Slate or Asbestos-Cement Shingles, Broken or Cracked. These are all made of rigid materials and are tricky to handle. Let the roofer replace them for you. In the meantime, protect the house by sliding a piece of copper or galvanized iron sheet-metal under the break. Anchor the metal there with roofing cement. Squeeze it in between the shingles that lie on top of the metal patch.

4. Sheet-Metal Roof, Nails Coming Loose. Winter ice can make these nails pop up. Hammer the nails down, then dab the heads with roofing cement.

5. Flashing Around Chimney and Vent Pipes. Play safe and cover the spots where the flashing and roof join with a new coat of roofing cement. In fact, all areas of the roof that have these metal borders should be coated with roofing cement at the joints. Leaks are prone to spring around their margins.

Coping With Ice Dams. You're likely to be "gifted" with a ghastly ice dam after a heavy snowfall. The dam builds at the edge of the roof (above the eaves). Water gets under the roofing there because the snow on warmer parts of the roof melts, and that water runs down to the colder edge of the roof, where it freezes. More snow will melt, water will pour down, and

it will then back up behind the dam. Now, you not only have an ice dam, you also have water seeping under your shingles and leaking into the house! And woe betide you.

The easy, inexpensive way to solve the problem is good old manual labor. Pull the snow off the edge of the roof after each heavy snowfall. Do this with a hoe or garden rake, and pull it off the *eaves* (to above the wall line; see diagram). Do as little *scraping* as possible—so that you don't pull shingles and nails up as you bring down the snow.

The surefire cure for ice dam leaks is better flashing. Have a roofing contractor put a wide piece of flashing on the roof. This metal roofing extends up the roof six inches beyond the wall line. If an ice dam forms, the water may back up, but the flashing prevents the water from seeping into the house.

ROTISSERIE AND BROILER-ROTISSERIE | portable electric

CAUTION: *Handling any electrical appliance requires care. Play safe and consult Section II,* ELECTRICITY AND WIRING, *p. 257, before you repair your rotisserie or investigate your broken-down broiler.*

Doesn't Heat. First, turn the switch to *off*, unplug the device, then inspect the heating coils. These may be on the sides, top, or bottom of the rotisserie. If there is a break in the heating element or its connection, a new coil will have to be installed. Usually, this means that the appliance must be sent back to the manufacturer.

If the heating element is intact, the rotisserie may not be heating because the plug needs repair. Examine it. If the prongs on the plug are in good condition—not wobbly or damaged—and the cord is intact, spread the plug's prongs a little with your fingers. Doing this may make for a better connection with the wall outlet. Your problem may be solved with this simple repair. If the appliance still won't work, check the *outlet itself,* by plugging a working lamp into the socket. A powerless outlet indicates a blown fuse or electrical failure. (Change the fuse, but first consult the section cited above.) If the outlet still doesn't work when the fuse is changed, the *outlet* should be fixed by an electrician.

Spit Doesn't Turn. If the unit heats but the spit doesn't revolve, there's probably a defect in the motor. Take the rotisserie to an appliance repair shop to be serviced.

RUG

Soiled or Stained. A hooked rug made by your great-grandmother, a priceless Oriental, or *any* valued rug, deserves special treatment from a professional rug cleaner. Home-shampooing is too risky for these treasures. However, you *can* home-shampoo other types of scatter rugs with cleaner that is specially marked for the particular fabric of the rug. We've found that the best results come from using rug shampoo with foam-cleaning action. (For complete details on rug cleaning, see CARPET—SOILED and CARPET—STAINED; also RUG SHAMPOOER.)

Frayed Edges and Worn Spots. When the binding wears away and the rug's border starts coming apart, trim and rebind the edge. (For details on sewing, see Section II, MENDING BY SEWING, p. 276.) If you are eager to have the job finished quickly, repair the damage by ironing on self-stick binding.

(For what to do with worn spots, see CARPET—FRAYED EDGES AND WORN SPOTS.)

Curled Edges. Take the border in hand and roll it in a direction opposite to the way it is curling. Then, steam the edge flat with a steam iron.

Limp. Take the rug to a professional rug cleaner for *sizing.*

Hooked or Braided Rug Coming Apart. Buy some burlap and sew it to the back of the rug to reinforce it. Then, go round and round or back and forth with needle and thread, attaching the backing to the rug. Use thread that matches the color of the rug, and work with a tapestry needle. The smaller the stitches, and the more rows of them you make in this repair, the stronger the rug will be. If you hate to sew, take the rug to the rug man and have him fix it for you.

RUG SHAMPOOER

CAUTION: *Turn to Section II,* ELECTRICITY AND WIRING, *p. 257, before you tackle any repairs on your rug shampooer. The more you know about coping with electrical appliances, the less you risk being shocked by them!*

Handle Coming Loose. Probably the screws that attach the handle to the base of the shampooer need tightening. (See FLOOR SCRUBBER-POLISHER —HANDLE COMES LOOSE.)

Shampoo Doesn't Reach Brushes. Check the plastic tube that feeds the shampoo from the canister to the rotating brushes. If the tube is clogged with dried shampoo or old wax from polishing jobs flush it clean with hot water. (For more details on the canister tube and valve, see FLOOR SCRUBBER-POLISHER—WAX DOESN'T FEED FROM CANISTER TO PADS OR FLOOR.)

Worn Brushes. Buy new ones from the local hardware store or dealer. Extend the life of the brushes by removing them from the shampooer when you put the machine away. (Store them separately.)

Doesn't Start. Make the basic electrical checks:

1. Is the plug firmly set in the wall outlet? If it's loose, take it out and examine it. The prongs may be wobbly or damaged. If they are, and if the wiring leading in and out of the plug is damaged, don't reinsert the plug in the outlet. Repair or replace the plug, but first consult the section cited above. If this wiring repair is too complicated for you, have the repairman do it: an appliance shop or service center will do the job.

2. If there is nothing wrong with the prongs of the shampooer cord plug, spread the prongs a little with your fingers. This should provide a better connection when the plug is inserted in the wall outlet.

3. If the shampooer still doesn't work, check the fuses for this circuit, and test the wall outlet. The fuse may have blown or the outlet may be defective. (Again, consult the section cited above.) You can change the fuse, but don't try to repair the outlet: this is a job for an electrician.

4. If all the above checks have been made, and if you're sure there is no power failure in the area, take the shampooer to the service repair center for an overhauling. Motor trouble or loose connections inside the machine will have to be repaired by an expert.

RUST, CORROSION

Things that can get corroded or rusty are all around you, and many of them are discussed in the pages of this book. Household appliances, fixtures, and fittings are subject to rust and/or corrosion. But did you know that corrosion can occur when *one* kind of metal (say, steel) touches *another* kind of metal (say, aluminum)? And did you know that if you have hard water in your plumbing or heating system it can corrode the pipes that carry the water? It can. Calcium can act on those metal pipes and really do a job of corrosion—making white rust.

The best advice we can give you in this deteriorating situation is: keep your metal surfaces dry. And if you can't keep them *dry*, keep them covered with a paint that protects against this metal-eater. The hardware dealer and plumber—and many other experts—can tell you which protector is best for a particular metal surface. Be guided by them and by the specific instructions in this book. See listings under: ALUMINUM, IRON, STEEL, DOOR/SCREEN, and GUTTER.

SASH CORD

Replacing. See WINDOW.

SCISSORS

Blades Are Dull. To sharpen your scissors blades, the technique you use is slightly different from the one used to sharpen a carving knife. Sharpen only the beveled, *outside* portion of each blade with straight, even strokes on a flat-surfaced stone. (See diagram.) Never try to sharpen scissors or

shears on the insides of the blade. If you do, you'll ruin the cutting edge.

Don't Cut Well. The repair is just a matter of bringing the two blades closer. To do this, tighten the screw that joins the blades with a screwdriver (but not too tight, or the blades won't move).

SCREEN

See DOOR, and WINDOW.

SEPTIC TANK

Full. There's very little you can do once a septic tank has filled, and the drains stop working, except to call the plumber or septic tank company. Have the tank emptied. But you *can* take precautions to prevent the tank from filling too quickly, and to make the system work more efficiently. Save on these otherwise expensive repairs by following these rules:

1. Never throw paper towels, facial tissue, wads of cotton, or tampons into a toilet that drains into a septic tank.

2. Don't use chemical or chlorinated cleaners in basins, sinks, or toilets that drain into a septic tank. They stop the bacterial action needed to keep the tank functioning.

SEWING MACHINE | electric

CAUTION: *Always play safe when you're handling electrical appliances. Consult your owner's manual and our instructions in Section II,* ELECTRICITY AND WIRING, *p. 257, before you make adjustments on a sewing machine.*

The pedal-switch, light, dials, and motor of your sewing machine should be repaired by an expert. Take the appliance to the service center for this. Many new models have added features to make sewing easier, but there are slight variations in the way you handle the different makes of machine. It's important, for this reason, that you use your owner's manual—if you lose it, get another from the dealer.

Needle Broken. Replace it with a new one. Follow the instructions in your owner's manual.

Noisy or Sluggish When Running. Probably the sewing machine needs oil. The old oil may have gotten dust-filled or coagulated, especially if you haven't used the machine recently. First, brush the lint out from under the needle plate. Then, do the same for the feed dog. Wipe the machine clean—use a clean, soft cloth to do this. Then, follow the owner's manual in oiling the machine. *Be sure that you use the oil that comes with the machine.* If you don't have any, buy some at your service center. Wipe the machine again, then sew a few seams on a scrap of cloth, using it to soak up any excess oil. (Don't put good work in the machine until you've done this.) Remember to keep the machine covered when you're not using it so that dust and lint won't clog the works again.

Jamming. Lint and thread that collect in the shuttle can cause this. Follow the instructions in your owner's manual to clean the machine.

Machine Works But Light Doesn't Go On. Turn the machine off, unscrew the light, and take it to your service center. (Never try to replace one of these with an ordinary bulb of the same size.) Insert the new light and go to work.

Machine Doesn't Run. Do some preliminary investigation before you go to the trouble of hauling the machine to the service center, or before you call a repairman to come and fix it. First, is the cord plugged into the outlet? Be sure it is, then try the machine again. Next, follow this routine:

1. Take out the plug that fits into the electric wall outlet. Is it broken? Are the prongs loose? Wiggle them to see if they're damaged. If they are, and if you want to do this repair yourself, consult the section cited above. Replace the plug.

2. If the plug is intact, test the wall outlet. Use a working lamp. If the lamp doesn't light, the trouble is with the *outlet,* not the machine. (So move it away to *another* outlet and *sew away! Don't* try to repair the outlet. Call the electrician and let him do the job.)

3. If the outlet works, check the fuse in the fuse box for this circuit. If it has blown, follow the instructions in the section cited above, then change the fuse. *Note:* If the fuse blows again, there are too many appliances working on this circuit. Move the machine to another outlet which is on *another* circuit, or else turn off some lights and appliances on *this* one before you start the machine. If the fuse is intact and the machine *still* doesn't run, it's time to have an expert investigate and repair it.

SHINGLE

Replacing. See ROOF.

SHOWER

See CERAMIC TILE, DRAIN, and FAUCET.

SHOWER CURTAIN

See BATHROOM ACCESSORIES/SHOWER AND WINDOW CURTAIN.

SHOWER HEAD

Water Holes Clogged. When the little ports clog up it's likely that minerals in the water are to blame. (If you live in a hard-water area the calcium will be deposited on the inside of the shower head, gradually closing up the water ports.) Unclog the ports with a thin wire or darning needle. Poke it through the holes while you stand in the shower. If you want to do a first-rate job, remove the cap, then scrape away the whitish deposits from the inside of the device. And if you plan to replace the shower head, get the self-cleaning type: in this model water comes through little notches around the edge of the disk—not through those cloggable holes.

SIDEWALK

Patching. See CEMENT.

SIDING

Cracks or Splits in Clapboard or Board-and-Batten. These can develop as the wood weathers. Protect horizontal (clapboard) siding or vertical (board-and-batten) siding by keeping an eye out for small splits. Treat them before they enlarge. (This may save you the trouble and expense of replacing a whole board or section of the siding.) To do this, fill small cracks and splits with plastic wood or wood putty. CAUTION: *Plastic wood is extremely flammable. Don't work near a flame, or even a lighted cigarette.* Sandpaper these smooth when the filler dries, then cover the repairs with paint to match the rest of the exterior.

Overlapping Clapboard Badly Split. If the damage is severe, and if a lower section of the clapboard is about to break off, start your repair as soon as a spell of dry weather comes. Use epoxy glue (see Section II, GLUING AND CLAMPING, p. 248). Squeeze this deep into the split, and coat both sides of the split *thoroughly*. To exert pressure on the repair until the epoxy cures, drive a board into the ground, then wedge the top end of the board into the mend. Angle this buttress so that it forces the split sides of the clapboard together. Drive some finishing nails into the lower half of the split. (Drive them at an angle—and only *partway in*. You need to remove these after the glue dries.) Take the nails out, fill the nail holes with plastic wood or wood putty. CAUTION: *Plastic wood is extremely flammable. Don't work near a flame or lighted cigarette.* Sandpaper the area smooth. Sand the mended portion, too. Paint the clapboard to match the rest of the siding.

Leaks Around Trim. Leaks usually start around the windows and doors—where the siding and trim join. The joints may have been caulked when the siding was installed. But caulking can shrink and leave cracks, which weather and water will discover. And if these areas weren't caulked, the siding and trim sometimes can shrink apart, leaving cracks for water to explore. Keep out the weather with this remedy:

1. Remove the old caulking. Scrape out the joint between the trim and siding with a screwdriver or a beer-can opener.

2. Brush out the crack. Use a stiff-bristled brush to do this.

3. Apply a new bead of caulking all around the door or window trim. Be sure to do this on a dry day. Apply the caulk with a caulking gun (see Section II, CAULKING, p. 271). You can buy disposable caulking guns at the hardware store. The caulking compound in these comes in colors to match house paint.

SILVER

Tarnished. Make your silver pieces shine with liquid, cream, or paste polish. Apply according to the instructions on the package, then wipe the silver with a soft cloth. Rinse the surface thoroughly. Dry with a clean, soft cloth.

Badly Tarnished. If your silver is almost black with tarnish, especially if it's *plated* silver, you won't want to scrub away at it to clean it. The job is time-consuming, and when you do this with silver-plated pieces, you're taking down a layer of silver (and getting that much closer to the other metal beneath). We suggest you boil away the tarnish! Here's how:

1. Get out an aluminum pot that's big enough to hold the silver pieces you're detarnishing. Make a solution of baking soda and water—one teaspoon of soda to one pint of water.

2. Put the silver and solution in the pot, bring it to a brisk boil on the stove. And soon, wonder of wonders, the black tarnish will leave the silver and go to the aluminum pot! (You can scour the pot without worrying about its surface.)

Note: If your silver has embossed or etched designs that show up best when the *background* is dark and the *foreground* is light, this is not the cleaning method to use. With the soda-water-aluminum treatment the *whole surface*—background *and* foreground—will be brightly polished, and the design will be less visible.

Dented. Be on guard against dents in your silver pieces. Use and store them with loving care. (Silver is a soft metal and rough handling will mar the surface.) Try to take a small dent out by pressing it with your fingers. And if you're cautious, you can work the dent out with a soft hammer. Wrap the hammerhead in a soft, clean coth, then tap the dent ever so lightly from the wrong side. Rest the bowl or pitcher on a soft padded surface (made with layers of towels).

Note: Don't try to fix any silver pieces this way if they're valuable collector's items. Take them to a jeweler or antique dealer for care and repair.

Broken. If one of your silver knives has come apart, or if there's a hole in a silver pitcher you treasure, take the pieces to the jeweler. He'll solder the silver and banish the blemish.

SINK

See also, DRAIN, FAUCET, and PIPE.

Porcelain Nicked or Scratched. The porcelain finish on the sink or basin is a pleasure to see when its gleaming and smooth, but almost nothing looks as dreary as a sink or basin that's pocked and scarred. To avoid wear and tear on these porcelain finishes, treat them with care:

- *Don't* use harsh abrasive cleansers that will scratch them.
- *Do* make a habit of cleaning the sink with soap or detergent and a sponge.

If you've just chipped the surface of the sink by dropping something heavy and sharp—like a meat cleaver—on it, don't give up hope of fixing it. A special enamel-patching compound, that you buy at the hardware or plumbing supply store, will do the job. Long scratches can be masked with porcelain enamel—buy it where you buy the patching compound. Before you apply either of these to the sink, be sure the surface is *bone dry*. Follow directions on the container.

Porcelain Sink Stained. The common cause here is a drippy faucet. The repair for this sink-stain is fixing that faucet washer! (See FAUCET.) If you can't get the stain out with soap and water, then do a *very light* scrubbing with a very *mild* abrasive cleanser. If this fails, cover the stain with a small rag and soak the rag with laundry bleach. Let this stay on overnight, then wash the area and rinse it. Sometimes you can get the stain up with an old toothbrush and bleach. (Don't let too much bleach go down the drain if you have a septic tank. See SEPTIC TANK.)

Stainless Steel Sink Stained. In spite of its name, stainless steel will sometimes look stained. If you let coffee or tea stand in the sink for several hours, there'll be some temporary discoloration on the sink's surface. You should, the experts say, rinse out the stainless sink once a day (to keep its steely-satin patina).

Note: Discoloration is apt to show up around a sink strainer, where coffee grounds, and other such things, drain before you dump them in the garbage. First, try household bleach (a small amount) on this area. If that doesn't take out the stain, use one of the metal polishes you use on stainless pots and pans. Buy this at a hardware or department store.

SOFA BED | convertible

Won't Close Properly. Convertible sofas are wonderfully convenient when they work, but they'll make you fume when they don't. Be on the alert for minor mechanical breakdowns that foretell larger malfunctions. If you hear a clicking sort of sound—of metal working against metal—when you fold or unfold the bed, small moving parts may be breaking or broken. Look around on the floor and under the bed for small bolts, rivets, nuts, or other metal pieces that may have come loose. Save any of these: they'll be useful when you go to buy replacements for the repairs you may have to do.

Convertible Has Collapsed. This can, and does, happen! Raise the mattress and examine the frame and springs. Look around for the trouble. Most likely, you'll find that it's a rivet or bolt. Sometimes these are sheared (or sliced) off by the other moving metal parts when you open and close the bed. The usual place for the trouble is the so-called *elbow* of the bed frame. It's right where the bed opens *flat* or *folds up double,* and it does most of the tricky mechanical work. You can usually get replacements for damaged metal parts from the manufacturer. Remember: you need to give the bed's serial number (it's stamped somewhere on the frame), and to explain which joint or part is broken. If you have part of a rivet or bolt (or all of it), send this with the other information to the manufacturer. (If all this seems too time-consuming, go to the hardware store with the broken bolt. Find one that will fit the bed frame, but choose the thickest variety, so that there will be maximum strength from the new part.)

It's a somewhat sticky operation to *install* the bolt. You have to get the holes in the frame into matching position, but the tension exerted by the springs on the inner hole will make this difficult. To make the job easier, either unhook the coil springs at this section of the bed, then join the frame together with the bolt, *or* let a C clamp draw the resisting parts together. Insert the bolt. (Hook up the springs—or remove the C clamp.) Remember that this frame joint you're fixing is supposed to bend like an elbow: don't tighten the bolt too much. Leave room for the parts to work back and forth. If you don't, you'll have a hard time opening and closing the bed.

If all this is beyond your coping, get in touch with the manufacturer's representative (you'll find the listing in the phone directory), or call the store where you bought the sofa bed. Either source can probably supply repairmen to put the sofa back into sound working condition.

Springs Sag. The sleeping-comfort of your sofa bed lies chiefly in its inner-spring mattress. But the mattress *itself* is supported by a series of small coiled springs along the sides of the frame which are joined by a wire mesh. If any of the wires break or any of the coil springs stretch out of shape, the mattress will sag. Replace any of the broken parts by contacting the manufacturer's representative (see above). Or, make your own connecting wires for the mesh from pieces of a wire coat-hanger. Follow the pattern of the unbroken pieces to make the new pieces. If the coil spring is stretched, replace it. (You can't fix it.)

Upholstery Damaged. See CHAIR/UPHOLSTERED.

SOFA

See CHAIR/UPHOLSTERED.

STAIR

Unsealed Staircase Creaks. You can decreak the stairs with fairly simple repairs if the stairs are open *underneath,* and if you can get under there. One way to make the stairs quieter is to insert little wedges of wood in the place where the *tread* sits on the *stringer.* (Consult the top diagram below.) Or, again working from underneath the stairs, put screws up through the treads and into the *risers.* If you do this, drill holes *first.* Make

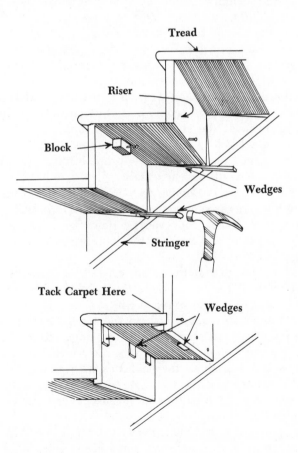

them slightly smaller than the screws. If neither method appeals to you, spray silicone lubricant into the squeak. (Sometimes this will be at the joint—where the risers meet the tread.) Buy the spray at the hardware store.

Sealed Staircase Creaks. Work on the topside of the stairs—because the underside is sealed over with wood or plaster. First, tap the tread along the edge until you come to a place where the sounds are solid rather than hollow. This is where the tread rests on the stringer. Mark this, then drive finishing nails along the edge of the tread and *into* the stringer. Countersink these nails with the tool that's called a *nailset*. Fill these little indentations over the nailheads with plastic wood. CAUTION: *Plastic wood is extremely flammable. Don't work near a flame or a lighted cigarette.* Sandpaper the spots when the plastic wood dries. Then, just crayon over the repair—use a color that matches the finish of the wood on the stairs. You also can squirt silicone lubricant into the squeak, as above.

Carpet Loose. Ordinary carpet tacks are not long enough to anchor stair carpeting. *Buy new tacks that are at least an inch long.* Get them at the hardware store. Tack down the carpet where the stair riser meets the tread. (See bottom diagram, p. 193.) Make this repair as soon as you can—before someone trips or falls down the stairs.

Treads Hollowed by Wear and Tear. If you want to make do with the treads you have, build up the worn spots. Just lay felt building paper in the hollows, then cover the stairs with carpeting. Be sure to tack the building paper down before you put the carpeting over it. If you don't use carpets and want to have the treads properly taken care of, have the carpenter replace the treads with new ones.

Banister Shaky, Balusters Coming Out. Wobbly banisters can throw you off balance when you're coming down the stairs, especially if you lean on them for support. They can even be downright dangerous. But you can mend the balusters and firm up the banisters with a little glue and some elbow grease. Here are the procedures:

1. Put plastic resin glue at the joints where the balusters set into the handrail. Put more of the same where the balusters join the stair tread. (See Section II, GLUING AND CLAMPING, p. 248.)

2. If the balusters are nailed flush to the tread (instead of being set into holes in the tread), renail them with finishing nails as soon as you've glued them. Do this *before* the glue sets. Countersink the nails with a tool called a *nailset*. Fill above the nailheads with plastic wood. CAUTION: *Plastic wood is extremely flammable. Don't work near a flame or a lighted cigarette.* Crayon over the plastic wood (to match the finish on the wood), then shellac over this coloring.

3. If the newel post is wobbly, sooner or later it can shake the whole banister loose. To make it secure, drill some deep-angled holes two inches above the base of the post. Do this on all four sides, and make the holes go down into the tread, if the post is set on it, or on the floor, if the post

sits there. Countersink these with a *larger* drill (for half an inch). (You do this to make the screws fit down deeper.) Next, drive in sturdy 3½-inch screws. Then, fill the holes with plastic wood. CAUTION: *Plastic wood is extremely flammable. Don't work near a flame or a lighted cigarette.* Refinish over these, as above.

STATUE, STATUETTE

See CHINAWARE, IVORY, MARBLE; also Section II, GLUING AND CLAMPING, p. 248.

STEAM IRON

See IRON.

STEEL FURNITURE | painted

Paint Peeling, Rust Spots Showing. "Nonstainless" steel and iron furniture will rust if you don't apply some protective coating. Use paste wax (and polish this), *if you can't duplicate the color or design* on painted metal furniture. If you *can,* do a *real* refurbishing, as outlined below:

1. Sandpaper or steel-wool the flaking paint and rust marks.

2. Buy a rust-resistant metal paint from the hardware store. (This is the undercoat.)

3. Buy a topcoat—preferably a heavy-duty enamel—which matches the color scheme. Apply each paint according to the instructions on the container.

4. Coat the tops of serving and cocktail tables with a waterproof varnish for extra protection from spills and water rings (you won't need to use coasters if you do this). Remember to do painting and varnishing in dry weather and in dust-free surroundings.

STEEL FURNITURE | stainless

Spotted or Dirty. Stainless steel of the legs, arms, or trim on modern furniture is easy to live with because it's easy to clean. When the stainless *does* become spotted or dirty, wipe it clean with a kitchen cleaner-wax, or, if you'd rather, use a few drops of full-strength ammonia. Apply the cleaners with a soft rag, then wipe the steel clean.

STEP | wood, concrete

See also BASEMENT—FLOORS AND WALLS, SMALL CRACKS; CEMENT AND CON-
CRETE—SURFACE SCARRED OR UNEVEN; and Section II, BRICK AND MORTAR:
CLEANING, REPAIRING, AND REPOINTING, p. 273.

Wooden Step, Split or Broken. Replace the board or step. Before you
nail the new piece down, paint the *underside* of it with wood preservative.
Buy this at the hardware store. Use preservatives on the stringer supports,
too. Nail the new board down. Countersink these nails with a tool called
a *nailset*. Fill the dents over the nailheads with plastic wood. CAUTION:
*Plastic wood is extremely flammable. Don't work near flame or a lighted
cigarette.* Paint or stain the step to match the rest of the wood.

Concrete Step, Edge Broken. Have you been stumbling over the edge
of that concrete step? Do you hate the way it looks? The repair is easy
to do if you use the new latex cement. Buy it at the hardware or building
supply store. Clean the chipped edge with a stiff brush, then whisk off
any residue of dust. Mix up the latex compound. (You don't need water—
just follow the instructions on the package.) Mold the mixture to fit the
crack or follow the line of the step. If the cement starts to give way, place
a board along the edge of the step, then remodel the cement within this
wood frame. Remove the wood when the latex repair is firm.

STORM WINDOW

For ways to repair these and other windows, see also WINDOW—WINDOW-
PANE . . . BROKEN.

Note: In some of the new combination units (they're installed with tracks
for window screens and double windowpanes), the glass panel inserts have
to be returned to the dealer when the glass breaks. He will reglaze these
for you. We advise you to check the dealer before you attempt a home
repair if you have double-track metal combination window units.

Cold Air Leaking in from Storm Window. You can caulk or weather-
strip storm windows; for details on types of caulking see Section II, CAULK-
ING, p. 271. See also WEATHER STRIPPING. Some air *should* "leak" from storm
windows. If you leave the bottom portion and a few inches *above* this
unsealed, there's less chance of moisture condensation on the windows.
Experts say you should, therefore, weather-strip or caulk across the *top*
of the storm window, and then carry the seal down each side to six inches
from the sill. This will give the windows a chance to "breathe."

STOVE

See also, RANGE/ELECTRIC, and RANGE/GAS.

STOVE | wood or coal burning

CAUTION: *Smoke from small holes or flames visible through cracks in the sides of your stove are fire hazards. Put out the fire, and don't use the stove until the repairs are made.*

Holes and Cracks in Iron Sides. The Franklin fireplace (originally designed by Benjamin Franklin) and the old-fashioned or modern parlor and kitchen stove, made of sheet or cast iron, are sturdily built and long-lived. Even so, steady service and hot fires can eventually crack this kind of iron. Be sure to check the back and bottom of the stove—where the fire is the hottest. (But do this when the fire's out and the stove is cold!) If you find damage has been done, there are various ways the stove may be made usable again, but the professional (the ironmonger or blacksmith) stresses that these methods are *not always surefire guaranteed* (cracks can recur in the same spot). We suggest that you be guided by the opinion of a stove expert: he'll know if your stove can be repaired.

If the cracks are tiny, and the iron is otherwise in good condition, buy some of the new cement used to repair furnaces. It hardens like steel, and has a silvery finish. When this is dry, coat it with stove black. Buy both products at the hardware store. Follow the directions on the packages.

If the damage to the stove is extensive, the manufacturer can supply you with new panels to replace the damaged ones. These you just bolt into place—after you've removed the old ones, of course. Some of the damaged areas can also be rewelded or *brazed* by the blacksmith, but the repairs may be a bit costly, and, as we've said, they may not last.

Rust and Stains. Don't ignore the rust spots that may occur on the stove. The time to act is when you first see them—so that the rust won't eat deeper into the stove's surface. Steel-wool the rusted areas, then apply stove polish, and the stove will regain its special charm.

STOVEPIPE

CAUTION: Soot accumulation *inside the stovepipe is hazardous. Clean the pipe regularly to avoid the danger of a chimney fire. (For details on this, see* CHIMNEY.) *Holes in the stovepipe are also dangerous. They expose you to noxious fumes and the possibility of a damaging fire. See below for ways to cope with both problems.*

Clogged with Soot. Removing the stovepipe is not hard to do, but unless you're prepared, you can be overwhelmed with soot when you take the pipe out. Remove one end of the pipe—very gently. Cover the end with a garbage bag anchored there with rubber bands or with masking tape. Repeat the process at the other end. Now, take the pipe outdoors. Tap it gently to loosen the soot. The garbage bag will be filled; tie it up and dispose of it. Be sure the pipe is as clean as the proverbial whistle. Polish the outside with stove polish, then reinstall it.

Holes in Pipe. Replace the pipe right away. We suggest you buy a new pipe which is rust-resistant. It's more expensive than the regular, old-fashioned type because its finish is a baked enamel one.

TABLE

See also CARD TABLE.

Scratched, Burned, or Gouged. See Section II, REFINISHING WOOD, p. 301.

Legs Wobbly. Be as kind to yourself and your back as you will be to your table and its legs when you do this repair. Have someone help you with the preliminaries. Select a soft rug, put some clean rags (or plenty of paper) on it, then *with your helper,* turn the table upside down. Now examine the wobbly legs. To fix them, you have to know which of several ways they're attached to the rest of the table. Legs can be attached to the frame (under the tabletop) by gluing, by metal brackets, or by screws and other fasteners. Examine the "patient," then choose the remedy according to the diagnosis.

1. Leg Glued at Joint. (See diagram.) In this case the boards that make the frame are slipped into slots on the inner sides of the legs (as shown). Glue is used to make the joint strong. In addition, wedges of wood in triangular shapes are sometimes glued at the place where the leg and frame join. Take a closer look at the wobbly leg. Has one of the wedges fallen off? If not, is the leg moving back and forth in the frame slot because the glue has turned to dust? Either way, scrape off all the old glue with a small knife (a paring knife will do). Do this in the corner where the wedge was glued, or all around the slot where the leg is fitted. Brush

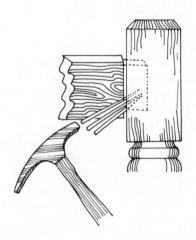

Table   **199**

off the surface and wipe it clean with a rag dipped in a mixture of vinegar and warm water. Wipe dry. Buy some toothpicks or kitchen matches, and some plastic resin (Weldwood) glue at the hardware store. Mix the powdered glue with water (follow the directions on the package; also consult Section II, GLUING AND CLAMPING, p. 248). Next, dip the toothpicks (or whittled matchsticks) into the glue, and push these into the slot to make the joint tight. Push them in as far as they'll go. Cut off the remainders of the toothpicks, so that they're flush with the surrounding wood surfaces. (You'll never know they're there, but they'll make that joint supersnug.) If the wedges have been lost, buy new ones at the lumberyard or building supply store. Give these a thin coat of glue, put another coat of glue into the corner (where the leg and frame join). Clamp the wedges in place (with C clamps) until the glue dries. Tie a rope around the table frame to keep the joint extra-tight, but be sure to protect the table's fancy finish with soft padding when you do this. Leave the table alone until the glue dries.

2. Leg Screwed or Fastened to Frame with Brackets or Bolts. If this is the way the table legs are attached to the frame, then merely tightening these fasteners may work away the wobble. Try this, with a screwdriver or monkey wrench, first, then test the leg. If the screws won't hold, or if they twirl around in the wood without tightening, take them out. Place kitchen matches (break off the heads) into the holes, then insert the screws and drive them in. (Keep filling the screw holes this way until the screws bite into the wood and tighten down.) If the table legs need new brackets, buy the same type at the hardware store.

Leaf Loose. To do any work on the leaf, you'll have to turn the table upside down (as you did for work on the legs, see above). First, look at the screws in the hinges that hold the leaf and the center of the tabletop together. Are they loose? If so, try tightening them. Chances are, though, that the screw *holes* are too big to hold the screws securely. To make the fit snug, take the screws out, fill the holes with matchsticks, as outlined above (item 2).

If the leaf is heavy and keeps coming loose, the problem is not with the screws themselves, but with the *hinges*. The experts say that a sizable table (like a dining table) should have three or more hinges, or, better still, a *piano hinge*—that is, a hinge that runs the entire length of the leaf. When you decide to rehinge the leaf, take extra care with the screws. Be sure that, when you drive them in, they don't burst through the other side of the wood—through the fine, finished surface of the table. (Mark the drill's bit with nail polish: when the bit sinks into the wood to this mark, stop drilling! Or, you can use what the carpenter calls a *stop*—it's like a clamp that fits on the bit and won't let you drill past a given depth.) Drill, screw the hinges to the leaf and to the center section of the table, then you and your helper can turn the table right side up.

Leaf or Top Split. These splits are often the result of wood-shrinkage. (Too much artificial heat in winter can dry the wood and cause it to split.) Below, we outline two ways to make the repair. One of these—in the cabinetmaker's eyes—is purely makeshift. The other is drastic, but experts think it's worth the effort. Take your choice, depending on your skills and the value of the table.

1. Simple Method. Fill the split with plastic wood. CAUTION: *Plastic wood is extremely flammable. Don't work near a flame or a lighted cigarette.* Force in as much wood filler as the split will hold. Sandpaper this smooth, after the filler has dried. Color the mend with a crayon that matches the table's finish. Shellac or varnish over this. (For details, see Section II, REFINISHING WOOD, p. 301.)

2. Cabinetmaker's Choice. There are several stages to this, and some preparations to make for the final one. *Note:* You'll be using clamps and glue for the leaf or the top, so you'll need to have plastic resin glue on hand, and either some lengths of laundry line (for "clamps"), or at least *three* belt clamps (buy these at the hardware store). In addition, you'll need some narrow boards to rest the mend on while the glue is drying, and some wax paper, to cover these boards, so that you don't glue the work to the boards! Now, muster your courage and make the mend.

- a. Cover a soft rug with clear rags and, with your helper, turn the table upside down to rest on it. Take out the hinge screws, take the leaf off. If it's split, see below. If you're going to mend the *center* section of the tabletop, remove the leaf, *then remove the top from the frame.* Do this by unscrewing the screws that hold it, and by gently whacking off the corner chocks glued to the frame on the underside of the table. (Use a padded hammer—that is, a hammer with its head wrapped in clean rags.)

- b. Consider the split. If you're unsure of yourself, just force glue into it, then clamp or tie the edges together as described below. If you're a purist, gently but firmly *complete the split,* so that you have *two separate pieces.* (This is a neater repair, and when it's finished, it should be almost invisible.)

- c. Apply plastic resin glue to both edges to be joined. *Always remember that the thinnest coat of glue makes the strongest and least visible mend.* Let the glue soak into the pores of the wood for a few minutes, then bring the two pieces together.

- d. Place the joined pieces on the wax-paper-covered boards. Tie the three belt clamps around the mend (be sure to pad the edges of the table to protect the finish). Keep the top (or leaf) right side up, so you can wipe off any excess glue that may be squeezed out of the join as the clamps or ropes are gradually tightened. Let the mend dry, then refinish (see Section II, GLUING AND CLAMPING, p. 248, and REFINISHING WOOD, p. 301, for details on these techniques).

Table **201**

Leaf or Top Warped. The experts say that any wood that will warp will also unwarp—which is good news to most of us. To take the warp out of the table leaf or the center section of the top, remove the leaf and/or top as described above, "Leaf or Top Split." Make a framework or stand that will hold the warped section. Put this stand about eight inches above the radiator or hot air duct (if you're doing the repair indoors in the winter). Now, put the warped wood on the stand, concave side up. (See diagram.) Into the troughlike curve of the warped wood, dump clean,

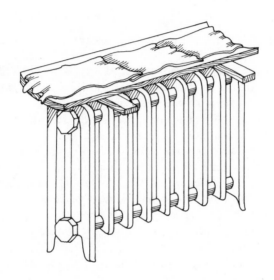

damp rags. Then let nature take its course! And it will: the heat on the underside will dry the wood fibers there, and the moisture on the topside of the wood will expand the fibers there! The result: in a few days, a nice flat tabletop (or leaf). But don't take chances. After the wood is flat, stand the piece on end against the wall. See if the warp stays out of it after it's rested there for a few days. If you've dewarped it for good, refinish *both sides* of the wood—to keep the moisture content on each side the same. (See Section II, REFINISHING WOOD, as cited above.)

Note: In fair weather, you can dewarp wood by using the great outdoors. But reverse the sides: the convex side should be up, so that the sun can dry it, and the concave side should be down, resting on the grass, where it will soak up some moisture. Weight the board down a little, to hasten nature's work. Stand the board on end for a few days, as above, to test the dewarping, then refinish both surfaces, as suggested above.

Marble Tabletop Damaged. See MARBLE.

Veneer Damaged. See VENEER.

TEAPOT

See CHINAWARE and SILVER.

TELEVISION ANTENNA

See ANTENNA.

TELEVISION SET | black-and-white, color

CAUTION: *What goes for any electrical appliance goes double for television sets. Handle them—if at all—with care. Keep away from the electrical connections in the back of the set, even after you've turned the TV off.* Remember that an electric charge may sometimes linger in the picture tube—if you touch any of the works in back, you may get a nasty shock. *Although most TV receivers are equipped with automatic* disconnect *plugs that work when the back of the set is removed, we* emphatically *urge you to keep the protective covering on the back at* all *times.* Leave the internal repairs of the set to the professional. *Always place your TV set so that air circulates behind it, because sets generate heat. If you've observed all these precautions, there are some simple things you can do to fix your set before you send for the repairman.*

Picture Has Double Exposure or Ghosts. The problem is often with the *antenna,* not the set. See ANTENNA.

Set Doesn't Turn On. First, take a close look at the plug. Has it been pulled out of the wall outlet by mistake? If so, plug it in. If nothing happens when you turn the tuning knob on, run through this checklist:

1. Turn the set off, then pull the plug out and examine both the cord and the plug. If the plug is cracked, and if the prongs are loose, don't use the set until the plug is replaced. You can do this yourself by following the directions in Section II, ELECTRICITY AND WIRING, p. 257. (If you don't trust yourself with this repair, have the electrician or TV repairman do it.)

2. If the cord and plug are not damaged, spread the prongs with your fingers—*just a little*—to get a better electrical connection. Plug the cord into the outlet. If the set *still* doesn't go on, take the plug out again.

3. Test the wall outlet you've been using by plugging in a working lamp. If the lamp doesn't go on, the outlet is faulty, and you should have an electrician do the repair work on it. Until he does, move the TV set to another outlet and plug it in. If the lamp *does* light, you know the problem is in your TV set or in its connections. Make one final test before you call the repairman.

4. If your set has a *tuning knob,* which turns but doesn't get results, the knob may simply be loose. Tighten the set screw on the side of the tuning knob. Do this with a small screwdriver. Now, turn the knob and if you *still* don't get sound and picture, call the repairman.

TERMITE

See Section II, PEST CONTROL, p. 307.

TERRA-COTTA

See CHINAWARE.

THERMOSTAT

See FURNACE.

TILE

See ACOUSTICAL TILE, CERAMIC TILE, and FLOOR TILE.

TOASTER | electric

CAUTION: *Handling any electrical appliance requires care. Play safe, and consult the procedures in Section II,* ELECTRICITY AND WIRING, *p. 257, before you tamper with your toaster.* Remember that the toaster's wires get red-hot when it's in use: never try to pull up toast that's stuck down in it with a fork, knife, or any metal implement. You're likely to get the shock of your life, if you do. *And because the wires of the toaster are exposed, be sure that you use the appliance far away from water that could splash it or flood it. Don't let your children play with the toaster, and tell them* never to put buttered bread into the toaster! (*Strange as it seems, children do this, thinking it's a shortcut to making buttered toast. It won't do that, but this* is *the speedy way to set the toaster, and perhaps something else, on fire.*)

Toaster Has Bad Odor. Disconnect the toaster and open the crumb tray— the metal panel on the bottom of the toaster. If there are lots of burned-on bread crumbs on it, scrub it with a scouring pad. Rinse the tray and *dry it super carefully!*

Smokes When You Use It. Crumbs or stray raisins are very likely sticking to the heating element (that is, the little wires that get red-hot). Turn the toaster off, *unplug it,* then open the crumb tray. With a clean paintbrush, gently whisk the incinerated raisins and anything else off the wires of the heating element. Wipe up the crumbs once they're loosened.

Doesn't Heat Up, Doesn't Make Toast. The toaster may not be faulty. First, be sure that the cord is plugged into the outlet. Then make these checks:

1. Is the plug firmly set in the wall outlet? If it's loose, take it out and examine it. Are the prongs wobbly or damaged? If they are, and if the wiring leading in and out of the plug is damaged, too, don't reinsert the plug in the outlet. (Repair or replace the plug, but first consult the section cited above. If this repair is too complicated for you, have the repairman do it: an appliance repair shop or the service center will do the job.) If there's nothing wrong with the prongs of the toaster's cord plug, spread the prongs a little with your fingers. (This may provide a better connection when you insert the plug into the wall outlet.)

2. If the toaster *still* doesn't work, check its circuit fuses, then test the wall outlet. The fuse may have blown or the outlet may be defective. (Again, consult Section II, as cited above. You can change the fuse, but don't try to fix the outlet: that is a job for an electrician.)

3. If all the above checks have been made, and if you're sure there is no power failure in your area that may have caused the toaster's breakdown, take the appliance to a service center for repair.

Toast Doesn't Pop Up or Go Down. When the toaster won't pop the toast up or take it down inside, there's something wrong with the latching mechanism. To fix this, the toaster will have to be taken apart. Take it to the expert at a service repair center.

TOILET

Even though you loathe the thought of doing toilet repairs, the time may come when—instead of being at the mercy of the plumber's schedule—you'll be glad you can cope with them yourself. To arm yourself against a possible "sea of troubles," have both a plumber's helper (rubber plunger) with a 2-foot-long stick and a toilet auger at hand. Buy them at the hardware store. If the toilet has a *flush tank,* examine the diagram below, then do a "field study" of the various valves and clever devices *inside* the tank. Get to know how these work in the several phases of their *normal* activity. (If the toilet has a *flushometer,* see the lone but simple remedy below.) To keep the whole sanitary-sewer-toilet-system functioning properly, read our section, SEPTIC TANK. If you do all this, *and* familiarize yourself with the items below, you'll be ready for minor and even major malfunctions, when they occur. And you'll be able to do something more helpful than tear your hair, waiting for someone else to do the repair.

Drains Slowly. You'll need the plumber's helper for this chore. See DRAIN—TOILET DRAINS SLOWLY.

Water on Outside of Tank Dripping onto Floor. Don't jump to the conclusion that the flush tank is leaking. If the bathroom is warm and the water supply to the toilet tank is cold, there is bound to be *sweat* on the tank surface (that is, condensation of the moist air in the room on the cold tank). Cope with this in one of four ways.

1. With a Terry Cloth Tank Jacket. Buy a new tank jacket made of stretch terry cloth (you can probably match the color of your towels). Department stores carry them. Slip the jacket over the *outside* of the tank.

2. With a Pan to Catch the Drips. Buy one at the store, and fit it under the tank.

3. With a Tank Liner. Empty the flush tank by turning off the water supply to it (usually the cold and hot water valves are near the toilet, just

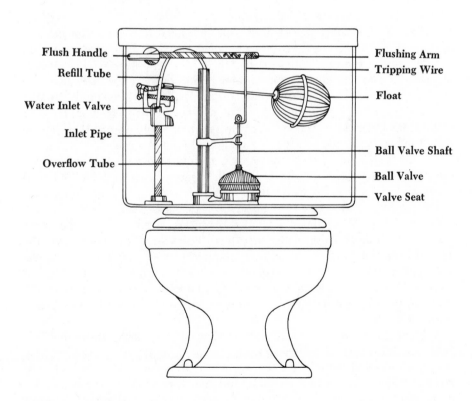

Flush Handle

Refill Tube

Water Inlet Valve

Inlet Pipe

Overflow Tube

Flushing Arm

Tripping Wire

Float

Ball Valve Shaft

Ball Valve

Valve Seat

above the floor; turn the cold one off). Next, flush the toilet. Then, clean and dry the inside walls of the tank. Buy some Styrofoam plastic sheets and some waterproof glue at the hardware store. (For details on glues, see Section II, GLUING AND CLAMPING, p. 248.) Cut the plastic sheets into pieces that exactly fit the interior walls of your tank, then spread the glue on the sheets. Apply the sheets the way you'd apply wallpaper. This liner will insulate the tank so that its outside surface will be less chilly, closer to the room temperature. Liner kits are also available. (Remember to turn the water supply to the tank back on when you're through.)

4. Change the Water Supply. If none of these remedies appeals to you, have the plumber take over. He can attach a hot-water pipe to the flush tank's water supply, to make a mix of cold and hot water in the tank. This repair will stop the tank from sweating for good.

Water Keeps Running into Toilet Bowl (Wasting Water and Making Annoying Sound). This can be caused by minor maladjustments of the devices within the tank. Study the diagram on p. 205 and check off the items below until you find the one that stops the water running. The first step is to take the top of the tank off, but do this gently, because the top is porcelain and breakable. Then proceed with your examination. Discover which of these is the cause:

1. Tank Ball Trouble. Get a flashlight, and shine it down to the bottom or floor of the tank. You'll see what's called the *tank ball* or *stopper ball* down there—it's the gadget that "corks" the tank after a flushing. If it doesn't fit properly into the hole at the bottom of the tank, water will leak into the pipe that supplies the toilet bowl. If the ball misses its mark, look at the stem or wire sticking up from the top of the ball. Is it straight or bent? If it's bent, this is the cause of the trouble. Straighten it, then let the ball drop back to a snug corking fit. And listen to the silence!

2. Tank Ball Damaged. If the stem that holds the tank ball is straight, the trouble may be with the ball itself. Reach down and feel it. Is it squishy? Are there holes in it? If so, replace it. Buy two extra tank balls at the hardware store (it's nice to have a spare around the house in case you have to do the repair on a Sunday, or in the evening, when the stores are closed). Turn off the water supply to the toilet at the valve near the floor. Flush the toilet to empty the tank. Unscrew the stem from the old stopper ball and screw the new one onto it. Then, clean the edge of the hole in the bottom of the tank by rubbing it with steel wool. This should give the tank a neater, surer corking-up. Turn on the water supply and enjoy the quiet.

3. Float Rod Bent. There's another ball in the tank, near the top. This one helps turn off the water supply to the tank by gradually rising with the incoming water until it reaches a certain level. At this level, the floating ball forces a valve to close, and the water supply is cut off. But if the float doesn't rise high enough to make this little door close, water

will keep running (into the overflow tube, and thence down into the toilet). Raise the float ball by hand, and see if the water stops running. If it does, just bend the float's rod *downward* to make the float rise higher. If this doesn't shut off the water supply valve, try the next repair.

4. Float Ball Damaged. The float ball may be so old that it doesn't float at all. Take a look at it; if it's damaged, buy a new one at the plumbing supply or hardware store. Unscrew the old one and take it with you when you buy the new one.

5. Intake Valve Needs Fixing. If raising the float by hand doesn't shut off the water supply (by closing the valve), then the valve is not working. Call the plumber and have him do this repair.

Flushometer Stuck, Toilet Keeps Flushing. To save water and to stop the constant din, turn off the water supply to the toilet. The supply valve is near the toilet, usually just above the floor. After this, call the plumber.

Toilet Overflows. The drain is clogged. First, try unclogging it with the plumber's helper, as suggested above, and if this doesn't work, reach for the auger. See DRAIN—TOILET CONTINUES CLOGGED AFTER WORKOUT WITH PLUNGER.

Tiny Cracks in Porcelain (Bowl, Tank, Tank Top). Hairline cracks that appear on any of the toilet's porcelain surfaces can be filled with epoxy glue (see Section II, GLUING AND CLAMPING, p. 248). Turn the water supply off at the valve near the floor, then empty the tank or bowl by flushing the toilet. Dry the surface you're going to fill, then force as much glue as possible into both sides of the crack. Let the glue dry before you fill the bowl or tank with water again.

Break in Porcelain Bowl. If you drop a heavy jar of skin cream into the toilet and it shatters the side of the bowl, woe to you. The whole bowl will have to be replaced. Call the plumber. Keep the lid down the next time you put face cream on!

TOOL

See Section II, GLOSSARY OF TOOLS, p. 225.

TOY

The most useful material for repairing toys is glue. For details on types you should use, see Section II, GLUING AND CLAMPING, p. 248.

Molded Plastic Toy—Broken. Use plastic cement. First, coat the edges of the break. Tape the parts together so that the glue can cure, overnight, then remove the tape. If the plastic is thin, it may then need reinforcement. Do this with a piece of polyvinyl (plastic) sheeting. Buy some at the hardware store if you don't have any scraps around the house. Cut the plastic patch wide enough so that it covers the break, and overlaps it, too. After you've glued, as above, cement the plastic to the back of the break.

Wooden Toy—Split or Broken. The damage can be mended with contact cement—which requires no clamping. Follow directions on the container.

Steel Toy—Broken. Clean both edges of the break and apply epoxy glue to them. Tape the parts together until the epoxy dries. Follow the directions on the container for drying time and handling.

All Materials—Parts Missing. Keep a box of usable parts salvaged from any broken toys you discard. Toy stores and hobby shops carry repair kits which have spare parts if you don't have the right ones for the job.

TRAY

Dented. Work out the dent in any metal tray (brass, copper, tin) by following the instructions given in ALUMINUM POT AND PAN—SIDES . . . DENTED. If, however, your tray is silver, see SILVER—DENTED.

Cracked or Broken. The break in the rim or bottom of your metal tray should be soldered by a metal craftsman, or, if it's a valuable piece, worked on by a restorer of antiques. You can find listings for each of these experts in the yellow pages of your phone directory. To repair a lacquer tray, see LACQUER WARE—BROKEN.

For other problems with trays made of these materials, see BRASS, LACQUER WARE, SILVER, and Section II, REFINISHING WOOD, p. 301.

VACUUM CLEANER

Won't Pick Up Lint or Dust. If your vacuum cleaner is doing a slovenly job—threads on the carpet don't come up, and the cat hair clings to a favorite chair—you know there's something wrong (but, if you're like the rest of us, you're not sure *what*). The several possibilities follow:

1. Dust Bag Problems. If the dust bag is full, change it or empty it. But if it's *not full,* and you've been using the vacuum to pick up fine particles— plaster dust or ashes from the fireplace—the air holes or pores in the bag can get clogged. If they *are,* the vacuum doesn't function as a *vacuum!* (Air must flow through the bag for the whole machine to work properly.) Change the bag, and be sure it's securely attached when you insert it.

Note: Don't reuse disposable bags—their pores are probably clogged after the first complete filling.

2. Tube (or *Wand*), Hose, or Attachment Problems. Any one of these parts can be blocked by something you've tried to vacuum up that gets

firmly lodged in the tubes, hoses, or pipes before it lands in the vacuum bag (where it belongs). Do some detecting to solve the problem. Start by exploring the attachments. Begin with the one (for obvious reasons) that you're *using!* Disconnect this part from the tube, and look at its neck portion. Are there fibers, twigs, and other obstructions, clogged with dust here? Clean the part out with a wire—a wire coat-hanger that you've straightened is dandy for this chore. If nothing's choking the neck of the attachment, try to look through the tube (*wand* is the appliance dealer's name for it). If there's something there, poke a broom or mop handle up through the tube—with luck it will *move.* If the obstruction isn't in this part of the works, try the flexible hose. (The *first* part of the hose isn't flexible and is curved, so here use the wire coat-hanger as a prod.) If you think the hose holds the source of the trouble, find a small wooden ball or steel ball bearing (from toys or games). Drop the ball down one end of the tube, then shake the tube furiously! The weight of the ball should dislodge the obstruction—both will tumble out. If nothing happens to free the lump in the middle of the hose, turn the hose upside down and let the ball fall out. Then, drop it down the *other* end. Shake furiously again. If still nothing comes of all this urgent activity, take the hose to the local service center and have someone there do the dislodging for you.

3. Filter Problems. Almost all vacuum cleaners have a second filter (that is, a filter slightly different from the dust bag, but a filter nonetheless). This additional filter is there to keep dust from leaking into the motor. Consult the owner's manual on the care and handling of this filter. *Note:* Some are made of paper, some of cloth, and some of plastic. *If yours is the washable variety, wash it, but don't reinstall it or run the vacuum until the filter is dry!* You may shock yourself and the vacuum if you do.

4. Beater Brush Problems. Upright vacuums with rug beaters, and canister types with beater attachments, are subject, sooner or later, to bristle fatigue. If the bristles on the beater are worn so that they don't sweep the carpet surface, lower the beater roller by ⅛ inch, if there's a gadget on your machines that lets you do this. If lowering the beater doesn't solve the problem, or you can't lower it, take the vacuum cleaner to the service center. Have the roller replaced. If the roller is jammed with threads and isn't rotating the way it should, pull off the threads and any other trouble-makers until you can get the roller to turn easily by hand. *Note:* If the roller isn't working at *all,* the drive belt may be broken. And though the wheels in the motor are turning, they can't turn the roller without the drive belt. Have the belt replaced at the service center or by a repairman.

Won't Start. Check the cord and plug for breaks and other damage. If you find any, disconnect the plug from the wall outlet immediately. (You can blow a fuse, if you don't.) Fix the cord, if you think you're handy, but see Section II, ELECTRICITY AND WIRING. p. 257 first. If you're not up to this repair, have the repairman at the service center or an electrician do it for you.

If the prongs in the cord plug are bent, try spreading them a little with your fingers. Doing so may make a better electrical connection when the plug is inserted in the outlet. If you *still* don't hear the happy hum of the vacuum when you flip the switch—try plugging the vacuum into another wall outlet. (The outlet you've been using may be faulty, but repairing it is a job for the electrician.) And if the outlet isn't the problem, check the fuse *for this circuit* in the fuse box. It may have blown. You can change the fuse, but don't before you consult the procedures in Section II, as cited above.

Overheats or Gives Off Oily Odors. Have the motor overhauled by the service center expert or by the repairman. Don't wait until the vacuum blows a fuse or catches fire. It can do either. *Beware.*

VALVE

Leaking. See FAUCET.

VENEER

Curling Up and Coming Loose. The veneer on old tables and antique furniture is more than a little vulnerable to dampness. When you see the surface wood loosen and curl, remember that there are ways to cope with the damage. Raise the loosened veneer a little (*but gently* so as not to break it!). Then scrape out the old glue under it—on the veneer and on the surface beneath. Blow out the dust. Reglue the veneer with plastic resin cement. Smooth the veneer down, wipe off any excess glue. If you've made the repair on a *horizontal* surface, cover the mend with wax paper, then weight the area down with books until the glue cures. If you've repaired veneer on the *vertical* side of a piece of furniture, cover a *dry* plastic sponge with wax paper, then tape it (or tie it) tightly over the repair. Let the glue dry overnight.

Bubbles or Blisters. Be bold and slit the blister with a razor blade—through its middle, *along the grain of the wood.* Press one side of the veneer down, then squeeze plastic resin glue under the other, *raised* side of the blister. Next, smooth this down, and squeeze glue under the second side. Press this down, then wipe up any excess glue. Weight the mend down as above.

Badly Damaged, Pieces Missing. Did you know that you can buy new veneer to match the damaged pieces? You can, at the hardware or wood-working shop. Get enough for the job and some to spare—in case you have trouble doing the repair the first time around. To make this patch first remove the damaged veneer. Woodworkers say that when you inlay or patch wood, you should do it *diagonally across the grain, not straight across it.* (See diagram opposite.) Diagonal cuts are harder to detect than

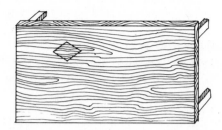

a right-angled one. Thus guided, you have a choice of patch patterns, according to the shape and extent of the damage. With a razor blade or sharp knife, cut out a diamond-shaped piece. The damage should be in the center of it. *Or,* cut out a rectangle, with a peak on the top and bottom, as shown. Then use a chisel (bevel edge down) to scrape up the old veneer. Don't gouge the wood beneath it. After this, use a razor blade to scrape up the old glue. Make a pattern for the patch or inlay. Do this by taping onionskin or tracing paper over the area to be patched and making a rubbing of the edge of the repair with a pencil. Trim the paper with scissors, and test it in the spot you're mending. When it fits *exactly,* cut the new veneer to conform to the paper pattern. Glue the patch with plastic resin cement. Smooth it down, then wipe off any excess glue. Weight the mend down as described above ("Curling Up and Coming Loose").

VENT

See FAN, or FURNACE—DOESN'T GIVE ENOUGH HEAT.

VENETIAN BLIND

See BLIND/VENETIAN.

WAFFLE IRON

CAUTION: *Handling any electrical appliance requires care. Don't try to fix your waffle iron until you consult the safety procedures in Section II,* ELECTRICITY AND WIRING, p. 257.

Waffles Stick. Disconnect the waffle iron. Then, use a scouring pad to clean any leftover burned waffles off the grill. Wipe the grill with a wet cloth or sponge, but don't rinse it under running water. (There's a chance that moisture might get into the electrical wiring.)

Brush cooking oil over the grill with a basting brush (use a paper towel to absorb the excess oil). Heat griddle, and you should have nonstick waffles!

Wipe the grill surface with paper towels to keep it clean. It's best to avoid further use of harsh detergents or scouring pads on the iron.

Doesn't Heat. Don't assume the waffle iron is the problem, until you make the following electrical checks:

1. Is the plug firmly set in the wall outlet? If it's loose, take it out and examine it. The prongs may be wobbly or damaged. If they are, and if the wiring leading in and out of the plug is damaged, don't reinsert the plug in the outlet. Repair or replace the plug, but first consult the section cited above. If this repair is too complicated for you, have the repairman do it: an appliance repair shop or the service center will do the job.

2. If there is nothing wrong with the prongs of the waffle iron's cord plug, spread the prongs just a little with your fingers. This should make a better connection when you insert the plug into the wall outlet.

3. If the waffle maker *still* doesn't work, check its circuit fuse and test the wall outlet. The fuse may have blown or the outlet may be defective. (Again, consult Section II, as cited above.) You can change the fuse, but *don't* try to fix the outlet: that is a job for an electrician.

4. If all the above checks have been made, and if you're sure there is no power failure in the area that may have caused the waffle iron's breakdown, take the appliance to a service center for repair.

WALL | indoor

See also BASEMENT—FLOORS AND WALLS, SMALL CRACKS, and CERAMIC TILE. See also Section II, BRICK AND MORTAR: CLEANING, REPAIRING, AND REPOINTING, p. 273.

Wall Wet, Discolored. Check for the leak that has caused the trouble. See ATTIC, PIPE, ROOF, and SIDING. After you've tackled the trouble, repair the wall surface as indicated below.

Plaster Wall—Damaged. See CEILING.

Plasterboard—Cracks and Small Holes. Small holes in plasterboard are repaired the way holes in plaster are repaired. See CEILING.

Plasterboard—Large Holes. If a large hole has been punched in your plasterboard wall, use a brand new piece or section of board for the repair. (Plasterboard usually comes in four-foot widths. Have the building supply store cut a piece long enough to fill the area. Be sure the new board is the same thickness as the old—take a piece of your old board with you when you buy the new section.) To make the mend, score above or beneath the hole with a sharp knife—in a straight line. (Cut *above* the hole if the damage is *near the floor,* and *below* the hole if the damage is *near the ceiling.*) Next, cut along the vertical edges of the old section of board. (Do this where the old section joins the sections on either side of it.) Break out the old plasterboard, then pry up the nailed edges. Nail the new piece in place. Fill the channels around the edges of the new piece with joint compound. (Buy it at the building supply store.) Cover this with a perforated tape that's sold with the compound. *Spot* nailheads (that is, cover them) with the compound. Follow directions on the box of compound when you smooth out the joint. Make the seal broad and even.

Other Wallboards, Including Cellotex. Replace sections of these panels as above. Seal the joints as above.

Wood Paneling. Fill the holes and gouges in wood paneling with plastic wood. CAUTION: *Plastic wood is extremely flammable. Don't work near a flame or a lighted cigarette.* Add the color (to match the rest of the wall) either to the plastic wood, or later, with a crayon. (Mix a wood stain in the plastic wood, coat the hole or gouge, let it dry. Sandpaper the mend, and you're done. If you prefer to apply the color *afterward,* fill the hole, let dry, then sandpaper. Crayon over the patch, then shellac the surface.) See also Section II, REFINISHING WOOD, p. 301.

WALLPAPER

Bubbles. Get rid of air bubbles in your wallpaper by slitting them with a razor blade. Then soak the area with water. Use an eyedropper to work paste underneath the slitted paper. With a clean, damp cloth, press the wall covering back into place. You can trim the edges, but it's all right to let them overlap.

Holes or Tears. If you have saved some leftover wallpaper, a hole or tear will be easy to patch. Remove the damaged section with a razor blade. Cut out a patch of wallpaper that matches the torn area, but make it slightly larger. The repair will be less noticeable if you trim the edges of the patch *unevenly.*

Then, apply a thin coat of wallpaper paste to the back of the patch, and position it in a way that makes it fit into the pattern on the wall. Use a damp cloth to smooth down the area.

Soiled. Many wallpapers are washable (clean them by wiping the surface with a soft sponge dipped in a solution of mild detergent and cool water). But before you begin to wash the paper, vacuum it. After this, test-wash a spot that is not conspicuous—try a small place behind the couch. If the colors don't run, begin to wash the wall by moving your arm in a circular motion. Clean a two-foot-by-two-foot area, and then move on.

Work this way until the entire wall has been scrubbed. Use very little water for the job—*don't soak the wall!* (Some papers will come unstuck with too much water.)

Note: There are special compounds available for cleaning nonwashable papers and for removing grease stains. Ask a wallpaper dealer to advise you, and follow the manufacturer's instructions on the cleaning compound's container. (When you notice only fingerprints, take them off with a *gum eraser* that can be purchased at an art supply store.)

WASHER, CLOTHES | electric

CAUTION: *Like other major appliances, automatic washers are complicated electrical devices, and, as such, should be handled gingerly if you notice anything wrong. Play safe and follow the procedures in Section II,* ELECTRICITY AND WIRING, *p. 257, before you give your balky washer a working over. If you heed the procedures and check the list below, you may be able to bring life back to the machine—without relying on the repairman for elementary repairs. And you'll be able to give him a better idea of what's wrong with the washer—if you know the significance of the symptoms we discuss.*

Clothes Come Out Grayish. The water temperature may be too low for white cottons and linens. Run some water from the hot-water tap to check the temperature, then turn up the temperature gauge on the hot-water heater. See WATER HEATER.

If the water is hot, check the owner's manual to be sure you're using the right amount of soap or detergent for the fabric.

Motor Runs But Machine Doesn't Spin. Check to be sure that the lid is properly closed. Close it firmly. (The washer won't spin until the lid is closed tight.)

Doesn't Drain. Check the drain hose to be sure that it isn't twisted or kinked up. If it is, straighten it. (If the washer still won't drain, call the repairman.)

Doesn't Fill. Check the hot and cold water faucets to which the washer's hoses are connected. Are both faucets on? If they aren't, double-check to be sure that the house water supply is working.

If the water supply *is* working and the faucets *are* on, watch the washer. Does it seem to lose water during the wash and drain cycles? If so, the hose may have been attached to a drainpipe that's too low. (This will often cause the water to be siphoned off, down the drain.) *Note:* The standpipe drain usually should be at least thirty inches high. If it isn't, have the plumber fix it for you.

Wash Is Too Sudsy. Consult the owner's manual. Are you using the correct amount of detergent or soap? (The amount of suds, by the way, is not necessarily an indication of the cleaning power of the detergent.) Use the low-sudsing variety and *don't be lavish* with the amount you feed the machine.

Machine Shakes, Rattles, Is Noisy. Take a look at the machine. Is it securely mounted, or does it jiggle around? (If it does, have the serviceman give it a firmer anchoring.) If the mounting seems to be strong enough, open the machine up. Are the clothes all bunched up? If the wash isn't well-balanced during the spin cycle, the machine may shake or vibrate. When this happens, the machine will turn off. Distribute the wash evenly, then start the washer again. If the machine is *still* noisy, and you hear rattling sounds, you may have to unload the wash and dig around for a button or pin or penny that's being spun around in the washer.

Doesn't Start. Are the controls properly set? Be sure that you haven't set the machine for a soak cycle, by mistake, when you expect it to *wash*. If you've set it correctly, run down this list:

1. Are both hot and cold water faucets (connected to the hose) turned on? If not, turn them on.

2. Is the electric cord plugged into the wall outlet? (If not, plug it in and try the machine.) If it is plugged in, turn off the machine, unplug the cord, then look at the plug and cord. Are they damaged? *If they are, don't reinsert the plug. Have the electrician or serviceman repair these before you use the machine again.*

3. If the cord and plug are in good condition, reinsert the plug. Now, check the fuse for this circuit in the fuse box. Has the fuse blown? If it has, you can change it, but not before you consult Section II, as cited above. *Note:* If the fuse blows a second time, it's possible there are too many electrical appliances and lights working on this circuit. Experts say that *ideally* your washer should have its *very own circuit*—with nothing else sharing the current. If this isn't practical, then turn off other lights and appliances when you run the washer. If the fuse blows when you do *this*, then there's trouble in the machine or in the wiring to it, and that's a job for the expert. Call the repairman, and take your clothes to the sink or to the laundromat for the time being.

4. If there's nothing the matter with the fuse, but the machine won't work, check the wall outlet. Just plug a working lamp into it. *If the lamp goes on, you know the trouble is in the machine.* Now call your friendly repairman. You have ample reason to ask for his help.

WATER HEATER | electric

CAUTION: *Handling any electrical appliance requires care. Play safe and follow the procedures in Section II,* ELECTRICITY AND WIRING, *p. 257, before you work with your water heater.*

Water Too Hot or Too Cold. Find the temperature regulator. Often this is under a plate screwed to the side of the heater. To get at it, use a screwdriver. Remove the screws, then set the temperature. If the temperature still doesn't go high enough (or low enough) to suit you, call the serviceman and have him regulate the heater.

No Hot Water. Check the fuse for the circuit the heater uses. Change it if it has blown, but first read Section II, as cited above. If there's nothing wrong with the fuse, and you *still* have no hot water, call the serviceman. (And if you change the fuse after it's blown, and it blows *again*, don't insert another. Call the serviceman.)

WATER HEATER | gas

CAUTION: *If there's a strong odor of gas around the heater, get your family out of the house and call the police first; then call the gas company.*

Water Too Hot or Too Cold. Check the thermostat which regulates the temperature of the water. If it has a gauge on it, reset this to the desired temperature. Otherwise, call a serviceman.

Pilot Light Out. If you feel you're wise enough in the ways of pilot lights, read the instructions on the tag or plate attached to the heater, then light the pilot. But, if you have *any* doubts about doing this, call the serviceman. Have him do it for you. (This is a trickier operation than lighting the pilot on your stove. *Don't experiment.*)

WEATHER STRIPPING

Worn, or Lets in Cold Air. Certain types of weather stripping are prone to wear out in time (especially the older type, made of felt and a strip of metal). Replace old weather stripping with new. If it's not worn, renail the old weather stripping closer to the door or window frame. This way it closes the cracks that let the cold air in.

If pieces of foam rubber stripping have become unglued, reglue them with contact cement (see Section II, GLUING AND CLAMPING, p. 248).

WINDOW

Sticks, Hard to Open. If your house has just been painted—inside or out, or both—chances are that the windows are stuck. To unstick them, follow this procedure:

1. Casement Windows. Force the window open, then scrape or sandpaper the paint bumps on the edge of the window *stop* molding (where

the molding touches the window itself). Also, sandpaper all the edges of the window. If your window is closed and opened by a metal cranking mechanism, spray silicone lubricant on the gear—the moving part, that is.

2. Double-Hung Windows. Break the window free of paint by running a thin *putty* knife between the window sash and the *stop* molding. Then, raise the *lower* sash, scrape the paint bumps from the inner edge of the *stop* molding. Sandpaper this smooth. Spray the track in which the window moves with silicone lubricant. Buy it at the hardware store. Lower the top sash, and repeat the process.

Window Drafty. There are many new types of cushioned weather stripping that will end most draft problems for *almost* all windows. Buy these at

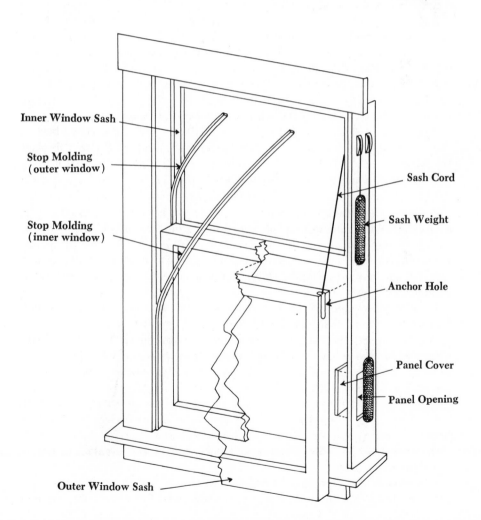

the hardware or building supply store, then simply nail or glue the stripping along the frame. Be sure the stripping *just touches* the window, yet doesn't impede its movements. *Note:* Permanent metal stripping with a spring edge can be installed in the window tracks, but the work is finicky, the job probably should be done by a professional.

Water Leaks in at Top or Sides. See SIDING, and ROOF.

Sash Cord Broken. This repair calls for some carpentry, so be prepared. If you don't want to call in a carpenter for the chore, do as follows (see diagram on p. 217):

1. Remove the *stop* molding on the inside of the window and on the side where the cord is broken. (See diagram on p. 217.) Pry it up—gently—with a wood chisel until all the nails are freed.

2. Swing *that* side of the sash into the room. Prop it up away from the side you're working on. (This will expose the panel cover behind which the sash weights rest. See diagram.)

3. Take off the panel cover by removing the screws that hold it. Behind this opening you'll find the sash weight.

4. Replace the broken cord with a metal chain. Buy it at the hardware or building supply store. Lower the chain over the pulley at the top of the sash channel *down to* the sash weight. Attach the dangling end to the weight, then pull the weight *up to* the pulley. Attach the other end to the top of the window sash (it goes in the hole designed for it). Replace the window sash in the channel. Renail the *stop* molding along it. Fill the nail holes with plastic wood, then repaint the molding. CAUTION: *Plastic wood is extremely flammable. Don't work near flame or a lighted cigarette.*

Windowpane Cracked or Broken. If the pane is cracked, you can keep it from breaking and falling out by gluing along the crack. Though you may hate the way this repair looks, it will, at least, give you protection from the weather until the cracked pane is replaced. Apply some household cement along the crack, inside and out. The repair is actually strong enough to last for years.

If the windowpane is broken and about to fall out, you'll want to replace it as soon as you possibly can. Here's how (see diagram opposite):

Window Sash. Pull out the broken glass with pliers, but wear heavy gloves when you remove the larger pieces. (Keep a cardboard box nearby so that you can dispose of the glass shards as you remove them.) Then, proceed, as follows:

1. Remove Old Putty. Take a small chisel and use it to cut out the old putty. Try not to gouge the wood of the sash while you're doing this. Also, "tick out" the triangular glazier's points that are embedded in the putty. Put a corner of the chisel blade under one point of the triangle, then give the chisel a twist.

2. Measure the Opening. Have the glazier or hardware dealer cut a piece of glass of the same thickness as the old pane. But remember: the new

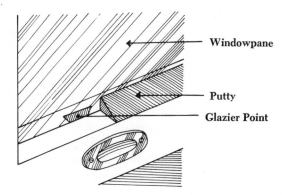

pane should be cut ⅛ inch smaller on each side than the opening. (Make accurate measurements or you'll have trouble later.) Before you place the glass in the opening, spread a thin coat of putty on the back groove of the wood against which the glass rests. Press the glass into place. With a screwdriver, drive the triangular glazier's points into the sash. They hold the glass in place. For small panes use two on each side. For larger panes use four.

3. Putty the Pane. Now you're ready to apply yourself to the art of puttying. Use regular putty or plastic putty—you can get both at the hardware store. Take a lump of putty out of the can and roll it into a half-inch strand. Start at one corner of the window, feeding this strand along the groove. Press the putty into a bevel with a putty knife. Once the four sides of the pane are *roughly* puttied, you can begin the "fine" work. Smooth out the putty in a straight stroke, but hold the knife so that the putty actually *slants from the glass at an angle down to the wood. Note:* the putty should cure for several days. It will have a "skin" on its exposed side when it's cured. Afterward, paint it. Run the paint *just onto the window*—to seal the putty-window-join.

Metal Sash. Follow directions for *"Wooden Sash,"* above. But with metal sash, use clips instead of glazier's points. The clips are removed, then pressed back into holes in the metal sash.

WINDOW, STORM

See "Storm Window."

WINDOW SCREEN

Screening Torn. See DOOR/SCREEN—SCREENING TORN.

Wobbly, Coming Apart at the Corners. As you might suppose, the weakest point of a window-screen frame is the corner, where the sides join. If the joint starts to open up, force the two sides together. Drive a metal fastener across the joint on the back side of the screen. These corrugated-type fasteners are available at hardware and building supply stores. If you prefer, screw flat, angle irons to each corner to give the joints greater strength. (See diagram under DOOR/SCREEN, DOOR RAILS SPLIT OR CRACKED.)

Replacing Screening. If the screening is so badly torn or so rotted that it can't really be patched, *replace* the entire piece of screening. The knack of this repair is to get the new screening in, and have it *taut enough* so that it doesn't have unseemly sags and bulges. To make the screen fit properly, follow this procedure:

1. Remove Molding and Screen. Remove the molding that covers the staples or the tacks that hold the screening in the frame. Do this extra-carefully. Take out the old screening, then pry out any staples or tacks that are left in the frame.

2. Screening. Buy a new piece of screening. Get it at the hardware or building supply store. The screening should be large enough to fit over the opening and molding areas *and* have a half-inch to spare all the way around. Fold the excess half-inch over—to make a hem that the staples or tacks will hold onto firmly. *Note*: Always use staples or tacks that are made of the same metal as the screening. Use copper tacks for copper screening, and so on. The reason: corrosion prevention! (For more on this, see RUST/CORROSION.)

3. Tacking. Start the tacking on a *long* side of the frame. Stretch the screen lengthwise as tightly as possible as you go along the side. Then, start down the other long side, stretching the wire tightly *across*, as well as lengthwise. Then, pull the ends tight and staple them or tack them down to the frame.

4. Finishing. Put the molding back, putty the nail holes, paint the frame.

ZIPPER

Won't Budge, All Jammed Up. Nothing can be more annoying, if you're in a big hurry! You probably know *why* this happens: the Y-shaped sliding mechanism has very likely been entwined with threads, or it's gotten caught in the fabric on the wrong side of the zipper placket. But that's cold comfort now. Our advice: jiggle the slider a bit. If you're careful and patient, you can free the slider from the cloth or threads, but it takes time. If you absolutely can't make the slider move, buy a zipper-repair kit at the five-and-dime store. This kit has a special tool that will release the slider.

Teeth Separate Down Below. If you've popped your zipper, check to see if the teeth have separated from the bottom up. Be sure not to push the slider down over them. Instead, join the teeth—two by two—by hand. If they mesh properly, the slider will move back down, and you can zip yourself up.

Teeth Missing. Buy a new zipper and follow the package instructions for sewing the zipper onto your dress.

SECTION II

GLOSSARY OF TOOLS

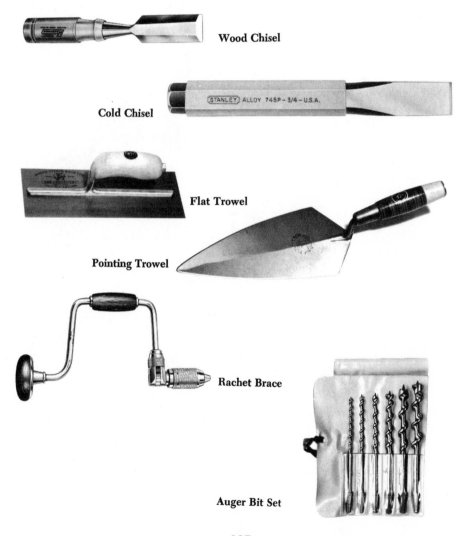

Wood Chisel

Cold Chisel

Flat Trowel

Pointing Trowel

Rachet Brace

Auger Bit Set

225

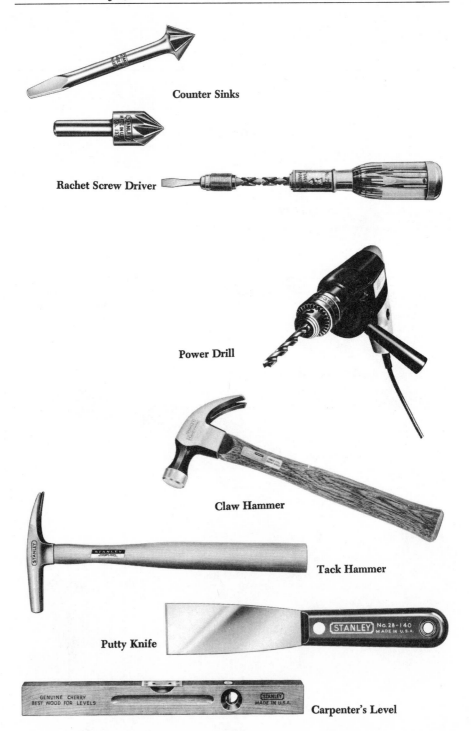

Counter Sinks

Rachet Screw Driver

Power Drill

Claw Hammer

Tack Hammer

Putty Knife

Carpenter's Level

 Nailset

Bench Plane

Block Plane

Scraping Tool

 Pliers

Needlenose Pliers

Folding Wood Rule

Tape Rule

Cross Cut Saw

Back Saw

Hack Saw

Keyhole Saw

Coping Saw

Scraper

Screw Driver

Phillips Screw Driver

Phillips Bit

Tin Snips

T-Square

Tack Claw

Adjustable Wrench

Pipe Wrench

GLOSSARY OF TERMS

Abrasive. Files, sandpaper, and scouring powder. The rough textures of these are used to smooth different kinds of surfaces (wood, metal, stone, etc.).

AC (alternating current). The type of electrical current most commonly used in the United States. The current reverses direction at intervals, like a shuttle going back and forth over the same route. (*Direct* current does *not* reverse, but flows steadily in one *direction.*)

Aerator. A small metal ring containing fine mesh screening which is screwed onto the water tap. When the tap is turned on, the aerator mixes air with the stream of water—thus reducing the force of the stream.

Amperes (amps). The term to designate the *intensity* of electrical current.

Angle Iron. In carpentry, a piece of metal used to strengthen joints of wood (windows, doors, and some furniture). The metal is steel (not iron) and is shaped like the letter L.

Appliqué. A stitched-on decoration. Also the art of sewing small, decoratively shaped pieces of cloth to a larger cloth backing.

Arcing. Sparking between two electrical connections.

Asbestos. Fibrous material used in fireproofing roofs, floors, heater cords, or anything else that may present a fire hazard.

Asphalt. Brown or black substance, similar to tar, used in cement, paving, and roofing mixtures.

Auger. The variety we discuss in this book is the one the plumber uses when he opens up clogged or impacted drains. This auger, otherwise called a *plumber's snake* is a coiled steel rope or spring, tipped with a "beak" or "claw" that bores into the obstructing material, making an opening in it. The plumber also uses the tool to reel in the obstruction, as one might wind in the reel of a fishing rod.

Axle. The shaft that runs through the center of a turning wheel, which it supports.

Barometer. A weather-forecasting instrument that measures atmospheric pressure.

Bearing. The part of a machine (in the wheels of a baby carriage, for example) that *bears the weight* of the machine and allows the *axle* to rotate freely.

Belt Clamp. A fabric or metal strip with buckle or locking device. Used to exert pressure on irregular-shaped objects that are being glued or being held in place.

Bevel. An angle (other than right angle) along the edge of wood, glass, or other material. Used to finish the edge of a mirror, counter top, etc.

Blonding. A process using a thin white lacquer to obtain blond tones on furniture. Can be made by adding one part white lacquer to four or five parts clear lacquer.

Bond. In carpentry and other crafts where glues are used, the term that describes the union of two parts brought about by a binding substance.

Bracket. In carpentry, a rigid vertical support, usually of metal, fastened to walls or cabinets to carry the weight of shelves.

Bulkhead. Originally, the term applied to a partition on a ship. On dry land it describes the outside cellar door and the structure holding it. Often this housing for the cellar door is pitched, like a roof, to facilitate rain runoff.

Butt. In carpentry, to join two flat surfaces squarely together.

Carnauba (or carnuba) Wax. Used to make candles and to restore artifacts made of alabaster. (It is also called Brazil wax because it is extracted from a palm tree native to Brazil.)

Caster. A small wheel on a swivel—usually attached to heavy furniture to facilitate mobility.

Caulking Compound. A puttylike, watertight sealer for cracks and seams—for example: outdoors, on the roof; indoors, around bathtub tiles.

Circuit. In electricity, the path of an electric current—from fuse box through wires, back to fuse box. There are several circuits in most homes. Usually, a label noting the circuit is put on or beneath the fuse box. (Sometimes a diagram is attached to the fuse box.)

Circuit Breaker. An automatic switch that stops the flow of electricity when a circuit is overloaded (carrying too much current). *Fuses* perform the same function but operate differently.

Cleat. Metal or wood piece that, when attached to another piece, gives support or stability to a structure. Used in many kinds of construction.

Conductor. In electricity, a substance that transmits an electric current—examples: water and copper wire.

Countersink. In carpentry, to drive nails, screws, or bolts *beneath* the receiving surface, or flush with it. (Nails are countersunk with nailsets. But you must drill a hole the size of the head to countersink a screw or bolt.)

Crochet. To do needlework using thread or yarn and a crochet hook. The yarn is looped over the hook and worked into chains of interlocking stitches.

Cure, Curing. In carpentry, used to describe the drying process of glues and caulking substances.

Damper. A movable metal plate in a chimney, furnace, or stove *flue* that controls the draft (or amount of air).

Darn. To mend holes in cloth, including knit goods, with yarn or thread and needle. There are various ways to fill the hole. Some are woven darns; others use blanket-stitches or "knit" stitches.

Decay. In carpentry, the decomposition of wood by fungi. *Advanced decay* makes wood "punky"—soft, spongy, stringy, and crumbly. The beginning of decay is indicated by a slight discoloration or bleaching of wood. During early decay, the wood is still hard.

Dowel. A round peg or pin (of wood or metal) which is used to join two pieces of wood or metal. The dowel extends from one piece and is inserted in a hole in the second piece to be joined.

Dry Rot. A term loosely applied to any dry, crumbly rot, but especially to that which, when in an advanced stage, permits wood to be crushed to a dry powder.

Dry Well. Drainage basin used to catch runoff water from gutters and downspouts.

Duct. A passageway for cool air or heat.

Epoxy. A strong adhesive, resin glue.

Ferrule. A metal ring or sleeve used to mend a broken tool handle or used to strengthen a fragile piece (such as the stem of a crystal goblet). Some ferrules are merely functional, others both functional and decorative.

Finial. Decorative knob or top part of a clock, bedpost, lamp, or fire tool (andiron, poker, etc.). Also an ornamental knob on the lid of a silver, china, or glass serving dish or tureen.

Flange. A protruding rim or edge on an object. The flange is used either to hold the object in place or to strengthen it.

Force Cup. A rubber suction-cup attached to a wooden handle. This is a plumber's tool—also known as the *plumber's helper,* and the *plumber's friend.* Its action, when pressed and released, opens up clogged drains.

Flue. In a chimney, the pipe or channel through which smoke and hot air escape. There may be several, separate flues within one chimney—one for the furnace, the others for each fireplace in the building.

Furring Strip. Wood or metal strip applied to the wall or ceiling. These strips are evenly spaced, and are put in place before new ceiling or wallboard panels are nailed or stapled to them.

Fuse. A small round or cartridge-shaped device that is used to safeguard an electric circuit. When a circuit is overloaded (too many lights and appliances are using it), a metal strip in the fuse melts. This breaks the circuit, stopping the dangerous flow of electric current, preventing heating of wires and possible fires. (When the fuse "blows" the lights or appliances will simply cease to operate.)

Gasket. Any leakproof material (such as rubber or plastic) usually ring-shaped, fitted around pipe joints or machine parts to prevent escape of liquid (water, fuel, etc.) or gas. The rubber seal on the inside of a dishwasher door is a gasket. So is the one on the inside of the refrigerator door—but that one's there to keep out hot air.

Glazier's Points. Tiny pieces of triangular metal used in setting windowpanes in a frame before puttying and painting around the frame and pane.

Gild. To cover a surface with a real or imitation gold pigment.

Gimp. A half-inch band or braid of cotton, rayon, silk, leather, or plastic used to finish edges or seams on upholstered furniture.

Grille. A metal or plastic grating, often used to screen a heating *duct,* cover the mechanism of an air conditioner or fan, or protect a window area.

Ground. In electricity, the connection between an electrical wiring system, or any part of it, and the earth. There are various ways electrical appliances are grounded, and these include *proper* and safe grounding with wires or special plugs, and *improper* grounding. For details, see ELECTRICITY AND WIRING, p. 269.)

Grout. Thin mortar used to fill in cracks and crevices, especially the ones between ceramic tiles.

Housing. The protective casing for the working parts of an appliance or a motor.

Jack Post. A metal pole with an extension device, used to push up or support sagging floors or decks.

Joint. In carpentary, the place where two pieces of wood, metal, or plastic meet. There are, for example, *butt* joints, *lapped* joints, *miter* joints, and *dado* joints— each used for a different purpose in construction and furniture-making.

Joist. A horizontal timber that supports the boards of a ceiling or floor.

Lath. Thin, narrow strip of wood or metal mesh used to form the supporting structure for plaster (ceilings and walls).

Louver (also Louvre). An opening for ventilation fitted with movable or fixed *slats*. The term also applies to a single slat. The slats may be of wood, metal, or glass, and are used in doors, windows, vents, or air conditioners.

Mastic. A gummy type of cement.

Molly (or Molly bolt). A type of bolt used on *hollow* walls. Part of the device opens up behind the wall to secure the bolt.

Mortar. A cement mixture used to join bricks, stone, or concrete blocks.

Mortar Hawk. A flat board with a handle, used to carry mortar from the mixer to the repair.

Mortise. A small cavity or rectangular recess in a piece of wood into which another piece (of wood or metal) is set. (Mortising makes the setting both durable and neat-looking.)

Mortise-and-Tenon. A type of joint used in carpentry. The tenon (a single, square-cornered "pin" at the end of a wood surface) fits into a corresponding hollowed *mortise* on another piece of wood. The two sections join like an angular version of the ball-and-socket *joint*.

Packing Nut. In plumbing or mechanics, this is a small metal ring, threaded, used to force packing (leakproof) material to fit snugly around pipes, etc.

Paraffin. A waxy white or colorless substance; solid when cold, it melts quickly when heated. Used for candles, etc.

Pendulum Bob. The weight at the end of a pendulum shaft.

Penetrating Floor Sealer. A penetrating finish for floors. Also good for simple finishes on furniture.

Picot. An edging used on fine linens, bedding, baby clothes. It is a series of tiny loops or twists made with embroidery stitches or with a crochet hook and thread.

Plastic Wood. A synthetic filler that dries and hardens like wood after it is used to seal a crack. Before it dries it is extremely flammable and must be used with caution—away from any flame (pilot light and lighted cigarettes included).

Plug Anchor. In construction and carpentry, a plastic or metal sheath used with special bolts and screws. The *sheath* is inserted in a drilled hole and when the *bolt* is inserted in this sheath and tightened, the sheath expands for a firm grip.

Plumber's Helper (or plumber's friend, or plunger). See FORCE CUP.

Plumber's Snake. An auger or boring tool used to open up badly clogged, impacted drains. (See AUGER.)

Plywood. Wood made of layers (plies) of *veneer*, or of veneer in combination with other cuts of lumber joined with adhesive.

Preservative. In carpentry, any substance that is effective in preventing the development of wood-rotting fungi, borers of various kinds, and harmful insects that deteriorate wood.

Rabbet. In carpentry, a groove along the edge of a piece of wood, metal, etc., that is fitted to receive a piece of wood, metal, or glass. A *rabbeted joint* is often used in furniture making.

Raffia. A fiber made from the leaves of an African palm tree. Raffia is used for mats, baskets, handbags, etc.

Rafter. One of the angled beams that supports a sloping roof.

Register. The adjustable *grille* covering an air *duct*.

Rivet. Various types of rivets are used to join metal pieces, wood, cloth, leather, and plastic. Metalwork rivets are like bolts or pins: a metal shank with a head. (The tail end of the rivet is hammered till it spreads out, to secure the materials being joined.) Rivets for cloth and leather may be in two parts —a shaft and a smaller shank which slips through it. These snap into place.

Runner. In a chest of drawers, the wood or metal track on which the drawer slides.

Sealer. A substance applied to wood, cork, wicker, cane, and cement, used to close the "pores" in these materials.

Screw Eye. A small metal screw with a doughnut-shaped head.

Shank. The straight or shaft portion of screws, nails, etc., as distinguished from the head portion.

Shellac. A coating used as a wood finish and sealer.

Shim. A tapered piece of metal or wood used to level an item of furniture or to raise structures. This wedge is inserted under or behind the object.

Silicone Lubricant. A synthetic, nongreasy lubricant.

Sisal. A stiff fiber often used for making rope—derived from the leaves of a Mexican plant.

Slat. A narrow strip of metal or wood, as in shutters and blinds, for example.

Solder. Molten metal used to cement metal parts.

Soldering. Joining metal pieces together with molten metal.

Solvent. A liquid used to thin or dissolve another substance (as, for example, turpentine is used with oil paint).

Spackle. Comes ready-mixed or in dry (plaster) form to be mixed with water. Used to fill small cracks and holes in walls, ceilings, etc.

Spirit Level. A tool used by carpenters to determine the true horizontal of stairs, counters, etc. The flat rulerlike tool contains liquid (sealed under glass) and a floating bubble. When the bubble is centered, the gauge reads level.

Stain. A pigment in liquid solution used to color wood floors, furniture, etc. Also applies to the accidental discoloration of wood or marble when food or liquids mar the finish.

Standard. An upright timber or rod used to support shelves or beams.

Standpipe. Used in plumbing. A pipe that extends above the surface and is part of the drainage or water system.

Stringer. The crosspieces of wood connecting walls and planks on a wood deck, floor, or boardwalk. Also, the timbers under risers and treads of a stairway.

Stripping. In refinishing wood, describes the process of removing the old painted, varnished, or shellacked surface.

Sump Pump. Pump placed in a well of the basement floor, used to drain away excess water.

Thermostat. A device that reacts to temperature changes so as to control the performance of an appliance. Air conditioners, furnaces, and refrigerators are among the appliances that use thermostats.

Toggle Bolts. Used to hang pictures, shelves, etc., on hollow walls. These bolts have winged nuts or other devices that open up behind the wall to hold them firmly in place. Various types and sizes are available.

Tongue-and-Groove. A small center tongue of wood fits into a groove of an adjacent piece of wood to form a *joint*. Most commonly used in flooring lumber.

Tourniquet. Originally a medical term—a band tightened around an arm or finger, for example, which limits the blood supply. In household repairs, a band tightened around a mend (as on a drawer or chair), left in place until the glue dries.

Turnbuckle. In carpentry, a device used to tighten or loosen two wires or rods attached to a framework. The tension of the wires gives strength to the structure of the framework.

Valve. Various devices to regulate the flow of water, gas, or steam by opening up or closing down a passageway.

Varnish Stain. General-purpose interior varnish tinted with dye colors, pigments, and all wood colors. This substance stains and varnishes in one operation, making refinishing quicker.

Veneer. A thin layer or sheet of wood.

Washer. A small ring or disc made of plastic, metal, or rubber. It is used in machinery and plumbing to distribute pressure, cut down friction, or prevent leakage of liquids.

Welting. Cord covered with fabric, leather, or plastic used to finish seams in upholstery, slipcovers, or cushions.

Wing Nut. In carpentry and construction, a nut with flared sides on it that make it possible to tighten the nut with your fingers.

WORKING WITH NAILS, SCREWS, AND FASTENERS

Working with Nails. Simple as it may seem, there's more to driving nails into walls or wood than meets the eye. Professionals—carpenters and cabinetmakers—use many different types of nails, and for good reason. Some nails are made for boats and barges, some for roofs, some for floors. And if you'll consult our charts, pp. 237–238, you'll see there are straight nails, thin nails, thick nails, and headless nails with crooked tails! The nail you choose should suit the material it goes into. It is visible or not after it's used, depending on the job you're doing. Some nails have names that are really *old-fashioned!* For instance, there's the *tenpenny* nail, which is three inches long. The name tells you that, long ago (before inflation) you'd have paid ten pennies for a hundred of these three-inch nails.

One rule of thumb is that *the nail you use for the job should be three times the thickness of the piece of wood (or whatever) and the other material you're joining together.* (In other words, two-thirds of the nail should be sunk down into the back, or holding piece. See diagram opposite.)

Note these other tips on nailing before you go to work:

1. The larger the nail is, the more it behooves you to drill a pilot hole into the wood or material you're nailing. (Doing this guards against the possibility of splitting the wood.)

2. Use a nailset (see GLOSSARY OF TOOLS, p. 227) to countersink the nailhead if you don't want the head to be visible. If you try to do this with your hammer you'll just leave dents in the surface around the nailhead.

3. If the nail starts to bend as you hammer, take it out and start over again, in *another* place (if you have the choice), and with a *fresh nail.* (Bending like that indicates some obstruction hidden beneath the surface—in wood it's usually a knot.)

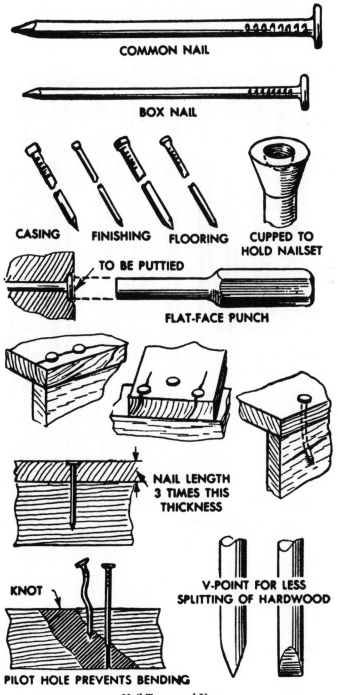

COMMON NAIL

BOX NAIL

CASING   FINISHING   FLOORING   CUPPED TO
HOLD NAILSET

TO BE PUTTIED

FLAT-FACE PUNCH

NAIL LENGTH
3 TIMES THIS
THICKNESS

KNOT

V-POINT FOR LESS
SPLITTING OF HARDWOOD

PILOT HOLE PREVENTS BENDING

Nail Types and Uses

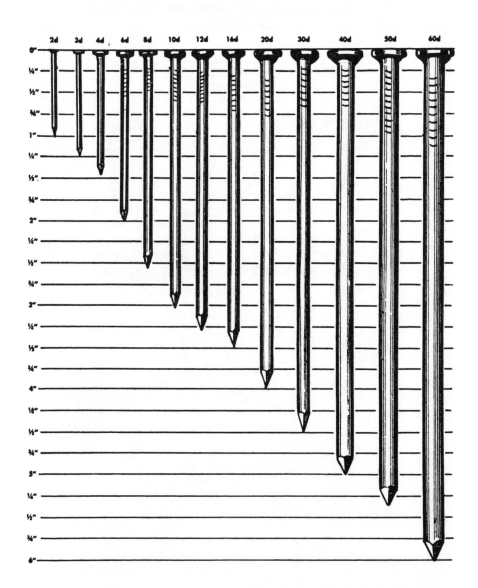

Nail Sizes

Working with Screws. The expert will choose screws instead of nails for special repairs because this way of fastening or joining two pieces of wood is stronger. The most obvious uses are furniture joints, where stress and strain make maximum firmness imperative. Chair arms and table legs are attached with screws for this reason.

Remember that—with one exception—you should drill a pilot hole for the screw. Don't try to start the screw just fresh on the surface of the wood—too much wasted effort. (The one exception: when you're using very small screws on very soft wood.) Remember also: the diameter of the hole you drill should be smaller than the diameter of the screw. Experts say the hole should be 90 percent of the screw core size for hardwood, and 70 percent of the core size for soft wood. (The core size is the diameter of the screw under the threads.) In other words, *the hole should be a little smaller than the screw if you're working on something like oak, and quite a bit smaller than the screw if you're working on something like pine.*

Wood screws (screws for wood) are made of steel, brass, bronze, and aluminum. You can also get steel screws that are coated with brass, zinc, cadmium, or chromium to make the surfaces rustproof. Screws come in various sizes and shapes. Some have flat heads, some have round heads, some have oval heads, and some (the lag screw) are square-headed. Screw heads are slotted. (Some of the roundhead-type screws have what are called *fillister* heads.) The single-slot-head screw is the most familiar, but the crisscross-slot head, on the *Phillips Screw,* is considered by some to be easier to use. (You need a special screwdriver to drive these screws.) Be sure the screwdriver you use fits snugly into the slot of the screw: if it doesn't you may damage the slot edges or even mar the wood surface, if the screwdriver slips. Take these tips for your repair work with screws:

1. Rub some soap along the screw threads: the screw will drive in more readily if you do.

2. Use a brace with a screwdriver bit when you're working with large screws. You'll do the work more quickly, and easily.

3. Be sure to buy screws with shanks that are long enough. The shank should go through the pieces being joined far enough to make the join firm. This means that the threaded part of the screw should penetrate all the way into the holding piece of material. (For example, if you're planning to attach a 1-inch-thick board to a 2-by-4, you should buy a 2½-inch-long screw. Its shank will be 1 inch.

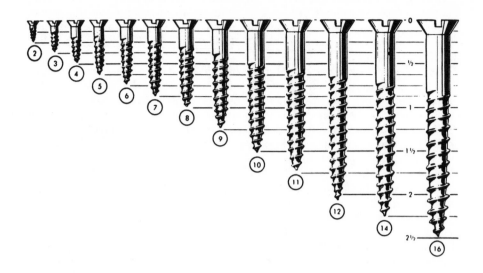

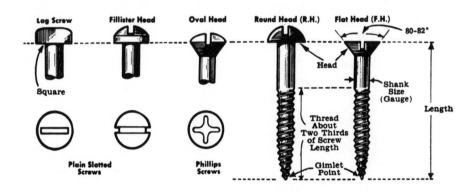

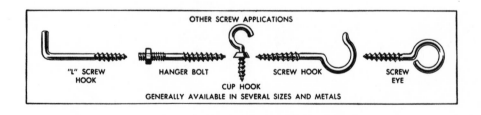

Screw Sizes and Types

Working with Machine Screws. See BOLTING AND RIVETING, p. 245.

Working with Fasteners. If you feel insecure about the way your mirror, pictures, or bookshelves are attached to the wall, make an inspection, then plan to put these items up with tried-and-true fasteners. The chart below shows what you should use.

One tip when you're working with hollow-wall fasteners: you need to know the thickness of the wall, that is, *where the hollowness begins.* To find out, drill a small hole through the wall. Next, push the *hook* end of a crochet hook through the hole. Now, "hook" the back of the wall surface—that is, pull the shank of the crochet hook toward you until the hook catches on the back surface of the wall. Mark the shaft at this point, or just place your thumbnail on the shaft on the room-side of the wall. Next, pull the hook out of the hole, then measure the inches (or parts thereof) from your thumbnail to the hook. *This gives you the thickness of the wall.* (*Sounds* complicated, but try it, it's simple.) All this measuring is necessary because you have to buy fasteners that will grip against the back, or inside, surface of the wall.

"ALL-PURPOSE" FASTENERS

Plastic Anchor

Nylon Expansion

Most brands come in three sizes. Where screws are not packaged with the anchors, use size recommended on package.

One size (about 1″ long, requiring a ⅜″ hole); serves all applications, comes with 1⅛″ self-tapping screw.

INSTALLATION

Except for larger sizes, anchors are molded in strips; break one off and force into hole of size recommended on card; insert screw through fixture and drive into anchor.

Drill hole at least 1½″ deep, pinch anchor between fingers and tap in place with hammer. Insert screw through fixture and tighten.

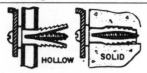 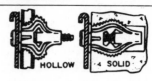

RECOMMENDED USES

Mounting any item normally held with wood screws—large pictures, mirrors, shelf brackets, drapery hardware, kitchen and bath accessories, awnings, mailboxes, Peg-Board hang-up panels . . . on concrete, tile, brick and hollow plaster walls.

Mounting any item such as drapery hardware, brackets and fixtures to any type wall: plaster, drywall, brick, marble, concrete, cinder block, stone, or even wood.

ADVANTAGES

Since anchor is rustproof, it's fine for bathroom fixtures, outdoor installations. Small hole means little wall damage. Screw can be removed and reinserted.

One type and size of fastener for all light hanging needs very thin lip lets you mount flush to wall.

DISADVANTAGES

Hole size is critical— anchor must fit snug, and is only as good as the wall material. For light loads only. Won't hold against much horizontal pull, especially in crumbly masonry.

Fairly large hole required; not satisfactory in hollow wall more than ⅜″ thick, so don't expand behind most plaster walls.

FOR HOLLOW WALLS ONLY

 **Toggle Bolt**

 **Expansion Bolt**

INSTALLATION

Insert bolt through fixture and spin the toggle head on several turns. Fold wings and push them through proper size hole in wall. Tighten bolt to

Insert unit in drilled hole, tap to embed cap teeth in wall surface, turn screw to draw split sleeve into "spider" against back of wall; remove screw

draw wings snug
against back of wall.

and reinsert after pass-
ing through mounting
hole of fixture.

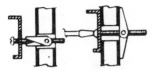

RECOMMENDED USES

Large hanging cab-
inets, heavy-duty shelf
standards, wall radi-
ators or vent fans,
bathroom grip bars.

Mirrors, wall cabinets,
lamps and clocks, ad-
justable shelf brackets,
window cornices,
shades and blinds,
coat hooks.

ADVANTAGES

Simple, immediate-
action installation,
great strength for com-
bination loads. Align-
ment of mounting
holes with wall holes
isn't critical.

Requires smaller hole
than toggle, centers
bolt precisely. Re-
mains in place for
reuse if fixture is re-
moved. Bolt is easily
inserted through fix-
ture *after* positioning
on wall.

DISADVANTAGES

Requires large insert
hole to pass wings, so
bolt "floats," does not
position fixture pre-
cisely. Mounting plate
must be big enough to
hide hole. If fixture is
removed, wings drop
off, are lost in wall.
Installation awkward
where fixture requires
several bolts, since all
must be inserted
through fixture before
positioning.

Slower installation.
Less strength, since
smaller bolt and
thinner anchor metal is
involved. Mounting
holes must exactly
align with fastener—
tricky where several
are involved.

MASONRY WALL FASTENERS

Fiber Anchor
(Lead Core)

Lead Screw Anchor

INSTALLATION

Use drill, plug and screw of same size. Clean hole of loose particles. Insert plug below surface, drive screw through fixture into lead core. Only threaded section should enter plug, so use proper-length plug, recess in deeper hole if necessary.

Screw length = thickness of mounting plate + length of anchor + ¼". Drill hole ¼" deeper than anchor, set it flush with wall surface, drive screw through fixture.

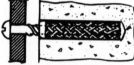

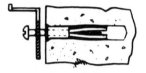

RECOMMENDED USES

Mounting any item you'd normally attach with wood, sheet metal or lag screws (for latter, there are larger sizes than listed)—outlet and fuse boxes, mirrors, bathroom fixtures, fireplace tools, awnings, etc.

Same as fiber anchor.

ADVANTAGES

Easy, inexpensive, versatile. Screw may be removed and replaced without affecting anchorage. Once screw is in, plug grips wall firmly.

Flared end prevents loss of fixture through drilled hole in concrete block, etc. also makes it easier to start screw.

DISADVANTAGES

Hole size is more critical than with most fasteners. Holding power depends on strength of wall material; poor in crumbly concrete, plaster.

Size for size, less holding power than fiber anchor; hole in wall must be exact fit.

BOLTING AND RIVETING

Working with Bolts. Many items that part company with lesser fasteners will be held together, *securely*, with bolts. And you'll find that bolts are the correct fasteners to use where the pieces to be joined also will rotate (like the axle you bolt in a wheelbarrow, bicycle, or baby carriage). The professionals have names for various bolts—*stove* bolts were used originally on stoves, *carriage* bolts were used, you guessed it, on carriages! Below are some tips on bolting.

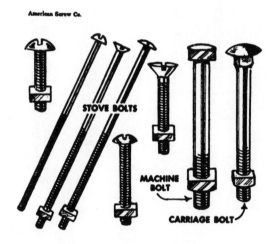

American Screw Co.

STOVE BOLTS

MACHINE BOLT

CARRIAGE BOLT

Bolts

1. When you're joining wood pieces with bolts, be sure to use washers at both ends—that is, under the *head* and under the *nut*. Do this so that the head and nut won't sink into the relatively soft surface of the wood as you tighten the bolt.

2. If the parts you're joining will be under constant stress, or if they'll be in motion or subject to frequent vibration, use what the hardware man calls a *locknut* washer. This special washer has a spring to it that doesn't come loose under stresses, strains, and jiggles.

3. Drill the *right size* hole in the material that's to be bolted. In wood, the hole should be exactly the diameter of the bolt, for a snug, firm fit. In metal,

the hole should be about ⅟₃₂ of an inch *oversize*—so the threads on the bolt won't be damaged by forcing them through a tight opening.

4. Buy bolts long enough. The nut at the far end should go all the way on the threaded portion of the bolt, and leave a little over.

Working with Machine Screws. These are half screw and half bolt-type fasteners. They're threaded for their entire length, as you'll see in the diagram. They have slotted heads, which means that you can drive them with a screw-driver. Machine screws are used mostly in the assembly of metal parts in house-hold appliances. They are used *without* nuts at the far end—the threads hold fast in the metal hole drilled to receive the screw. For this reason, when you replace a machine screw with a new one, be absolutely sure it's *exactly the size of the one replaced.*

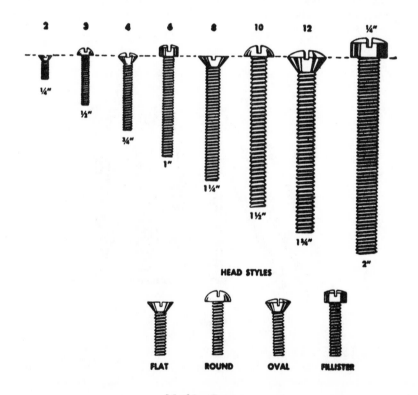

Machine Screws

Working with Rivets. As you know if you have kids who wear blue jeans, rivets can be used on soft things (denim and leather). They're also used on hard materials, like metal and wood. Metalware rivets are best used for *thin* surfaces—such as copper and aluminum cooking utensils—where nails, bolts, or screws would be cumbersome or not strong enough for a secure join.

In some respects rivets are like bolts, only smaller. The rivet head, like the bolt head, is larger than the shaft. But the rivet shaft-tip can be solid metal or it can be hollow.

To use a rivet, drill a small hole—*just the size of the rivet*—in each of the materials you plan to join. Insert the rivet through these holes. Then hammer or *peen* the tail end of the rivet so that the edges flatten out and grip the surface of the material you're riveting. The rivet that has a *scored end* (that is, partially slit) is more decorative-looking than other types. Insert the rivet, then set the scored end with a riveting tool (buy it at the hardware store). Doing this *spreads the scored sections out* so that they look like the petals of a flower. These petals hold the rivet and joined material in place.

One kind of rivet used on cloth and leather clothes is particularly simple to use. This type of rivet has *two parts,* each of them with a head and tail. One is larger and is hollow. This part is inserted in the material, then the other, smaller rivet is popped into this and snaps or locks into place. (Buy these at the arts and crafts shop or at the notions counter of a department store.)

GLUING AND CLAMPING

It's a safe bet that though all the king's horses and all the king's men couldn't put Humpty Dumpty together again, the *right glue* could make those mends! The variety and versatility of glues and adhesives available today make is possible for you to fix most things around the house—from chairs to stairs, chandeliers to wood veneers, and lots more! But you do need to follow certain rules in gluing and mending procedures:

- You must select the right glue for the materials you're repairing.
- You must know whether the glue will hold the pieces together without clamps or weights or some form of pressure, or whether clamps are a *must.*
- You need to study the nature of the glue. Read instructions on the container. Some glues give off vapors or fumes that are dangerous to inhale (the so-called airplane glues that children have been known to sniff for "kicks"). Other glues *cannot be used in the presence of any flame—including stove pilot lights and lighted cigarettes. The danger from these is explosion and fire.* Some glues must be mixed, and others will not take hold effectively if you're working in the cold or in rooms with temperatures below 50 degrees Fahrenheit. If you're repairing wood, don't start a project in a room or shed that may go from warm to very cold overnight—while the glue is drying. (Furniture glues usually require a temperature of 75 degrees Fahrenheit for twenty-four hours, and, according to the experts, the wood itself should be about the same temperature.)

For details on types of glue and how to use them, consult the chart opposite, see our suggestions on various ways to put pressure on your mending projects, and take our tips on gluing techniques.

GLUE CHART

Name	Characteristics	Uses	Special Directions
ACRYLIC RESIN GLUE	A two-part glue (liquid and powder). Drying and setting times are controlled by the proportions of liquid to powder. Extremely strong bond is made when glue dries—it takes a weight of 3 tons to break the glued joint apart!	Special glue for very special jobs. Good for heavy-duty repairs to objects immersed in water (such as boats), but useful in the home, too. Sticks to almost anything, including metal and wood. Good for filling gaps or cracks in objects that hold or are in water.	Must be mixed. Be sure to follow directions on container to get proper proportions for the job you're doing. Drying and setting controlled by the amounts mixed: for example, 3 parts of powder to 1 of liquid will set in about 5 minutes at 70 degrees Fahrenheit. Changing these proportions will allow for faster or slower drying and setting.
ALIPHATIC RESIN GLUE	Comes ready to use; looks like heavy cream. Advantage of this glue is that it can be "dyed" or pre-colored with water-soluble dyes to match the material being repaired. It's water-resistant but *not* waterproof.	Good general wood glue. It is water-resistant enough to be used for various indoor and covered-porch furnishings.	Will hold lightweight, small jobs together without clamping, but you should hold the mend in place for a minute or two to be sure it's dried.
BUNA-N BASE ADHESIVE	Made from synethetic rubber; tan in color; sold in tubes or bottles. Its great virtue is that, like rubber, it's flexible yet strong.	Special glue for bonding two materials with a flexible joint between them. This glue will bond *anything* to *anything*, allowing ample back-and-forth movement.	When this glue is used on porous materials, the moving parts can be assembled while the glue is wet. But when you want a flexible joint between two nonporous materials (such as two pieces of metal), apply the glue, let it dry, then soften it with heat just before bringing the parts together. Don't put *newly* glued items on good tabletops, etc., because the solvent in the glue may mar their finish.
CASEIN GLUE	The old reliable glue, made from milk. It comes as a light beige	A good furniture glue. This also works as a gap filler in wood that's	Can be worked with in any temperature above freezing.

GLUE CHART (cont.)

Name	Characteristics	Uses	Special Directions
CASEIN GLUE (cont.)	powder which you mix with water. The glue is not waterproof, but it is moisture-resistant, and has long been used on outside jobs. The unmixed powder will last for as long as two years.	cracked. Can be used outdoors. It makes a strong bond when it's set.	
CLEAR CEMENT OR PLASTIC CEMENT	Dries clear, sets quickly (in about 10 minutes) with some pressure put on the joint, but the cement takes 24 to 48 hours to set completely. Water-proof except on wood and *some* plastic sur-faces; it will discolor wood and *some* plas-tics. *Most cements are flammable before they're dry. The fumes are toxic and danger-ous.* When gluing plastic, use the cement best suited. Styrene glues are usually best for rigid plastics; vinyl glues best for flexible plastics.	Good for most plastics (but check the pack-age directions; some plastics resist gluing). Also good for wood, metal, paper, glass, ceramics. Fine for jewelry repairs.	Roughen nonporous surfaces to be mended. Clamp the joined pieces while cement is drying for a tight, firm bond. Some types (such as the ones used on model airplanes) give a good-enough bond if the pieces are held together for 15–20 seconds. *Be sure to work in a well-venti-lated room. Don't work near flame (including stove pilot light or lighted cigarette).*
CONTACT CEMENT	Bonds on contact and needs no clamping. *Most contact cements are flammable, and the fumes are toxic.* But some types (for kitchen-counter laminating) are water-based; use these if you're working in a room with a pilot light. Don't use contact cements on copper, brass, bronze, or manganese.	The best adhesive to use for bonding plastic laminates (such as plastic counter tops), linoleum, leather, or synthetic rubber, to wood. Good for china. Good for replacing tiles. Can be used with metals, *except* copper, bronze, brass, manganese.	Coat both surfaces generously, and allow to dry before joining them. Drying takes from ¼ to ½ hour, but you must finish the job in 2 hours. Once the glued surfaces touch they're impossible to adjust, so these must be aligned exactly be-fore you join them. Be sure that the tempera-ture in the room is at least 65 degrees Fahrenheit or the bond will be weak. Complete drying time requires 8 hours to several days, and sur-

GLUE CHART (cont.)

Name	Characteristics	Uses	Special Directions
CONTACT CEMENT (cont.)			faces to be joined must be absolutely dry or they will come apart. *Be sure to work in a well-ventilated room. Don't work near flame (pilot light on stove or lighted cigarette) unless you're sure the contact cement you're using is water-based.*
EPOXY GLUE	Provides a very strong bond, but not a flexible one. Doesn't shrink when it hardens. Is waterproof and heat-resistant; mends made with epoxy can be washed in a dish-washer, after the glue has set. The mixture must be used quickly. Clamp the repair while the glue cures. A little heat from a light bulb will shorten the curing time. If you work in low temperatures (50 degrees or less) the epoxy will not harden. Normal curing is ½ to 8 hours. (A new type of epoxy hardens in 5 minutes.) It's expensive, so use glue sparingly—for the job that needs this type of strength, waterproof-ing, and heat-resis-tance.	Good to use on metals and china. Also good for ceramics, glass, pottery, porcelain, marble, concrete, brick, most plastics (some resist gluing), rubber, cloth, and wood.	Must be mixed *exactly*, so follow the instruc-tions on the container. Usually, equal pro-portions of resin and hardener are called for. Mix these thoroughly (too little mixing and the mend will come apart). Wait 5 min-utes and mix again. Be sure to get the epoxy into all cracks and crevices on each surface. Be sure sur-faces are dirt- and grease-free. Use a thin coat of glue. Roughen all non-porous surfaces (such as metal) to make a better grip for the glue.
HIDE GLUE	The traditional *hot glue* of the cabinet-maker. Comes in two forms—solid flakes or strips, or liquid. Sets overnight. Not water-proof. The solid types must first be soaked, then heated, and mixed with the proper amount of water. You	If you're a purist and want to do repairs on fine furniture, this is an excellent glue for the job.	In all cabinetwork and furniture repairs, sur-faces should be care-fully prepared. All the old glue should be scraped from joints, then the surfaces given a soaking in warm vinegar and water to remove vestiges of old glue. Dry the surfaces

GLUE CHART (cont.)

Name	Characteristics	Uses	Special Directions
HIDE GLUE (cont.)	must use it quickly. Your best bet is probably the *liquid* type. The liquid glue is ready to use and allows plenty of working time.		to be joined, roughen them a little, wipe clean, then apply thinnest possible coat of glue. Let it soak into the pores of the wood for a few minutes, then join and *clamp tightly* overnight.
POLYVINYL RESIN GLUE OR WHITE GLUE	Dries quickly and doesn't stain. Is nontoxic, nonflammable. It requires little pressure and only short clamping time. Comes ready to use, usually in a squeeze bottle. Doesn't support great stress for long periods. A recent type of this glue is washable but not waterproof.	Good for paper, wood, cloth, leather, and other porous materials.	Not to be used on bare metal—causes corrosion. Sets fully in 72 hours, and when the work is clamped, the glue will give you a stronger bond.
RESORCINOL RESIN GLUE	Comes in 2 parts: a syrupy resin and a powder; these are mixed. Completely waterproof, and is stronger than wood.	Fine for outdoor furniture and for items immersed in water—such as boats (even toy boats).	Temperature of surroundings must be at least 70 degrees Fahrenheit. Will set in 8 hours in these conditions and in 1½ hours at 100 degrees Fahrenheit. Bonding strength increases for next 6 weeks. Keeps indefinitely.
RUBBER-BASE ADHESIVE	Comes in tubes and cans (for large-scale projects). It's usually black, sticks to most things, can be used on nonporous materials if there's a way for the solvent to evaporate.	Economy all-purpose adhesive. Can be used to caulk roofs, and will hold wall panels to brick or concrete. Can also be used to seal seams underwater.	Though this will glue wood to wood, there are other adhesives (see above) that are better for the job. When used for caulking, let this glue harden, then paint it and the seam will be less visible. You can make cleanups (of hands or tools) with kerosene (but be careful when you use kerosene—a flammable material).

GLUE CHART (cont.)

Name	Characteristics	Uses	Special Directions
STEEL AND ALUMINUM GLUES (PLASTIC STEEL, PLASTIC ALUMINUM, FURNACE CEMENT)	Most of these adhesives come in squeeze tubes. Best used as fillers for cracks. The furnace cement (Quick Metal) is actually used to repair furnaces, and hardens like steel.	For patching metal cracks and for bonding two metals together. The furnace cement is best to use where fire-proof mending is needed, but big or tricky metalwork on stoves, etc. is something you should consult a blacksmith about.	Be sure to follow directions for each type of metal sealer or bonder.
NEUTRAL LIBRARY PASTE (ALSO CALLED BOOK-BINDER'S PASTE)	Made of white flour and water. Is acid-free and thus is used for mounting art works.	The ideal paste recommended for original paintings and art works to be mounted and framed. Available at art supply stores.	Keeps well for a few days in cool temperatures. Discard it when it "sours."

CLAMPING AND CLAMPS

Repair projects that use glue almost always require pressure to set the mend. The surest and most professional way to exert this pressure is with various kinds of clamps. The basic types, shown below and on the next page, are available at hardware stores. You may want to use several clamps for one job, *or* you may use various sizes of one type of clamp for various repair jobs.

1. Band Clamps. These come in canvas or steel bands, and work like a belt that you pull tightly around your waist. They are indispensable for bringing strong pressure on irregular surfaces. The band encircles the work, is pulled tight through a self-locking device (like the buckle on a stretch belt), and is released with a flick of the fingers. You can buy the band clamp with four steel corners for special repairs on items like picture frames.

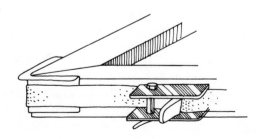

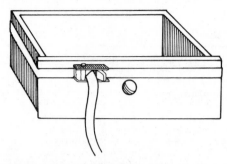

2. C Clamps. So called because they're shaped like the letter C. C Clamps come in about two dozen different sizes. You'll find the C clamp right for most of the gluing and clamping work you do. To use the clamp, insert the repair in the jaws of the clamp, then tighten the screw.

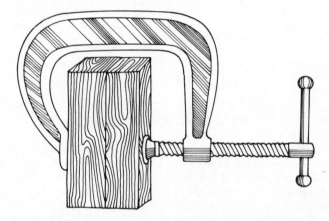

3. Spring Clamps. These look and operate like the clothespins you use to hang up your laundry, but they're made of steel, not wood, and their springs are stronger and grip the work more tightly than clothespins. Their tips are coated with plastic to protect fine finishes. These "extra hands" are good for many types of repairs: they'll hold the screening for your screen door in place, tautly, while you tack it to the frame. They'll do the same for canvas, plastic, metal, and wood, when you're gluing these or nailing them into place.

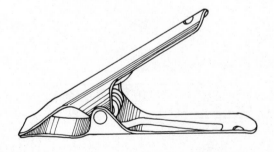

4. Hand Screws. These clamps have jaws made of wood, and are able to hold various shapes—including round shapes and irregular ones. Good for metal-, plastic-, fabric-gluing, and perfect for furniture repairs.

OTHER WAYS TO PUT PRESSURE ON GLUED REPAIRS

Don't fret if you have no fancy clamps handy. You can improvise and exert pressure in a number of ways (some simple and obvious, others a little trickier) with items around the house.

A Stretch-Elastic Belt. Use this the same way you'd use a store-bought band clamp (see opposite, top).

Clothesline and a Wood or Metal Stick or Bar. Make a tourniquet to hold the glued joints together. It's just like the tourniquet described in your First Aid kit. Wrap clothesline around the mend, then tighten the rope by turning the stick. Wedge the stick in place. (But remember to protect fine furniture finishes by padding under the rope with clean cloth.)

Clothespins or Stationer's Clips. Use these the way spring clamps are used (see opposite, bottom).

Various Weights. A stack of books can weight down a glued joint.

Two sacksful of marbles, beads, or lead shot, tied together and slung over an awkward join (a cup handle, for instance) will put pressure on the two surfaces of the mend. (See "CHINAWARE.")

Make splints with the weather stripping, as shown.

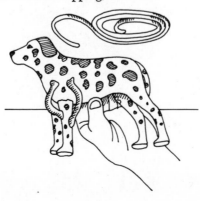

TIPS ON GLUING

If the object you're planning to mend is a treasure and you're not confident about your glue know-how, take the item to an expert. (Indicated in Section I: if it's china, see CHINAWARE, and so on.) If you are patient and eager to do the work yourself, follow these procedures:

Consult the Glue Chart. Select the glue, then use a scrap of material similar to what you're mending. Test the glue, after it dries, in these ways (depending on the material you're mending):

- Try to pull the joined pieces apart with your hands. There should be no give at all.
- Try to bend the joint. If the material is rigid, the mend should not bend.
- Drop the glued test piece. If there are any breaks, these should be *new* ones, and not along the lines of the earlier break.
- Soak the mended scrap in water: it should not come apart.
- Boil the test piece in water. If your mending job survives this test, you know the particular glue you're using for, say, a piece of chinaware will hold and stand up under washing and regular use.

Now, Start Your Serious Glue Repair. Be a fanatic about the following:

1. Clean the object thoroughly. Wash, rinse, and dry it. If glue from previous attempts at mending adheres to the surfaces you're about to join, remove that glue using steel wool or a solvent (nail polish remover, alcohol, or vinegar will usually dissolve most glues).

2. Apply a *thin* layer of glue. Coat each surface with glue, but remember that most glues bond best with the *thinnest possible* layer of glue.

3. Make an accurate join. Be sure the broken edges interlock exactly. Use a magnifying glass on fine work to be sure of your join.

4. Exert pressure. Use any of the methods we've suggested above. Be sure that the pressure you put on the join is at *right angles* to it. (If not, the pressure may force the two pieces askew.) It is all right if glue is squeezed from the seam. Just remove it according to the instructions on the glue container.

ELECTRICITY AND WIRING

Here we are, deep into the space age, and most of us still are in the dark about what happens when the kitchen lights go off. We're not about to explain how space flights and kitchen lights are related to each other (they are), but we *do* want to give you a notion about what electricity *is* and how you should handle it.

Scientists tell us that electricity is really a river of flowing particles (called electrons). Perhaps you can picture that river in your mind's eye if you think of it as being like an endless swarm of fireflies floating across the night sky. However you see it, this river of electrons is what comes to your house in cables and power lines—it literally *pours* into your house power plant.

The power company takes care of repairs to the lines leading to your house. But your responsibility starts where the lines attach to the house. The fuse box or circuit breaker panel, usually located in the basement, is where your household electricity begins its work. From here it travels through wires to the rooms of your house, giving power to your appliances and lighting your lamps. The slightly used current then travels back down through different wires to the basement again, to be given more pep by the power plant downstairs. (Think of the electrical system in your home as being something like steam heat. The boiler in the basement heats water to steam, the steam goes up the pipes to a radiator, which it heats, the radiator turns the steam back into water, and this water travels down to the basement to be heated *again!* This is similar to the route of your electricity.) The continuous path the electric current travels is known as a *circuit*.

The flowing current of electricity in your house is carried in a pair of wires— one called supply, the other ground. The supply wire or line (also known as the hot line) is sheathed in *black*, and thus is readily identifiable. The ground line is sheathed in *white*. When you turn on the lamp by your bed, the current surges up through the black line, goes through the bulb giving off light, then travels back downstairs through the white line. To light your lamp, *the current must have this uninterrupted route.*

There are probably four or more circuits in your house (depending on how many electrical appliances you use, and on how many rooms you have). Each circuit has its own circuit breaker or fuse. Fuses and circuit breakers are the indispensable little devices—the safety valves—that protect you if something goes wrong with your appliances or with the wiring in your house. The fuse or circuit breaker literally *breaks into* the circular path of the dangerous current and shuts it off, so that no damage will be done to your home. Below, we give you details on these events, and indicate how you can handle them. Since these devices are so important to your electrical system, it's essential that you know where they are and what they look like. You should also know the location of your main switch (the connection between the power lines *outside* the house and the lines *inside*). If you don't know now, ask the electrician or the power company representative to show you the location of these switches.

Working circuits should be labeled, showing the rooms they serve and the appliances they power. (*Note:* In newer houses, the contractor may install extra circuits, to be hitched up to new appliances you may use at a later date. They're usually so designated and don't have fuses set in them.)

One circuit may serve several rooms where usage is low. A single circuit may bring power to three or more lamps and small appliances in another part of the house. The wires for each light or appliance will then sprout from the circuit (between your walls) to the outlets they serve, like twigs on the branch of a tree.

Or, a single circuit may bring electricity to just *one* large, power-hungry appliance—such as a washer. (In many parts of the country, the electrical codes insist that this be the practice.)

When malfunctions occur in your electrical system, and in the lights and appliances it feeds, you need to know *which circuits* are affected. You must know the condition of the lamp or appliances involved, and you also need to know something about the *connections* between the circuit and the lamp or appliance. These links are the *cords, plugs, and electrical outlets* all around your house. As it happens, these connections are perhaps the weakest links in the electrical chain—because they're subject to so much wear and tear and outright abuse. But they are easy to inspect and not complicated to repair.

Read on and you'll learn the techniques to use on the various parts of your electrical system, when things go wrong. But first, *always be sure to follow the safety procedures outlined below.*

SUPER SAFETY RULES

- *Don't* use electrical appliances, equipment, or cords unless they bear the Underwriters' Label (UL). The label comes in various shapes, sizes, and colors, but whatever its form, it indicates that the item that wears it has been designed for safe use, in compliance with the National Electrical Code. When you buy electrical appliances and connections such as cords, ask to see the UL seal on *both* the appliance and the cord *before* you put your money down!
- *Do* inspect electrical cords and plugs on lamps, appliances, etc., to be sure they're safe. Replace frayed cords and cracked or loose plugs *before* you use the appliance or lamp.
- *Don't* work with electrical appliances in moist or damp areas, and be sure any major appliance is grounded.
- *Don't ever* touch or change fuses while the electric power is on. If a fuse blows, first turn off the main switch (this cuts off all current in your house). Then, with a flashlight to light your work, replace the fuse. (For details, see below.)
- *Don't* let well-meaning helpers fool with your fuses. Never let anyone re-

place a fuse with a penny or a metal strip. Doing this destroys the safety system in your circuit and can cause a fire.

- *Don't* use heavier (say 30-amp) fuses where you should use 15-amp fuses! Most household circuits are made for 15-amp fuses (though kitchen and dining rooms may have circuits that require 20-amp fuses). Have a stack of new 15-amp fuses handy. (For details see *Note,* p. 262.)
- *Don't* use too many extension cords. Be sure the ones you *do* use are hefty enough (that is, the correct gauge) to carry the amount of power your appliance requires. If you have any doubts as to which gauge you need, consult your electrical supply or hardware store. Heating or motor-driven appliances require a heavy-duty cord.
- *Don't* let your electrical cords trail under rugs and carpets. Be sure no heavy furniture is pressing down on cords, wearing through their insulation. The risk is that the exposed wires will short-circuit and possibly cause a dangerous fire.
- *Don't* try tacking an electrical cord with small nails, thumbtacks, etc., to get the cord off the floor. Do use insulated staples for this job. (The hardware store sells them.)
- *Do* unplug appliances that are not in use if there's danger that a child or pet could touch the interior electrical wires—as, for example, the heating wires of a toaster.
- *Don't* inspect or repair lamps or appliances *until you've disconnected them* or turned off the house current at the main switch.
- *Don't* try to repair a faulty electrical wall *outlet* or *switch.* This is a job for the professional electrician.
- *Do* ask your electrician or appliance repairman to *ground* major appliances, in accordance with the demands of the National Electrical Code. (For details on grounding, see below.)
- *Do* turn off all major appliances (furnace, freezer, washer, dryer, etc.) if there's a power failure in your area. After power is restored, turn on the appliances one by one. Doing this is a precaution that may save your electrical system from a sudden overload. (For details on overloading, see below.)
- *Don't* use metal ladders when you're fixing electrical appliances or ceiling lights and lamps.
- *Do* use insulated tools: rubber or plastic-handled pliers and screwdrivers give extra protection from electric shock.
- *Don't* try to do repairs involving electrical gadgets unless you're sure of yourself. Improper repairs expose you and yours to serious hazards, including fire or shock—even electrocution.

ELECTRICAL DANGER SIGNALS

The signals below warn you about minor and major malfunctions involving your electrical system and appliances. Actual appliance failures are treated in Section I. See the specific appliance, for example: AIR CONDITIONER, RANGE/ ELECTRIC, etc.

Flickering Lights, or Lights Dimming When Appliances Go On. Usually this is an indication of an overload on the circuit—that is, you're asking a circuit with a given amount of power to do too much work by plugging too many lamps and appliances into it. Have your electrician check the load on the circuit; or figure out how much your circuits *should* carry, and how much they actually *are* carrying now. (See table and chart and explanation of how to do this below.)

Sometimes, however, a flickering light merely indicates a poor connection: the lamp bulb may not be properly screwed into the lamp socket, or, the cord plug may be loose in the outlet. Check to be sure these are not the causes and, if the condition continues, call your electrician.

Fuses Blow Frequently, Circuit Breakers Trip Frequently. There are two reasons why fuses blow or circuit breakers trip. The most frequent cause is overloading of circuits: the fuse blows to tell you that the circuit is heating up to the danger point (because you're trying to run too many appliances and lights on the circuit). When the fuse blows, the power is temporarily shut off, and you are thus protected from the danger of fire coming from the overheated circuit. The circuit breaker also breaks the flow of electric current in this type of situation. You can test to discover the cause, as we outline below.

If overloading the circuit is not the problem, then a short circuit in one of your lamps or appliances or in the wiring of the circuit may well be. See how to test for short circuits below. But if you suspect a short and don't want to bother making the test, call the electrician and have him take care of the problem as soon as possible.

Appliance Motors Seem to Slow (Function Below Capacity). This can also be an overload symptom. Appliance motors will also slow if there's a power dim-out—that is, the utility company is feeding less than its usual amount of power to your neighborhood or general area. Listen to your battery-operated radio or check with your neighbors or the utility company to see if this is the case. *But first, it's a good idea to turn off the appliance until full power is restored.*

Strange Odors from Appliance or Electrical Equipment. This should warn you of malfunction—the insulation on a wire may be heating to the danger point, or, a motor may be about to burn out. Whenever you detect strange odors in any electrical device, disconnect the items from its power source. If necessary, remove the fuse in this circuit. Then, call the electrician.

You Feel Electric Shocks When You Touch the Toaster, Refrigerator, etc. The hazard is *serious.* Disconnect the units immediately. There are various causes for this: damaged wiring inside the unit is one. In any case, you need professional help. Don't use the unit until the electrician has made the appropriate repairs.

Arcing. A serious malfunction in any electrical unit. Arcing is an actual spark or shower of sparks that you can see. These jump a gap between wires or metal parts of a machine. The danger here is both shock and fire. Disconnect the unit from its power source *immediately,* then call the repairman.

HOW TO TEST FOR ELECTRICAL OVERLOADS ON YOUR HOUSE CIRCUITS

According to experts, overloading circuits with too many electrical appliances, lamps, etc., is the top cause of home fires. That should be enough to persuade you to learn how to check for overloads. But if you can't do it yourself, have an electrician do it for you. The first and most obvious indication that the circuit may be overloaded is, as we've said above, a *blown fuse*. What you *notice* is that the lights in part of the house suddenly go off. To test, follow this routine:

Unplug All Appliances and Lamps or Lights That Went Out When the Fuse Blew. It's important to disconnect all the electrical appliances *and* lights—from furnace blowers, garbage disposers, to overhead ceiling and closet lights—that work on this circuit. That means turning off the switches that normally control the lights, etc. Next, arm yourself with a flashlight and a new 15-amp fuse.

Turn Off the Main Switch. This is usually in the basement, near the fuse box or circuit breaker panel, and it's probably labeled, if you don't know its location. Once you turn off the main switch, all the power in the house is shut off.

Remove the Blown Fuse. Locate the blown fuse from among those in the fuse box. If the fuse isn't labeled or numbered, flash your light on the little glasslike window on the surface of the fuses. If the fuse has blown, the tiny metal strip that shows through this window will be broken, as you see in the illustrations on page 265. Remove the fuse by unscrewing it counterclockwise (turning to the left). Insert the new fuse by screwing it in clockwise—*but, again, be absolutely sure that the fuse is 15-amps* or the proper one for the circuit.

Turn On Main Switch.

Now, One by One, Switch On the Lights and Appliances Served by this Circuit. If the fuse blows just after you've plugged in the last electrical appliance, it's more than likely the circuit's suffering from overloading. (The alternative possibility is that this *last* appliance is short-circuiting. For details, see below, HOW TO TEST FOR SHORT CIRCUITS. . . .") To cope with the overload, unplug this or some other appliance or, if it's more convenient, disconnect a series of lamps.

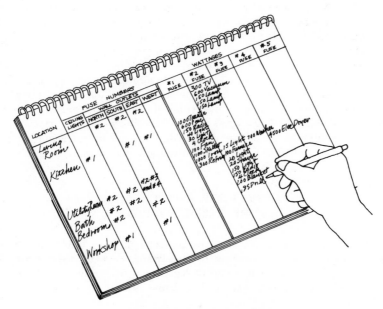

Chart: Wiring System Inventory

Again, Insert a New Fuse. (Be sure to follow the procedure given above.) You can live with this overload until you have a new circuit installed by the electrician *if* you limit the number of appliances working simultaneously on the circuit. For instance, if you want to use the toaster, unplug some lamps, a radio, or something else. When you've finished with the toaster, turn on the lamps, etc., again.

Note: If your circuits are controlled by circuit breakers instead of fuses, follow the procedures above—except for the replacement of fuses. With a circuit breaker, merely flip the switch to *on* again (after it's been tripped by an overload to *off*).

If you're interested in discovering the power problems and needs in your home, we suggest you do a bit of basic research. Consult the table, below, to get an idea of the power your lights and appliances require. Then, go to the fuse box or circuit breaker panel and attach a label under or near each circuit fuse: The first fuse on the left is numbered 1, the next 2, and so on. Go upstairs and turn on every light in the house. Go back to the fuse box. First, turn off the main switch, then remove fuse #1. Turn *on* the main switch, and go back upstairs. Now, with a chart like the one below, *mark all of the lights that have been turned off by removing fuse #1.* Test wall outlets by plugging working lamps into them. If they fail to turn on, these outlets are also on the #1 fuse circuit.

Turn off the main switch and restore fuse #1, then follow the same routine with fuse #2.

Note: Number circuit breakers the same way; then, one by one, trip them to determine which circuit handles which lights and appliances.

The maximum *safe load* for a 15-amp house circuit is 1800 watts. When you total the columns of power being used in your house, following the form given in the chart, you may discover just which circuits you're overloading and by how much. If it's at all practical, move some of the lamps or appliances to other circuits that don't carry so many electrical devices. If it's not easy to do this, call your electrician (at least now you'll know where and what your new power requirements are). He can install a new circuit for you.

Note: Often, in new homes, the electrician will install special, heavy-duty circuits for large, power-hungry appliances: water heater, furnace-blower, clothes dryer, etc. These are separate circuits that take more than a 15-amp fuse. They're installed with heavier gauge wires, and operate on fuses suited to the appliance. We suggest that you consult your electrician if you have problems with these circuits. *But we do caution you: don't mix up your 15-amp and higher amp fuses.* Keep them separated, in boxes that are clearly labeled. Make it a rule, until you have real expertise, to handle only the 15-amp circuits and fuses.

HOW TO TEST FOR SHORT CIRCUITS IN YOUR HOUSE WIRING

Short circuits produce sparks, and sparks can light fires. If you inspect your electrical appliances—check their cords and plugs regularly—and treat them kindly, you may never have to come face-to-face with a short circuit. But, for that one possible encounter, you need to know how short circuits occur and what to do about them.

TABLE OF AVERAGE WATTAGES

LIGHTING

Wall, Ceiling (per bulb)	25–150
Table Lamp (per bulb)	60–150
Pin-up Lamp	40–150
Floor Lamp (per bulb)	25–300
Night Light	7½
Fluorescent Circlines	22–32
Fluorescent Tubes	15–40

KITCHEN, DINING ROOM

Blender, Food*	250–380
Casserole (6-quart)	330
Clock	2
Coffe Grinder*	150
Corn Popper	500
Dishwasher (heated)*	1250
Dishwasher (unheated)*	400
Disposal Unit, Food Waste*	500
Egg Cooker	500
Electric Knife	100
Exhaust Fan*	250
Fryer, Deep-fat	1350
Hot Plate (per unit)	700–1250
Iron, Hand (dry or steam)	1100
Knife Sharpener*	110
Microwave Oven (portable)	1450
Mixer, Food*	150
Pan, Sauce	1000
Polisher, Floor*	350
Percolator (6-cup)	600
Refrigerator (12 cu. ft.)*	300
Roaster-Rotisserie*	1400
Sandwich Grill	800–1160
Skillet, Frying	1100
Toaster	1200
Trash Compactor	400
Waffle Iron	1100

LIVING ROOM, FAMILY ROOM

Air Conditioner (5,000 BTU)	575–930
Air Conditioner (8,000 BTU)	800–1400
Fan, Ventilating*	150
Fan, Floor (large)*	650
Radio, Table (small)	50
Radio, Console-type	150
Record Player*	75

Television Set	55–300
Vacuum Cleaner*	630–800

BEDROOMS, BATHROOMS

Blanket	200
Bottle Warmer	400
Fan, Window (large)*	200–500
Hair Dryer*	275–380
Heater, Reflecting (portable)	1200
Heater, Wall (built-in)	1250
Heating Pad	60
Lamp, Heat, Infra-red	250
Lamp, Sun, Ultra-violet	400
Shaver	15

BASEMENT, UTILITY ROOM

Dehumidifier*	160–250
Dryer, Clothes (gas-type)*	350
Freezer*	350
Furnace, Coal Stoker*	400
Furnace, Gas-fired*	100
Furnace, Oil-fired*	800
Incinerator	600
Ironer-Mangle*	1650
Lawn Mower*	300
Pump, Well or Sump*	300
Washer, Clothes (automatic)*	500–700

WORKSHOP

Drill (¼-in.)*		150–375
Grinder		185–375
Lathe, Wood or Metal (⅓ hp.)*		250
Sander, Portable (1 hp.)*		746
Saw, Band (12-in., ⅓ hp.)*		250
Saw, Bench (8-in., 10-in.)*	375,	560
Saw, Jig (18-in., ⅓ hp.)*		250
Saw, Radial Arm (10-in.)*		1500
Saw, Sabre (⅙ hp., ⅓hp.)*	100,	250
Soldering Iron		150

240-VOLT APPLIANCES
(*Use Separate Circuits, Fusing*)

Air Conditioner (12,000 BTU)	1600–2100
Dryer, Clothes*	4500
Range, Cooking*	8000–16000
Water Heater (50-gal.)	2000
Water Pump, Deep-well*	1250

* Motor-driven appliance. All motors consume much more power for a few seconds when started.

The obvious symptom of short-circuiting in any wiring in your house, or in any of your appliance motors, is just the same as for the overload: the lights in one part of the house will suddenly go out, and the appliances that share this circuit will stop working. Again, as with the overload, the circuit fuse has blown. But there's a difference in the way the fuse blows, and a difference in the way the fuse looks after it's been hit by a short circuit. To cope with the situation, arm yourself (as before) with a flashlight and a new 15-amp fuse. Then follow this procedure:

Unplug Small Appliances and Lamps That Went Out When the Fuse Blew. Turn Off Major Appliances. (This part of the routine is just the same as the preparation to test for an overloaded circuit.)

Turn Off the Main Switch. The house will be dark, just as it was when you tested for an overload.

Remove the Blown Fuse. (If the fuse isn't labeled or numbered, and you don't know which fuse to remove, shine the flashlight on the little glasslike windows of the fuses. If there's been a short in one of the circuits, *the fuse window will be blackened.* Note that this is different from the way a fuse looks after an overload has caused it to blow. When there's a short, the small metal strip under the window is given such a scorching that filament burns and leaves a telltale signature. Remove the damaged fuse. See FUSES, below, p. 265.)

Now at least you know that you have a short somewhere along this circuit. Your problem is to *locate* it.

Insert the New Fuse, Using the Same Size.

Turn On the Main Switch. If the fuse blows immediately (scorching the window as it did with the previous fuse), you've discovered that the short is in the *wiring of the circuit.* At least you know that it's *not* in your lights or appliances, because you haven't yet connected them to the circuit. Small comfort, maybe, but it will save the electrician some time if you've gone this far with the investigation. Take the old fuse out or leave it there, then go upstairs and call the repairman. (He may have to open your walls to find the damaged portion of the circuit.)

If you've inserted the new fuse in the circuit and it *doesn't blow* when you turn on the main switch, you'll have more detective work to do to locate the short.

One by One, Switch On the Lights and Appliances. If, for example, you've turned on two lights and the lights stay on, and then you turn on a third lamp and the lights or appliances on the circuit go dead again, you know that the *third lamp* is the source of trouble. Unplug this lamp. Insert a new 15-amp fuse downstairs (as you've done previously), turn the main switch on, then go upstairs and look at lamp number three and its cord and plug. Most likely you'll find exposed wiring where the insulation has worn off the cord, or burn marks to explain why you had a short circuit. Have the lamp cord repaired, or do it yourself, with instructions given below. (If your inspection doesn't show you where on the lamp the trouble is, take the lamp to the electrician—you've done what you can, and now it's time for an expert to take over.)

Note: If your circuits are controlled by circuit breakers you won't have any visual proof as to whether the lights go out because of an overload or a short circuit. But you *can* complete the test for a short circuit. Unplug the lamps and appliances, as above, then flip the circuit breaker switch from *off* to *on.* If the circuit breaker trips to *off* at this point, you know the short is in the circuit wiring. Call the electrician and have him do the repairs. If the circuit breaker doesn't trip to *off* until you've plugged in lamp number three, you know that the short is in the lamp or its cord. Replace or repair these or have an expert do so.

FUSES AND CIRCUIT BREAKERS

Plug Fuses. These are the fuses you normally use in your fuse box. They're screwed into the fuse sockets. There are three types, the last two being preferable to the first.

1. Edison Base Fuse. Until recently, this type was most widely used in homes in the United States. Note that the metal filament or strip that breaks with an overload or burns up with a short is visible through the window on the face of the fuse.

2. Time-Delay Fuse. These fit the same socket as the Edison Base, and are recommended for home use because of an added aspect of their performance that makes them more convenient. Note that they're as safe as the Edison Base—that is, they'll blow as quickly when there's a short circuit, and thus give your home proper protection. But these fuses are also made to take higher electrical loads for a few seconds—as when, for instance, the motor in your portable heater goes on. In effect, this fuse can handle brief periods of overloads, without blowing. (Appliance motors, when they start up on a circuit that's serving near capacity, will often blow ordinary fuses.) We suggest you install time-delay

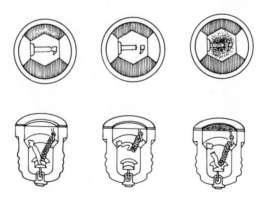

fuses when you replace your ordinary types. You buy them at the hardware store in the appropriate size.

3. S-Type Fuse. This type does the same job as the time-delay, and it incorporates a special safety feature that prompts the National Electrical Code to insist on its use wherever possible. The S-type fuse has two parts: an adapter

base that screws into the socket the way the fuses above do, and a smaller fuse section. The adapter, once installed, *can't be removed* by careless fuse-changers. The top of the adapter will take only the size fuse it is designed for—or smaller. That means no meddlers can mess up your circuits by inserting a 30-amp fuse in a 15-amp circuit. You may want to buy these super-safety, tamper-free fuses for your circuits.

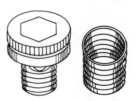

Cartridge Fuses. These are the types used in heavy-duty appliances and in the special circuits that serve them. Consult your hardware man and electrician if you want to replace any cartridge fuses, but it's probably best to let the expert handle this chore.

 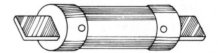

Circuit Breakers. These usually look like extra-large light switches, which is what, in effect, they are. They're favored in new homes because they're permanent, and do not need changing as the blown fuse does. When a short or overload occurs, the circuit breaker trips open, cutting off the flow of electricity. This means that the switch flips to *off*, and that lights on the circut go out and appliances stop working. When you're ready to bring the current back into the circuit, you merely switch the circuit breaker to its *on* position. (It will automatically trip open again if you haven't taken care of that short or overload.) Your electrician can install circuit breakers for you in place of fuses, if you choose to make the alteration.

REPAIRING PLUGS AND CORDS

If you're nimble-fingered, neat, and patient in *other* chores, you've got what it takes to do repairs on the most vulnerable links in your household's electrical chain. Repairing plugs and cords can save money *and* the aggravation of carting your lamps and appliance cords to the local service center or electrician. *But we stress that your work must be careful and exact.* If you're forgetful or fumble-fingered, doing these repairs can expose your family and home to the dangers of electric shock and fire.

You may notice trouble in the plug or cord when you're making a regular inspection of your electrical connections and appliances. Below are the problems and the ways to cope with them. (First, be sure to *disconnect* the cord from electrical power source.)

Small Strands of Wires Loose Around Terminals of Plugs. If the *prongs* seem steady and they're not corroded, and if the plug *case* is sound, then all you have to do is *fix the loose wires.* The repair is simple, but the condition you've discovered *is dangerous.* (If the loose strands from the two separate cables of wire ever *touch,* they'll cause a short circuit. You'll have sparks, and possibly a fire, as a result.) To make the repair:

1. Loosen the little terminal screws slightly with a screwdriver.

2. Twist one bunch of the tiny copper wires, beside one terminal, into a tight, firm cable. (The result should look the way a strand of tightly twisted knitting yarn looks.)

3. Wrap this strand or cable around one of the terminal screws. Be sure to wrap it clockwise (left to right) around the screw.

4. Tighten the screw by driving it in clockwise with a screwdriver.

5. Repeat these procedures with the second bunch of tiny copper wires, making a *firm, tight cable,* etc.

6. Inspect your work, to be sure no wirelets are visible. *Be sure all wires are covered by the screwheads.* (If any small wires do stick out, clip them with wire cutters or unscrew the terminal and redo your work.)

7. Insert the cardboard insulation-cover (slip it over the prongs). Test the plug by inserting it in a working wall outlet.

Cord Leading into Plug Is Frayed. Disconnect, and inspect as above to be sure that the prongs of the plug are not loose or corroded. To make the repair:

1. Cut through the frayed cord with a sharp kitchen paring knife, to get rid of the frayed portion of the cord.

2. Slip the good cord back through the plug and push it *through* to the prong side so that there's at least 2½ inches of cord sticking out between the prongs and remove the outer covering on the cord for about 1½ inches.

3. Strip the insulation off one of the wires, exposing the cable of twisted copper wire, for *about ½ inch.* Twist these exposed wires into a tight cable.

4. Repeat the process with the second wire.

5. Now tie what's called an *Underwriters' Knot* in the two insulated wires. *This is the important, safety-first part of the repair, so follow the steps as shown in the diagram on p. 268,* to prevent the cord from being yanked from the plug, and to keep the little copper wires around the two terminals from touching each other and igniting whatever they're in contact with. This knot, in other words, keeps the final step of the repair secure.

6. Loop one wire around one prong, as shown, and the other around the *other* prong, as shown.

7. Finish the repair by twisting one strand, or cable, of the exposed wires *clockwise* around *one* terminal screw, twisting the other, also clockwise, around

the second screw. Clip off any wirelets not anchored and covered by the screw-heads, as below.

8. Insert the cardboard cover on the plug, as above. Test the plug.

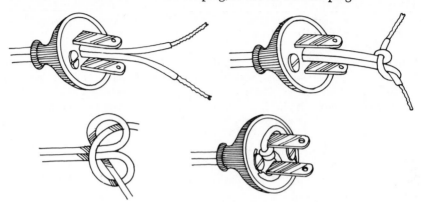

Note: There are new types of *male* plugs on the market that save you all the bother of doing this job. Just cut off the damaged portion of the cord, then clamp the new plug onto the wire, near the end. (This plug makes its *own* connection with the wires, by piercing the insulated sheaths around them.) Buy these at the hardware or electrical supply store. It should be noted, however, that experts favor the *old-fashioned plug* we've described above, *because its wires can be secured inside the plug case with the Underwriters' Knot.* This, they say, makes the older plug much *safer* to use.

Repairs to *female* plugs are essentially the same as the repairs given above. The case (unless it's molded of plastic or rubber) can be unscrewed and taken apart, and the repairs to the wires are then made. (See illustration.)

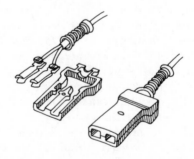

Damaged, Wobbly, or Corroded Prongs. Cracked Plug Case. Replace the plug, or buy a new cord with new plug attached.

Cord Outer-Covering Cracked. If you're sure that the inner insulation isn't damaged, make a temporary repair. Wrap the cracked part of the cord securely with overlapping layers of electrician's plastic tape. (Buy it at the hardware store.) Don't use substitutes.

EXTENSION CORDS

The best advise we can give you about extension cords is: use them *seldom—if at all!* For one thing, the extension cord *diminishes the power your appliance receives;* and the greater distance from the source of power, the poorer the performance of your appliance. Move your appliances and lamps closer to an outlet, if possible. Or, have new outlets installed adjacent to the appliance. Be guided by the safely rules, p. 258, which apply to *all electrical cords—*if you *must* use extension cords. Check with your hardware dealer or electrician about the correct cord to use for the appliance. Ordinary lamp-cord extensions will heat up dangerously if you attach them to a heavy appliance like a vacuum cleaner or toaster. *Be sure to use heavy-duty cords for these—again, if you must use extension cords.*

GROUNDING

If you've ever scuffed across a carpeted room, touched a metal door handle, then been jolted by a tiny spark of static electricity, you don't have to be told you're a dandy conductor. This minor encounter with the forces of nature gives you a rough idea of the problems of grounding. Large appliances that use lots of electrical power (air conditioners, washers, dryers, ranges) can give off even more powerful jolts unless they're properly connected with wires to the ground, or earth. Leaking current has to reach the ground somehow, and unless it's channeled safely, it'll go through you or whatever touches the surface of the appliance to get to mother earth.

In many parts of the country, the electrical codes specify certain grounding practices. You may have noticed on some appliances that the plug at the end of the cord has *three—*not two—prongs. The third prong is the grounding device. When such a plug is inserted into a special three-prong outlet, the appliance is grounded, and you can't be shocked when you touch it.

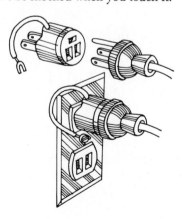

If you buy a new refrigerator which has a three-prong plug, but discover that your wall outlet has only two slots for the plug, you can buy (or have the electrician install) an *adapter*. In this particular case, the adapter *adapts* the three-prong plug to the two-slot outlet. (It fits between them, with two prongs inserted into the outlet and with three prongs in *it*.) The adapter also has a special grounding wire which is attached to the metal case of the wall outlet. This wire is usually hooked around the screw in the center of the outlet plate (see Illustration.) *Be sure this ground wire is attached to the outlet.* (Turn off the power before you attempt to attach it.) If you're uneasy about the work, have your electrician install a grounded wall outlet which will match the plug.

CAULKING

CAULKING CHART

Name or Type of Material	Characteristics	Uses	Remarks and Special Directions
SILICONE CAULK	Mildew-resistant. Comes in colors to match the objects being sealed: white, gray, black, and natural stone. A translucent variety for invisible caulks is available; this adapts to any surface color. Very versatile for joints where bending and compressing of materials is necessary (pliable weather stripping for example).	For bathtub and tile joint sealing, metal plumbing fixtures, gutters, and downspouts. Also can seal rubber and canvas pieces inside and outside your house.	Don't use this caulk on sidewalk cracks.
BUTYL RUBBER CAULK	Comes in several shades of white and in tan, gray, stone, brown, aluminum, limestone, and for a small extra charge, any special colors you may need.	For seals around windows and outdoor house siding. Especially useful for sealing chimney flashings and for roof-shingle repair. Makes seals between dissimilar materials—for instance: wood and glass; metal and concrete; plastic and wood.	A good replacement for putty, in window repairs, because it lasts longer and doesn't get brittle *Note:* Not quite as flexible as silicone caulk. You can paint over rubber caulk after a skin forms on its surface, depending on the weather. Must be applied when temperature is over 40° Fahrenheit.
LATEX CAULK	White-colored, easy to use. Its surface can be smoothed with water when you apply it, and you can apply it with	Inside the house. This is the best caulk to use around tiles of the shower, or for filling areas around counter-	Probably a good idea to stock this for most of your routine caulking and sealing inside the house. Remember:

271

CAULKING CHART (cont.)

Name or Type of Material	Characteristics	Uses	Remarks and Special Directions
LATEX CAULK (cont.)	your moistened finger or a damp knife or small applicator. When dry this caulk is water-resistant. Can be sand-papered and painted. Cleanup is easy—just wash it off with water.	tops of tile or plastic. Works on glass and is good for seals around windowpanes. Also good to fill nail holes.	it is less elastic and resilient than the rubber caulk described above.
ASPHALT CAULK	Is black, and similar to the blacktop of roads, but it can be painted over with oil-base paint.	Roof repairs, especially leaks, and cracks around drains, vents, and flashing.	Can be bought in a large can or in a tube (which makes application relatively simple).
ACRYLIC LATEX CAULK	Comes in "bright" white; do cleanup after applications with water.	Especially made for use on cracked, latex-painted surfaces (outside or interior walls or trim).	Can be painted over; when this is done it actually *merges* with the latex paint to make a durable, invisible seal.

BRICK AND MORTAR: CLEANING, REPAIRING, AND REPOINTING

Though we don't plan to preempt your mason's mastery of bricks and mortar, we do suggest you try your hand at some simple masonry repairs. Whether you try these repairs or not, do get to know your brick walls and chimney exterior. Inspect them and be alert to signs of serious trouble. *Be aware of the differences between these and minor masonry maladies.* (A line of badly cracked bricks, for example, or smoke leaking through the mortar joints of the chimney when it's in use, should warn you to send for the mason or building contractor immediately. Don't use the chimney until repairs have been made by a professional. For additional details, consult CHIMNEY and FIREPLACE in Section I.)

If you're the puttering type, the minor repairs we take up below can often (but not always) forestall deterioration, and they'll probably bring back the beauty of the brickwork.

Cleaning Brick. Start with the everyday household remedies when you tackle dirty brick.

1. Vacuum the surface. Use your vacuum cleaner or a soft brush to dust off grime and smoky particles.

2. Scrub with detergent and water. Use a stiff brush, but scrub gently: be careful not to chip out the mortar. Rinse with clear water, and allow the surface to dry for about an hour. If the smoke and grease stains are still visible, it's time to resort to harsher methods.

3. Make a mixture of trisodium phosphate and water. Buy the trisodium phosphate at the hardware store. Follow the directions on the container; be sure to wear rubber gloves to protect your hands. Use a stiff brush, but scrub the surface *gently*. Rinse off with clear water and allow the bricks to dry for about an hour. If the stains are still there, try the next method.

4. Rub the surface with carborundum. Use the rod that sharpens your carving knives—it's carborundum—or buy a carborundum block at the hardware store. Be careful when you rub the surface, because doing this is really taking off a thin layer of brick and mortar. Vacuum or brush the dust off.

CAUTION: *Don't try* muriatic acid *as a cleaner, even though some masons and experts suggest it.* The acid is dangerous, and should only be handled by professionals.

Note: If none of the above remedies banish the stains, buy some latex "water-base" paint, and touch up the stained surfaces. Paint or hardware stores carry latex paints for indoor and for outdoor use in colors that match bricks.

Repairing and Repointing. When repairs are made on brick it's called *repair-*

ing. When *mortar* between the lines of bricks is fixed it's called *repointing*. We give the simple steps for both below:

1. Clean out damaged brick or mortar. If the mortar's crumbly, scrape it out from between the bricks (go as deep as ¼ to ½ inch to get the old mortar out). Use a screwdriver or a *cold chisel*. (See GLOSSARY OF TOOLS, p. 225.) If one brick is damaged, repair or replace *that one*. (Remove the cracked brick with the chisel, but be careful not to chip into the neighboring, undamaged bricks.) Clean the hole to get rid of the old mortar, as described above.

2. Dust off area. Be sure the surfaces are free of grit and dirt.

3. Soak the area. If you're planning to replace a damaged brick, soak the *new brick* in water for a few minutes. Then, soak the area the brick will go into—be sure all nooks and crannies are really wet.

4. Have mortar ready. Buy prepared (dry) mortar at the hardware store or lumberyard or at your brick dealer. Mix this with just enough water to make a thick, buttery spread. Dampen a small piece of wood (a plywood scrap is good) then put dabs of the mortar on it. Take this mortar *hawk* and clean trowel or kitchen spatula to the repair station, and go to work. (You use the hawk the way an artist uses an oil-paint palette—troweling the mortar from it to the repairs.)

5. Apply mortar. If you're inserting a new brick, "butter" all but the front of the brick with the mortar. Slip the brick into the hole left by its predecessor. Pack in *more* mortar around the edges of the brick. (*Note:* If you're only doing a repointing job—*not* replacing a brick—pack mortar into the spaces left by the old mortar.) Be careful not to dribble mortar onto the rest of the wall or chimney —it's hard to clean mortar off after it sets.

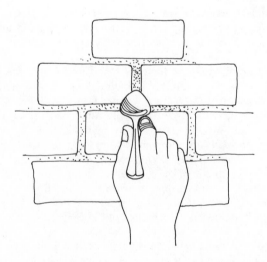

6. Finishing or *striking*. Let the mortar set for a few minutes, then run a small tube or pipe, or an old but clean teaspoon, across the fresh mortar joints. This indents the mortar and forms a concave groove between the line of bricks. (See diagram.) It's a finishing touch that's called *striking the joint*. And there's a purpose beyond just looks to the strike. The indentation keeps rain and snow from getting into the mortar seams, and thus prolongs the life of the wall or chimney.

Note: Little, hairline cracks or small gouges in bricks can be repaired as above using mortar. Touch up the repairs with a matching indoor or outdoor latex paint.

MENDING BY SEWING

There's more *reason* than rhyme to the old proverb, "A stitch in time saves nine." Many's the sweater, afghan, or bedspread that really fell apart for want of a stitch at the right moment in the right place. Below, we give you a brief summary of mending techniques, to help you catch little tears before they become big tatters.

Note: Experts suggest that hand mending is the best way to fix fabrics that are ripped and damaged—especially on accessories that *show*—cushion covers, bedspreads, and curtains, for instance. But mending by machine is sometimes easier and often stronger. A zigzag machine-stitched mend across a tear in canvas or denim may outlast the cushion cover *itself!* In any case, if you own a machine, you'll probably know how to handle it and when to use it for quick and strong mending jobs. You may choose the machine, or you may prefer some of the hand methods we suggest.

Tips on Tools and Supplies. Be sure you have these at hand when the time to repair arrives:

1. Needles. Most packets of needles contain the three basic types: sharps, betweens, and crewels. The medium-length sharps are the good, general-use type. Betweens come in handy for awkward places and teensy spaces (where long needles can't go) and they do fine-stitching on heavy fabrics. The large-eyed crewels (or embroidery needles) are dandy for yarn when used for darning, for blanket-stitching over a worn blanket border, and can be used for regular sewing if you prefer fairly big-eyed needles. The practice with needles is to match them to the material: generally, big, heavy needles are the ones to use on coarse, heavy fabrics. Fine needles work best on fine, delicate weaves.

Note: Be sure to have some of the special needles. Buy a curved upholstery needle, and one of the extra-long upholstery or mattress needles. You may want to pick up a special three-sided needle to be used for mending leather clothes and coverings. All of these are available at the sewing counters of department stores.

2. Thread. Keep all the colors of the rainbow on hand in your sewing basket. Also, be sure to have the old reliables: black, brown, gray, tan, and white threads. Experts say to use thread that is a shade *darker* than the fabric you're mending. Off the spool and in the *seam*, the strand of thread will *seem* lighter!

As with the needle you use for the job, the thread or yarn should match the weight of the material it goes into. Lightweight fabrics take best to fine threads. Medium-weight fabrics are best mended with medium-weight thread, and heavy threads go in heavy fabrics.

Mercerized cotton threads are used for cotton, linen, silk, wool, and synthetic fabrics. But, if you prefer, use silk for mends made on silks and wools. (You can use silk thread on synthetics, too, but experts suggest using synthetic threads for these materials.)

3. Shears and scissors. The best for large work are the tailor's favorite: 8-inch, bent-handle shears. Buy them at sewing counters. Trimming scissors, 4 to 6 inches long, are indispensable for darns, patches, and other smaller jobs.

4. Thimble and pins. Save your finger by wearing a thimble. Save time by using pins in your work. (We suggest the nonrust type.)

5. Tape measure or ruler. Many mends will need to be measured for new material.

Note: You'll also use an iron and ironing board to finish off your mending.

Basic Stitches (By Hand). These are diagramed so that you can see the end product.

1. Basting. A quick, large stitch used to keep cloth in place temporarily, removed when the fine, finished stitching is done. (There are varieties of basting, but the type pictured here suffices for simple mends. (See illustration.)

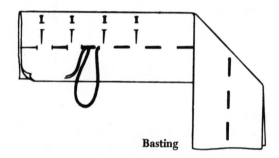

Basting

2. Running stitch. Used for seaming delicate fabrics. All stitches are small as possible, *and the same size!* The beginner can take up one stitch at a time on the needle; the practiced mender will run several stitches at a time on the needle. (See illustration.)

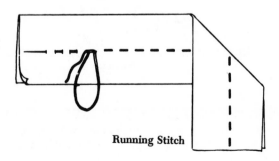

Running Stitch

3. Backstitch. A strong stitch that can take the place of machine sewing. Start with a small stitch: put the needle down through the fabric and, on the wrong side, make a stitch running from right to left. Bring the needle up through the material. Now do your first *backstitch*. Bring the needle and thread back to the beginning, where the knot in your thread is (that is, from left to right). Put the needle down through the fabric to the wrong side again, and this time make a stitch *twice* as long as the first, stitching from right to left. Pull the needle up to the top again, and bring it back (from left to right) again, to the left end edge of the first stitch. Continue this process to the end of the work. On the under, or wrong side, you'll have what looks like a continuous line of overlapping stitches. On the "show" or top side, you'll have stitches in a line, the end of one stitch abutting the beginning of the next. (See illustration.)

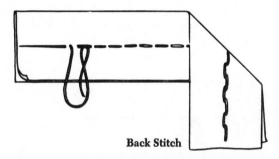

Back Stitch

4. Hemming. Fold the edge of the material under, pin in place. Baste to hold fabric in place, then do the hemming by making a series of small, slanted stitches: slip your needle through the fewest possible threads of fabric, then up, at a slant, through the folded-under hem. (See illustration.)

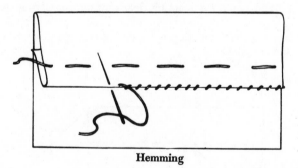

Hemming

5. Slip stitch (or invisible stitch). You can make an invisible hem or other mend with this stitch. Pick up one or two strands of the fabric with the needle, then slip the needle into the underside of the folded hem, as shown. (See illustration.)

Slip Stitch

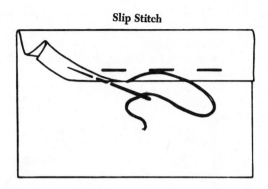

6. Whip stitch. A much-used stitch, the whip stitch joins two folded or hemmed edges together. The needle is inserted in the fabric slantwise (pointing from right to left, *if* you're right-handed). (See illustration.)

Whip Stitch

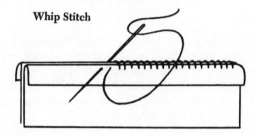

7. Overhand stitch. Another version of the whip stitch, in which the needle is pointed straight at the needle wielder.

8. Overcasting. Used to keep raw edges of material from fraying. The needle is slanted to make diagonal stitches, which are inserted far enough into the fabric to make the stitches and edge secure. (See illustration.)

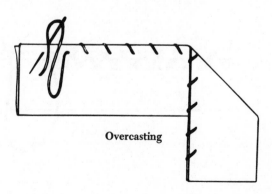

Overcasting

9. Blanket stitch. Good for edging thick materials—like *blankets!* You work from left to right. Bring the needle out very close to the edge of the blanket or other fabric. Then, take an upright stitch to the right with the needle pointed down, keeping the thread *under* the needle. Bring needle out again near fabric edge. Consult the diagram. (See illustration.)

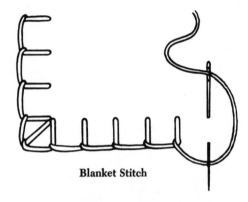

Blanket Stitch

10. Buttonhole stitch. If you use this around frayed buttonholes, work from right to left, using a finer, closer version of the blanket stitch above. If you use it decoratively, for embroidery, work from left to right, as above, but with stitches very close together. Buttonhole loops are made by using this stitch. First, make a loop with several strands of thread anchored to the material on each side. Then, go over these with buttonhole stitch.

11. Catch-stitch hemming. Good for heavy fabrics, and for finishing a ribbon binding on a blanket edge. Work from left to right. With a backstitch, catch your needle first in the edge of the ribbon or fabric, then in the fabric above it. Work this way, back and forth, using the diagram as a guide. (See illustration.)

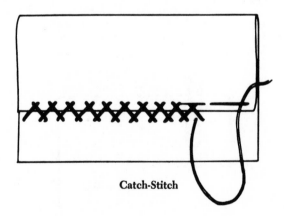

Catch-Stitch

12. Gathering. Just use the running stitch (see above), then gently pull the thread to make the gathers in the material.

Darning. Neat, precise darning can give new life to various types of woven fabrics and to knitted clothes and accessories. The trick is to use matching yarn for the mend. If the fabric is woven, take the threads from the turned-under portion of a hem, or from the seam edges. If the item is knitted, duplicate the color and *ply* (thickness) of the yarn from yarn or needlework stores. There are several techniques to use:

1. Ordinary or woven darn. As you'll see from the diagrams, this type of darn is really an elaboration of the running stitch (see above). *Don't* knot the yarn, and *do* work on the right side of the fabric so that you can be sure you're making the stitches as inconspicuous as possible. (If the fabric is torn, fit the edges together. Reinforce with fabric on the underside if necessary.)

- Three-Cornered Tear. Notice that the second application of stitches is *woven through* the running stitches of the first, to give the mend added strength. (See illustration.)

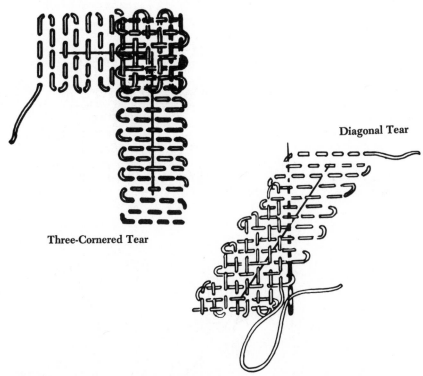

Diagonal Tear

Three-Cornered Tear

- Diagonal Tear. Again, weave the stitches for strength. (See illustration.)
- Darning a Hole. Trim the edges to get rid of loose ends. Use a sock darner or piece of cardboard as a base for your operations when you start to sew—to keep the material evenly stretched. Use running stitches, going from top to bottom as shown, then turn and fill the hole with more running stitches, woven through the vertical strands, as shown. (See illustrations.)

Darning (Woven)

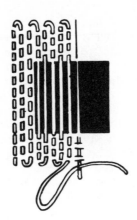

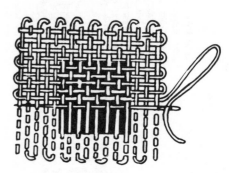

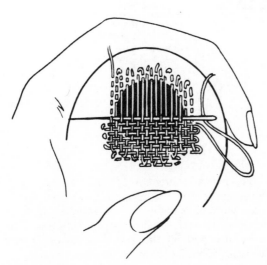

2. Blanket-stitch darn. Prepare the hole with running stitches in one direction, as above, then, instead of weaving, cover the hole by using a blanket stitch across it. (See illustration.)

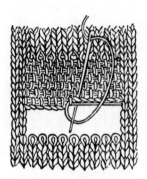

Blanket Stitch Darn

3. "Knitted" darns for knit goods. The finished work in any of these darns will look like knitting. If the yarn matches, the mend will be *undetectable on the right side*.

- Mending a Run with a Crochet Hook. Insert the hook, as shown, and just go up the ladder, pulling the stitches through as you do in chain-stitching. (See illustration.)

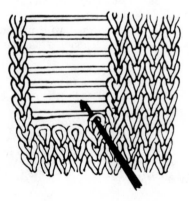

Mending with Crochet Hook

• Reinforcing Worn Spots with Duplicate Stitch. With needle and matching yarn, work rows of duplicate stitch over the area, as shown.

Reinforcing Worn Spot

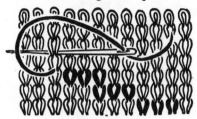

Duplicate Stitch

Note: This is also the way you can "embroider" knitted items, making the design look as if it were originally knitted in. (See illustration.)

• Weaving a Hole Using Knit Stitch. Prepare the hole by unraveling any broken stitches. Make the hole either square or rectangular. Secure the stitches along the sides of the hole (tack them lightly on the wrong side of the knitwear as shown in diagrams). (See illustrations.)

With needle and matching yarn, pick up stitches at top and bottom of hole, as shown. Make your pickups one stitch beyond the hole on either side, to give added strength to the mend. (See illustration.)

Fasten yarn in lower right corner on wrong side, turn to right side then "knit" over the hole, using vertical strands. Work in rows, using a variation of the duplicate stitch (see above). Be sure to keep the stitches in proportion to the actual knitted portion of the piece. (See illustration.)

Patching. Large holes are better covered with patches than darns. There are three types of patches you can use, depending on your skills and on the item you're mending.

**Weaving a Hole, Using
Knit Stitch**

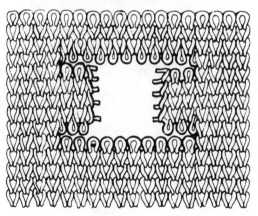

1. unraveling

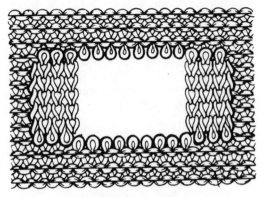

2. tack stitches on back

3. pick up stitches
top and bottom

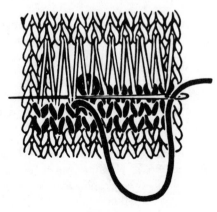

4. "knitting in"
the hole (with
knit stitch)

1. Ordinary sewed-on patch. Be sure to follow the grain, or weave, of the fabric when you use this method. Trim the hole to make it square or rectangular and to take off raveling threads. Cut a patch from matching fabric: if you can't duplicate it at the store, then steal some fabric from a wide hem or a corner that won't be visible later. Again, be sure the patch is cut on the grain of the fabric—and if it's patterned, match the patch to the design. *Wash the patch if the material is new* so that it won't shrink when it's sewn in place. Pin, then baste in place. Then slip-stitch, on the right side of the patch, to the fabric. (See above for slip stitch.)

2. Hemmed patch. Good for many kinds of fabrics. Cut a patch at least 1 inch larger than the hole. Clip the trimmed hole at the corners (about ¼ of an inch) so that you can turn under the edges of the good side of the material— that is, *fold* the rough edges of the hole to the wrong side of the material. *Be sure that you fold on the grain of the fabric.* Baste around the edges on the wrong side, while attaching the patch. Turn the fabric to the *right side,* and hem the turned-under edges of the hole. Turn to the wrong side again, and stitch the patch in place. You can also use a catch stitch to hold the patch: work it on the wrong side.

Note: You can *darn in* the patch, applying it first, by basting. Then use tiny running stitches around the edge of the hole and the patch. See above, "Darning."

3. Rewoven patch. This mend is best for coarsely woven fabrics, and if you're patient you can make the work *invisible.* First, outline the hole by clipping and pulling out one horizontal thread above the hole and another horizontal thread below it. Then, do the same on each side of the hole with a vertical thread.

Next, cut a patch from a matching piece of fabric. Make the patch an inch larger than the hole. Now, fray the edges of the patch. These frays on all four sides should make the *unfrayed* part of the patch fit exactly into the rectangle of material when one is placed on top of the other.

Tack the patch in place on the right side of the material.

You'll probably want to use a magnifying glass for the next operation, though it's not imperative that you do so. (You may want to buy the kind that expert needleworkers use: the glass has a cord that goes around your neck, and a device that keeps the glass at right angles, in place against your chest, so that you can look through it and have your hands free to do your needlework and darning.)

Now, with a small crochet hook, pull the frayed yarns one by one down through the pulled-out spaces of the material. If you've matched the patch to the material you're mending, each frayed yarnlet will find a perfect home in the weave of the fabric beneath it, going through the space left by the pulled-out strands.

As a finishing touch, turn the work to the wrong side, where the woven frayed yarns are, and tack each yarnlet with *tiny, tiny* stitches to secure them. Press the mend, and it should appear absolutely invisible on the right side! This, by the way, is what "invisible" reweavers do when they mend your clothes.

Appliqué. This is really a variation of the patch. Cut a piece of fabric in a decorative shape, tack or baste the fabric in place on the larger piece, then, with tiny running stitches, sew the appliqué to the larger piece. Turn the patch edge under as you do this, to make the work neat and to keep the edges from fraying.

Binding Edges. Sew ribbon or binding to the edge of the blanket or fabric you're mending. Do this on the right side, near the edge of both the binding and the blanket, as shown. Then, fold the binding over the edge and sew in place on the wrong side of the blanket, as shown. (See illustration.)

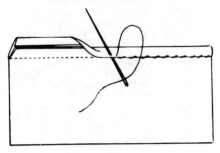

Binding

Tufting. (**For Mends Only.**) If you've patched your tufted bedspread and now need to disguise the patch by tufting the *bald* patch, follow these procedures. Buy some matching tufting yarn. Double the strands to make thick tufts, and thread these through a large-eyed needle. Push the needle straight down through the spread, then send it back up, ¼ inch away. Tie the yarn with a double knot, and trim the yarn to match the length of the undamaged tufts. (See illustrations.)

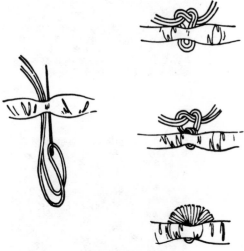

Tufting

Mending Lace. Repair a hole in your favorite piece of lace by weaving horizontal threads as you would for ordinary darning (see above). Next, weave *diagonally* from the upper right corner to the lower left corner, catching or looping around the horizontal threads as you go. If necessary, weave *again*, from the opposite diagonal. (See illustrations.)

Mending Lace

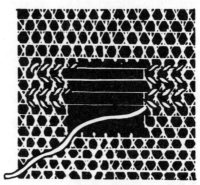

1. weaving horizontal
threads

2. weaving diagonally
(upper right)

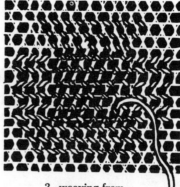

3. weaving from
opposite corners
(lower left)

CANING

Natural cane—the type used for chair seats and backs—comes all the way from jungles in Borneo, Sumatra, and Malaysia. As you might guess, it's related to rattan: in fact it's the *outer peeling* (or bark) of rattan, and as such comes in various sizes. Perhaps you hanker to replace the broken caning of an antique rocker with wider or narrower cane. But remember, the holes in the wood frame, through which the cane must pass and be secured, dictate the size of the cane you can use. If you have any doubt about the size of the cane strands you need to reweave your chair seat, clip a piece from the old caning before you discard it. Take the sample (or send it) to the cane supplier. Find the listings in the yellow pages of your phone directory under "Caning." (The cane supplier will also include binder cane and small wood pegs, both of which are used in the repair.) Be sure to do any refinishing or repairing to the chair *frame before* you weave the cane seat. Consult REFINISHING WOOD, p. 301, and Section I, CHAIR/SIDE OR ARM—WOOD, for details. See also CHAIR/CANE SEAT AND/OR BACK, for the technique used to apply *prewoven* cane to certain types of chairs.

Weaving the Seat. Before you begin the work, sharpen the cane ends to make them slip easily through the holes in the frame. Cut them with a knife or razor blade. Then, soak the cane in water for about an hour—this makes it pliable and supple. Study all of the diagrams below, and take your time on this project—go slowly until you get the knack of the work.

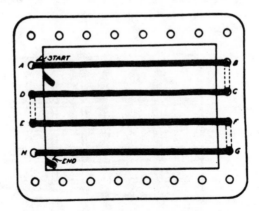

Fig. I. Inserting First Layer of Strands

Figure I. Begin as shown, at A and fasten the strand of cane in the hole with a peg. Carry the strand across to B. From here, carry the cane *underneath the frame* to C. Now, go up through C and across the frame to D. Keep the strand fairly tight. (It will be tighter later, with weaving, and *tightest* when the work is complete and the cane dries out.) Use a wood peg at C to keep the strand from slipping back to B. Continue the process, carrying the strand across the frame, from left to right, then right to left, *until you reach the last left-hand hole in the next-to-last row.* Peg the strand there. If the strand isn't long enough to finish this first run across the frame, insert a new strand where the old one leaves off, and tie them both. (See illustration.)

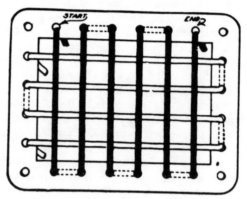

Fig. II. Inserting Second Layer of Strands

Figure II. This phase of the work adds a *second layer* of strands—at right angles to the first, as shown in the diagram. Note that this layer is *not* woven into the first—it merely lies atop the first layer. Begin this layer at the top left-hand portion, in the *second hole on the left.* Run the strand from top to bottom of the frame, then from bottom to top, ending at the top right corner, in the *second hole from the right.* (See illustration.)

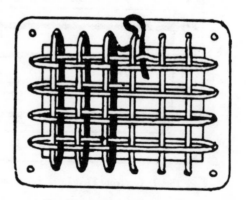

Fig. III. Weaving the Strands

Next add a *third* layer of strands. This layer runs parallel to the first layer, and is placed on top of the previous two layers. To apply it, follow the instructions given in Figure I. *Note again, that* no *weaving is being done with these first three layers of cane.*

Figure III. With this layer of cane, the actual weaving begins. Start in the upper left corner, in a hole where only *one strand of cane has been threaded.* Take the cane, first under, then over the two crosswise strands. Repeat this weaving with the next series of strands until you reach the bottom left portion of the frame. Carry the cane underneath the frame and up through the hole immediately to the right. Now, weave the cane up to the top of the frame. Continue across the seat. Be sure to keep the vertical pair of strands (as shown in the diagram) pushed close together. (See illustration.)

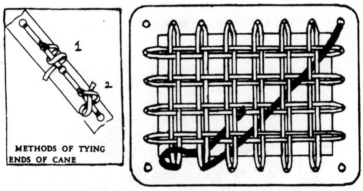

METHODS OF TYING
ENDS OF CANE

Fig. IV. First Diagonal Weave

Figure IV. With this new application of cane, you start the first *diagonal weave.* Before you do, though, make some preparations. Dampen the strands already on the seat—*thoroughly!* Then, force the *pairs of strands close together.* You do this to form hollow squares, all of the same size, all over the seat panel. Experts say that if you hold wood pegs in each hand, you can force the strands into position. Be sure to do this part of the work carefully, or you'll have difficulty with the diagonal weavings. (See illustration.)

Start the diagonal weave from the *empty upper right-hand hole.* Go left and down, first over the pair of horizontal strands, then under the pair of vertical strands. Bring the strand down through the third hole from the left at the bottom of the panel, and up through the second hole from the left. Weave back to the upper right hole, first going *under* the verticals and *over* the horizontals.

Note: All four corner holes of a rectangular frame always carry *two* diagonals. Be sure, when you're weaving the edges of the frame, that the weaving strand is run over or under all strands.

Figure V. Again you are weaving diagonal strands, but this time you start in the third hole, upper left, and weave down to the lower right corner hole. Then, start another diagonal next to this one, in the second hole from the left, and carry it down to the *same right-hand hole* occupied by the previous one. In this diagonal, you are weaving *over the verticals,* and *under the horizontals.*

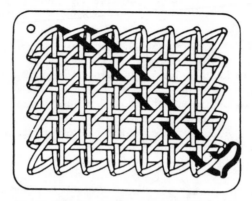

Fig. V. Weaving the Second Diagonal Strands

Figure VI. Check your weaving with the diagram to be sure you filled all the holes and have woven every strand correctly. (See illustration.)

Fig. VI. The Completed Weave

Figure VII. The finishing touch. Place the *binder* cane over the holes around

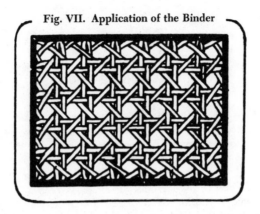

Fig. VII. Application of the Binder

the edge of the panel or seat. Then with loops of fine cane, secure the binder. Do this by pushing the fine cane up through a hole, over the binder, and back down through the hole, much the way you'd overcast with thread and needle. Pull the fine cane very tight. Finish by overlapping the binder cane, then fastening these ends down securely. Pull the ends to the underside of the seat and tie them as shown in insert above. (See illustration.)

Note: Finish the seat, when it's *thoroughly dry,* with a coat of clear lacquer or shellac. Coat both the under and upper sides. This protects the cane from deterioration caused by moisture—*and* it gives the chair a surface that's easier to clean.

Permission to reproduce caning drawings granted by Peerless Rattan & Reed Mfg. Co., Inc.

PAINTING, INDOOR

Before you take on a big job of painting, read the label on the paint can. The paint manufacturer knows how the paint should be handled: some paints need stirring and others don't; some paints go on best with rollers, others can be sprayed on the walls or furniture. Whichever paint you choose comes with its own special rules—you'll be happier at work *and* with the results if you follow them.

Tips for Beginners. Rub a creamy hand lotion on your hands and you'll find that the paint droplets will be much easier to clean off later, when you're finished painting. *Be sure to cover the floor and furniture with old sheets or canvas cloths to protect against paint drips and drops.*

Painting Do's and Don'ts. Before you buy the paint and other supplies, be guided by these:

- *Don't* use glossy paint on walls or ceilings—unless you want a shiny surface.
- *Do* study paint color samples both in daylight and electric light. (The colors change with artificial lighting.)
- *Don't* make a small room look cluttered by using different colors for woodwork or trim and walls. Paint them all the same color.
- *Do* remove all hardware from the doors and windows (except hinges, etc.) before painting. If you can, loosen the bases of lighting fixtures before you paint. (You'll be able to slip the paint brush just under the edges to make the work look neat.)
- *Do* apply *two coats.* Make the first one thin, and let it dry thoroughly, then apply the second. (One heavy coat tends to get tacky and messy-looking.)
- *Don't* store brushes by standing them on end. After you've cleaned the brush, wrap it in wax paper, then hang it up or lay it on a flat surface.

Tips on Tools to Use.

1. Brushes. These are still the way to get the best results. The brush gets around corners, tackles uneven surfaces with ease, and is tops for painting trim. Paint applied with a brush makes the best bond with the surface being painted. Make sure that the brush you choose is of high quality—with nylon or with natural bristles. The best bristles have what the experts call *natural split ends.* They may also have commercially *flagged* or split tips that grab onto the paint. On good brushes there's also a mix of long and short bristles—all tapered to an appropriately serviceable edge.

When you paint large, flat surfaces, use a wide brush. Pick a small round or flat brush for hard-to-reach nooks and crannies, and for trim. All natural-bristle brushes can be used on *any surface*—with *any type of paint. Note:* Nylon brushes cannot be used to apply shellac. But experts say that nylon brushes are superior to naturals for latex—or "water-base" paints.

2. Rollers. The most popular roller is the one you just dip into a paint tray. There may be times and places, though, when you'll want to use the *pressure-release* roller. It holds the paint inside until you want it—then provides the paint when you press a mechanical *releaser.*

Rollers are either made with synthetic fibers or of wool. Remember that the rougher the surface to be painted, the longer the nap (fibers) should be. On stucco surfaces, for instance, use a deep-pile roller. For a smooth, glossy look, use a short-pile roller.

3. Spray guns. For small, awkward paint jobs (louvered shutters, for instance), you can attach a spray gun to your vacuum cleaner. Use water-base paint for this: it sprays easily and will not clog the gun as oil paint tends to do. If you prefer a supersprayer, rent one of the electrical spray guns. These are easy to handle: the unit contains the sprayer and a canister that holds the paint. And if neither type of sprayer tempts you, just buy an aerosol spray paint at the hardware store.

Preparing the Surface. Before you get to the work that shows, remember that all walls—especially those in the bathroom and the kitchen—should be washed down with a household cleaner and warm water. (*Note:* If your walls are plasterboard, don't overdo this—too much water will make plasterboard swell up.) When the walls have been cleaned, inspect them. Patch, if necessary, following the procedures given in Section I, CEILING/PLASTER, and WALL/INDOOR. If necessary, remove old paint with a paint remover and scraper (for details, see REFINISHING WOOD, p. 301.

Removing Wallpaper. It's possible to paint over one evenly applied layer of wallpaper (though the experts aren't keen on the idea). But more than one layer of wallpaper on the wall will be a problem. Remove it as follows:

1. Cut the paper. Slice the paper into vertical strips. Loosen the wallpaper paste behind each strip with a brush soaked in warm water—just brush the surface of the paper. You can add wallpaper remover to the water if you want to speed the process. Or, if you don't have any remover, use a detergent in the water. Pull off the strips of paper, one by one, after they've soaked. Scrape off any remaining paper with a putty knife, but don't gouge the plaster!

(*Note:* If the paper refuses to budge, you may need the help of a professional paperhanger. Even though some sources suggest that you rent a machine that will steam the paper off the wall, we think the steamer is too cumbersome and too tricky for an amateur to handle.)

Using Primers. Consult the chart on the next page to find out which surfaces need primer coats before painting. (Buy the primer at the paint or hardware store when you buy the other supplies.)

The Right Paint for the Job. There are three main types of paint, as follows:

1. Oil-base paint. The base is linseed oil. Thinned with turpentine or mineral spirits *only.*

2. Enamel. Has a glossy-finish; it's an oil-base paint with varnish added to give the shiny look.

3. Latex paint (the so-called "water-base" paint). Though latex is thinned with water, and you clean the wet paint up with water, its *base* is actually plastic! (*Water-soluble* is probably more apt terminology for this paint.)

What to use ... and where

	FLAT PAINT	SEMI-GLOSS PAINT	ENAMEL	CASEIN	INTERIOR VARNISH	SHELLAC	WAX (LIQUID OR PASTE)	WAX (EMULSION)	STAIN	WOOD SEALER	FLOOR SEALER	FLOOR VARNISH	ALUMINUM PAINT	SEALER OR ENAMEL	METAL PRIMER SEALER OR UNDERCOATER	LATEX TYPES
PLASTER WALLS & CEILING	✓•	✓•	✓												✓	✓
WALL BOARD	✓•	✓•	✓												✓	✓
WOOD PANELING	✓•	✓•			✓	✓	✓		✓	✓						✓•
KITCHEN & BATHROOM WALLS		✓•	✓•												✓	
WOOD FLOORS						✓	✓	✓•	✓•	✓	✓	✓•				
CONCRETE FLOORS								✓•	✓•	✓		✓				✓
VINYL & RUBBER TILE FLOORS							✓	✓								
ASPHALT TILE FLOORS								✓								
LINOLEUM						✓	✓	✓			✓	✓				
STAIR TREADS						✓				✓	✓	✓				
STAIR RISERS	✓•	✓•			✓	✓				✓	✓					
WOOD TRIM	✓•	✓•			✓	✓	✓			✓				✓		✓•
STEEL WINDOWS	✓•	✓•											✓		✓	✓•
ALUMINUM WINDOWS	✓•	✓•											✓		✓	✓•
WINDOW SILLS					✓											
STEEL CABINETS	✓•	✓•												✓		
HEATING DUCTS	✓•	✓•											✓		✓	✓•
RADIATORS & HEATING PIPES	✓•	✓•											✓		✓	✓•
OLD MASONRY	✓	✓		✓									✓	✓		✓
NEW MASONRY	✓•	✓•													✓	✓

✓• Black dot indicates that a primer or sealer may be necessary before the finishing coat (unless surface has been previously finished.)

Consult the chart for details on which of these to use for the job.

Applying the Paint. At last we come to the technique of painting!

1. Painting with a brush. Never put too much paint on your brush—it will drip all over! Dip the brush just one third of its length into the paint can. Then tap the brush lightly to get rid of the excess (do this *instead* of wiping the brush against the rim of the can). Use light, long strokes to brush the paint onto the surface. First, brush up and down, then brush across, then go up and down

again (to get rid of any bristle marks). When you're painting walls and vertical surfaces, start at the top and work down.

2. Painting with a roller. If you're working on a wall, start with a *brush*. Paint a border about two feet deep, starting at the ceiling line. Do the same with the side or corners. Take the paint-dipped roller, and roll upward. (Do this just below the border you've brush-painted, rolling up to it.) After you've covered an area of about 2 feet by 3 feet with vertical strokes of the roller, turn the roller at right angles, and roll across the painted surface. Use a brush at the bottom of the wall. *Note:* If you're doing a ceiling, use a long-handled roller. This means you won't have to stand on a ladder to do the job.

3. Spraying the paint on the surface. Before you begin, be sure to protect windows, etc., against spray droplets. Buy or rent a painter's face mask to keep the spray out of your lungs, mouth, and eyes. Hold the gun six to ten inches from the wall or other item you're planning to paint. Point it directly at the surface. Spray up and down—don't arc with the gun. Apply a light coat (to keep the paint from dripping and running down the surface). *Note:* Begin a stroke *before* you press the trigger of the spray gun, and finish the stroke *after* you've released the trigger. Doing this makes the coat neat and trim.

PAINTING, OUTDOOR

Painting the outside of the house yourself may be a bigger job than you realize. But it *will* save you money. (Just ask for the contractor's estimate and you'll discover how much!) If you plan to do the work, with some help from your friends or family, use this guide to the job:

Choosing the Paint. Two basic types of exterior house paint are available: oil base and latex (the so-called "water-base" paint that actually has a plastic base, but is *thinned* with *water*). Either type will give a good, lasting coat if it is applied properly. *Note:* There are a few guidelines to buying one or another *brand* of paint—your best bet is to be sure of paint dealer, and to select from a well-known paint maker. Don't try to save money on the project by buying the cheapest paint: the work itself demands that you get the best, so you won't have to do the whole thing over again another season.

Until recently, oil-base paints were always used for outside paint jobs. But latex paints also offer advantages for outside work. Latex dries faster than oil-base—so insects buzzing around in the breeze don't have as much chance to fly into the new coat of paint and stick there. Also, latex cleanups are easier: brushes are rinsed in water, and paint splatters are wiped up with water and a little soap or detergent. Finally, latex allows you to paint on *damp* days, and to start before the dew is dry!

Tips on Outdoor Painting. (Consult the previous section, PAINTING/INDOOR, for additional information.)

1. Use oil-base paint over old coats of oil paint. If you plan to switch to latex, be sure to apply a primer-sealer first. Then cover with latex paint.

2. Buy enough paint for the entire job (see estimator chart, p. 299, for help with this). Most paint stores offer a lower price per gallon for quantities over 5 gallons. (It doesn't hurt to have some paint left over from this particular batch: use it for touch-ups later on.)

3. If the previous paint job on your house has been discolored—by mildew or industrial smoke—buy a fume- and mildew-resistant type of paint this time around.

4. If you're changing colors, plan on *two* coats of paint. (Be wary of claims for one-coat coverage.)

Preparing the Surface. A good outdoor paint job requires careful preparation and the correction of conditions that have caused the previous coat of paint to blister, peel, or "check." And moisture is usually the problem *outdoor* walls encounter. (Moisture can build up within the walls and attack the paint from the underside. Or, rain, snow, and heavy dew can leak in, behind the outside wall, from areas that aren't properly sealed—around windows and doorframes,

298

PAINT ESTIMATOR

1. FIND PERIMETER OF HOUSE AT TOP OF TABLE
2. MOVE DOWN COLUMN TO FIGURE OPPOSITE HEIGHT OF HOUSE — THAT'S THE NUMBER OF GALLONS YOU'LL NEED FOR ONE COAT

	100'	125'	150'	175'	200'	225'	250'	275'	300'	325'
24'	5½	6½	7½	8½	10	11½	12½	14	15½	17
22'	5	6	7	8	9	10½	12	13	14½	16
20'	4½	5½	6½	7½	8½	9½	11	12	13½	15
18'	4	5	6	6½	7½	9	10	11	12½	13½
16'	3½	4½	5	6	7	8	9	10	11	12
14'	3½	4	4½	5½	6	7	8	9	10	11
12'	3	3½	4	5	5½	6½	7	8	9	10
10'	2½	3	3½	4	5	5½	6½	7	8	9

for example.) Experts suggest that you vent moisture buildup by installing small metal plugs here and there in the wall. Consult the hardware dealer about these plugs. If your window and doorframes allow moisture to attack the walls, then you'll need to do a careful *caulking* job. (For details, see Section II, CAULKING, p. 271.) Here's the routine *before* you paint:

1. Scrape off loose paint. Use a scraper to remove blistered or flaking paint, then sandpaper over this area to smooth the edges of old paint. Brush off particles of paint and dust.

2. Drive nails in. Inspect for any loose nails in the siding. Drive them in *below the surface* (with a nail set). Fill the indentation with plastic wood.

CAUTION: *Plastic wood is extremely flammable. Don't work near flame—including lighted cigarettes.* Touch up this repair work with your oil paint and allow it to dry before you start the *first coat*. If you're going to use latex, touch up exposed nailheads with the primer before you paint. (Rust stains will appear if a water-base paint is used over unprotected metal.)

3. Remove screen doors, window screens, and window shutters. Paint these separately.

Applying the Paint. Late summer or early fall—or even when the temperature hovers around 70 degrees Fahrenheit—is the time to paint, the experts say.

The temperature is good for *you* and for the paint, too. All types of paint flow on with ease. (*Note:* If oil paint is your choice, consider the humidity, too, and pick the drier days for painting. Wait twenty-four hours after a rainfall before you use oil paint.) Here's the routine:

1. Mixing. Be sure the paint is thoroughly mixed. Shake the can before you open it. Then mix it with a wooden paddle.

2. Brushes. Use a 3½- to 4-inch brush with 4-inch bristles for the job.

3. Where to begin: Start at the top, painting with the grain of the wood, working toward the wet edge. If you have to stop for the day before the job is done, finish all the way to the corner of one board (the result will be smoother).

4. Keep in the shade. Paint on the shady side of the house. Move to the next side *as the sun moves from it.*

REFINISHING WOOD

Furniture—Small Scratches on the Surface. The easiest way to make these disappear is with an ordinary wax crayon. Pick a matching color and simply crayon over the scratch. (Paste waxes and furniture oils will also obliterate these little marks.)

Dents on Surface. Some of these are worth keeping—they give character and age to an "antique." But if you're bothered by a new and unsightly dent, *raise the wood* to get rid of it! Here are the steps:

1. Remove the varnish from the surface with varnish remover. (For details on various types of removers, see below, "Stripping the Furniture.")

2. When the wood is bare (that is, with no finish) give it a few droplets of water. Be sure to drip these on the dented portion *only.* Wait for the wood to rise! These droplets will moisten the wood fibers so that they'll swell and come up to the level of the surrounding wood. (*Note:* If this treatment doesn't banish the dent, moisten the spot again, cover the area with a clean, folded cloth, and apply heat to the spot with your iron. Check the area every few minutes by lifting the pad. When the dent disappears, let dry and refinish the spot to match the rest of the wood. For details, see below.)

Surface Chipped or Gouged. Save any wood chips that break off your furniture. You can glue them back in place and make a mend that will be almost invisible. Here are the steps:

1. Apply the thinnest possible coating of white glue (polyvinyl acetate), or of contact cement, to both surfaces.

2. Fit the wood chip into the gouge. Press down, and cover the patch with padding. Apply more pressure—with clamps, or a tourniquet (made of string wound tight with a pencil), or with a stack of books. Let the mend stand for twenty-four hours. Touch up with one of the finishes described below. *Note:* If you've lost the wood chip, fill the gouge with a substitute. Experts say you should use wood putty, and after it, a shellac stick that you melt over the mend. (Do this by holding the shellac stick like a lighted candle: just drip the hot shellac onto the surface.) Shellac sticks come in colors to match most wood finishes. After the shellac is set, sandpaper *lightly* with very fine sandpaper. This brings the new surface flush with the wood around it.

Burns on the Finish But Not in the Wood Beneath. If these are small and haven't penetrated to the wood, rub off the discoloration with fine steel-wool or sandpaper. Wipe clean. If the finish is varnish, cover the spot with clear nail polish. (For other finishes, see below.)

Burns into the Wood. If the burn is deep enough to char the wood, follow the procedure above (with steel wool or sandpaper). When the scar goes, the wood will probably be raw (that is, the stain will have been rubbed away), and the site will be a small valley. You can use the wood putty and shellac stick technique (above) for this repair. Or, if you prefer, color the wood with a crayon, then fill the valley with clear nail polish.

Finish Is Badly Marred. Refinish the entire piece. In most cases, this is a big job. Don't start until you have prepared thoroughly. Allow enough time to complete each phase of the work. Here are the steps:

1. Remove any hardware. Metal handles, hinges, and knobs usually are screwed or bolted onto a piece of furniture and should be taken off so an even finish can be applied later. (It is difficult to strip or finish a piece around the hardware.) Wooden knobs and handles can also be removed if they are bolted or screwed on. If they're firmly glued onto a piece, leave them in place—you may do real damage getting them off. Refinish around them.

2. Clean off wax or polish. Before stripping furniture with a chemical remover, wash the piece with warm water and soap or detergent. This takes off old wax or polish (which might keep the chemical from doing its job). Don't use water around glued joints. Dry thoroughly!

3. Stripping the furniture. Many brands and types of paint remover and varnish remover are available. For home use, the easiest and safest should be considered first. We suggest the *nonflammable, wax-free types.* These require no after-rinse or neutralizing when the job is done.

CAUTION: *Fumes from removers are dangerous to inhale. These chemicals should be used out of doors or in a well-ventilated room. Wear rubber gloves to protect your hands. Don't splash any of the chemical into your eyes. If any gets in, flush your eyes immediately with cold water.* To apply chemical finish-remover, follow the directions on the container. Be sure to let the chemical stand on the wood surface exactly the specified time *before* you start rmoving the finish. When the old finish is *thoroughly softened,* scrape it off with a putty knife or wipe it off with burlap. If you used a water-soluble remover, the softened finish can simply be hosed off, with a strong jet from your garden hose out-of-doors. On grooved, carved, or indented surfaces, wrap a cloth around a pointed stick or use wads of steel wool. An old toothbrush is handy in getting at intricately carved surfaces!

Note: If all this seems too messy and too laborious, furniture repairing and refinishing firms (which can be found in the yellow pages of your telephone book) will do the work for you. They take the finish off, down to the bare wood, by soaking the piece in a large vat until the old finish is completely dissolved.

Finishing. When the old finish is off and the wood is dry, you can decide what color, gloss, and wearability you want for the new finish. Color is the first consideration: remember, you can't change it once the new finish is completed. Also, if you want the piece lighter, you bleach. If you want it darker, you stain it.

1. Bleaching. First, try a strong solution of laundry bleach. Spread it on and let it stand until it's dry. Then wipe the piece with *water to which vinegar has been added* (two tablespoons to a cup of water). This neutralizes the bleach. If sanding is done at this time to smooth the wood, use very fine sand-

paper and rub lightly. (Otherwise, you may take off the lighter-colored surface of the wood, and make the piece *dark again!*)

Two-step commercial bleaches are available from the hardware or paint dealer, but remember, *these strong chemicals must be handled with care.* Follow instructions. Wear rubber gloves and old clothing. Rinse off (immediately!) any splatters that get on your skin.

2. Staining. Before you start to stain, the unfinished or stripped wood should be wiped off with denatured alcohol, to remove any grease that might make the stain coat uneven. Varieties of ready-mixed stains are available in paint and hardware stores: they are dyes or pigments mixed into a solvent. The solvent can be water, oil, or alcohol. If you are trying for a particularly subtle shade or unusual color, *and* you want to combine colors of ready-mixed stain to get this, *be sure to use stains with the same solvents!*

Test the stain on the piece of furniture. Do this where your test will be hidden—say, on the undersides of tables, chairs, or the backs of bureaus. Once you have the right color, follow the directions on the container for using the stain. Spread it on evenly with a brush or cloth. Apply, then wipe off in the direction of the wood grain. *Allow stains to dry overnight before continuing with finish coats.*

3. Fillers. Some hardwoods (such as mahogany, oak) have an open grain. For a smooth finish these woods need to have the pores filled. Paste wood-fillers are available at paint and hardware stores, and come in colors to match the stain you choose. These paste fillers must be diluted to brushing consistency before you use them. Follow the container's directions, or mix the filler with equal parts of turpentine or mineral spirits.

Apply fillers *across the grain.* Let dry until the surface is firm, but not hard. Wipe off the excess with a cloth, using a circular motion. Then finish off lightly with a swipe along the grain. *Allow fillers to dry for twenty-four hours before continuing a refinishing job.*

CAUTION: *When the work is finished (or you break for the day), burn the rags or store them in a pail of water. If left in a heap, spontaneous combustion can occur. These rags are serious fire hazards.*

4. Final coat. Several choices are available for the finish coat. Consider what type of wear and tear the piece of furniture will undergo when you choose the finish for it. Some finishes are easy to apply, but may not be as durable as the finishes that take more time and know-how.

Varnish. For the *most durable* finish, a good varnish is hard to beat. Varnishes are available in many kinds of glosses, from the mirrorlike *high gloss* to the low, or *satin gloss.* Varnishes, it's important to know, are resistant to *water, alcohol, and hot liquids.* New, synthetic varnishes (such as alkyd or urethane products) used on wood furniture give tough, durable finishes.

Two or three thin coats of any varnish are preferable to one heavy coat. Do a light sanding *along the grain* between coats to take out any bubbles or imperfections. (Use very-fine grade sandpaper.) Tips on using varnish:

- *Do not stir varnish in the can.* This will cause bubbles to form. (Varnish *does not separate out* like paint, which does need stirring.)
- *Dip only one third of your brush into the varnish.* Tap the brush gently against the inside of the can. (If you squeeze the brush against the edge of the can lip, bubbles will form in the brush—which you *don't* want.)

- Flow the varnish on liberally (with the *least number of brush strokes* and a moderate amount of pressure). Finish the application with a light stroke *along the grain of the wood with a nearly dry brush.* Allow varnish to dry thoroughly between coats.

Shellac. Shellac finishes are easy to apply. *But when shellac finishes are dry they're not impervious to heat, alcohol, or water.* (Shellac finishes should be applied to bookcases or any surfaces that don't come in contact with food and drink.) Shellac comes in ready-to-use cans, and it also comes in containers that specify a thinner of wood alcohol. Obviously, directions on the can should be observed. Tips for using:

- Brush on a thin coat of shellac with long, sweeping strokes. *Two thin coats are better than one thick one.*
- Sand with very-fine grade sandpaper between each coat.
- Buy only enough shellac for the job to be done. (Shellac can deteriorate when opened or when left on the shelf unused.)

Linseed oil. A rubbed linseed-oil finish is time-consuming, but repeated coats of it give a lasting, softly glowing, handsome finish. (The finish, however, is *not highly water-resistant.* It does withstand heat.) One advantage to this surface: it doesn't show scratches the way varnish or shellac finishes do. To apply:

- Spread boiled linseed oil over the surface with a cloth pad. Allow the oil to soak into the wood until no more can be absorbed.
- Rub as much oil into the wood as you can. Wipe off any excess with a clean cloth.
- Allow the piece to dry overnight. Repeat the same process the next day. *At least three coats can be applied to start.* Additional touchup coats can be applied from year to year, if you wish.

CAUTION: *Burn (or store under water) all rags you use for this work: they are fire hazards.*

Floors. The various plastic finishes available these days can bring a durable and handsome surface to the floor that's suffered wear, tear, and scratches beyond compare. Below, we tackle some typical problems on various types of floors.

Worn Spots in Some Areas. You may be tempted to fix just the areas that show wear, and leave the rest alone. But experts say that your floor is bound to look patchy if you do. Our advice is to set aside the time, and to close off the space, and do the *entire* floor.

Flooring: Hardwood and Fir. Most contemporary flooring is made of 2-inch to 3-inch boards, and these take readily to refinishing. (Antique and wide-board floors are treated below—and they take more doing.) Here are the steps:

1. Remove the old finish. The easiest way to do this is to rent a sanding machine, or hire a professional to do the job for you. Varnish, shellac, or linseed-oil finishes will be taken off with a sanding machine—and don't let anyone tell you that it's easy to do it without a machine. (You have to get down on your hands and knees, apply varnish remover, or alcohol for shellac, or a strong detergent for linseed oil. The work is not only hard but smelly, and the fumes can be dangerous.) When you rent the sanding machine (at a hardware store or appliance shop), be sure to get detailed instructions on how to use the machine. Get some extra sanding belts, too. Remember: a large belt-sander *must* be run smoothly and in even strokes over the floor. If you stop in any area with the

machine running, you'll make a nice little valley in your floor. *Turn off the machine when it's not being moved across the surface.* The large sander can't get all the way over to the baseboard, so rent a small, hand-held circular sander, too. This will take up the finish around the peripheral (or border) portion. Also, you will want to protect both your lungs and the rest of the house from the fine sawdusty polution the sander produces. Close doors tightly, and stuff blankets or newspapers into cracks around them. Rent a face mask! (Vacuum area carefully.)

2. Apply new floor stain. This is the coloring material for your new floor. There are charts in the hardware or paint store that give you a wide selection. The type of floor you have will dictate the type of stain you use:

- Hardwoods: oak, maple, teak: Experts suggest a stain with an alcohol solvent, because hardwoods, being *hard,* don't absorb readily. Alcohol will penetrate their grains just enough to carry the stain.
- Fir and Other Softwoods: Use a linseed-oil stain. Softwoods are more porous than hardwoods, and tend to soak up moisture. Linseed oil controls this process so that the right amount of stain gets into those pores.

Apply the stain with a brush or a rag dipped in a bowlful of the stain mix. Work it onto the surface with even strokes. Allow the stain to soak in for 3 to 5 minutes, then remove the excess by wiping the area with a clean rag. Now, if you think the result is too *light,* apply another coat of the stain. *Note:* It's easier to go step by step to *darken* the floor. Trying to lighten it if you've applied too many coats, or left the stain to soak in for too long, is much more work than you need.

Now wait for the stain to dry. If you use an alcohol stain, you can go on to the next phase of the work the next day. With linseed-oil stains, wait several days—until the surface is dry (not tacky).

3. Sand over the surface, very lightly (or use a steel-wool pad on a floor polisher). This is done to smooth off any little floor fibers that have been rubbed up in the staining process.

4. Apply the finish coat or coats. You have a choice here, and we recommend the first type:

- Polyurethane Plastic Varnishes. (There are several trade names on the market.) These come in dull, satin, or gloss finishes. Apply with a roller, usually three coats, for best results. Allow forty-eight hours' drying time before you use the floor (even though some of these products claim to dry to the touch in thirty minutes). The care, after this, is just dusting—no waxing necessary. Touch up worn surfaces when they appear, to protect the stain beneath.
- Shellac. Follow directions on the container, but remember that this surface will show water and alcohol splatters and splashes.
- Varnish. Follow the directions on the container. But remember that this surface will show scratches. And you'll be waxing it just about every month to keep it shiny and fresh.

Old (Antique) Flooring: Wide Boards of Pine and Spruce. There's no denying the charm and old-world look these floors give to a room. But refinishing them is a chore, and hard on your knees. (You can't use sanding machines here if you treasure the old look these floors have. The sander will make them flat, new-looking, and uniform.) To tackle the treasured old boards, follow these steps:

1. Remove the old finish. You can use solvents, but we don't recommend them: the work is odious, odorous, and the old finish runs into the cracks of the wood and sticks there. We suggest that you sandpaper by hand! Before you sand, start on the surface with a 2-inch paint scraper. Work along the grain of the wood. *Don't gouge the boards by putting too much pressure on the scraper. Note:* Replace the scraper blade if it gets too dull. And remember: if the boards have been nailed down from the top surface, use a punch and hammer to sink the nailheads below the surface. Do this before you start the scraping. Get any little spots of resisting finish up with a razor blade or sandpaper. (Use a single-edged razor blade. Hold it at right angles to the surface, and stroke it along the wood as if you were stroking with a paintbrush, back and forth.)

2. Apply new floor stain, as above under fir and other softwoods.

3. Apply finish coats as above. *Note:* Before you apply the polyurethane finish, use a few coats of penetrating sealer. It will soak into the wood and keep those old fibers firm. Buy the sealer that goes with type of plastic varnish you'll be using.

PEST CONTROL

Prevention or speedy action are the watchwords for pest control. To avoid the damage that insects and rodents can inflict on your home or its furnishings, keep the pesky creatures *out!* If they're already *in*, starting to gnaw, get rid of them right away! Most pests can be eliminated by the combination of good housekeeping and the proper (and cautious) use of pesticides. (For details on pesticides, see the *Special Note* at the end of this section.) But before you resort to the chemical cure, you need to identify the pest. In addition to the information we give, you can get expert, detailed help on the pests particular to the region from your county agent. (Reach him by contacting the Federal-State Extension Service in the region. If you have any trouble finding him, contact the local 4-H Club or the regional office of the U.S. Department of Agriculture.) Exterminators can also be called in for advice, and will take on the job of pest control if you feel the job is too big or too tricky to handle yourself. Below, we give pointers on pests that may pervade your home, the damage they *may* do, and the expert's suggestions on dealing with them.

Bee, Wasp, Hornet. These stinging insects can enter a house through cracks around the windows and doors. Most frequently, they'll get in through attic-peak vents (between the louvers). Strictly speaking, these insects won't *damage* the house, if they get in. But not many of us would relish a flourishing hornet's nest in the attic. Tight-fitting screen doors and proper caulking around window-frames and attic louvers can keep these pests out of the house.

If you find the beginning of a nest in the attic—or just outside it, under the eaves—get rid of it. First. spray the nest with a pesticide (but see *Note*, p. 310). *Spray the nest at night when all the insects are safely in the hive.* When the hive is inactive, remove it with tongs: loosen it and plop it into a garbage bag. Burn the bag.

Bat. More and more bats are infected with rabies, so it's prudent, if not imperative, to keep these flying rodents out of your house. Be sure to block up all possible entrance holes. If you find bats in the vicinity and want to get rid of them, spread naphthalene flakes on the bat-infested areas. CAUTION: *Do not pick up or touch a dead or dying bat. If you've been bitten by a bat, go to the doctor immediately.* If possible, take the bat body with you. Pick it up with tongs and put it into a garbage bag (discard the tongs).

Carpenter Ant. Although other types of ants may invade your home and create a nuisance there, these large (½ inch) black ants can actually drill through parts of the house. They will head for the wooden supports, where they'll build their homes. To do this, they tunnel through the wood, then make their nests. If you see any of these large black ants—even one or two of them—this is a clue that there's a nest nearby. Or, if you see the ants' expelled borings beneath splits in wood, you should realize that you may be hosting a convention of carpenter ants. Try to trace the ants to their lair. When you find it, spray it with the proper pesticide (see below). Often these ants are hard to track. If you have problems about finding the nest and depesting your house, call an exterminator: have an expert do the job for you.

Carpenter Bee (**Boring Bee**). These are large brown bees, bigger than the yellow-and-black bumblebee. They're not harmful to humans, but they do relish rafters and wood siding. To make their nests, they bore neat ¼-inch holes in the eaves or siding or other exterior woodwork of the house. These holes are "bee-lines" to the nesting tubes. All this boring work can weaken the supports and other wood members of the house. To control this carpenter, spray the holes at night with the appropriate pesticide (see below).

Carpet Beetle, Clothes Moth. The larvae (or unhatched young) of these insects attack fabrics of animal origin—wool, silk, fur, etc. Your best protection from this sort of damage is cleaning, care, and correct storage. Be sure that all fabrics are washed or dry-cleaned. Get a *sealed* container for fabric storage. Put *methoxychlor* balls or crystals into the container with the clothing or other storables. (*Note:* Always air clothing, blankets, and rugs in the sun for several hours *after* storage. The methoxychlor vapor is harmful if inhaled by living things—*including* your pets.)

Cockroaches. These creepy, crawly bugs are not only unsightly: they're probable health hazards when they're around (they are thought by some to be disease-carriers). Roaches can also do damage to decorative fabrics, clothes, books, and paper accessories. They habitually hide in cracks and crevices that are awkward to reach or repair. When you can, prevent an infestation of roaches by sealing nooks, crannies, cracks, crevices. Do this around doors, baseboards, openings around pipes and ducts. Try an insecticide (see below) and if this fails to dislodge and destroy the pests, call in a professional exterminator.

Cricket. You may like the gentle chirp of the cricket outdoors, but you'd best be on guard if there's a cricket in the house, for crickets are a type of *chewing* beetle. They munch on clothing or any fabrics—especially soiled things. If there are crickets in the house and you're kindhearted, try to remove them by hand when they emerge from their hiding place (usually cracks around the fireplace). If you're just plain anticricket, spray with a pesticide (see below).

Fly. Though houseflies usually breed outdoors, they like to forage *indoors*—that is, in the home. The best control here is to make your house as impenetrable as possible. Repair all window and door screens. *Be sure door screens are hung so that they open out.* This way, the door shoos the flies away as you go in or out. If you've done your best to block flies from entry, just swat the occasional flies that arrive. Sprays aren't called for here—their residues tend to settle on kitchen work surfaces and on pots and pans and other utensils. (In warm weather, be extra careful with garbage. Neglecting it can sometimes bring a whole host of odious baby flies, called maggots.)

Mouse, Rat. To make a wooden house absolutely rodentproof is difficult, often impossible, as some of us know. These pests will try to find ways to the spaces between the inner and outer walls of the house, where they'll settle happily and build nests. Then, after they've established a home, they'll gnaw holes through the inner walls and enter the house. Inspect your house for possible mouse- and ratholes. Cover these immediately. (You can nail the cleaned top of a soup can over the hole.) Place the rat bait that contains *warfarin* in crawl spaces and in crevices under the house. (*Remember: Certain pesticides are highly poisonous*—not just to rats, but to people and pets. Put the bait where only the rat or mouse will find it. See below.) Call an exterminator if you suspect a serious infestation.

Silverfish, Book Louse. Wallpaper, books, and clothing can be damaged by these starch-eating insects. To control them, spray cracks and crevices with a pesticide (see below).

Spider. Only two types are poisonous (the others may be a nuisance, but as fly-catchers, they're also beneficial). Guard against and learn to identify the black widow and the widely known brown spider (found mainly in the midwest). When any of these spins webs in the basement or in doorways, spray with pesticides (see below). *Note:* Don't aim the spray directly over your head, if that's where the spider is. It may drop from its web and bite you.

Termite. Many a homeowner trembles at the thought of termite infestation— and with reason. But remember that these wood-eaters will have to be in residence for several years before they can, literally, bring the house down around your ears. If you inspect regularly for signs of infestation, and take proper precautions, you'll avoid the trembles and termite damage. If the colony has just *begun* to make its home in your home, you needn't fear the worst. Call the pest controller immediately, and have him do the necessary chemical depesting.

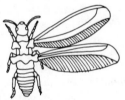

Termite (thick waist)

Flying Ant (narrow waist)

Detection in this case is your best protection. There are two types of termite, and each leaves its distinctive calling card.

1. Ground-nesters (or subterranean termites). These are found in most of the eastern parts of the United States. They are the most destructive of the species. The ground-nester must make his way from the *ground* to your home.

If you notice long, flattish earthen "tubes" over the surface of the cement foundation or in spaces next to the pipes that lead into your house, it's likely you're hosting ground-nesting termites. If you see a sudden swarming of the winged members of the colony around doors or windows, be on guard against infestation (see illustrations). You may mistake the breeding members of the termite tribe for flying ants, but study the illustrations and notice the differences between the ant and the termite. Finally, if you happen upon a little cluster of discarded wings, on the basement floor or near a door, it's time to call the local termite-exterminator. The ground-nester won't reduce the wood beams in your house to powder—as his cousin, the *dry wood* termite will do. But he'll honeycomb the interiors of any wood structure with his tunnels to the nests, eating the wood as he goes. In several years, although the outside of one of your beams may *look* durable and sound, the *inside* may be fragile as lace (and about to fall on your face). Until your pest control expert arrives to cope with the infestation, you can help: fill any cracks in the masonry, ventilate the basement, and keep wood scraps and cellulose leftovers out of the house.

2. Dry wood termites (and powder post beetles). Both of these are found throughout the United States. The dry wood termite tends to flourish in Florida and California. Both pests will eat hard and soft wood, including furniture, if they have the chance. And they leave as evidence of their efforts a powdery wood residue. The presence of this wood dust (where once perhaps you had a wood box or table leg) is the clue to infestation. If you see anything of this sort, call the pest controller. Let him make the identification, then have him go to work on the problem. Before he comes, you can protect the furniture and woodwork by sealing it with wax polish, varnish, or applications of linseed oil.

Note: Pesticides and Pest Control. In recent years great controversy has surrounded the use of many pesticides (particularly DDT). At the same time the production of pesticides has been *increasing* yearly. Both situations make it more difficult for you to decide which of several hundred currently available preparations are safe for use in and outside of your home.

Many states have already passed legislation restricting or prohibiting the use of DDT and other *persistent* pesticides. (Persistent pesticides are those suspected of leaving—or known to leave—toxic residues in the environment for years.) These include *chlorinated hydrocarbons* (you may know them as dieldrin, endrin, heptachlor, chlordane, benzene hexachloride, and lindane). Also included are compounds containing arsenic, lead, or mercury.

In 1970, after the regulation of pesticides was transferred from the U.S. Department of Agriculture to the new Environmental Protection Agency (EPA), the U.S. Court of Appeals ordered that the agency *cancel registration of DDT for all purposes.*

Current research, according to most experts, indicates that certain chemicals *are safe* for use in your home. These are the pesticides that are not persistent and those that don't contain highly toxic (poisonous) chemicals. But you should know that *all* pesticides are under constant review, and that it's impossible to approve any one of them *absolutely.* What looks good today may turn out to be hazardous tomorrow or next year. With that in mind, use pesticides containing the following active chemicals for garden and household bug control. Check the label for these ingredients before buying or using any preparations:

1. **Pyrethron with Synergists** (such as Piperonyl Butoxide and Dicarboximide). This usually comes in an aerosol container. Must be sprayed directly at the insects. Because of this, it's good for flying insects. Not as effective against cockroaches and crawlers, whose control is better accomplished by spraying walls, nooks, and nesting places.

2. **Diazinon.** This chemical is preferable to the often-used chlordane for cockroach control because, in some instances, cockroaches have developed a biological resistance to chlordane. Other pests controlled by diazinon are ants, spiders, and ticks.

3. **Carbaryl (Sevin).** Representative of a new class of insecticides developed to replace persistent pesticides, this is a good chemical for *outside* use. It's particularly good for controlling chewing insects—grasshoppers, potato beetles, and certain cutworms. Not very effective against plant lice.

4. **Malathion.** This chemical is good for controlling sucking insects (plant lice, mites, squash bugs, stink bugs, and thrips) in home gardens. It's also an excellent household insecticide, although it is odorous.

5. **Methoxychlor.** As noted above, this also is effective against certain chewing insects and for fabric pests—clothes moths, for instance. *Note:* ineffective against roaches.

Although these five compounds should be sufficient to meet most household needs, there are many other products on the market. Anyone who needs highly toxic chemicals for household use can get help from a public health officer or from a pest control expert. You should be guided in your purchase by pesticide labels. The products with CAUTION marked on them are of *low toxicity* (that is, not very poisonous). The next level of toxicity is indicated by a WARNING sign on the label: this indicates that *the substance should be handled with great care. The pesticide product with a skull-and-crossbones symbol should never be used in the home.* Most household pest problems can be handled with the least hazardous chemicals—those marked "caution," or "keep out of reach of children."

The Good Housekeeping Institute recommends that before using pesticide products in your home, try to get rid of unwanted bugs and insects by using *nonpesticide measures*. First, build permanent defenses against them with a complete set of screens on windows and doors. Next, make sure there are no pest-breeding grounds (uncovered garbage cans and such) near your home. Paint areas where insects tend to hide with white paint. Insects hate light. Be sure to keep food covered—*always!*

LADDER SAFETY RULES

For all its apparent simplicity, the common ladder can be a dangerous tool. In *mis*using it, you may not realize that you're defying certain physical laws (of gravity, equilibrium, friction, tension, and stress). And these, sad to say, can't be broken without disaster. To keep you within these laws—and out of the hospital—here are a few ladder-safety do's and don'ts from us, and several *more* from the Ladder Institute and the National Safety Council.

- *Don't* ever use a makeshift ladder someone has nailed together from boards and materials at hand.
- *Don't* ever use a ladder as a horizontal gangplank. It's not made to stand strain in that position.
- *Do* place the ladder correctly. Study the diagram, and you'll see that the distance between the *foot of the ladder and the bottom of the wall is exactly ¼ the distance to the top (where the ladder meets and is supported by the top part of the wall)*. In this case, the ladder rests against the wall 10 feet up the wall. Thus, the space between the foot of the ladder and the bottom of the wall is 2½ feet. If you place the ladder farther out from the wall, it may sag and break in the middle when you climb it. If you place it closer, it may topple away from the wall when you go up or down it. (See Diagram.)
- *Do* make sure that the ladder is on firm, level ground. If necessary, use some wood blocks or planks under a low ladder leg.
- *Do* keep your shoes and the ladder's rungs free of oil, grease, mud, snow, and ice.
- *Do* use extension ladders properly. Be sure the *overlap* of the two parts is sufficient. If the ladder is 36 feet long (including the extension), the overlap should be at least 3 feet. If the ladder is from 36 to 48 feet long, the overlap should be at least 4 feet. If the ladder is from 48 to 60 feet long, the overlap should be at least 5 feet.
- *Don't* stand on, or climb down, a ladder the way you would stairs. *Always face the ladder,* grip it firmly with both hands, and place your feet squarely on its rungs.
- *Don't* carry large, heavy, or bulky items up or down a ladder. Raise or lower these with a rope.
- *Do* secure the ladder, when possible, with a rope. For instance, if you're going to the roof to inspect your chimney, throw a rope around the chimney. The rope should be *long enough* so that both ends are at the roof edge. Attach one end to a straight ladder and pull the ladder snugly against the chimney. Fasten the other end of the rope—securely—to a tree, porch beam, or other solid support.

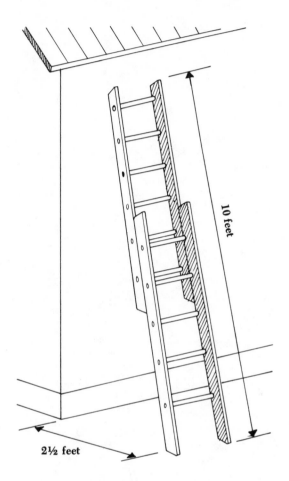

10 feet

2½ feet

- *Do* work facing the ladder, and hold on with one hand. (If you must have both hands free for work, hook a leg over one rung to give yourself better balance.)
- *Don't* ever climb *over* the top of the ladder and onto the roof. If you're climbing from the ladder to the roof, be sure the ladder's top extends 3½ feet above the roof's edge.
- *Do* check your stepladder before you climb it. Be sure that it's fully spread and locked into position. Be sure that all four legs rest on a level base.
- *Don't* use aluminum ladders when you're doing electrical work or repairs.
- *Don't* depend on a "nonslip" ladder if you're using it on a waxed floor. The "nonslip" feet can pick up wax and become *very* slippery.
- *Do* store your wooden ladder in a dry place—*away from steam pipes and radiators.*